lonely planet

W9-BTF-627

THE PACIFIC NORTHWEST'S

BEST TRIPS

33 AMAZING ROAD TRIPS

This edition written and researched by

**Mariella Krause,
Celeste Brash, Korina Miller,
Brendan Sainsbury**

SYMBOLS IN THIS BOOK

 Top Tips

History & Culture

Essential Photo

Link Your Trips

Family

Walking Tour

Tips from Locals

Food & Drink

Eating

Trip Detour

Outdoors

Sleeping

🕿 Telephone Number

@ Internet Access

English-Language Menu

🕒 Opening Hours

🛜 Wi-Fi Access

Family-Friendly

P Parking

Vegetarian Selection

Pet-Friendly

Nonsmoking

Swimming Pool

Air-Conditioning

MAP LEGEND

Routes

Trip Route
Trip Detour
Linked Trip
Walk Route
Tollway
Freeway
Primary
Secondary
Tertiary
Lane
Unsealed Road
Plaza/Mall
Steps
Tunnel
Pedestrian Overpass
Walk Track/Path

Boundaries

International
State/Province
Cliff

Population

Capital (National)
Capital (State/Province)
City/Large Town
Town/Village

Transport

Airport
Cable Car/ Funicular
Parking
Train/Railway
Tram
Underground Train Station

Trips

1 Trip Numbers
9 Trip Stop
Walking tour
Trip Detour

Highway Route Markers

97 US National Hwy
5 US Interstate Hwy
44 State Hwy
16 Trans-Canada Hwy

Hydrography

River/Creek
Intermittent River
Swamp/Mangrove
Canal
Water
Dry/Salt/ Intermittent Lake
Glacier

Areas

Beach
Cemetery (Christian)
Cemetery (Other)
Park
Forest
Reservation
Urban Area
Sportsground

PLAN YOUR TRIP

ON THE ROAD

WASHINGTON TRIPS 31

CONTENTS

British
Columbia
p261

Washington
p31

Oregon
p145

Contents cont.

Classic Trips

Look out for the Classic Trips stamp on our favorite routes in this book.

Mt Hood A symbol of the Pacific Northwest's grandeur (Trip 16)

WELCOME TO
THE PACIFIC NORTHWEST

What's the Pacific Northwest got that other regions don't? Plenty. Start with hundreds of miles of coastline and throw in a stunning natural landscape: thousands of years of geological events have dramatically shaped this region, leaving behind snow-capped mountain ranges, rocky islands, hundreds of waterfalls, natural hot springs and one particularly lovely gorge.

Because almost every drive in the Pacific Northwest is a scenic one, there's no better way to see it than by road trip. We've put together 33 of the very best routes and listed all the great stops along the way, from historical sites to natural wonders to roadside attractions.

You can cruise along the coast, explore volcanic remnants, sample regional wines, or even travel in the footsteps of Lewis and Clark. And if you've only got time for one trip, make it one of our nine Classic Trips, which take you to the very best of the Pacific Northwest. Turn the page for more.

➔

THE PACIFIC NORTHWEST'S
Classic Trips

WHAT IS A CLASSIC TRIP?

All the trips in this book show you the best of the Pacific Northwest, but we've chosen nine as our all-time favorites. These are our Classic Trips – the ones that lead you to the best of the iconic sights, the top activities and the unique Pacific Northwest experiences. Turn the page to see the map, and look for the Classic Trip stamp throughout the book.

ALASKA STOCK ©

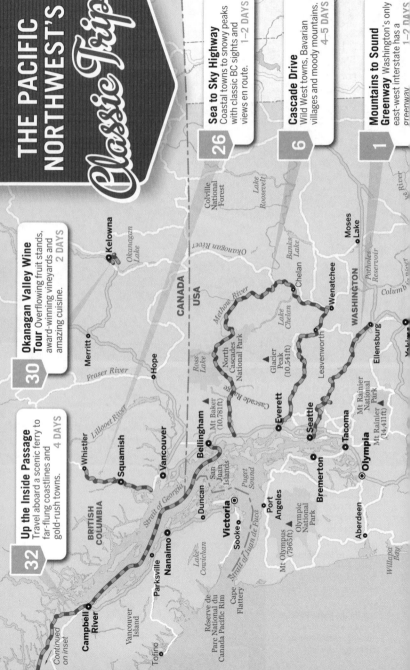

THE PACIFIC NORTHWEST'S Classic Trips

26 Sea to Sky Highway Coastal towns to snowy peaks with classic BC sights and views en route. 1–2 DAYS

6 Cascade Drive Wild West towns, Bavarian villages and moody mountains. 4–5 DAYS

1 Mountains to Sound Greenway Washington's only east-west interstate has a greenway 1–2 DAYS

30 Okanagan Valley Wine Tour Overflowing fruit stands, award-winning vineyards and amazing cuisine. 2 DAYS

32 Up the Inside Passage Travel aboard a scenic ferry to far-flung coastlines and gold-rush towns. 4 DAYS

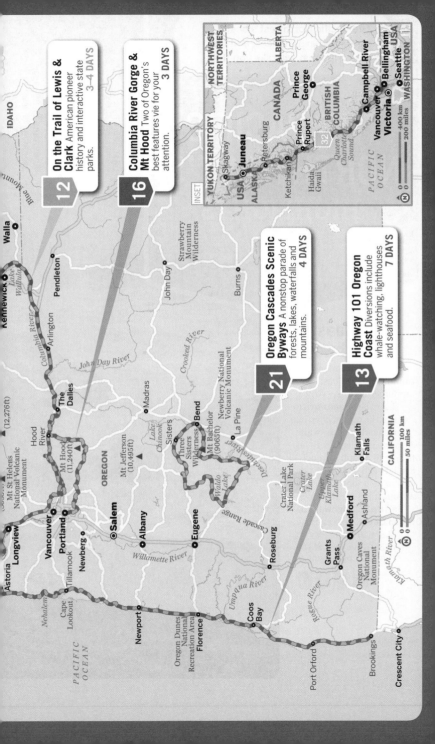

12 **On the Trail of Lewis & Clark** American pioneer history and interactive state parks. **3–4 DAYS**

16 **Columbia River Gorge & Mt Hood** Two of Oregon's best features vie for your attention. **3 DAYS**

21 **Oregon Cascades Scenic Byways** A nonstop parade of forests, lakes, waterfalls and mountains. **4 DAYS**

13 **Highway 101 Oregon Coast** Diversions include whale-watching, lighthouses and seafood. **7 DAYS**

The Pacific Northwest's best sights and experiences, and the road trips that will take you there.

THE PACIFIC NORTHWEST'S
HIGHLIGHTS

Coastal Highways

Cruising along the stunning Pacific Coast is an unforgettable experience. Lofty headlands reach out to the ocean, offering spectacular views, while steep mountains of rock jut offshore like giant sentinels. Stroll beaches, explore tide pools, watch for whales and eat your fill of fresh seafood on **Trip 13: Highway 101 Oregon Coast**, or get a taste of maritime history on **Trip 3: Graveyard of the Pacific Tour**.

TRIPS

Coastal Highways Highway 101 winds past Cape Sebastian (Trip 13)

13

Back Roads & Byways Mt Hood rises in the distance

The Cascade Mountains

The Cascades stretch from British Columbia to California, and you don't have to leave the cities to enjoy them: snow-capped peaks make natural backdrops to the urban bustle in Seattle, Portland and Vancouver. Want to get closer? Explore the northern Cascades on **Trip 6: Cascade Drive** and the Oregon Cascades on **Trip 21: Oregon Cascades Scenic Byways**.

TRIPS

John Day Fossil Beds

Within the soft rocks and crumbly soils of eastern Oregon's John Day region lies one of the world's greatest fossil collections. Over 2200 plant and animal species dating back millions of years have been identified at the John Day Fossil Beds, and the amazing rock formations make **Trip 17: Journey Through Time Scenic Byway** particularly memorable.

TRIP 17

Back Roads & Byways

Ditching the interstate is richly rewarded around these parts. Experience one of the West Coast's most spectacular coastal back roads on **Trip 5: Chuckanut Drive & Whidbey Island**. Get lost in a maze of forests, lakes and hot springs in **Trip 21: Oregon Cascades Scenic Byways**. Or go back in time with the amazing **Trip 17: Journey Through Time Scenic Byway**.

TRIPS

Willamette Wineries View over a vineyard

BEST ROADSIDE FUN

Oregon Vortex Defy physics at a classic roadside attraction. **Trips** 22 23

Prehistoric Gardens Where the dinosaurs are more fun than ferocious. **Trip** 13

Stonehenge Washington's answer to the UK monument. **Trips** 12 17

The Glass House A quirky house made of embalming fluid bottles. **Trip** 11

Marsh's Free Museum Right across from the World's Largest Frying Pan. **Trip** 3

Willamette Wineries

Pinot Noir lovers unite! It's Oregon's most famous grape, finicky as a superstar and the foundation for some exceptional wine. Cruise around the towns of Newberg, Dundee and McMinnville and sample the local favorite, along with chardonnay, Riesling and Pinot Gris. Bring a designated driver and hit all the high points on **Trip 15: Willamette Valley Wine Tour**.

TRIP

Volcanoes & Craters Hikers admire Crater Lake (Trip 23)

Volcanoes & Craters

Volcanoes have a way of wreaking havoc upon the landscape, but give them an eon or two to settle down and you get some gorgeous results. The eruption of Mt Mazama left behind the unique geological gift of Crater Lake, which you'll see on **Trip 23: Crater Lake Circuit**, or you can witness more recent volcanic aftermath on **Trip 8: Mt St Helens Volcano Trail**.

TRIPS 8 23

BEST HOT SPRINGS

Terwilliger Hot Springs
A popular place at Cougar Reservoir. **Trips** 20 21

Breitenbush Lovely, developed springs with on-site accommodations. **Trip** 20

Bonneville A luxurious spa complex on the Lewis & Clark Trail. **Trips** 12 16

Umpqua An unbeatable location, perched on a cliff above the Umpqua River. **Trip** 23

Belknap A resort built around two giant pools. **Trip** 21

Columbia River Gorge Spectacular cascades tumble over mossy cliffs

Olympic National Park Deer frolic in a lush meadow

Columbia River Gorge

Carved out by the mighty Columbia as the Cascades uplifted, the Columbia River Gorge is a geological marvel. With Washington state on its north and Oregon to its south, the gorge provides both states with dramatic views, countless waterfalls and great hikes. Take your time following the gorge on **Trip 16: Columbia River Gorge & Mt Hood**.

TRIP

Olympic National Park

Within this park you can hike through old-growth forests, waltz through flower-filled meadows, swim in pure mountain lakes or try to summit Mt Olympus. You can even go trout fishing, beachcombing, hot-spring soaking and skiing. Learn about some of the park's best features, including the intensely green Hoh Rainforest, on **Trip 2: Olympic Peninsula Loop**.

TRIP

Waterfalls

Tiered falls, plunging falls, curtain falls, ribbon falls – hundreds of waterfalls in the Pacific Northwest give you ample opportunity to witness firsthand all the variations in the waterfall vernacular. You'll find abundant waterfall-peeping opportunities on **Trip 16: Columbia River Gorge & Mt Hood**, and you can even hit 10 falls within one state park on **Trip 20: To Bend & Back**.

TRIPS 20 21

19

The Inside Passage

Park your car on a ferry and let the captain do the driving on this epic journey that takes you along the Canadian coast and all the way up to Alaska – further both north and west than anywhere else in the Pacific Northwest. Wildlife, scenery, lighthouses and quiet fishing towns line the way along spectacular **Trip 32: Up the Inside Passage**.

TRIP

Microbreweries

Love beer? Welcome to paradise. The Pacific Northwest has some of the best microbrews in the world and plenty of them. In fact, Portland (aka 'Beervana') holds the distinguished record of 'most microbreweries of any city in the world.' Almost any city worth its malt has multiple brews to sample; head out to Bend and check out their nine local microbreweries in **Trip 20: To Bend & Back**.

TRIPS

Left: **The Inside Passage** Mendenhall Glacier

Below: **Island Exploration** Gwaii Haanas National Park Reserve (Trip 31)

Island Exploration

Hundreds of islands litter the Pacific Northwest coastline, ranging from uninhabited to barely inhabited, and you'll feel like you've left the world behind the moment you drive onto the ferry. Go off the grid on **Trip 4: San Juan Islands Scenic Byway**, or make your escape with **Trip 31: Haida Gwaii Adventure** or **Trip 32: Up the Inside Passage**.

TRIPS 4 28 31 32

BEST SKIING

Whistler Follow in the ski tracks of the 2010 Winter Olympians. **Trip** 26

Methow Valley A cross-country skier's paradise with over 125 miles of groomed trails. **Trip** 6

Crystal Mountain Washington's largest ski resort, with more than 50 named runs. **Trip** 7

Mt Hood You can ski here every month of the year. **Trip** 16

IF YOU LIKE...

Alert Bay Totem poles in the wilderness (Trip 29)

History

History buffs can follow in the footsteps of Native Americans, explorers, pioneer families and gold rush prospectors, and the area's maritime history is reflected all along the Pacific Coast. Too recent? Explore fossil beds that date back millions of years.

3 Graveyard of the Pacific Tour Lighthouses, nautical museums and shipwrecks illuminate maritime history.

12 On the Trail of Lewis & Clark Follow the trail of America's greatest explorers.

17 Journey Through Time Scenic Byway Dig deep into Oregon history with fossil beds, ghost towns and more.

25 Vancouver & the Fraser Valley East of Vancouver, learn more about British Columbia's pioneer past.

The Great Outdoors

It's no wonder the Pacific Northwest attracts so many outdoorsy types. The Great Outdoors is what the area is all about, whether you're trekking through forests, finding remote hot springs, or biking down the coast.

2 Olympic Peninsula Loop From beaches to mountains, explore the treasures of the Olympic Peninsula.

4 San Juan Islands Scenic Byway Whale-watching, kayaking and biking are the main attractions in these islands off Washington's coast.

16 Columbia River Gorge & Mt Hood This area reveals some of Oregon's most dramatic work.

21 Oregon Cascades Scenic Byways Waterfalls, hot springs and lakes break up the almost nonstop greenery.

Food & Drink

The Pacific Northwest leads the continent in locally grown, sustainable and organic products. And since great wine demands great food, you can get your fill of both in the wine regions of Oregon, Washington and British Columbia, where tasting things has been raised to an art form.

5 Chuckanut Drive & Whidbey Island Nosh your way from cheese shops to oyster farms and farm-to-plate restaurants.

9 Washington Wine Tour Columbia Valley's laid-back wine country is emerging as a major winemaking destination.

15 Willamette Valley Wine Tour Oregon's wine country showcases some of the area's best food and wine.

30 Okanagan Valley Wine Tour Explore Canada's hill-lined, lakeside wine region.

Olympic National Park Trek through forests for superb views (Trip 2)

Family Travel

From aquariums full of sea life to cowboys riding bucking broncos, the Pacific Northwest will spark a child's imagination. Whether you head to the coast, the mountains or farmland, you'll be greeted with kindness by locals who know how to treat families right.

1 Mountains to Sound Greenway Waterfalls, aquariums and interesting museums make this trip fun for everyone.

13 Highway 101 Oregon Coast Enjoy tide pools, ocean surf and lots of small-town stops along the way.

22 Essential I-5 This trip packs in the fun, with stops that range from roadside attractions to light history moments.

26 Sea to Sky Highway The Britannia Mining Museum is a hit with road-weary kids.

Off the Beaten Track

No one does remote like the Pacific Northwest. It's easy to lose yourself out here, with undeveloped land masses that stretch on and on, from the unpopulated eastern regions of Washington and Oregon, to the vast expanses of British Columbia that stretch into Alaska.

11 International Selkirk Loop Find the forgotten corners of Washington, Idaho and British Columbia.

19 Hells Canyon Scenic Byway Few roads access the canyons in this remote corner of Oregon.

32 Up the Inside Passage How far are you willing to go to escape crowds? Alaska? Good.

29 Vancouver Island's Remote North Head north from Vancouver to see the less-well-known side of the island.

Mountains

One of the benefits of being in a geological area known for earthquakes and volcanoes is the unique landscape they leave behind. Snow-capped ranges dominate the landscape, providing scenic backdrops and abundant recreational opportunities – from skiing to hiking to searching for Bigfoot.

6 Cascade Drive This altitudinous route through the northern Cascades is alive with rugged beauty.

7 Mt Rainier Scenic Byways At 14,411ft, volcanic Mt Rainier is the highest peak in the Cascades.

8 Mt St Helens Volcano Trail See the destruction left behind after its 1980 eruption.

33 Circling the Rockies Get a taste of national parks, hot springs, and the Canadian Rockies.

NEED TO KNOW

CELL PHONES

The only foreign phones that work in North America are GSM multiband models. SIM cards are relatively easy to obtain in both countries.

INTERNET ACCESS

Wi-fi is available in most lodgings and cafes; some larger hotels add $10 to $20 for access. Internet cafes charge $4 to $10 per hour.

FUEL

Gas stations are easy to find, except in national parks and some mountain areas. Expect to pay $3.50 to $4.50 per gallon.

RENTAL

Budget (📞800-527-0700; www.budget.com)

Enterprise (📞800-261-7331; www.enterprise.com)

Hertz (📞800-654-3131; www.hertz.com)

IMPORTANT NUMBERS

American Automobile Association (AAA; 📞800-444-8091)

Canadian Automobile Association (CAA; 📞604-268-5500)

Emergencies (📞911)

US travel info (📞511)

Climate

Desert, dry climate

Warm to hot summers, mild winters

Mild to hot summers, cold winters

Vancouver
GO Jun–Sep

Victoria
GO Jun–Sep

Seattle
GO Jun–Sep

Eastern Washington
GO May–Oct

Portland
GO Jun–Sep

Eastern Oregon
GO May–Oct

Oregon Coast
GO Jun–Sep

When to Go

High Season (Jun–Sep)

» Sunny, warm days throughout the region.

» More crowds and higher prices for accommodations and sights.

» For ski resorts, busiest times are December to March.

Shoulder Season (Apr–May & Oct)

» Crowds and prices drop off.

» Temperatures remain mild, although there can still be snow at high altitudes.

» Services are more limited, but there's less competition for them.

» Some roads are closed at this time of year.

Low Season (Nov–Mar)

» Colder days, less sunlight, more rain.

» Some services may close along the coast, and high passes can be blocked by snow.

» Indoor activities such as theater and music are at their best.

Daily Costs

Budget: Less than $100

» Cheap motel room: $50–$75

» Fast-food or food-truck meal: $5–$10

» Museums: $0 on free-admission days

Midrange: $100–$175

» Hotel room with bath: $100

» Meal in a good restaurant: $15–$20 plus wine

» Museum admission: $10–$20

Top End: More than $175

» Upscale hotel room: $150

» Fine-dining meal: $25 and up, plus wine

» Theater performances and major attractions: $50–$100

Eating

Food trucks Cheap, creative and often delicious.

Cafes Pick up a pastry with your morning coffee.

Roadside diners Cheap and simple.

Restaurants All price ranges and cuisine types are represented.

Vegetarians Most restaurants offer vegetarian options.

Eating price indicators represent the cost of a main dish:

$	less than $10
$$	$10–$20
$$$	more than $20

Sleeping

Hostels Budget options let you share a room on the cheap.

Motels Cheaper than hotels and ubiquitous along highways.

B&Bs Personal service, often in former homes, breakfast included.

Hotels The higher the rate, the more amenities.

Sleeping price indicators represent the cost of a double room with private bathroom:

$	less than $100
$$	$100–$175
$$$	more than $175

Arriving in the Pacific Northwest

Sea-Tac Airport (Seattle)

Rental Cars Reserve online and pick up at the airport.

Link Light Rail Connects to downtown Seattle in 30 minutes; adult/child $3/1.25.

Bus Metro buses stop outside baggage carousel 5; $2.75/1.25.

Shuttle Frequent services from $11 one way.

Taxi $35; about 25 minutes to downtown.

Portland International Airport

Rental Cars Reserve online and pick up at the airport.

Max Light Rail Connects to downtown Portland in 40 minutes; $2.40/1.50.

Shuttle Frequent services from $14 one way.

Taxis $30; around 20 minutes to downtown.

Vancouver International Airport

Rental Cars Reserve online and pick up at the airport.

SkyTrain Connects to downtown Vancouver in 25 minutes; from CAN$7.50/6.75.

Taxi CAN$35; around 30 minutes to downtown.

Money

ATMs widely available. Credit cards accepted at most hotels, restaurants and shops.

Tipping

15% to 20% of restaurant bill; 10% to 15% for taxis; $1 per drink or 15% for bartenders; $1 to $2 per bag for valets; $1 to $2 daily for housekeeping.

Opening Hours

High season hours:

Restaurants ⊘7–11am breakfast, 11:30am–2:30pm lunch, 5–10pm dinner

Shops ⊘9am or 10am–5pm or 6pm (malls 9pm) Monday to Saturday, noon–5pm Sunday

Supermarkets ⊘24 hours in large cities

Useful Websites

Lonely Planet (www.lonelyplanet.com/usa/pacific-northwest)

Oregon Tourism Commission (www.traveloregon.com)

Tourism British Columbia (www.hellobc.com)

Washington State Tourism (www.experiencewa.com)

For more, see the Pacific Northwest Driving Guide (p350).

CITY
GUIDE

SEATTLE

Lively, progressive and endlessly green, Seattle is Washington state's largest city. Rainy days are a great time to wander historic Pike Place Market, take the Seattle Underground Tour or visit Seattle's most rocking museum, the Experience Music Project. When the sun comes out, head for the Olympic Sculpture Park or take our walking tour (p138).

Getting Around

All Seattle taxicabs operate at the same rate, currently $2.50 at meter drop, then $2.50 per mile. Metro Transit buses (fares $2 to $2.75). Traffic can be messy, but freeway high-occupancy vehicle (HOV) lanes make it easier for two or more people.

Parking

Downtown parking is scarce and expensive, and some hotels charge a premium overnight, so check before booking. Metered parking goes from 8am to 6pm and extends until 8pm in popular areas; Sundays are free if you can find a spot.

Seattle City skyline

Where to Eat

Some of Seattle's favorite restaurants are tucked into Pike Place Market, where you can also forage for top-notch picnic fixings. The historic core of the city, Pioneer Square, has a surprising number of budget-friendly dining options, and the International District has amazing Asian cuisine.

Where to Stay

Belltown and the Pike Place Market areas of downtown offer lots of choices ranging from hostels to boutiques to large chains. The University District offers more budget-conscious options, and Capitol Hill is a good choice for inns and B&Bs.

Useful Websites

Visit Seattle (www.visitseattle.org) Official site of the Convention and Visitors Bureau.

Lonely Planet (www.lonelyplanet.com/usa/seattle) Travel tips, accommodations and travelers' forum.

Trips Through Seattle: 1 7

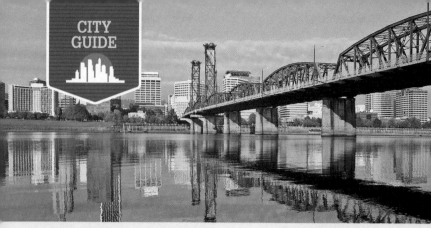

CITY GUIDE

Portland Willamette River

PORTLAND

Laid-back Portland has a vibrant downtown and charming neighborhoods full of friendly (and often zany) people. People-watching is a favorite pastime, best enjoyed while noshing at food carts, catching live music, or wandering though local gardens or the aisles of Powell's Books. Check it all out on our walking tour (p254).

Getting Around

One of downtown Portland's greatest features is the Free Rail Zone, which lets you ride MAX Light Rail and the Portland Streetcar for free within Downtown, the Rose Quarter and the Lloyd District. Or join the locals and take a bike in this exceedingly bike-friendly city.

Parking

You can get lucky with metered street parking, but there are six convenient SmartPark buildings downtown that charge $1.50 per hour. Check www. portlandonline.com/ smartpark for locations and hours.

Where to Eat

Downtown offers everything from fine dining to food carts where you can find the perfect combination of good, cheap and fast. For good midrange options, including great brunches and a mélange of ethnic cuisines, head across the river to northeast and southeast Portland.

Where to Stay

You'll find Portland's swankiest digs downtown, along with some nice midrange options. On the east side of town are some of the city's coolest independent hotels, as well as lots of midrange and budget chain offerings near the convention center.

Useful Websites

City of Portland (www. portlandonline.com) Portland's official website.

Food Carts Portland (www. foodcartsportland.com) A guide to Portland's food carts.

Travel Portland (www. travelportland.com) What to do, where to go, how to save...

Trips Through Portland: 14 15 16 22

Vancouver Stanley Park

VANCOUVER

Vancouver is a sparkling, cosmopolitan city set against a backdrop of rugged natural beauty. Its welcoming downtown (see our walking tour, p344) is flanked by the forested seawall of Stanley Park, and the neighborhoods contain easily walkable shopping streets. Wander historic Gastown, artsy Granville Island and the colorful West End 'gayborhood.'

Getting Around

You don't really need a car in Vancouver: it's easy enough to get around on foot, by bus or by cab. TransLink network – which includes buses, SkyTrain and SeaBus – starts at CAN$2.50 for travel within one zone. An all-day, all-zone pass costs CAN$9/7 per adult/child.

Where to Eat

Top streets include downtown's Robson St for Japanese *izakaya,* Yaletown's Hamilton and Mainland Sts for splurge-worthy dinners, Gastown for resto-bars, Commercial Dr for ethnic-flavored joints, and the West End's Denman and Davie Sts for midrange options.

Useful Websites

City of Vancouver (www.vancouver.ca) Resource-packed official city site.

Inside Vancouver (www.insidevancouver.ca) What to do in and around the city.

Trip Through Vancouver: 25

Parking

Parking is at a premium downtown. Some streets have metered parking, but your best bet is to head for pay-parking lots (from CAN$4 per hour). Underground parking at Pacific Centre mall or Vancouver Public Library will put you in the heart of things.

Where to Stay

Swanky sleepovers abound downtown, as do midrange options. To split the geographical difference between downtown and the great outdoors, head to the North Shore. Hostels are scattered across the city; there are good digs near the University of British Columbia.

Washington Trips

THERE IS NO QUINTESSENTIAL WASHINGTONIAN. So banish that stereotypical image of a Prius-driving, latte-supping Seattleite from your mind. Instead, the spinal Cascade Mountains cut the state metaphorically in half. In a few hours you can drive from the wet, urban, liberal, evergreen coast, via a dramatic volcano-punctuated mountain range, to the arid, conservative, vineyard-patterned and scrublike east.

On the way you'll find literary inspiration in the footsteps of Jack Kerouac, geological epiphanies near Mt St Helens, vampire apparitions on the Olympic Peninsula and miles and miles of expertly engineered strips of winding asphalt that seem to defy the icy, precipitous terrain.

Mt Rainier National Park Snow-capped Mt Rainier (Trip 7)

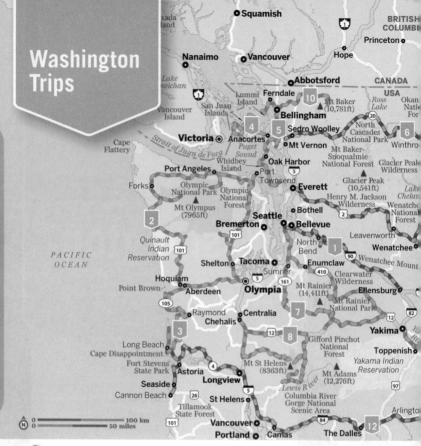

Washington Trips

DON'T MISS

Ross Lake Resort

A floating hotel on a wilderness lake; no wonder Kerouac loved the cold, almost terrifying, beauty on Trip 6

Cape Disappointment

Few leave Cape Disappointment disappointed, thanks to its spectacular end-of-the-continent setting. Drop by on Trips 3 12

Leavenworth

German theme towns rarely work in the US except when the alpine backdrop looks positively German. See it on Trip 6

Northwest Railway Museum

Snoqualmie community saves a slice of American heritage: a moving museum on a train. Visit on Trip 1

North Woven Broom

Long before Harry Potter, North Woven Broom was making artisan broomsticks. Sweep by on Trip 11

Cascade Mountains Bucolic trails and small towns await off the I-90

Classic Trip

Mountains to Sound Greenway

1

Busy I-90 zaps you from the Yakima River Valley to the metro sophistication of Seattle in less than two hours. But meander off the main road and more serendipitous adventures lurk.

TRIP HIGHLIGHTS

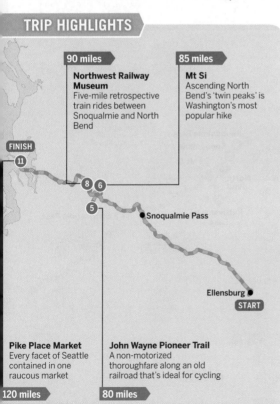

90 miles

Northwest Railway Museum
Five-mile retrospective train rides between Snoqualmie and North Bend

85 miles

Mt Si
Ascending North Bend's 'twin peaks' is Washington's most popular hike

FINISH
11

8 6

5

Snoqualmie Pass

Ellensburg
START

Pike Place Market
Every facet of Seattle contained in one raucous market
120 miles

John Wayne Pioneer Trail
A non-motorized thoroughfare along an old railroad that's ideal for cycling
80 miles

1–2 DAYS
120 MILES/193KM

GREAT FOR...

BEST TIME TO GO

May to September when the museums are open and the weather is less fickle.

ESSENTIAL PHOTO

Snoqualmie Falls for a mixture of raw natural power and 1990s TV flashbacks.

BEST FOR FAMILIES

Northwest Railway Museum and its spring/summer train rides.

35

Classic Trip

1 Mountains to Sound Greenway

Dramatic changes in scenery and radically contrasting ecosystems are par for the course in Washington, a land bisected by the climate-altering Cascade Mountains. With Interstate-90 as its main artery, this drive ferries you from the dry east to the wet west via 3046ft Snoqualmie Pass on an ostensibly busy road. But a mile or two off the interstate a parallel 'greenway' of bucolic trails and small-town preservation societies prevails.

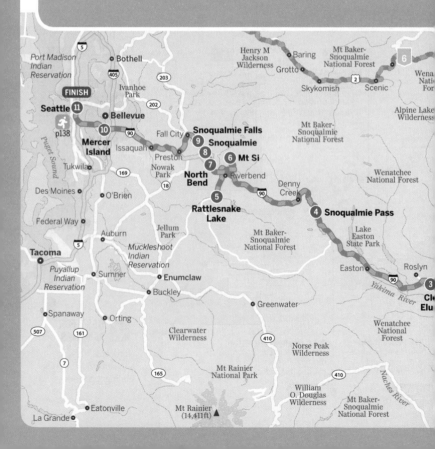

❶ Ellensburg

Take an archetypal American small town with a stately college and a smattering of historic buildings; then throw in the largest and most lauded rodeo in the Pacific Northwest. Welcome to Ellensburg, town of improbable juxtapositions.

Here, erudite college undergraduates rub shoulders with weekend cowboys in a small yet salubrious collegiate town where two-thirds of the 16,000 population are registered students. Like most Washington towns, Ellensburg has its fair share of peripheral motel/mall infestations, but body-swerve the familiar big boxes and you'll uncover a compact but select cluster of venerable red-bricked buildings in a downtown **historic district**. Also worth checking out is the **Kittitas County Historical Museum** (www. kchm.org; 114 E 3rd Ave; donations accepted; 🕑10am-4pm Mon-Sat), housed in the 1889 Cadwell Building, known mostly for its petrified-wood and gemstone collections, but also hosting a cleverly laid out history section documenting the backgrounds of Croatian, Arabic and Welsh immigrants.

✕ 🛏 p43

The Drive » To avoid the clamor of the busy interstate, take US-97 northwest out of Ellensburg before branching onto SR-10 to the small rural settlement of Thorp.

❷ Thorp Grist Mill

In the small town of Thorp (population 240) 9 miles northwest of Ellensburg, the **Thorp Grist Mill** (www.thorp.org; admission free; 🕑11am-3pm Thu-Sat, noon-4pm Sun May-Sep) was once a de-facto meeting place for local farmers. Today, its well-preserved shell gives an interesting insight into the pioneer famers who plowed the fields of the Kittitas Valley in the late 19th century. Converted to a rural museum, the mill originally dates from 1883 when its primary purpose was to grind flour using water power from the nearby Yakima River. It ceased operation in 1946, but, thanks to the foresight of local community activists, was placed on the National Register of Historic Places in 1977.

The Drive » Continue northwest on SR-10, 18 miles to Cle Elum through quiet bucolic farmland.

🔗 LINK YOUR TRIP

6 Cascade Drive

Both ends of this trip will deposit you close to entry points for the Cascade Drive, another mountain-punctuated driving extravaganza (p77).

9 Washington Wine Tour

Do this drive backwards starting in Seattle and the essence of local wine in Ellensburg might inspire you to travel on to Yakima and beyond (p105).

Classic Trip

❸ Cle Elum

Cle Elum's location on the cusp of the Eastern Cascades and the bald treeless grasslands of the Kittitas Valley pulls in two radically different types of visitor. Seattleites regularly cross Snoqualmie Pass to sup the local wine and enjoy seemingly endless summer sunshine. Easterners stop by to gaze west at the snowier, more topographically interesting mountains. A posh resort, the **Suncadia** (www.suncadiaresort.com; r from $169), just west of Cle Elum and complete with golf, spa and a brand-new winery, caters for both groups.

Though small, the town has a couple of esoteric museums conceived and maintained by vivacious community groups. The best is the **Telephone**

Museum (221 E 1st St; admission free; ⊙noon-4pm Sat & Sun May-Sep) with old switchboards, phones and some insightful local history.

Up the road, Roslyn stood in for Alaska in the 1990s TV show *Northern Exposure* (plot spoiler: there's more TV nostalgia two stops further on).

The Drive ❱❱ Time to brave I-90! Access the road at exit 84 and motor 30 miles progressively uphill to Snoqualmie Pass. Just before the summit you'll pass Keechelus Lake, the source of the Yakima River, on your left.

❹ Snoqualmie Pass

One of the easier routes across the Cascades and the only one to carry an interstate (the I-90), Snoqualmie was first prospected by white settlers in the 1850s. By the 1930s a fledgling road was being plowed year-round and the pass had spawned a nascent ski area which has since morphed into four separate areas

known (and managed) communally as the **Summit at Snoqualmie** (www.summitatsnoqualmie. com). This is the nearest day-use ski area to Seattle (read: long lines). Should you summit the pass in summer, consider a hike. The **Pacific Crest Trail** briefly descends to the hustle of the interstate here but blissful tranquility stretches for many miles in either direction.

The Drive ❱❱ Descend on I-90 until exit 32. Go south on 436th Ave SE which becomes Cedar Falls Rd. Within 3 miles you will be deposited at Rattlesnake Lake.

TRIP HIGHLIGHT

❺ Rattlesnake Lake

An important nexus on the Mountains to Sound Greenway, tranquil Rattlesnake Lake was once a more tumultuous place. A town called Moncton existed here until 1915 before it was flooded, evacuated and condemned after an abortive damming project. From 1906 to 1980 an erstwhile railway, the 'Milwaukee Road', passed through. The railroad bed has been reworked into a non-motorized thoroughfare known as the **John Wayne Pioneer Trail** which is popular with cyclists. A summer shuttle called **Bus-up 90** (www.busup90. com; adult/child $22/18)

ELLENSBURG RODEO

Outside of the Calgary Stampede, Ellensburg's Labor Day weekend rodeo (which dates from 1923) is the biggest of its kind in the Northwest and one of the top 10 in the USA. Not surprisingly, it attracts fine riders, big prize money (up to $250,000) and huge crowds, so, if you're going to be attending, book early for both tickets and accommodation. A good online portal is www.ellensburgrodeo.com.

TWIN PEAKS

Recognize *that* Snoqualmie Valley mountain, *that* waterfall, *that* cafe and *that* hotel? If you're under 40 and have never heard of Kyle McLachlan or vexed over who murdered the unfortunate Laura Palmer, then *Twin Peaks* may need a bit of explaining. The TV drama series was conceived, written and directed by Mark Frost and legendary US film director David Lynch in the late 1980s. The latter's work *(Blue Velvet, Wild at Heart)* became so influential that he even had an adjective named after him: 'Lynchian' denotes anything that's surreal, dreamy, unsettling and – occasionally – freakishly funny. *Twin Peaks,* which ran for 30 episodes over two series between 1990 and 1991, was set in a fictional Washington town of the same name (and filmed in North Bend and Snoqualmie). It starred Kyle McLachlan as FBI agent Dale Cooper investigating the mysterious death of a pretty blonde homecoming queen. The series, with its complex plot and surreal, but suspenseful, storyline, quickly gained a large audience and was heaped with critical praise earning numerous Golden Globes and Emmys. Time has done little to diminish its appeal. Like all great art, *Twin Peaks* proved to be powerfully influential and, over 20 years later, it still inspires obsessive geekdom with cult followers everywhere from Japan to Scandinavia.

As for those recognizable landmarks; the mountain (the fictional 'Twin Peaks') is Mt Si, the waterfall (seen in the show's opening credits) is Snoqualmie Falls, the cafe (where Kyle McLachlan extolled the virtues of piping hot black coffee) is Twede's (p39) and the hotel (the Great Northern in the show) is the Salish Lodge & Spa (p43).

whisks cyclists three times daily, 22 miles and 1700ft uphill. From here you can descend to the lake, a journey that includes careering through the 2.3-mile Snoqualmie tunnel (bring headlamps). The lake is also the starting point for the **Snoqualmie Valley Trail** and a 4-mile round-trip hike up to Rattlesnake Ridge. There are toilets and a kayak launch lakeside and a small interpretive center.

The Drive ⟩⟩ Return to I-90 but this time, rather than join it, head underneath on 436th Ave SE to the junction with E North Bend Way. Turn left and then go right on SE Mt Si Rd.

TRIP HIGHLIGHT

6 Mt Si

Brooding moodily behind the town of North Bend, 4167ft Mt Si is allegedly the most climbed mountain in the state (approximately 40,000 hike it every year) and an annual fitness test for many Seattleites. The trail starts 2.5 miles down SE Mt Si Rd from a parking lot and is an 8-mile round-trip including 3150ft of ascent. Though popular and predictably crowded in summer, the switchbacking path is no cakewalk. Dress appropriately for the

mountains and bring water. The lofty meadow that acts as the summit for most walkers (the actual summit is a precipitous haystack-shaped rock) is revered for its hard-earned Puget Sound views.

The Drive ⟩⟩ Retrace your route along SE Mt Si Rd to the intersection with E North Bend Way, where you turn right into North Bend.

7 North Bend

If your memory stretches back to pre-Clinton era America and/or you nurture a secret penchant for cult US TV mini-series, your first sight of North Bend could

NIK WHEELER / ALAMY ©

JOEL W. ROGERS / CORBIS ©

FARMERS

LOCAL KNOWLEDGE
SCOTT DAVIES,
PUBLIC
INFORMATION
SPECIALIST, PIKE
PLACE MARKET

The North Arcade in Seattle's Pike
Place Market is where farmers and
craftspeople sell their wares. Look
out for the numerous flower sellers,
many of whom are Hmong people
originally from Laos and Thailand. In
the market's North End are some of
the neighborhood's best restaurants
and takeouts, including the Russian
bakery Piroshky Piroshky and
artisan cheese-maker Beechers,
both of whom make their products
from scratch in their front windows.

Top: Ellensburg's downtown historic district
Left: Pike Place Market, Seattle
Right: Snoqualmie Falls

require an eerie double take. This is where David Lynch's weird and wonderful *Twin Peaks* was filmed in the early 1990s and the town – a sleepy, if salubrious, place these days – is still playing on the fact. **Twede's** (www.twedescafe. com; 137 W North Bend Way; ☺8am-8pm, from 6:30am Sat & Sun), the 'Double R Diner' in the TV show, proudly advertises its *Twin Peaks* credentials with cherry pie and 'a damn fine cup o' coffee,' along with 50 – yes 50 – different types of burger. Down the road, the **Snoqualmie Valley Historical Museum** (www. snoqualmievalleymuseum.org; Bendigo Blvd; ☺1-5pm Sat-Tue) charts the pre-Lynchian history of the valley with pioneer and Native American exhibits.

The Drive » From Bend take Bendigo Blvd crossing the South Fork of the Snoqualmie River and continuing 3 miles into Snoqualmie.

- - - - - - - - - - - - -

TRIP HIGHLIGHT

❽ Snoqualmie

Located a mile east of the famous falls, Snoqualmie is a diminutive town of esoteric shopfronts that ply hardware, organic coffee and Native American art. Across the tracks, the lovingly restored **Northwest Railway Museum** (www. trainmuseum.org; 38625 SE King St; ☺10am-5pm) is the largest of its type in

Classic Trip

Washington. Its hook is its retro steam-train trips (adult/child $15/10) which chug (four times daily from April to October) 5 miles down the line to North Bend and another equally cute Thomas-the-Tank-Engine station.

Snoqualmie is also an ideal place to jump onto the **Snoqualmie Valley Trail**, the region's longest greenway (31 miles) that parallels the Snoqualmie River along the course of an old railway line. Access is best gained from the north end of Meadowbrook Way SE.

The Drive » From Snoqualmie follow Railroad Ave northwest out of town and within a mile you'll be at Snoqualmie Falls.

9 Snoqualmie Falls

Come between April and June during the spring snow melt and you'll see why this 268ft mini-Niagara has been producing hydroelectric power since 1899. New observation decks and an overlook park stand face-on against the supersonic spray, while perched awfully close to the giant falls' rim is the luxurious **Salish Lodge & Spa** (p43), the second incarnation of a hotel that was first built here in 1918.

A half-mile trail that drops down through spray-fed rainforest to the original 1910 powerhouse was being renovated at the time of research and is due to reopen in early 2013.

 p43

The Drive » Take the Fall City–Snoqualmie Rd to Fall City where you turn left onto the Preston–Fall City Rd opposite the Fall City Roadhouse and Inn. Merge west onto I-90 again at Preston (exit 22).

10 Mercer Island

You don't have to get out of your car to experience Mercer Island's greatest engineering marvel. The community's two colossal parallel bridges that carry traffic over to metro Seattle are the second and fifth longest floating bridges in the world. An initial bridge, built here in 1939, was destroyed by a storm in 1990. Hence, the current structures, the **Homer M Hadley Memorial Bridge** (westbound traffic) and the **Lacey V Murrow Memorial Bridge** (eastbound) were built in 1989 and 1993 respectively.

The Drive » Coming off the floating bridges, traffic is directed through the Baker Tunnel before coming out with surprising suddenness in Seattle's downtown core close to King Street Station.

TRIP HIGHLIGHT

11 Seattle

Put aside some time to enjoy Seattle at the end of this drive which deposits you on the cusp of downtown and its cluster of craning skyscrapers – check it out on our walking tour (p138). For dazzling city views ascend the **Columbia Center** (701 5th Av; admission $5), built in 1985, which at 932ft high is the loftiest building in the Pacific Northwest and a lot cheaper than the Space Needle. Pioneer Square is Seattle's oldest quarter and home to the **Klondike Gold Rush National Historical Park** (www.nps.gov/klse; 117 S Main St; admission free; 9am-5pm), a shockingly good free museum about the 1897 Alaska gold rush. Another good family-orientated attraction is the **Seattle Aquarium** (www.seattleaquarium.org; 1483 Alaskan Way at Pier 59; adult/child $19.95/13.95; 9:30am-5pm;), the centerpiece of which is a glass-domed room where sharks, octopuses and other deepwater denizens lurk in the shadowy depths. For a post-drive picnic decamp to **Pike Place Market** for artisan cheeses, Russian pastries and Italian deli meats.

 p43

Eating & Sleeping

Ellensburg ❶

✕ Yellow Church Café Brunch, Fusion $$
(www.yellowchurchcafe.com; 111 S Pearl
St; brunch $8-12, dinner $13-23) Top in the
Ellensburg 'quirky' stakes is this former bright
yellow church built by the German Lutherans in
1923 and now converted into an unconventional
restaurant that serves spiritually enlightening
food. The breakfast has won widespread
recommendations, while the elegant dinner
options are matched with local wines from the
expert owners who also run a nearby winery.

🛏 Inn at Goose Creek Hotel $$
(☏509-962-8030; www.innatgoosecreek.
com; 1720 Canyon Rd; r from $99; 🛜) Surely
one of the most imaginative motels around,
this establishment off I-90 is not your standard
fancily restored period piece – at least, not
from the outside. Inside is a different story.
Eclectic themed rooms include the Victorian
Honeymoon Suite, the Ellensburg Rodeo Room,
and the I Love Christmas Room.

Snoqualmie Falls ❾

✕🛏 Salish Lodge & Spa Hotel $$$
(☏360-647-0092; www.salishlodge.com; 6501
Railroad Ave SE; r $209-309; ❄🛜) Out-acted
only by Kyle McLachlan in *Twin Peaks* (when it
was the Great Northern Hotel), the Salish needs
little introduction. All of the luxury rooms face
the waterfall which is so close you can literally
drink the spray. Good job they've also all got
traditional wood-burning fires. The acclaimed
restaurant and spa point to a steep asking price.

✕🛏 Fall City
Roadhouse & Inn Inn, Diner $
(☏425-222-4040; www.fcroadhouse.com; 420
Preston-Fall City Rd SE; r $70-100; ❄🛜) A
traditional building given a 2008 makeover, the
Roadhouse has been reborn as an eye-catching
distraction in otherwise run-of-the-mill Fall City.

Seattle ⓫

✕ Wild Ginger Asian $$
(www.wildginger.net; 1401 3rd Ave; mains
$15-28) All around the Pacific Rim – via China,
Indonesia, Malaysia, Vietnam and Seattle of
course – is the wide-ranging theme at this
highly popular downtown fusion restaurant. Try
the fragrant duck first.

✕ Top Pot Hand-Forged
Doughnuts Cafe $
(www.toppotdoughnuts.com; 2124 5th Ave;
🕑6am-7pm Mon-Fri, 7am-7pm Sat-Sun) Top Pot
are to doughnuts what champagne is to wine – a
different class. And their cafes – this one in an
old car showroom with floor-to-ceiling library
shelves and art-deco signage – are equally
legendary.

✕ Zeitgeist Cafe $
(www.zeitgeistcoffee.com; 171 S Jackson St;
🕑6am-7pm Mon-Fri, 8am-7pm Sat & Sun; 🛜)
Plug into the spirit of the times with the rest of
the laptop crew at this lofty, brick-walled cafe
near the train station.

🛏 Belltown Inn Hotel $$
(☏206-529-3700; www.belltown-inn.com;
2301 3rd Ave; s/d $109/119; ❄@🛜) Can it
be true? The Belltown is such a bargain and
in such a prime location that it's hard not to
believe it hasn't accidently floated over from a
smaller, infinitely cheaper city. But no, those
clean functional rooms, handy kitchenettes,
free bikes and – vitally important – borrow-and-
return umbrellas, are all yours for the price of a
posh dinner.

Hoh Rainforest Dense, wet, green and intensely surreal

Olympic Peninsula Loop

2

Freakishly wet, fantastically green and chillingly remote, the Olympic Peninsula looks like it's been resurrected from a wilder, pre-civilized era.

TRIP HIGHLIGHTS

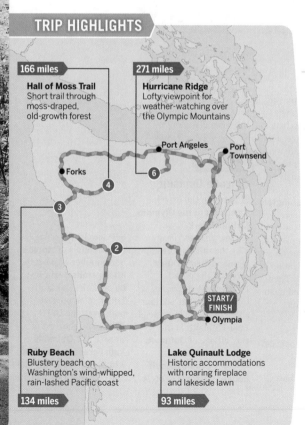

166 miles

Hall of Moss Trail
Short trail through moss-draped, old-growth forest

271 miles

Hurricane Ridge
Lofty viewpoint for weather-watching over the Olympic Mountains

● Port Angeles

Port Townsend

● Forks

4

6

3

2

START/ FINISH

● Olympia

Ruby Beach
Blustery beach on Washington's wind-whipped, rain-lashed Pacific coast

134 miles

Lake Quinault Lodge
Historic accommodations with roaring fireplace and lakeside lawn

93 miles

4 DAYS
435 MILES/700KM

GREAT FOR...

BEST TIME TO GO

June to September when your chances of getting drenched by continuous rain are slightly diminished.

 ESSENTIAL PHOTO

Hoh Rainforest to snap shades of green you haven't even seen yet.

 BEST FOR WILDLIFE

Hoh Rainforest offers rare glimpses of Roosevelt elk.

45

2 Olympic Peninsula Loop

Imagine *Wuthering Heights* fused with an American Mt Olympus, with a topical slice of Stephanie Meyer's *Twilight* saga thrown in for good measure and you've got an approximation of what a drive around the Olympic Peninsula might look like. This is wilderness of the highest order where thick forest collides with an end-of-the-continent coastline that hasn't changed much since Juan de Fuca sailed by in 1592. Bring hiking boots – and an umbrella!

① Olympia

Welcome to Olympia, city of weird contrasts, where street-side buskers belt out acoustic grunge, and stiff bureaucrats answer their ringtones on the lawns of the expansive state legislature. A quick circuit of the **Washington State Capitol** (admission free; ⊗8am-4:30pm), a huge Grecian temple of a building, will give you a last taste of civilization before you depart. Then load up the car and head swiftly for the exits.

 p51

The Drive » Your basic route is due west, initially on Highway 101, then (briefly) on SR-8 before joining US-12 in Elma.

In Gray's Harbor enter the twin cities of Aberdeen and Hoquiam, famous for producing William Boeing and the grunge group Nirvana. Here, you swing north on Highway 101 (again!) to leafier climes at Lake Quinault.

TRIP HIGHLIGHT

② Lake Quinault

Situated in the extreme southwest of the **Olympic National Park** (www. nps.gov/olym; vehicle entry $15), the thickly forested Quinault River Valley is one of the park's least-crowded corners. Clustered on the south shore of deep-blue glacial Lake Quinault is the tiny village of **Quinault**, complete with the luscious **Lake Quinault Lodge** (p51), a US Forest Service (USFS) office, plus a couple of stores.

A number of short **hiking trails** begin just below Lake Quinault Lodge; pick up a free map from the USFS office. The shortest of these is the **Quinault Rain Forest Nature Trail**, a half-mile walk through 500-year-old Douglas firs.

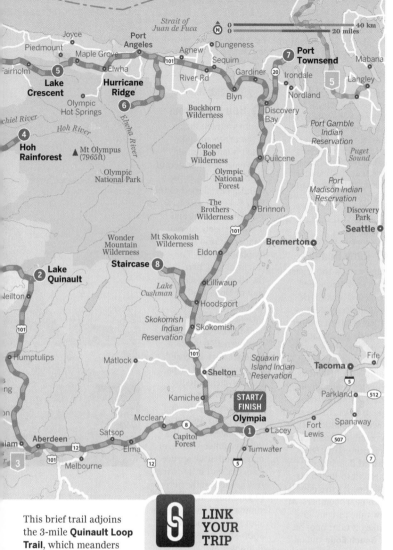

This brief trail adjoins the 3-mile **Quinault Loop Trail**, which meanders through the rain forests before circling back to the lake. The Quinault region is renowned for its huge trees. Close to the village is a 191ft Sitka spruce tree (supposedly over 1000 years old), and nearby are the

S LINK YOUR TRIP

3 Graveyard of the Pacific Tour

Continue down the coast where rough seas have acted as a watery cemetery for many historic ships (p53).

5 Chuckanut Drive & Whidbey Island

Across the Port Townsend ferry, Whidbey is a gentler and – traditionally – dryer contrast to the Olympics (p69).

world's largest red cedar, Douglas fir and mountain hemlock trees.

 p51

The Drive ›› West from Quinault Lake, Highway 101 continues through the Quinault Indian Reservation before entering a thin strip of national park territory that protects the beaches around Kalaloch (*klay*-lock). This is some of the wildest coastal scenery in the US accessible by road. Various pullovers allow beach forays.

TRIP HIGHLIGHT

❸ Ruby Beach

Inhabiting a thin coastal strip that was added to the national park in 1953, Ruby Beach is accessed via a short 0.2-mile path that leads down to a large expanse of windswept coast embellished by polished black stones and wantonly strewn tree trunks. To the south toward Kalaloch, other accessible beachfronts are unimaginatively named Beach One through to Beach Six, all of which are popular with beachcombers. At low tide, rangers give talks on tidal-pool life at **Beach Four** and on the ecosystems of the Olympic coastal strip.

 p51

The Drive ›› North of Ruby Beach, Highway 101 swings sharply northeast and inland, tracking the Hoh River. Turn right off 101 onto the Hoh River Rd to explore one of the national park's

most popular inner sanctums. Suspend your excitement as the trees eerily close in as you (re) enter the park.

TRIP HIGHLIGHT

❹ Hoh Rainforest

Count yourself lucky if you arrive on a day when it isn't raining! The most popular detour off Highway 101 is the 19-mile paved road to the Hoh Valley, the densest, wettest, greenest and most intensely surreal temperate rain forest on planet earth. The essential hike here is the short but fascinating **Hall of Moss Trail**, an easy 0.75-mile loop through the kind of weird, ethereal scenery that even JRR Tolkien couldn't have invented. Old-man's beard drips from branches above you like corduroy fringe, while trailside licorice ferns and lettuce lichens overwhelm the massive fallen trunks of maple and Sitka spruce. Rangers lead interesting free guided walks here twice a day during summer and can help you spot some of the park's 5000-strong herd of Roosevelt elk.

The Drive ›› Rejoining Highway 101, motor north to the small and relatively nondescript settlement of Forks. Press on through as Highway 101 bends north then east through a large logging area before plunging back into the national park on the shores of wondrous Lake Crescent.

-----

❺ Lake Crescent

Before you've even had time to erase the horror of teenage vampires from your head the scenery shifts again as the road winds along the glittering pine-scented shores of glacial-carved Lake Crescent. The lake looks best from water level, on a rental kayak, or from

Ruby Beach This windswept coast is embellished by polished black stones

high above at its eastern edge on the **Storm King Mountain Trail** (named after the peak's wrathful spirit), accessible via a steep, 1.7-mile ascent that splits off the Barnes Creek Trail. For the less athletic, the **Marymere Falls Trail** is a 2-mile round-trip to a 90ft cascade that drops down over a basalt cliff. Both hikes leave from a parking lot to the right of SR 101 near the **Storm King Information Station** (☺summer only). The area is also the site of the Lake Crescent Lodge, the oldest of the park's trio of celebrated lodges which first opened in 1916.

✕ ⊨ p51

The Drive » From Lake Crescent take Highway 101 east to the town of Port Angeles, a gateway to Victoria, Canada, which is reachable by ferry to the north. Starting in Race St, the 18-mile Hurricane Ridge Rd climbs up 5300ft toward extensive wildflower meadows and expansive mountain vistas often visible above the clouds.

TRIP HIGHLIGHT

❻ Hurricane Ridge

Up above the clouds, stormy Hurricane Ridge lives up to its name with fickle weather and biting

49

THE TWILIGHT ZONE

It would have been impossible to envisage a decade ago: diminutive Forks, a depressed lumber town full of hardnosed loggers, reborn as a pilgrimage site for 'tweenage' girls following in the ghostly footsteps of two fictional sweethearts named Bella and Edward. The reason for this weird metamorphosis is the *Twilight* saga, a four-part book series by US author Stephanie Meyer about love and vampires on the foggy Olympic Peninsula that in seven short years has shifted over 100 million books and spawned three Hollywood movies. With Forks acting as the book's main setting, the town has catapulted to international stardom. **Dazzled by Twilight** (www.dazzledbytwilight.com; 11 N Forks Ave; ◷10am-6pm; 👶) runs two Twilight merchandise shops in Forks and daily **Twilight Tours** (adult/child $39/25; ◷departing 8am, 11:30am, 3pm & 6pm) visiting most of the places mentioned in Meyer's books.

winds made slightly more bearable by the park's best high-altitude views. Its proximity to Port Angeles is another bonus; if you're heading up here be sure to call into the museum-like **Olympic National Park Visitor Center** (3002 Mt Angeles Rd, Port Angeles; park admission $15; 👶) first. The smaller **Hurricane Ridge Visitor Center** (◷9:30am-5pm daily summer, Fri-Sun winter) has a snack bar, gift shop, toilets and is the starting point of various hikes. **Hurricane Hill Trail** (which begins at the end of the road), and the **Meadow Loop Trails** network are popular and moderately easy. The first half-mile of these trails is wheelchair accessible.

The Drive » Wind back down the Hurricane Ridge Rd, kiss the suburbs of Port Angeles

and press east through the retirement community of Sequim (pronounced 'squwim'). Turn north on SR-20 to reach another more attractive port, that of Port Townsend.

---

⑦ Port Townsend

Leaving the park momentarily behind, ease back into civilization with the cultured Victorian comforts of Port Townsend, whose period charm dates from the railroad boom of the 1890s, when the town was earmarked to become the 'New York of the West.' That never happened but you can pick up a historic walking tour map from the **Port Townsend visitors center** (www.enjoypt.com; 2437 E Sims Way; ◷9am-5pm Mon-Fri, 10am-4pm Sat, 11am-4pm Sun) and wander the

waterfront's collection of shops, galleries and antique malls. Don't miss the old-time **Belmont Saloon** (Water St), the **Rose Theatre** (www.rosetheatre.com; 235 Taylor St), a gorgeously renovated theater that's been showing movies since 1908, and the fine Victorian mansions on the bluff above town, where several charming residences have been turned into B&Bs.

🍴 🛏 p51

The Drive » From Port Townsend retrace your steps to the junction of Highway 101, but this time head south passing Quilcene, Brinnon, with its great diner (p51), and the Dosewallips park entrance. You get more unbroken water views here on the park's eastern side courtesy of the Hood Canal, a serene contrast to the wind-whipped waves of the open Pacific. Track the watery beauty to Hoodsport where signs point west (right) off Highway 101 to Staircase.

---

⑧ Staircase

It's drier on the park's eastern side and the mountains are closer. The Staircase park nexus, accessible via Hoodsport, has a ranger station, campground and a decent trail system that follows the drainage of the North Fork Skokomish River and is flanked by some of the most rugged peaks in the Olympics. Nearby **Lake Cushman** has a campground and water sports opportunities.

Eating & Sleeping

Olympia ❶

🍴 Spar Cafe Bar — Pub, Diner $

(114 4th Ave E; breakfast $4-6, lunch $6-9; ⊘7am-9pm) A long-established local cafe and eating joint now owned by Portland's McMenamin Brothers who have maintained its authentic wood-panel interior. You could spend all morning here eating brunch, shooting pool, tasting the microbrews and listening to the buskers on 4th Ave outside.

Lake Quinault ❷

🍴🛏 Lake Quinault Lodge — Lodge $$

(☎360-288-2900; www.olympicnationalparks. com; 345 S Shore Rd; d $150-289; ❄ ⛵) Everything you could want in a historic national park lodge and more, the 'Quinault' has a huge, roaring fireplace, peek-a-boo lake views, a manicured cricket-pitch-quality lawn, huge comfy leather sofas, a regal reception area and – arguably – the finest eating experience on the whole peninsula. The latter is thanks to the memorable sweet potato pancakes served up for breakfast.

Ruby Beach ❸

🍴🛏 Kalaloch Lodge — Historic Hotel $$$

(☎360-962-2271; www.olympicnationalparks. com; 157151 US 101; d $248-360; ❄) A little less grand than the Lake Quinault and Lake Crescent Lodges, the Kalaloch (built in 1953), nonetheless, enjoys an equally spectacular setting perched on a bluff overlooking the crashing Pacific.

Lake Crescent ❺

🍴🛏 Lake Crescent Lodge — Historic Hotel $$

(☎360-928-3211; www.olympicnationalparks. com; 416 Lake Crescent Rd; d $160-290; ⊘May-Oct; ❄ 📶) Built in 1915 as a fishing

resort, this venerable shake-sided building is the oldest of the Olympic National Park lodges and, along with the Lake Quinault Lodge, leads the way in style and coziness. To add star appeal, President FD Roosevelt stayed here in 1937 – a year before he made the Olympics a national park.

Port Townsend ❼

🍴 Waterfront Pizza — Pizza $$

(951 Water St; large pizzas $11-19) Quite simply the best pizza in the state, this buy-by-the-slice outlet inspires huge local loyalty and will satisfy even the most querulous of Chicago-honed palates. The secret: crisp sourdough crusts and creative but not over-stacked toppings.

🛏 Palace Hotel — Hotel $

(☎360-385-0773; www.palacehotelpt.com; 1004 Water St; r $59-109; ❄ 📶) Built in 1889, this beautiful Victorian building is a former brothel that was once run by the locally notorious Madame Marie, who did her dodgy business out of the 2nd-floor corner suite. Reincarnated as an attractive period hotel with antique furnishings and old-fashioned claw-foot baths, the Palace's former seediness is now a thing of the past.

Brinnon

🍴 Halfway House — Diner $

(Hwy 101, Brinnon) This is one of those 'great find' places that pepper the byways of rural America – an embellishment-free diner with friendly staff, lightning-quick service and crusty fruit pies that taste like they were made by someone's treasured grandma. It sits aside Highway 101 in Brinnon, halfway between Port Townsend and Staircase.

Cape Disappointment *Stay in the lighthouse keepers' residences*

Graveyard of the Pacific Tour

3

The typically calm Pacific Ocean turns fiendish where tide meets current at the mouth of the Columbia River. Explore shipwrecks and lighthouses in this landlubber's tour of the nautical Northwest.

TRIP HIGHLIGHTS

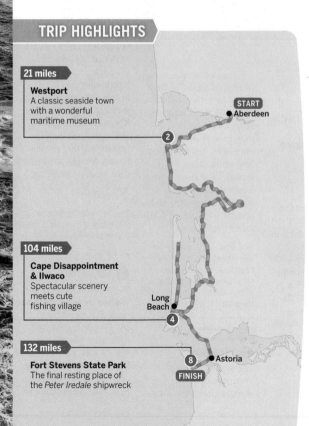

21 miles

Westport
A classic seaside town with a wonderful maritime museum

START
● Aberdeen

104 miles

Cape Disappointment & Ilwaco
Spectacular scenery meets cute fishing village

Long Beach

132 miles

Fort Stevens State Park
The final resting place of the *Peter Iredale* shipwreck

●Astoria
FINISH

**2 DAYS
110 MILES/177KM**

GREAT FOR...

BEST TIME TO GO

From April to September when the weather's on its best behavior.

 ESSENTIAL PHOTO

The wreckage of the *Peter Iredale*.

 BEST SHIP SIGHTING

The tall ship *Lady Washington* docks up and down the coast.

Graveyard of the Pacific Tour

3

They call it the Graveyard of the Pacific. The area from northern Oregon to Vancouver Island is known for its unpredictable weather, unforgiving coastline, and bad habit of gobbling up ships. Thousands of vessels have been lost, from war ships to barges to countless smaller craft. Dive in to this area with its unique seafaring character and fascinating maritime history.

❶ Aberdeen

Start your trip in Aberdeen's Grays Harbor, home port of the tall ship **Lady Washington** (📞800-200-5239; www.ladywashington.org; 320 S Newell St; sailings $35-60, tours by donation), the Official Ship of the State of Washington. This impressive reproduction of a 1788 tall ship – featured in *Pirates of the Caribbean* if that helps give you a visual – is available for dockside tours and adventure sails all along the state's coast. Check the online schedule to find out where along the way you might catch her.

Fans of Nirvana frontman Kurt Cobain might be interested in the self-guided **walking tour** (www.aberdeen-museum.org/kurt.htm) offered by the Aberdeen Museum of History. It includes the store where Kurt's uncle bought him his first guitar and several seen-better-days former residences.

The Drive » From Aberdeen, take Highway 101 across the Chehalis River bridge, then follow Grays Harbor southwest on Hwy 105 for 20 miles to reach the coastal town of Westport.

`TRIP HIGHLIGHT`

❷ Westport

The seaside town of Westport has two worthwhile stops. First, head to **Grays Harbor Lighthouse** (1020 W Ocean Ave; tours $5; ⊙10am-4pm Apr-Sep, noon-4pm Fri-Mon Oct-Nov & Feb-Mar), the tallest lighthouse in Washington. It's always available for photo ops, and tours up the 135-step circular staircase (pant, wheeze) are available seasonally.

Next, head over to the **Westport Maritime Museum** (www.westportwa.com/museum; 2201 Westhaven Dr; adult/child $5/2; ⊙10am-4pm Apr-Sep, noon-4pm Fri-Mon Oct-Mar), a noteworthy Cape Cod–style building at the northern tip of town. It offers your typical array of nautical knickknacks, but most impressive is the authentic Fresnel lighthouse lens. It's a first-order lens, which is really impressive if you know about lens rankings; loosely translated, that means it's big enough to need its own separate building.

 p59

The Drive » Continue on Hwy 105, following the coast 30 miles southeast to Raymond.

❸ Raymond

Raymond is home of the **Willapa Seaport Museum** (www.willapaseaportmuseum.org; 310 Alder St; admission by donation; ⊙noon-4pm Wed-Sat or by appointment). Small and cluttered, the exhibits sometimes seem more like a fisherman's

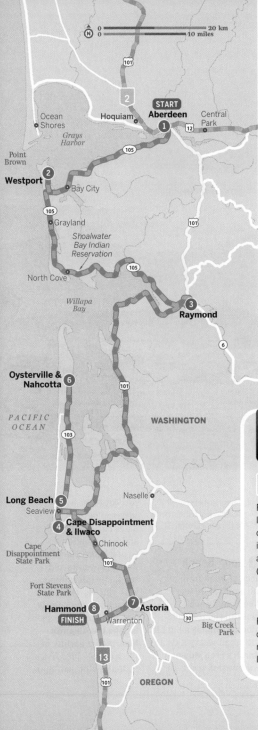

garage sale than a formal museum, but that's part of its charm, and it's a good leg-stretch on your way to your next stop.

Before you leave, though, you might want to stop to pay your respect to Willie Keils at **Willie Keils Grave State Park** (443 Hwy 6; ⏰dawn-dusk), just south of town. Nineteen-year-old Willie died in 1855 right before his family left Missouri to travel west, but they couldn't bear leaving him behind; instead, they filled his coffin with whiskey and brought him along, turning their wagon train into a very slow funeral procession.

The Drive » Pick up Highway 101 west and head 45 miles south. When you get to Seaview, follow the signs for Cape Disappointment.

LINK YOUR TRIP

2 Olympic Peninsula Loop

From Aberdeen, pick up this loop that features the best of northwest Washington, including more coastline and Olympic National Park (p45).

13 Highway 101 Oregon Coast

From Astoria, continue down the coast for seafood, razor clams, tide pools and lighthouses (p149).

NATALIA BRATSLAVSKY / DREAMSTIME ©

TRIP HIGHLIGHT

❹ Cape Disappointment & Ilwaco

Just over the Astoria Bridge in Washington, two lighthouses within **Cape Disappointment State Park** (244 Robert Gray Dr, Ilwaco; ☺dawn-dusk) have been warning sailors away from the shore for over 100 years. If you aren't up for the hike, you might find the **Cape Disappointment Lighthouse** lives up to its name – it's not open to the public and it's at the end of a hilly, muddy, nearly mile-long path. Passing by dramatic Dead Man's Cove makes the hike worthwhile (as long as you're not disappointed there aren't any dead men there).

If that sounds like too much work, drive five minutes north to the easy-access **North Head Lighthouse**. It welcomes visitors with a flat, quarter-mile hike, public tours, a gift shop, and even overnight accommodations in the keepers' residences.

Just north, you'll pass through the cute seaside village of **Ilwaco** that's decorated with driftwood, glass floats and fishermen's nets.

🛏 p59

The Drive ≫ Head back north on Highway 101, which continues on to become SR-103; Long Beach is just 6 miles north of Cape Disappointment.

- - - - - - - - - - - - - -

❺ Long Beach

Need a break from all the nautical history? Wee Long Beach packs in the roadside goodness and is a big hit with road-weary kids. **Marsh's Free Museum** (www.marshsfreemuseum. com; 409 Pacific Ave S; admission free; ☺9am-6pm) dates back to the 1930s and isn't a museum so much as a place where souvenirs and sea shells intermingle with sideshow-worthy attractions and oddities. The real star of the show is **Jake the Alligator Man**, media darling of the *Weekly World News*. Half-alligator, half-man,

Fort Stevens State Park *Peter Iredale* shipwreck

his suspiciously plaster-like remains hold packs of tweens in his thrall. Across the street from Marsh's is the **World's Largest Frying Pan**, measuring over 18ft tall.

Want to find out just how long Long Beach is? Primary **beach access** points in Long Beach are off 10th St SW and at the end of Bolstad Ave;

a 0.25-mile boardwalk links the two entryways.

 p59

The Drive ➔ Head north up the peninsula for 15 miles to find the quiet, undeveloped part of Willapa Bay.

- - - - - - - - - -

6 Oysterville & Nahcotta

Purists might prefer the Willapa Bay side of

the peninsula, with its old towns, oyster beds and wildlife viewing. The charm of these old communities – the only ones on the bay side of the Long Beach Peninsula – derives not just from their history but also from the absence of the beachfront towns' carnival atmosphere. Tiny Oysterville stands largely unchanged since

✓ TOP TIP:
WHICH WAY TO THE
PETER IREDALE?

It's not like a shipwreck has a street address. And asking the locals for directions can be more confusing than helpful. So: Go over the bridge from Astoria to Hammond and turn right on East Harbor Dr, which becomes Pacific Dr. Take a left at Lake Dr (referred to locally as 'that four-way stop...honey, what's that street called?'). Take a right at the KOA campground and go straight until you see the signs.

its heyday in the 1870s, when the oyster boom was at its peak.

Oysterville is filled with well-preserved Victorian homes including the 1863 **Red Cottage** (Territory Rd), near Clay St, which served as the first Pacific County courthouse, and the **Big Red House** (cnr Division St & Territory Rd), built in 1871. Other historic buildings include a one-room schoolhouse and the 1892 **Oysterville Church** (cnr Clay St & Territory Rd); pick up a walking-tour brochure here.

 p59

The Drive » Head back south down the Long Beach Peninsula, then take Highway 101 south. After 9 miles you'll cross the Columbia River and arrive in Astoria.

❼ Astoria

Astoria sits at the mouth of the Columbia River, where you'll find some of the most treacherous waters of the Pacific, thanks to river currents rushing out where ocean tide is trying to get in. The town has a long seafaring history and has seen its old harbor attract fancy hotels and restaurants in recent years, thanks in part to Astoria's popularity as a film location. *Kindergarten Cop, Free Willy* and *Into the Wild* were all filmed there, and fans of the cult hit *The Goonies* can seek out the house where Brandon and Mikey Walsh lived.

You can explore both flotsam and jetsam at **Columbia River Maritime Museum** (www.crmm.org; 1792 Marine Dr; adult/child $12/5; 9:30am-5pm). It sits right on the edge of the Columbia River, offering a look at everything from old boats to maritime mementos that have washed up in the area.

A Coast Guard exhibit – featuring a rescue boat plying dramatic, fake waves – makes you really appreciate the danger of their job.

 p59

The Drive » Head west for the 10-mile drive to Hammond and Fort Stevens State Park.

TRIP HIGHLIGHT

❽ Fort Stevens State Park

Thousands of vessels have been lost in the Graveyard of the Pacific, from war ships to barges to freighters, and those are just the ones on record. There are likely countless smaller craft littering the ocean floor. A few are still visible occasionally at low tide, but the easiest one to spot is the **Peter Iredale**, resting peacefully at Hammond. The ship was driven onto the shore by rough seas on October 25, 1906, and the wreckage has sat embedded in the sand for over a century. Today, kids have made a jungle gym out of the rusted skeleton and families picnic and build sandcastles on the nearby sand at low tide. (As a reassuring side note, no lives were lost in the shipwreck, so don't let the thought of ghostly sailors dampen your fun.)

Eating & Sleeping

Westport ②

✕ Brady's Oysters   Seafood $
(☎800-572-3252; www.bradysoysters.com;
3714 Oyster PI E, Aberdeen; ☺9am-6pm) Stock
your coolers with a sailor's snack of delicious
bivalve mollusks at this family-owned institution
just a few miles south of Westport (though
listed as Aberdeen). It's nothing fancy, but,
seriously, you won't care.

✕ Mermaid Deli   Deli $
(☎360-612-0435; 200 E Patterson; ☺11am-7pm;
sandwiches $7-15) Hot and cold sandwiches – 6in
or foot-long – plus a mean clam chowder make
this dependable stop-off a favorite among locals
and vacationers alike. Did we mention the full bar,
mermaid mural and live music?

Cape Disappointment & Ilwaco ④

⮞ North Head Lighthouse   House $$$
(☎888-226-7688; parks.wa.gov/
vacationhouses/capedisappointment; Cape
Disappointment State Park; house $224) Play
lighthouse keeper in one of three comfortably
furnished keepers' residences; each residence
sleeps up to six people and comes with the
requisite lighthouse ghost lore.

⮞ Inn at Harbor Village   Hotel $$
(☎360-642-0087; www.innatharborvillage.com;
120 Williams Ave NE, Ilwaco; r $115-185; 🛜) This is
the church, this is the steeple, open the doors and
see – your guest room? One of Washington's most
surprising accommodations is this refurbished
1928 Presbyterian church with nine lovely rooms.

Long Beach ⑤

✕ Depot Restaurant   Seafood $$
(☎360-642-7880; 1208 38th PI, Seaview; mains
$20-29; ☺from 5pm Wed-Mon) Located in a
former train depot, this wildly popular place has
a selective menu that includes both seafood and
'landfood,' not to mention small plates.

Oysterville & Nahcotta ⑥

✕ Bailey's Bakery &
Café   Bakery, Cafe $
(☎360-665-4449; 26910 Sandridge Rd,
Nahcotta; snacks from $3; ☺9am-3pm Thu-
Mon) Sharing digs with Nahcotta post office,
this small nook serves locally roasted Long
Beach coffee and the lauded 'thunder buns':
currants, pecans, honey butter glaze and a
whole lot of bun.

⮞ Moby Dick Hotel &
Oyster Farm   Hotel $$
(☎360-665-4543; www.mobydickhotel.com;
25814 Sandridge Rd, Nahcotta; d incl breakfast
$90-150) Eclectic themes and bold colors
characterize the 10 well-appointed rooms in
this 1929 structure that once served as a Coast
Guard barracks. Added bonus: a substantial
three-course breakfast is included.

Astoria ⑦

✕ Baked Alaska   Northwestern $$$
(☎503-325-7414; www.bakedak.com; 1 12th
St; dinner mains $18-24; ☺11am-10pm) One
of Astoria's finest restaurants, Baked Alaska
sits right atop a pier on the water – views are
excellent. Lunch means 0.5lb gourmet burgers
and blackened sirloin salad, while dinner mains
range from grilled wild salmon to the 10oz
rib-eye steak.

⮞ Cannery Pier Hotel   Hotel $$$
(☎503-325-4996; www.cannerypierhotel.com;
10 Basin St; r $199-329) A former fish cannery,
this thoroughly modern hotel has luxurious
rooms, each one of which has a window seat
facing the Columbia River so you can watch the
boats floating by.

Haro Strait One of the best places
in the world to view whales

San Juan Islands Scenic Byway

4

More a float trip than a drive, this voyage will leave you swearing that you've dropped off the edge of the American continent and landed somewhere less clamorous.

**3 DAYS
136 MILES/220KM**

GREAT FOR...

BEST TIME TO GO

April to September for smooth sea journeys and more common whale sightings.

ESSENTIAL PHOTO

View from top of Mt Constitution on Orcas Island.

BEST FOR WILDLIFE

Fantastic whale-watching trips can be organized in Friday Harbor, San Juan Island.

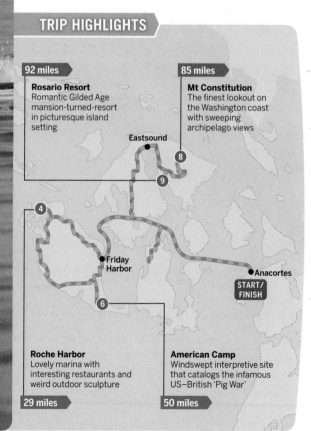

92 miles

Rosario Resort
Romantic Gilded Age mansion-turned-resort in picturesque island setting

85 miles

Mt Constitution
The finest lookout on the Washington coast with sweeping archipelago views

Eastsound

8

9

4

Friday Harbor

Anacortes

START/FINISH

6

Roche Harbor
Lovely marina with interesting restaurants and weird outdoor sculpture

29 miles

American Camp
Windswept interpretive site that catalogs the infamous US–British 'Pig War'

50 miles

San Juan Islands Scenic Byway

4

A thousand metaphoric miles from the urban disquiet of Puget Sound, the nebulous San Juan archipelago conjures up Proustian flashbacks from another era (the 1950s, perhaps?). Street crime barely registers here, fast-food franchises are a nasty mainland apparition, and cars – those most essential of US travel accessories – are an optional luxury on the three most easily reachable islands of Orcas, Lopez and San Juan Island.

1 Anacortes

This voyage starts at **Anacortes Ferry Terminal** (www.wsdot. wa.gov/ferries; 2100 Ferry Terminal Rd; adult/child/car $12.45/10/57.35; ⏱7am-9pm), where you'll board the ferry for Friday Harbor. Drivers might end up waiting for hours in the busy summer months. Two alternatives are to: 1) spend the night in Anacortes and get to the ferry early, or, 2) park at the terminal and make the trip on foot or by bike.

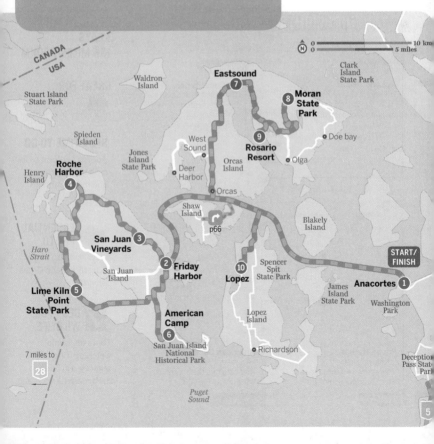

The Drive » If you're taking your car, today's drive is limited to sliding in slow motion onto the ferry where you'll be packed tightly in with several hundred others. Don't stay put; rather climb upstairs and enjoy the journey (and it is a *great* journey) from the passenger lounge.

❷ Friday Harbor

After an 80-minute ferry ride, you'll land at Friday Harbor, the San Juans' only real town and a blueprint for the archipelago as a whole, where the worst kind of hassle you're likely to face is a badly pitched baseball. Restaurants, shops and a couple of

LINK YOUR TRIP

5 **Chuckanut Drive & Whidbey Island**

A short hop from Anacortes, this pastoral trip acts like a decompression chamber before re-entering metro Puget Sound (p69).

28 **Southern Vancouver Island Tour**

Located a handful of watery miles from Vancouver Island, the San Juans provide an ideal opportunity to visit Canada without crossing the 49th parallel (p293).

interesting museums embellish the settlement's diminutive grid.

San Juan Island has the good fortune to be right in the migration path of three pods of orcas (aka killer whales), unimaginatively named the J, K and L pods. (Pod members' names aren't much better: 'K-17, meet L-9.') To learn more about the island's unofficial mascots, stop by the **Whale Museum** (www.whale-museum.org; 62 First St N; adult/child $6/3; ◷9am-6pm). To see the real thing – a regional highlight – hook up with **San Juan Excursions** (☏360-378-6636; www. watchwhales.com) who stand by their boast: 'see whales or come again free.'

✕ 🛏 p67

The Drive » Navigation on San Juan Island is a no-brainer. Take Roche Harbor Rd northwest out of Friday Harbor as far as Sportsman Lake.

❸ San Juan Vineyards

Washington's most westerly **vineyard** (www. sanjuanvineyards.com; 3136 Roche Harbor Rd; ◷11am-5pm) has a tasting room adjacent to its on-site, 1896-vintage schoolhouse 3 miles northwest of Friday Harbor. The vineyard also has an outlet in town. For the real home-grown stuff, you're looking at Siegerrebe and Madeleine

Angevine varietals with the occasional Pinot Noir thrown in. They also make wines using grapes imported from East Washington.

The Drive » Continue northwest on Roche Harbor Rd. At a T-junction with West Valley Rd, turn right.

TRIP HIGHLIGHT

❹ Roche Harbor

A sublime rurally inclined 'resort,' Roche Harbor is a scenic mix of swanky yachts, historic houses and picnicking vacationers. At the entrance gate sits the eccentric **Westcott Bay Sculpture Park** (Westcott Dr & Roche Harbor Rd; ◷dawn-dusk) where you can wander among more than 100 sculptures scattered over 19 acres. Half the fun is the sheer variety; each was made by a different artist, and materials range from aluminum to granite to recovered redwood.

Around the corner, Roche Harbor proper has a lovely marina packed with millionaire boats and backed by the historic buildings of the lime-mining McMillan clan, the oldest of which dates from 1886. Explore the manicured gardens, browse the plush shops or even play boules.

The Drive » Heading back down the Roche Harbor Rd, take the West Valley Rd south at the first junction. Just past the alpaca farm, turn right on

Mitchell Bay Rd and then left on West Side Rd which skirts the lapping waters of Haro Strait.

GREG VAUGHN / ALAMY ©

❺ Lime Kiln Point State Park

Clinging to the island's rocky west coast, this beautiful park overlooks the deep Haro Strait and is one of the best places in the world to view whales from the shoreline. There is a small **interpretive center** in the park open from Memorial Day to Labor Day along with trails, a restored lime kiln and the landmark **Lime Kiln lighthouse** built in 1919. Orca and minke whale sightings are more common in summer after the June salmon run. Offering exceptional views of Vancouver Island and the Olympic Mountains, the park is best enjoyed at sunset, camera poised.

The Drive >> West Side Rd swings east and becomes Bailey Hill Rd and Little Rd before joining with Cattle Point Rd. Turn right here toward the island's wild treeless southern tip.

TRIP HIGHLIGHT

❻ American Camp

On the southern flank of the island, the American Camp hosts a small **visitors center** (admission free; ☺8:30am-4:30pm Thu-Sun Oct-May, daily Jun-Sep) and is a good place to learn about the islands' history and the infamous 'Pig War' with Britain in 1859, a military standoff ignited

after an American settler shot a pig belonging to a homesteading Irishman on San Juan Island. The ensuing squabble led to a border dispute and near conflict between Britain and the US. Among the remnants of an old fort are the officers' quarters and a laundress' house, while a series of interpretive trails lead to earthwork

fortifications, a British farm from the dispute era and desolate South Beach. The 1.8-mile trail along the ridge of **Mt Finlayson** makes for a pleasant hike with splendid views and unlimited birdwatching potential.

The Drive >> Head north on Cattle Point Rd back to Friday Harbor and catch an inter-island ferry to Orcas Island. Here you'll find a wilder, less manicured

Moran State Park View over Rosario Strait from Mt Constitution

landscape than on San Juan Island, with the residents tucked away down long gravel drives. There's not a lot to see or do around the ferry landing so head straight down Orcas Rd to Eastsound.

- - - - - - - - - - - - -

⑦ Eastsound

Orcas Island is shaped like a pair of saddlebags, with the main town, Eastsound, diplomatically in the middle. From the ferry landing, it's just over 8 miles through hilly farmland to get there, and that's where you'll find most of the dining. The town does shut down early, though, so don't wait till you're hungry to plan dinner.

Paddling around the island gives you an entirely different view of things, and **Shearwater** **Adventures** (☎360-376-4699; www.shearwaterkayaks. com; 138 North Beach Rd, Eastsound; 3hr tour $69) offers guided excursions from the north side of the island. Take anything from a quick, one-hour splash-about to an all-day outing in their hand-crafted, Aleut-style kayaks.

✖ ⊨ p67

65

DETOUR: SHAW ISLAND

Start: **7** Eastsound

The quietest and smallest of the four main San Juan Islands, tranquil Shaw is famous for its restrictive property laws and handsome Benedictine monastery. Twelve ferries arrive here daily (car and driver $25.10 on westbound trips only; 15 minutes), but with only one campsite offering just 12 overnight berths, opportunities to linger are limited. For the curious, Shaw is worth a slow spin on a mountain bike or an afternoon of quiet contemplation on a pebbly beach. History buffs can break the reverie at the **Shaw Island Historical Museum** (Blind Bay Rd), while perennial peace-seekers can find lazy solace on quiet South Beach in **Shaw Island County Park**, a stop and potential camping spot on the aquatic Cascadia Marine Trail – doable on nonmotorized boats and kayaks – that starts in southern Puget Sound.

The Drive ›› East of Eastsound, Olga Rd gives access to the island's eastern saddlebag dominated by Moran State Park.

TRIP HIGHLIGHT

8 Moran State Park

Ex-Seattle mayor, Robert Moran's generous gift to the island was **Moran State Park** (Mountain Rd & Olga Rd; ⊙6:30am-dusk), where over 5000 acres of forest lie draped over two mountains. On a clear day, the view from **Mt Constitution** is incomparable; you can see mountains, islands, even Vancouver. Sadly, on a foggy day, you can only see the person standing next to you. Thirty miles of trails give you ample opportunity to explore

on foot, but there's also a road straight to the top if you have a ferry to catch.

🍴 p67

The Drive ›› Just after exiting the park's northern gate a road turns left to the Rosario Resort.

TRIP HIGHLIGHT

9 Rosario Resort

Orcas' resort is a refined place unsullied by modern clamor where seaplanes dock, kayaks launch and discerning vacationers bask in a heady kind of F Scott Fitzgerald–style romance. Its centerpiece is the seafront Rosario mansion built by former shipbuilding magnate Robert Moran in 1904 with 180 modern rooms sprawled across the

surrounding grounds along with a swimming pool, tennis courts, a marina and elaborately tiled spa facilities. A **museum** (Rosario Way; ⊙9am-8pm) encased in the mansion tells the life and times of Moran, a former Seattle mayor who lived here from 1906 until 1938. Look out for the ship memorabilia and the huge custom-made organ.

 p67

The Drive ›› There's only one way back to the ferry terminal – the way you came! Inter-island ferries leave five times daily for Shaw and Lopez Islands.

10 Lopez Island

Lopez – or *Slow-pez* as it's sometimes known – is the ultimate friendly isle where local motorists give strangers the 'Lopezian wave' (two fingers raised from the steering wheel) and you can leave your bike outside the village store and it'll still have both wheels when you return several hours later. A leisurely pastoral spin can be tackled in a day with good overnight digs available in the clustered settlement that passes for the main village. If you arrive bike-less, call up **Lopez Bicycle Works** (www.lopezbicycleworks. com; 2847 Fisherman Bay Rd; ⊙10am-6pm May-Sep) who can deliver a bicycle to the ferry terminal for you.

🍴🛏 p67

Eating & Sleeping

Friday Harbor ②

✕ Market Chef · Deli $

(225 A St; ⊙10am-6pm Mon-Fri) **Several hundred locals can't be wrong, can they?** The chef's specialty is deli sandwiches and very original ones at that. Join the queue and watch them prepare the goods with fresh, local ingredients.

🛏 Earthbox
Motel & Spa Boutique Motel $$$

(☎360-378-4000; www.earthboxmotel.com; 410 Spring St; r from $177; 🛜🏊) **Reaching out to retro-lovers, Earthbox styles itself as a 'boutique motel,'** a hybrid of simplicity and sophistication that has taken a former motor inn and embellished it with features more commonly associated with a deluxe hotel.

Eastsound ⑦

✕ Allium International $$$

(☎360-376-4904; www.alliumonorcas.com; 310 E Main St; dinner mains $30; ⊙5-8pm Thu-Mon, 10am-2pm & 5-8pm Sat & Sun) **Orcas got a destination restaurant in 2010 with the opening of the illustrious Allium** where the secret is very simple: 'simplicity' (local ingredients, limited opening hours and only five mains on the menu). The result: food worth visiting the island for.

✕ Passionate for Pies Pies $

(460 Main St; ⊙9am-6pm Wed-Sat & Mon, 11am-6pm Sun) **You *will* be after visiting this newish Eastsound nook** offering savory (roasted organic chicken) and sweet (coconut cream) pies concocted on the premises.

🛏 Outlook Inn Hotel $

(☎360-376-2200; www.outlookinn.com; 171 Main St, Eastsound; r with shared/private bath $79/99; 🌀🛜) **Eastsound village's oldest building (1888) is an island institution** that has kept up with the times by expanding into a small bayside complex. Also on-site is the rather fancy New Leaf Café.

Moran State Park ⑧

✕ Cafe Olga Cafe $

(11 Point Lawrence Rd, Olga; mains $9-11; ⊙9am-6pm Mon-Fri, 9am-8pm Sat & Sun, closed Wed Mar-Apr) **Tucked inside a barn alongside a crafts gallery 1.5 miles south of Moran State Park, Olga specializes in homemade pies** and provides a sweet treat for cyclists and hikers who've just conquered lofty Mt Constitution.

Rosario Resort ⑨

🛏 Rosario Resort & Spa Resort $$

(☎360-376-2222; www.rosarioresort.com; 1400 Rosario Rd; d/ste $129/179; 🌀🛜🏊) **A magnificent seafront mansion built by former shipbuilding magnate Robert Moran in 1904** and now converted into an exquisite, upscale resort and spa.

Lopez Island ⑩

✕ Bay Cafe Seafood $$$

(www.bay-cafe.com; 9 Old Post Rd; mains $15-36) **Lopez's one and only attempt at fine dining** offers romantic sunset views right on the water with classic fish dishes, including Dungeness crab and seafood tapas. Keeping it local are island-raised beef and wine from the local vineyard.

🛏 Lopez Islander Resort Resort $$

(☎360-468-2233; www.lopezfun.com; 2864 Fisherman Bay Rd; d from $120; 🌀🛜🏊) **Next to the marina just south of the village, this midrange sprawler is Lopez's only resort.** It has a restaurant, gym and pool and offers free parking in Anacortes (another incentive to dump the car).

Chuckanut Drive *Trees frame island-speckled water views*

Chuckanut Drive & Whidbey Island

5

Veer off the congested interstate at Bellingham and you quickly enter a parallel universe of sinuous back roads, tulip fields and spectacular ribbons of coastal asphalt.

TRIP HIGHLIGHTS

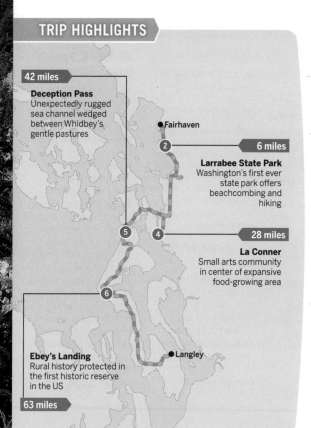

42 miles

Deception Pass
Unexpectedly rugged sea channel wedged between Whidbey's gentle pastures

● Fairhaven

2 **6 miles**

Larrabee State Park
Washington's first ever state park offers beachcombing and hiking

5 **4** **28 miles**

La Conner
Small arts community in center of expansive food-growing area

6

Ebey's Landing
Rural history protected in the first historic reserve in the US

● Langley

63 miles

1–2 DAYS
89 MILES/143KM

GREAT FOR...

BEST TIME TO GO
March to June when fields of spring flowers are in bloom.

 ESSENTIAL PHOTO
The daffodil and tulip fields around La Conner are the best this side of Holland.

 BEST FOR FOOD
La Conner – food from farm to plate in yards rather than miles.

Chuckanut Drive & Whidbey Island

5

Short but very, very sweet, this winding sojourn along Chuckanut Drive and through Whidbey Island is the kind of dreamy pre-interstate era drive you see in car commercials: sunlight through the trees, glimpses of sparkling ocean and a dozen broccoli-colored islands shimmering in the mid-distance. If you've got a convertible, it's roof down time, weather permitting, as you glide between oyster restaurants, beaches and scenic state parks.

❶ Fairhaven

Of Bellingham's four original towns, Fairhaven is the best preserved; a four-square-block historic district of handsome red-bricked Victorians testifies to a rich, if sometimes rambunctious, past. Today, the same buildings harbor bookstores, cafes and arty nooks – take a look on our walking tour (p140). Fairhaven is also an important transport nexus, and home of Bellingham's Amtrak station and ferry terminal with regular ferries up the Inside Passage to Alaska (p327).

✕ 🛏 p75

The Drive ❯❯ The thrill of Chuckanut Drive is that you don't have to wait long for its beauty to unfold. Vistas open out immediately south of Fairhaven where homes hug million-dollar lots high above Puget Sound. Cut into the cliff, the road winds spectacularly through trees that frame island-speckled water views. Paralleling it on the right is the railway.

TRIP HIGHLIGHT

❷ Larrabee State Park

At the southern end of the Interurban Trail (p74), just 6 miles south of Fairhaven, sits **Larrabee State Park** (www.parks.wa.gov; Chuckanut Dr; ☾dawn-dusk; ♿), a square chunk of emerald green forest

that spills into the bay at popular Clayton Beach and Wildcat Cove. Poking around in the tide pools or hiking up to **Fragrance Lake Trail** (5.1 miles return) are the most popular activities, though the trails can be crowded at weekends.

The Drive ❯❯ Chuckanut's precipitous topography continues for a few miles after Larrabee. Then, with dramatic suddenness, the landscape opens out into the flat agricultural pastures of the Skagit River Valley. Pass the Oyster Bar and Chuckanut Manor (both on the right) and you'll arrive at Bow Hill Rd, the first main intersection since Fairhaven.

❸ Bow & Samish Bay

As you continue the drive south several pullouts lure you with fine views over Samish Bay as they explain the history of the road and its oyster industry. Oysters adore the brackish waters of the bay and nearby **Taylor Shellfish Farms** (www.taylorshellfish.com; 2182 Chuckanut Dr, Bow; ☾9am-6pm) has been hand harvesting and shucking 1800 acres of seabed here since the 1880s. Staff can lead you through oyster etiquette as you learn to differentiate between a buttery Shigoku or a creamy Kumamoto.

Both Taylor and nearby Blau, across the bay on Samish Island, deliver

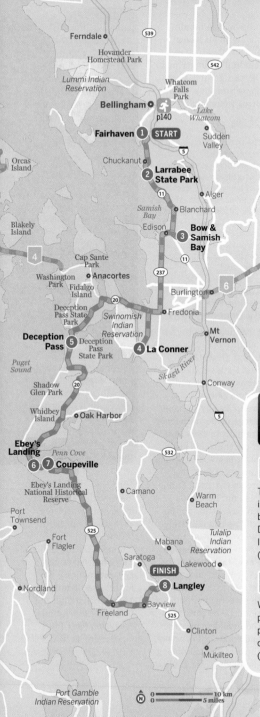

their freshest catch to a pair of Chuckanut Drive restaurants that between them boast the region's most hypnotic views, the **Oyster Bar** (www.theoysterbar. net; 2578 Chuckanut Dr; ⏱11:30am-10pm) and **Chuckanut Manor** (www. chuckanutmanor.com; 3056 Chuckanut Dr; ⏱lunch & dinner Tue-Sun).

South of Blanchard Mountain, Bow junction holds a few surprises, including the gourmet Goudas (and other treats) of **Samish Bay Cheese** (www.samishbaycheese. com; 15115 Bow Hill Rd, Bow; ⏱10am-4pm Mon-Fri, noon-4pm Sat & Sun), **available for tasting at their tiny store.**

The Drive » Back at the Bow Hill Rd–Chuckanut Drive intersection take the W Bow

LINK YOUR TRIP

4 San Juan Islands Scenic Byway

The San Juan archipelago is never out of view as you breeze down Chuckanut Drive and across Whidbey Island, begging you to visit (p61).

6 Cascade Drive

Bisected by SR-20, Whidbey Island, though physically flat, is actually part of the official Cascade drive. Join it in Burlington (p77).

Hill Rd through the pinprick community of Edison whose artisan bread store and Tweets Café merit a quick stopover. Continue south on the ruler-straight Farm to Market Rd to busy SR-20 which you join briefly heading west before turning left onto the La Conner–Whitney Rd.

TRIP HIGHLIGHT

❹ La Conner

Celebrated for its tulips, wild turkeys, erudite writer's colony, and (among other culinary treats) soccer ball–sized cinnamon buns; La Conner's myriad attractions verge on the esoteric. Jammed with gift shops and classy B&Bs, it also has three decent museums; the best is the **Museum of Northwest Art** (www.museumofnwart.org; 121 S 1st St; admission $5; ⌚10am-5pm Tue-Sun). The zenith of La Conner's cultural calendar is the annual **Tulip Festival** when the surrounding fields are embellished with a colorful carpet of daffodils (March), tulips (April) and irises (May). To see the flowers in all their artistic glory detour a few miles to the **Roosengaarde Display Garden** (www.roosengaarde.com; 15867 Beaver Marsh Rd, Mt Vernon; admission $5; ⌚9am-6pm Mon-Sat, 11am-4pm Sun) halfway between La Conner and Mt Vernon. This renowned 3-acre garden plants 250,000 tulip bulbs annually and, with Mt Baker and a Dutch-inspired windmill glimmering in the background, photo opportunities abound. Bring a camera!

✕ 🛏 p75

The Drive » Retrace your tire tracks north to SR-20 and turn left with the Anacortes traffic toward the San Juan Islands ferry terminal. After crossing the Swinomish Channel turn left on SR-20 following signage to Whidbey Island. Although you probably don't realize it, you're now on Fidalgo Island, separated from the mainland by a narrow sea channel.

TRIP HIGHLIGHT

❺ Deception Pass

Emerging from the flat pastures of Fidalgo Island, Deception Pass leaps out like a mini Grand Canyon, its precipitous cliffs overlooked by a famous bridge made all the more dramatic by the sight of the churning, angry water below. The bridge consists of two steel arches that span Canoe Pass and Deception Pass, with a central support on Pass Island between the two. Visitors to the 5.5-sq-mile **Deception Pass State Park** (41229 N State Hwy 20) usually introduce themselves to the spectacular land and seascape by parking at the shoulders on either end and walking across the bridge. Built during the 1930s by the Civilian Conservation Corps, the bridge was considered an engineering feat in its day.

BRAD MITCHELL / ALAMY ©

Besides the dramatic bridge overviews, the park's attractions include over 15 miles of saltwater shoreline and 27 miles of forest trails. **Deception Pass Tours** (www.deceptionpasstours.com; adult/child $25/21) organizes

Deception Pass Bridge Walk across and enter a spectacular land and seascape

jet boat tours through the turbulent waters daily.

The Drive » The rugged terrain of Deception Pass disappears almost as soon as it materialized and you're soon in the pastoral fields that characterize Whidbey Island. After passing the entrance to the Naval Air station on your right, you'll skirt the rather ugly mall infestations of Oak Harbor. Traffic lights will slow your progress here. Keep on SR-20 to Penn Cove.

TRIP HIGHLIGHT

⑥ Ebey's Landing

The nation's first national historic reserve, listed in 1978, was created in order to preserve Whidbey Island's historical heritage from the encroaching urbanization that had already partly engulfed

Oak Harbor. Still 90% privately owned, **Ebey's Landing** (admission free; ☺6:30am-10pm Apr 1–Oct 15) comprises 17,400 acres encompassing working farms, four historic blockhouses, two state parks and the small historic town of Coupeville. A series of interpretive boards shows visitors how the patterns of croplands,

INTERURBAN TRAIL

For a break from the car, you can join Bellingham's fleece-wearing weekend warriors and savor a bit of Chuckanut Drive by bike along the 6-mile Interurban Trail, a deliciously flat former electric trolley bed that parallels the tarmac past deep forest and lovely views of Chuckanut Bay to Larrabee State Park. **Fairhaven Bike & Ski** (www.fairhavenbike.com; 1103 11th St, Fairhaven; ☺9:30am-7pm Mon-Thu, 9:30am-8pm Fri, 10am-6pm Sat, 11am-5pm Sun) will set you up with a bike ($24; four hours) for the easy two-hour ride.

woods and even roads reflect the activities of those who have peopled this scenic landscape, from its earliest indigenous inhabitants to 19th-century settlers.

The museum in Coupeville distributes a brochure on suggested driving and cycling tours through the reserve. Highly recommended is the 3.6-mile **Bluff Trail** that starts from a small parking area at the end of Ebey Rd. The energetic can walk or cycle here 2.5 miles from Coupeville, thus crossing the island at one of its narrowest points.

The Drive >> Veer off SR-20 just past Penn Cove to visit Coupeville.

---

7 Coupeville

Tiny Coupeville is Whidbey Island personified: fresh

mussels and clams, old-world B&Bs, historic clapboard shop-fronts, and instant access to a National Historical Reserve. Call in at the **Island County Historical Society Museum** (908 NW Alexander St; admission $3; ☺10am-5pm May-Sep, 10am-4pm Fri-Mon Oct-Apr) for the lowdown on Washington state's second-oldest settlement (founded in 1852) and walking tour maps of the town's handsome vintage homes.

🍴🛏 p75

The Drive >> SR-20 veers right at the southern end of Ebey's Landing toward the Keystone Ferry and Fort Casey State Park. The latter was once part of an early 1900s military defense system and is worth visiting for its old cement batteries, underground tunnels and lighthouse. Otherwise continue south on SR-525 through Freeland to Bayview where you take a left for Langley.

8 Langley

Langley, like Coupeville, is a small seafront community that is little changed since the late 19th century. Encased in an attractive historical center lie small cafes, antique furniture shops, funky clothes boutiques and a couple of decent B&Bs. While there's little to do here activity-wise, Langley provides a perfect antidote to the hustle and bustle of nearby Seattle and is a great place to relax and unwind, after numerous hours packed bumper to bumper on I-5.

Langley is 8 miles north of **Clinton** and the 20-minute ferry service from **Mukilteo** (www.wsdot.com/ferries; adult/child/car $4.65/3.75/9.75), making this the closest of the Whidbey Island communities to the urban areas of northern Seattle.

 p75

Eating & Sleeping

Fairhaven ❶

✗ Colophon Cafe   International $

(www.colophoncafe.com; 1208 11th St, Fairhaven; mains $7-10) **Linked with Fairhaven's famous literary haven, Village Books, the Colophon is a multiethnic eatery for people who like to combine their paninis with Proust.** Renowned for its African peanut soup and chocolate brandy cream pies, the cafe has indoor seating along with an outside wine garden and is ever-popular with the local literati.

🛏 Fairhaven Village Inn   Hotel $$$

(📞360-733-1311; www.fairhavenvillageinn.com; 1200 10th St; r with bay/park view $179/199; ❄🛜📶) **Downtown Bellingham lacks a decent number of well-appointed independent hotels, but one good alternative option is this prime place in genteel Fairhaven.** Well in keeping with the vintage tone of the historic district, the Village Inn is a class above the standard motel fare, with prices to match.

La Conner ❹

✗ Seeds
Bistro & Bar   Modern American $$$

(📞360-466-3280; www.seedsbistro.com; 623 Morris St; mains $18-25) **Situated in the old Tillinghurst Seed building, Seeds Bistro offers that rare combo of classy food and brunch-cafe-style friendliness.** The key lies in harnessing the fresh flavors of the surrounding farmland and mixing it with equally fresh fish plucked from the nearby ocean. The result: unparalleled ling cod and off-the-ratings-scale crab cakes.

🛏 Heron Inn   B&B $$

(📞360-399-1074; www.theheroninn.com; 117 Maple Ave; r $99-180; ❄🛜📶) **Under new management and all the better for it, the Heron has jumped back into the fray with La Conner's B&B big guns and landed on its feet.** Above-and-beyond service is propped up by its onsite spa, French toast breakfast, and inclusive kids-are-welcome policy.

Coupeville ❼

✗ Christopher's   Modern American $$$

(📞360-678-5480; www.christopherson whidbey.com; 103 NW Coveland St; mains $17-26) **Go where the locals go and bring a good appetite.** Christopher's does exciting and creative modern cooking in huge portions. The mussels and clams are the best in town and the seafood alfredo pasta is wonderfully rich. Then there are the desserts – anyone for chocolate mousse?

🛏 Captain Whidbey Inn   Inn $$

(📞360-678-4097; www.captainwhidbey.com; 2072 W Captain Whidbey Inn Rd; d incl breakfast $103, cabins $175, cottages $230) **They don't come any more outlandish than this.** The Captain Whidbey is a 1907 inn built entirely out of rust-colored madrone (arbutus) wood. With its low ceilings, creaky floors and cozy lounge strewn with faded copies of *National Geographic*, it feels more like something out of a medieval forest than a 21st-century tourist island.

Langley ❽

✗ Cafe Langley   Mediterranean $$

(www.cafelangley.com; 113 1st St; mains $16-20) **Ah, at last: some choice Mediterranean cuisine; with a few deft Northwest seafood infusions (eg mussels) thrown in for good measure.** There are some amazing lamb options here, an Andalucian steak, Italian pasta, Greek moussaka and a memorable baklava for dessert. Delicioso!

North Cascades National Park
High-altitude scenery at its best

Classic Trip

Cascade Drive

6

Rugged and inaccessible for half the year, this brawny mountain drive is etched with the kind of monumental, Alaskan-style beauty that once inspired Jack Kerouac.

TRIP HIGHLIGHTS

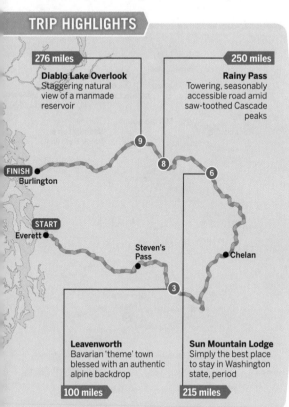

276 miles

Diablo Lake Overlook
Staggering natural view of a manmade reservoir

250 miles

Rainy Pass
Towering, seasonably accessible road amid saw-toothed Cascade peaks

FINISH
Burlington

START
Everett

Steven's Pass

Chelan

Leavenworth
Bavarian 'theme' town blessed with an authentic alpine backdrop

100 miles

Sun Mountain Lodge
Simply the best place to stay in Washington state, period

215 miles

4–5 DAYS
350 MILES/563KM

GREAT FOR...

BEST TIME TO GO
June to September when all roads are snow-free and passable.

ESSENTIAL PHOTO
View from the Sun Mountain Lodge over the Methow Valley.

BEST FOR HIKING
The Maple Pass Loop Trail from Rainy Pass.

Classic Trip

6 Cascade Drive

Nature defies modern engineering in the North Cascades where high-altitude roads succumb to winter snow storms, and the names of the mountains – Mt Terror, Mt Fury, Forbidden Peak – whisper forebodingly. Less scary are the scattered settlements, small towns with esoteric distractions such as Bavarian Leavenworth and 'Wild West' Winthrop. Fill up the tank, put on your favorite Springsteen track and prepare for one of the rides of your life.

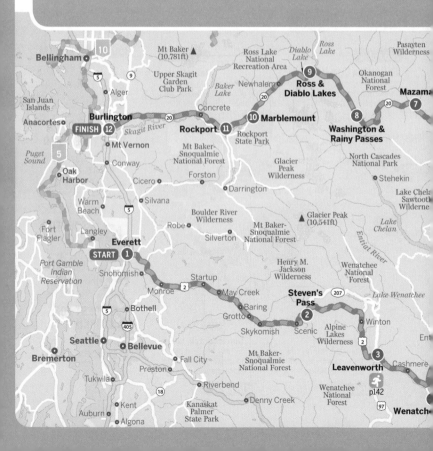

1 Everett

This drive incorporates four-fifths of the popular 'Cascade Loop.' You can complete the other fifth by taking in the second half of Trip 5 through Whidbey Island. There's not much to detain you in Everett, the route's starting point 30 miles north of Seattle. It's known mainly for its Boeing connections and as the genesis for countless Seattle-region traffic jams. Head directly east and don't stop until Steven's Pass.

The Drive ›› The starting point of US-2, a 2579-mile cross-continental road that terminates in Maine, is in Everett. Crossing I-5, the route, which parallels the Great Northern Railway and Skykomish River for much of its journey, passes the small towns of Startup, Sultan and Index, climbing toward Steven's Pass. If you're thirsty, stop at one of the ubiquitous drive-through espresso huts en route.

2 Steven's Pass

Accessible year round thanks to its day-use **ski area** (www.stevenspass.com), Steven's Pass was only 'discovered' by white settlers as recently as 1890. Despite its lofty vantage – at 4045ft it is over 1000ft higher than Snoqualmie Pass – the Great Northern railroad chose it for their cross-cascade route. Notwithstanding, you won't see any train tracks here. Instead, the railway burrows underneath the pass via North America's longest rail tunnel (7.8 miles). The long-distance

Pacific Crest Trail also crosses the highway here. Tempted?

The Drive ›› From Steven's Pass the descent begins immediately with subtle changes in the vegetation; the cedars and hemlocks of the western slopes are gradually replaced with pine, larch and spruce. The road threads through the steep-sided Tumwater canyon alongside the turbulent Wenatchee River. Suddenly, German-style houses start to appear against an eerily familiar alpine backdrop.

TRIP HIGHLIGHT

3 Leavenworth

Blink hard and rub your eyes. This isn't some strange Germanic hallucination. This is Leavenworth, a former lumber town that underwent a Bavarian makeover in the 1960s after the re-routing of the cross-continental railway threatened to put it permanently out of business. Swapping loggers for tourists, Leavenworth today has successfully reinvented

anogan
ational
Forest

Conconully
State Park

Conconully ○ —— 97

Winthrop

Omak ○

wisp

Okanogan ○

Malott ○   Colville
             Indian
Carlton   Reservation

153

Pateros ○   ○ Monse

Bridgeport
State Park

○   17

ason

5   Mansfield

Chelan
Lake Chelan
State Park

2

Lenore
Lake

Soap Lake ○

Ephrata ○

20 km
10 miles

N

Columbia River

LINK YOUR TRIP

5 Chuckanut Drive & Whidbey Island

For a complete break from the mountain madness, veer north in Burlington to Bellingham and sample the coastal and pastoral joys of Puget Sound (p69).

10 Mt Baker & Lummi Island

For more mountain madness, head north to Bellingham and then head back inland into another North Cascadian wilderness (p113).

Classic Trip

itself as a traditional *Romantische Strasse* village, right down to the beer and sausages. The *Sound of Music*-style setting helps, as does the fact that Leavenworth serves as the main activity center for sorties into the nearby **Alpine Lakes Wilderness** and **Wenatchee National Forest**.

A surreal stroll through the gabled alpine houses of Leavenworth's Front St with its dirndl-wearing waitresses, wandering accordionists and European cheese-mongers is one of Washington state's oddest, but most endearing experiences – see it on our walking tour (p142). For whitewater rafting trips, call by **Osprey Rafting Co** (www.ospreyrafting.com; 4342 Icicle Rd) who offer excursions from \$78.

✖ 🛏 p85

The Drive » The 22 miles between Leavenworth and Wenatchee highlight one of the most abrupt scenery changes in the state. One minute you're in quasi-Bavaria surrounded by crenellated alpine peaks, the next you're in a sprawled couldn't-be-anywhere-but-America town amid bald hills and a Nile-like river valley. East of Leavenworth US-2 shares the road briefly with US-97.

❹ Wenatchee

Fruit stands start peppering the highway soon after you leave Leavenworth, paving your entry into Wenatchee, the self-proclaimed – and who's arguing? – Apple Capital of the World. Something of an ugly sister after cute Leavenworth, Wenatchee's a place to go local and taste the apples from the nearby orchards before swinging north. The best fruit stands enliven Hwy 2/97 on the way to Chelan. As an overture to your tasting experience, check out the **Washington Apple Commission Visitors Center** (☎509-663-9600; www.bestapples.com; 2900 Euclid Ave; ☺8am-5pm Mon-Fri, plus 9am-5pm Sat, 10am-4pm Sun May-Dec) on the way into town where you can bone up on the relative merits of a Gala versus a Braeburn over a surprisingly interesting video.

The Drive » Hwy 2/97 plies the east side of the Columbia River between Wenatchee and Chelan. This is one of the best places to 'shop' at impromptu seasonal fruit outlets run by enterprising local farmers who haul their freshly plucked produce from the nearby fields and orchards to sell roadside from semi-permanent stores, carts or just plain old boxes.

❺ Chelan

Lake Chelan shelters some of the nation's cleanest water and has consequently become one of Washington's premier water recreation areas. Not surprisingly, the place is cheek-to-jowl in summer, with all number of speedboats, jet-skis and power-craft battling it out for their own private slice of water. To avoid any high-speed collisions, try renting a kayak from **Lake Rider Sports** (www.lakeridersports.com; Lakeshore Waterfront Park, W Manson Hwy; single/double per day \$50/70) and paddling up the lake to see some undiluted Cascadian nature at first hand.

There are public beaches at **Lakeside Park**, near the west side of Chelan town, and at **Lake Chelan State Park**, 9 miles west on S Lakeshore Rd.

If you have kids, don't even think they'll let you sneak past **Slidewaters Water Park** (www.slidewaters.com; 102 Waterslide Dr; day pass adult/child \$18/15; ☺10am-7pm May-Sep; 🚸) on a hill above the *Lady of the Lake* boat dock.

The Drive » Rejoin US-97 and follow it north through the grand coulees of the Columbia River Valley to the small town of Pateros. From here SR-153 aka the Methow Hwy tracks the younger, faster-flowing Methow River north to Twisp. At a junction with US-20 turn left, and continue on the highway into Winthrop.

6 Winthrop

Winthrop is – along with Leavenworth – one of two themed towns on this Cascade Drive. Once a struggling mining community, it avoided 'ghost town' status in the 1960s when it was madeover to look like a cowboy settlement out of the Wild West. Although on paper it sounds more like corny Hollywood than *Gun Fight at the OK Corral*, the Gary Cooper touches are surprisingly authentic. Winthrop's *High Noon* shopfronts hide a genuine frontier spirit (the road ends in winter not far beyond here), and hide some fantastic eating places and accommodations.

The facades of downtown Winthrop are so realistic it's easy to miss the collection of homesteader cabins that make up the **Shafer Museum** (285 Castle Ave; admission by donation; ⏱10am-5pm May-Sep). But best of all is the unmissable **Sun Mountain Lodge** (www.sunmountainlodge.com), a sporting and relaxation dreamscape 10 miles out of town overlooking the valley.

✕ ⛏ p85

The Drive » SR-20 out of Winthrop enters the most bucolic and endearing stretch of the Methow Valley whose broad

LOCAL KNOWLEDGE: METHOW VALLEY TRAILS

The Methow's combination of powdery winter snow and abundant summer sunshine has transformed the valley into one of Washington's primary recreation areas. You can bike, hike and fish in the summer, and cross-country ski on the second-biggest snow-trail network in the US in the winter. The 125 miles of trails are maintained by a nonprofit organization, the **Methow Valley Sport Trails Association** (MVSTA; www.mvsta.com), and in the winter it provides the most comprehensive network of hut-to-hut (and hotel-to-hotel) skiing in North America.

valley floor scattered with farms gives little hint of the jagged wilderness that lies beyond. If you thought Winthrop was small, don't blink in Mazama, a small cluster of wooden buildings reminiscent of a gunslinger movie.

7 Mazama

The last outpost before the raw, desolate, occasionally terrifying North Cascades, Mazama's half-dozen wooden abodes sit at the western end of the Methow Valley. Fuel up on brownies at the **Mazama Store** (50 Lost River Rd; ⏱7am-6pm Sun-Thu, to 7pm Fri & Sat), aka The Goat, an espresso bar for outdoorsy locals, but also a great place to pick up trail tips.

The Drive » You'll be working through your gears soon after leaving Mazama as the North Cascade Mountains start to close in. This part of US-20 is unlike any other trans-Cascade road. Not only is the scenery

more spectacular, but the road itself is a major engineering feat. Only completed in 1972, it still remains closed November to May due to snow blockage.

8 Washington & Rainy Passes

Venture less than 100yd from your car at the **Washington Pass overlook** (5477ft) and you'll be rewarded with fine views of the towering Liberty Bell and its Early Winter Spires, while the highway drops below you in ribbonlike loops. By the time the highway reaches **Rainy Pass** (5875ft) a couple of miles further west, the air has chilled and you're well into the high country, a hop and a skip from the drive's highest hiking trails. The 6.2-mile **Maple Pass Loop Trail** is a favorite, climbing 2150ft to aerial views over jewel-like Lake

NIK WHEELER / CORBIS ©

LOCAL KNOWLEDGE
ARLENE WAGNER, CURATOR, NUTCRACKER MUSEUM (P142)

Leavenworth is the most authentic German-flavored town in the US. The Bavarian theme was laid out in the 1960s and many German people came to live here later on. For souvenirs look for German clocks, German smokers (wood-carved incense burners), candle pyramids (ornate models where candle-heat turns a fan to rotate figurines and images) and nutcrackers. The Nutcracker Museum exhibits over 6000 nutcrackers, the oldest dating from 200 BC.

Top: Washington Pass
Left: Main St, Winthrop
Right: Leavenworth

Ann. The epic **Pacific Crest Trail** also crosses Hwy 20 nearby, so keep an eye open for wide-eyed and bushy-bearded through-hikers popping out of the undergrowth. Perhaps the best choice to shake the crowds is the excellent climb up to **Easy Pass** (7.4 miles return), hardly 'easy,' but offering spectacular views of Mt Logan and the Fisher Basin below.

The Drive » Surrounded by Gothic peaks, the North Cascades Scenic Hwy makes a big swing north shadowing Granite Creek and then Ruby Creek where it swings back west and enters the Ross Lake National Recreation Area near Ruby Arm.

TRIP HIGHLIGHT

❾ Ross & Diablo Lakes

The odd thing about much of the landscape on this trip is that it's unnatural, born from the construction of three huge dams that still supply Seattle with much of its electricity. The wilderness that surrounds it, however, is the rawest you'll get outside Alaska. **Ross Lake** was formed in the 1930s after the building of the eponymous dam. It stretches north 23 miles into Canada. Soon after the **Ross Lake overlook** a path leads from the road to the dam. You'll see the unique Ross Lake Resort floating on the other side.

Classic Trip

A classic photo op comes a couple of miles later at the **Diablo Lake overlook**. The turquoise lake is the most popular part of the park, offering beaches, gorgeous views and a boat launch at **Colonial Creek campground**, with nearby hikes to Thunder Knob (3.6 miles return) and Thunder Creek.

🛏 p85

The Drive » From Diablo head west alongside the sinuous Gorge Reservoir on US-20. Pass through Newhalem (where you can stop at the North Cascades National Park Visitor Center). As the valley opens out and the damp west coast air drifts in from the Pacific, you'll enter Marblemount.

⑩ Marblemount

Blink and you'll miss the town of Marblemount, but the thought of buffalo burgers may entice you to pull over at the **Buffalo Run Restaurant** (60084 Hwy 20; lunch $7-9, mains $15-20; ⊗closed Wed; 🖢), the first (or last) decent restaurant for miles and a friendly one at that, as long as you don't mind being greeted by the sight of several decoratively draped animal skins and a huge buffalo head mounted on the wall.

🛏 p85

KEROUAC AND THE VOID

A turnout at milepost 135 on US-20 offers the drive's only roadside views of **Desolation Peak**. The peak's lookout tower was famously home to Zen-influenced Beat writer Jack Kerouac who, in 1956, spent 63 days here in splendid isolation, honing his evolving Buddhist philosophy, raging at 'The Void' of nearby Hozomeen Mountain (also visible from the turnout) and penning drafts of *Desolation Angels*. It was the last time Kerouac would enjoy such anonymity; the following year saw the publication of *On the Road*, and his propulsion to the status of literary icon.

The Drive » The Skagit River remains your constant companion as you motor the 8 miles from Marblemount to equally diminutive Rockport. Look out for rafters, floaters and bald eagles.

⑪ Rockport

As the valley widens further you'll touchdown in Rockport where the miragelike appearance of an Indonesian-style Batak hut, aka the **Cascadian Home Farm** (📞360-853-8173; Mile Post 100, Hwy 20; ⊗May-Oct; 🖢), begs you to stop for organic strawberries, delicious fruit shakes and lifesaving espresso, which you can slurp down on a short self-guided tour of the farm.

Nearby, a 10-mile stretch of the Skagit River is a wintering ground for over 600 bald eagles who come here from November to early March to feast on spawning salmon. January is the best time to view them, ideally on a winter float trip

with **Skagit River Guide Service** (www.ackerlunds.com; Mount Vernon), whose boats use propane heat and are equipped with comfy cushioned seats. Three-hour trips run early November to mid-February and cost $65.

The Drive » From Rockport head west on US-20 through the Cascade Mountain foothills and the ever-broadening Skagit River Valley to the small city of Burlington that sits just east of busy Interstate-5.

⑫ Burlington

The drive's end, popularly known as the 'Hub City', is not a 'sight' in itself (unless you like looking at shopping malls), although the settlement's location in the heart of the Skagit River Valley means its acts as a hub for numerous nearby attractions including the tulip fields of La Conner, Chuckanut Drive (which officially ends here) and the San Juan Islands.

Eating & Sleeping

Leavenworth ③

✗ Pavz Cafe Bistro   European $$

(www.pavzcafe.com; 833 Front St; mains $15-25) The first culinary rule in Leavenworth is: don't assume you have to dine on bratwurst. Pavz, nestled underneath the timbered gables of Front St, justifies its bistro tag with its signature crepes (savory and sweet) and some outstanding Mediterranean dishes with a northwestern twist. The scallops with pesto-doused angel hair pasta are a highlight.

🛏 Enzian Inn   Hotel $$

(☎509-548-5269; www.enzianinn.com; 590 Hwy 2; d/ste $155/255; P 🛈 🏊) Most hotels get by on one quirk, but the Enzian broadcasts at least a half-dozen, the most obscure of which is the sight of long-term owner, Bob Johnson, giving a morning blast on his famous alphorn before breakfast. If this doesn't grab you, look out for the free putting green, swimming pools, or the nightly pianist in the lobby.

Winthrop ⑥

✗ Duck Brand Cantina   Mexican $$

(www.methownet.com/duck; 248 Riverside Ave; mains $7-15) No standard Mexican restaurant, the 'Duck' nonetheless serves quesadillas, enchiladas and tacos that could roast the socks off any authentic Monterey diner. Closer to home, the Wild West saloon–style cantina churns out a mean American breakfast. In the winter the hearty porridge will keep you skiing all day.

🛏 Sun Mountain Lodge   Hotel $$$

(☎509-996-2211; www.sunmountainlodge.com; lodge r $235-460, cabin $385-595; 🌫 🛈 🏊 🐎) Without a doubt one of the best places to stay in Washington, the Sun Mountain Lodge benefits from its incomparable natural setting perched like an eagle's nest high above the Methow Valley. Inside, the lodge and its assorted cabins manage to provide luxury without pretension, while the adjacent trail network could keep a hyperactive hiker/biker/skier occupied for weeks.

Ross & Diablo Lakes ⑨

🛏 Ross Lake Resort   Cabins $$

(☎206-386-4437; www.rosslakeresort.com; d cabin $150, q cabin $216; ⏱mid-Jun–Oct) The floating cabins at this secluded resort on Ross Lake were built in the 1930s for loggers. There's no road in – guests can either hike the 2-mile trail from Hwy 20 or take the resort's tugboat-taxi-and-truck shuttle from the parking area near Diablo Dam. Cabins vary in size and facilities, but all feature electricity, plumbing and kitchenettes. Bring food.

Marblemount ⑩

🛏 Buffalo Run Inn   Motel $

(☎360-873-2103; www.buffaloruninn.com; 58179 Hwy 20; shared/private bath $59/89; 🌫 🛈) Situated on a sharp bend on Hwy 20, the buffalo doesn't look much from the outside. But within its wooden walls is a clean, scrubbed mix of modern motel (kitchenettes, TVs and comfy beds) and backcountry cabin (kitschy bear and buffalo paraphernalia). Five of the 15 rooms share baths and a sitting area upstairs. The Buffalo Run Restaurant is across the road.

Reflection Lakes See Mt Rainier mirrored in these tranquil waters

Mt Rainier Scenic Byways

7

Emblazoned on every Washington license plate and visible throughout the western state, Rainier is the contiguous USA's fifth-highest peak and, arguably, its most awe-inspiring.

TRIP HIGHLIGHTS

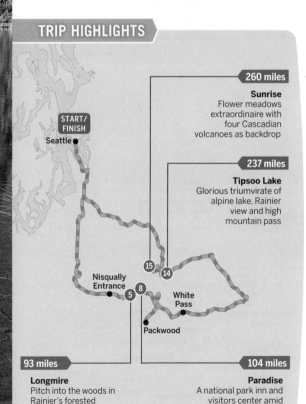

260 miles

Sunrise
Flower meadows extraordinaire with four Cascadian volcanoes as backdrop

237 miles

Tipsoo Lake
Glorious triumvirate of alpine lake, Rainier view and high mountain pass

START/FINISH
Seattle

Nisqually Entrance

White Pass

Packwood

93 miles

Longmire
Pitch into the woods in Rainier's forested lowland nexus

104 miles

Paradise
A national park inn and visitors center amid high-altitude trails

2–3 DAYS
354 MILES/570KM

GREAT FOR...

BEST TIME TO GO

June to October when fabulous alpine flower meadows are in bloom.

ESSENTIAL PHOTO

Rainier's snow-topped summit reflected in the appropriately named Reflection Lakes.

 BEST FOR ALPINE MEADOWS

A toss-up between Paradise and Sunrise, which wins by a point.

Mt Rainier Scenic Byways

Wrapped in a 368-sq-mile national park, and standing 2000ft higher than anything else in the Pacific Northwest, Rainier is a mountain of biblical proportions. Circumnavigate it by car and you'll quickly swap the urban melee of Seattle for forest-covered mountain foothills strafed with huge old-growth trees and imbued with Native American myth. Closer to Paradise (the inn), lucid flower meadows cower beneath Rainier's ice-encrusted summit during an intense summer season.

❶ Seattle

Seattle is an appropriate place to start this epic circuit around what locals refer to reverently as 'the Mountain.' On our walking tour (p138), you can seek out the soul of the city in **Pike Place Market** (for that's where it hides) and, on the days when Rainier reveals itself from the cloudy heavens (a minority annually), you can wander down to the waterfront for a glimpse of the high-altitude glories to come.

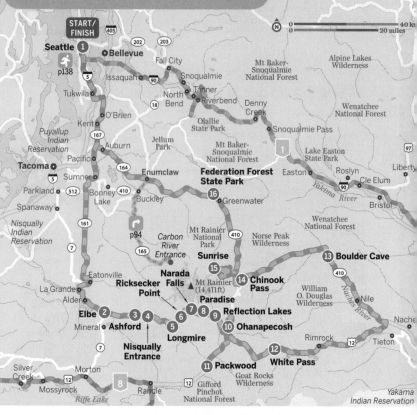

The Drive » Getting out of Seattle and its suburbs is a means to an end and there is little to delay you until the small town of Ashford. Drive south on I-5 to exit 154A, then east on I-405, and south again on SR-167 and SR-161. Just southwest of Eatonville, SR-161 merges with SR-7; follow this road into Elbe on the cusp of the national park.

- - - - - - - - - - - - -

❷ Elbe

The pinprick settlement of Elbe (population 29) has two claims to fame: its tiny white Lutheran **church** built by German immigrants in 1906 (and positively ancient by Pacific Northwest standards), and the heritage **Mt Rainier Scenic Railroad** (☏360-492-5588; www.

LINK YOUR TRIP

8 **Mt St Helens Volcano Trail**

A logical link and an easy one given the proximity of the two mountains – Packwood, near Rainier's Ohanapecosh entrance, serves both drives (p97).

1 **Mountains to Sound Greenway**

Seattle is the finish point of this roller-coaster drive, which is equally spectacular if done in reverse (p35).

mrsr.com; 54124 Mountain Hwy E; adult/child $21/16) that runs summer steam trains between Elbe and Mineral (7 miles south). Trips depart three times daily from May to September. Aping the railway theme is the **Hobo Inn & Diner** (www.rrdiner.com; 54106 Mountain Hwy E; r $115), whose restaurant, bar and rooms all inhabit vintage, but lovingly tended, cabooses (train carriages).

The Drive » From Elbe take SR-706 (the National Park Hwy) due east to Ashford.

- - - - - - - - - - - - -

❸ Ashford

Situated a couple of miles outside the busy Nisqually entrance, Ashford is the national park's main service center with some medium-ranking accommodations, an info center and **Whitaker's Bunkhouse**, a hostel-cafe conceived by legendary local mountaineer Lou Whitaker in the early 1990s. It would be heresy to leave town without popping inside for an espresso before grabbing brunch (or lunch) down the road at the **Copper Creek Inn**, where the wild blackberry pies have fuelled many a successful summit attempt.

 p95

The Drive » Just east of Ashford on SR-706 you'll encounter the park entrance gate.

- - - - - - - - - - - - -

❹ Nisqually Entrance

The southwestern Nisqually entrance (named for the nearby river, which in turn is named after a local Native American tribe) is the busiest in **Mt Rainier National Park** (park fee $15) and the only year-round entry gate. The simple entrance arch was built in 1922. Pay your park fee at the ticket window. As you drive through the entrance, you'll notice how, almost immediately, the trees appear denser and older. Many of these moss-covered behemoths date back over 700 years and measure up to 200ft in height.

The Drive » Follow the road alongside the Nisqually River for a couple of miles to Kautz Creek, where the summit of Rainier appears like a ghostly apparition.

- - - - - - - - - - - - -

❺ Longmire

Worth a stop to stretch your legs or gain an early glimpse of Rainier's mossy old-growth forest, Longmire was the brainchild of a certain James Longmire who first came here in 1883 during a climbing trip when he noticed the hot mineral springs that bubbled up in a lovely meadow opposite the present-day National Park Inn (p95). He and his family returned the following year and established Longmire's Medicinal Springs, and in 1890 he built the Longmire Springs Hotel. Since 1917 the National Park Inn has stood on this site – built in classic 'parkitecture' style – and is complemented by a small store, the tiny **Longmire Museum** (admission free; ⊙9am-6pm Jun-Sep, to 5pm Oct-May) and a number of important trailheads. For a laid-back look at some old-growth forest and pastoral meadows, try the **Trail of the Shadows** loop, a 0.8-mile circuit that begins across the road from the museum.

 p95

The Drive ›› After Longmire the road slowly starts to climb, passing the Cougar Rock campground and Christine Falls, both on the left. A couple of miles after the falls, bear right onto a short stretch of summer-only one-way road (signposted 'Viewpoint') for a view stop at Ricksecker Point.

- - - - - - - - - - -

❻ Ricksecker Point

One of the park's premier viewpoints beloved by photographers, professional or otherwise, Ricksecker Point is a fine place to study five of Rainier's 26 glaciers – Nisqually,

Pyramid, Success, Kautz and Wilson. The summit you see here is actually a false one (Point Success); the obscured *true* summit is 257ft higher. Equally majestic to the southeast is the saw-toothed Tatoosh range.

The Drive ›› Rejoin the main road and continue uphill.

- - - - - - - - - - -

❼ Narada Falls

Eight miles east of Longmire, a parking area marks the starting point for a steep 0.2-mile trail that leads down through flowers and ferns to the misty 168ft Narada Falls. The falls, often embellished by brilliant rainbows, carry the Paradise River over a basalt cliff. In high season, expect to get a face-full of water spray and an earful of oohing and ahhing as this is the park's most popular waterfall. In winter the falls freeze over and attract daring ice-climbers.

The Drive ›› Soon after the falls, the road forks; stay left for Paradise. Follow the winding asphalt for another 2 miles to the Upper Parking Lot, where you'll find the Paradise Inn and Henry M Jackson Visitor Center.

- - - - - - - - - - -

TRIP HIGHLIGHT

❽ Paradise

'Oh, what a paradise!' exclaimed the daughter of park pioneer James Longmire on visiting this

spot for the first time in the 1880s. Suddenly, the high mountain nirvana had a name, and a very apt one at that. One of the snowiest places on earth, 5400ft-high Paradise remains the park's most popular draw with its famous flower meadows backed by dramatic Rainier views on the days when the mountain decides to take its cloudy hat off. Aside from hiding numerous trailheads and being the starting point for most summit hikes, Paradise guards the iconic Paradise Inn (p95; built in 1916 and refurbished in 2008) and the informative **Henry M Jackson Visitor Center** (⊙10am-7pm Jun-Oct), completely rebuilt and reopened in 2008. Park naturalists lead free interpretive hikes from the visitors center daily in summer, and snowshoe walks on winter weekends.

⚒ 🛏 p95

The Drive ›› Drive out of the east end of the Paradise Upper Parking Lot, cross the Paradise River (looking out for marmots) and descend the one-way road for 2 miles to a junction. Turn left and rejoin the main two-way road heading toward Reflection Lakes and Steven's Canyon.

- - - - - - - - - - -

❾ Reflection Lakes

Rainier eyes itself in the mirror on calm cloudless days at Reflection

Narada Falls Mt Rainier National Park's most popular waterfall

Lakes, formed during a violent volcanic eruption nearly 6000 years ago. You can pull over for double-vision photos of the mountain framed by tufts of precious wildflowers. The main lake used to have a boat concession, but now it's deliciously tranquil bar the odd passing tour bus.

The Drive ≫ Avalanche chutes plague the U-shaped Steven's Canyon Rd in the winter, ensuring it remains closed outside peak season (unlike Paradise on the western side). Seen from above, the canyon is rather spectacular. Stop for a bird's-eye view a mile or so after Reflection Lakes before the trees close in. From here it's downhill all the way to Ohanapecosh.

- - - - - - - - - - -

🔟 Ohanapecosh

Ohanapecosh (o-*ha*-nuh-peh-*kosh*) – the name means 'at the edge' – in the park's southeastern corner is usually accessed by the small settlement of Packwood, 12 miles to the southwest

on US 12, which harbors a small number of eating and sleeping options. Shoehorned between Mt Rainier and it two southern neighbors, Mt St Helens and Mt Adams, this is a good base for travelers wanting to visit two or more of the mountains.

Just inside the Steven's Canyon gate, you'll find the 1.5-mile **Grove of the Patriarchs Trail**, one of the park's most popular short hikes. The trail explores a small island in the Ohanapecosh River replete with craning Douglas fir, cedar and hemlock trees, some of which are over 1000 years old. To reach the Ohanapecosh Visitors Center, turn right at the Steven's Canyon entrance onto SR-123 and drive 1.5 miles south. Alternatively, you can hike down from the Grove of the Patriarchs.

The Drive ≫ Go right at the Steven's Canyon entrance and follow SR-123 south past

the visitors center to the intersection with US 12. For Packwood, bear right.

- - - - - - - - - - -

🔟 Packwood

A service center for Mt St Helens, Mt Rainier and the nearby ski area of White Pass, Packwood is what in the Old West they called a 'one-horse town.' A few low- to mid-ranking eating and accommodation joints glued to US 12 provide a good excuse to pull over and mingle with other road-trippers. Chin-waggers congregate in **Peter's Inn** (www.peters-inn. com; Hwy 12, near Skate Creek Rd; mains $11-15), a no-thrills diner with elk-watching opportunities from the window.

The Drive ≫ Retrace your route to the intersection of US 12 and SR-123. The climb to White Pass begins here. Stop at a pullover soon after the intersection to appreciate the indelible sight of Mt Rainier as it appears briefly above the trees.

🛏 p95

SUMMER WONDERLAND

You've circumnavigated it in a car; now how about walking it? Rainier is not only encircled by a road; you can also walk around it on foot via the long-distance Wonderland Trail. Laid out in 1915, the 93-mile-long precipitous path initially served as a patrol beat for park rangers and in the 1930s it was briefly earmarked as a paved ring road for cars. Fortunately, the plan never reached fruition and today the unbroken trail (which gains 21,000ft in cumulative elevation) is one of the most challenging and iconic hikes in the Pacific Northwest. You'll need food, camping gear, eight to 12 free days and a permit from the Wilderness Info Center in Ashford to do Wonderland. Longmire is a popular start point. There are 18 backcountry campgrounds en route; reservations ($20) are advisable in peak season (July and August). The official park page (www.nps.gov/mora) has more information.

Ohanapecosh River A suspension bridge on the Grove of the Patriarchs Trail

12 White Pass

Higher than Snoqualmie and Stevens Passes to the north, White Pass carries a quieter, open-year-round road that, at various points, offers glimpses of three Cascadian volcanoes: Mt Rainier, Mt Adams and Mt St Helens. The pass itself, perched at 4500ft, is home to an understated but recently expanded **ski area** (www. skiwhitepass.com) which has one condo complex for overnighters. Otherwise, people stay in nearby Packwood or drive up for the day from Yakima.

🛏 p95

The Drive » A classic east–west Washington scenery shift kicks in soon after White Pass as you follow US 12 amid increasingly scattered trees and bald, steep-sided river coulees. At the intersection with SR-410,

swing north on the Chinook Scenic Byway just west of the town of Naches.

13 Boulder Cave

Among the many excuses to pull over on this stretch of the Chinook Scenic Byway is **Boulder Cave** (⊙May-Oct), a rarity in the relatively cave-free terrain of the Pacific Northwest and doubly unique due to its formation through a combination of volcanic and erosive processes. A 2-mile round-trip trail built by the Civilian Conservation Corp in 1935 leads into the cave's murky interior, formed when Devil's Creek cut a tunnel through soft sedimentary rock, leaving hard volcanic basalt on top. Up to 50 rare big-eared bats hibernate in the cave each winter, when it is closed to the public. Bring a flashlight.

The Drive » Continue west and uphill toward Chinook Pass as the air cools and the snowdrifts pile up roadside.

TRIP HIGHLIGHT

14 Chinook Pass

Closed until May and infested with lingering snowdrifts well into July, Chinook Pass towers 5430ft on Rainier's eastern flank. The long-distance **Pacific Crest Trail** crosses the highway here on a pretty stone bridge, while nearby **Crystal Mountain** (www. crystalresort.com) comprises Washington's largest ski area and only bona fide overnight 'resort.' Rather than stop at the pass, cruise a few hundred yards further west to **Tipsoo Lake**, another reflective photographer's dream where a paved trail will return the blood to your legs.

DETOUR: CARBON RIVER ENTRANCE

Start: ⑯ Federation Forest State Park

The park's northwest entrance is its most isolated and undeveloped corner, with two unpaved (and unconnected) roads and little in the way of facilities, save a lone ranger station and the very basic Ipsut Creek Campground. But while the tourist traffic might be thin on the ground, the landscape lacks nothing in magnificence or serendipity.

Named for its coal deposits, Carbon River is the park's wettest region and protects one of the few remaining examples of inland temperate rain forest in the contiguous USA. Dense, green and cloaked in moss, this verdant wilderness can be penetrated by a handful of interpretive trails that fan off the Carbon River Rd.

The Drive » From Tipsoo Lake the road winds down to relatively 'low' Cayuse Pass (4694ft). Turn north here and descend a further 1000ft in 3 miles to the turning for Mt Rainier's White River entrance. This is the gateway to Sunrise, 16 miles uphill via a series of switchbacks.

TRIP HIGHLIGHT

⑮ Sunrise

Sunrise, at 6400ft, marks the park's highest road. Thanks to the superior elevation, the summer season is particularly short and snow can linger into July. It is also noticeably drier than Paradise, resulting in an interesting variety of subalpine vegetation, including masses of wildflowers.

The views from Sunrise are famously spectacular and – aside from stunning close-ups of Rainier itself – you can also, quite literally, watch the weather roll in over the distant peaks of Mt Baker and Mt Adams. Similarly impressive is the glistening Emmons Glacier, which, at 4 sq miles, is the largest glacier in the contiguous USA.

A trailhead directly across the parking lot from the Sunrise Lodge Cafeteria provides access to **Emmons Vista**, with good views of Mt Rainier, Little Tahoma and the glacier. Nearby, the 1-mile **Sourdough Ridge Trail** leads to pristine subalpine meadows for stunning views over other volcanic giants.

The Drive » Coast downhill to the White River Entrance and turn north onto the Mather Memorial Pkwy in order to exit the park. In the small community of Greenwater on SR-410 you can load up with gas and food.

⑯ Federation Forest State Park

Just when you thought you'd left ancient nature behind, up springs Federation Forest State Park, created by a foresighted women's group in the 1940s in order to preserve a rapidly diminishing stock of local old-growth forest from logging interests. Today its fir, spruce, hemlock and cedar trees cluster around the lackadaisical White River, while the **Catherine Montgomery Interpretive Center** (⊙9am-4pm Wed-Sun May-Sep) offers a rundown of the contrasting ecosystems of east–west Washington state. There's also a bookstore and 12 miles of trails, most of them family-friendly.

The Drive » Continue on SR-410 west to the small city of Enumclaw, then switch onto SR-164 heading northwest to Auburn. Briefly join SR-18 before filtering north on SR-167, whereupon you can retrace your steps to downtown Seattle.

Eating & Sleeping

Ashford ③

✖ Copper Creek Inn
Brunch $

(www.coppercreekinn.com; 35707 SR-706 E;
breakfast $7-10; ⏰7am-9pm) This is one of the
state's great rural restaurants, and breakfast
is a rite of passage for anyone heading off for a
knee-shattering hike inside the park. Perched
just outside the Nisqually entrance, the Copper
Creek has been knocking out dessert pies and
their own home-roasted coffee successfully for
over 50 years. Why stop now?

✖ 🛏 Whittaker's Motel
& Bunkhouse
Hostel $

(☎360-569-2439; www.whittakersbunkhouse.
com; 30205 SR-706 E; dm/d $35/85) Down-
to-earth and comfortable, this place is part of
Rainier's 'furniture' with a good old-fashioned
youth-hostel feel and cheap sleeps available
in six-bed dorms. The alluring on-site
Whittaker's Café & Espresso (⏰7am-
9pm, weekends only in winter) is a fine place
to hunker down for breakfast – none of those
saran-wrapped day-old muffins here.

🛏 Nisqually Lodge
Motel $$

(☎360-569-8804; www.escapetothemountains.
com; 31609 SR-706 E; r $95-125; ❉📶) With
an expansive lobby complete with crackling
fireplace and huge well-stocked rooms, this
lodge is far plusher than an average motel. The
outdoor Jacuzzi, simple help-yourself breakfast
and easy park access pretty much seal the deal
in this price bracket.

Longmire ⑤

✖ 🛏 National
Park Inn
Historic Lodge $$

(☎360-569-2411; www.mtrainierguestservices.
com; r with shared/private bath $114/159; ❉)
The pride of Longmire, parts of which date from
1917, goes out of its way to be rustic with no TVs

or telephones in the rooms and small yet cozy
facilities. But who needs HBO and the Discovery
Channel when you've got fine service, fantastic
surroundings and delectable complimentary
afternoon tea and scones in the dining room?

Paradise ⑧

✖ 🛏 Paradise Inn
Historic Lodge $$$

(☎360-569-2413; www.mtrainierguestservices.
com; r with shared/private bath $112/163;
⏰mid-May–Sep) A historic 'parkitecture' inn
constructed in 1916, the Paradise has long
been part of the national park's fabric and was
an early blueprint for National Park Rustic
architecture countrywide. Reopening in 2008
after a two-year, $30 million, earthquake-
withstanding revamp, the small-ish rooms
retain their close-to-the-wilderness essence,
while the communal areas are nothing short
of regal.

Packwood ⑪

🛏 Cowlitz River Lodge
Motel $$

(☎360-494-4444; www.escapetothemountains.
com; Hwy 12, at Skate Creek Rd; s/d incl breakfast
$80-95; ❉📶) Probably the most convenient
accommodations for both Mt Rainier and Mt
St Helens, the Cowlitz is the sister motel to
Ashford's Nisqually Lodge and offers 32 above-
average motel rooms along with the obligatory
outdoor Jacuzzi.

White Pass ⑫

🛏 White Pass Village Inn
Condo $$$

(☎509-672-3131; www.whitepassvillageinn.
com; 38933 US 12; studio $80, 1-bed condo $110;
📶❉) Adjacent to the White Pass skiing area,
this condo complex is open year-round. The
outdoor pool is heated to spa temperatures in
the winter, and a store and laundry are next door.

Mt St Helens Enter a blast zone full of eerie landscapes

Mt St Helens Volcano Trail

8

Fiery infamy was made in 1980 when Mt St Helens blew megatons of molten ash into the atmosphere. Its devastated but recovering landscape looks and is like nothing else on earth.

TRIP HIGHLIGHTS

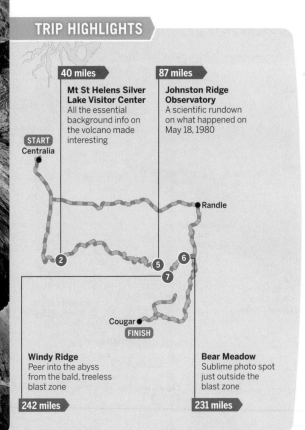

40 miles

Mt St Helens Silver Lake Visitor Center
All the essential background info on the volcano made interesting

87 miles

Johnston Ridge Observatory
A scientific rundown on what happened on May 18, 1980

START
Centralia

● Randle

② ⑤ ⑥
⑦

Cougar ●
FINISH

Windy Ridge
Peer into the abyss from the bald, treeless blast zone

242 miles

Bear Meadow
Sublime photo spot just outside the blast zone

231 miles

3 DAYS
366 MILES/589KM

GREAT FOR...

BEST TIME TO GO
July to October – the mountain's best sights and roads are open.

 ESSENTIAL PHOTO
Bear Meadow, from where Gary Rosenquist took his famous shots of the mountain exploding.

BEST FOR FAMILIES
Silver Lake Visitor Center's interactive exhibits.

97

Mt St Helens Volcano Trail

The name Mt St Helens has a fearful resonance to anyone who was alive on May 18, 1980, when a massive volcanic eruption set off the largest landslide in human history. Over 30 years later, you can drive through the embattled but slowly recovering landscape, stopping off at strategically placed interpretive centers that graphically document the erstwhile environmental carnage. It's a unique if sometimes disconcerting ride.

❶ Centralia

The main reason to make this rather mundane mining and lumber town the starting point for your volcanic excursion is to stay at a converted brothel! The **Olympic Club Hotel** – a 'venue hotel' run by Portland's McMenamin brothers – dates from 1908 when it opened as a 'gentlemen's resort' designed to satisfy the various drinking, gambling and sexual vices of transient miners and loggers. In 1996 the turn-of-the-century

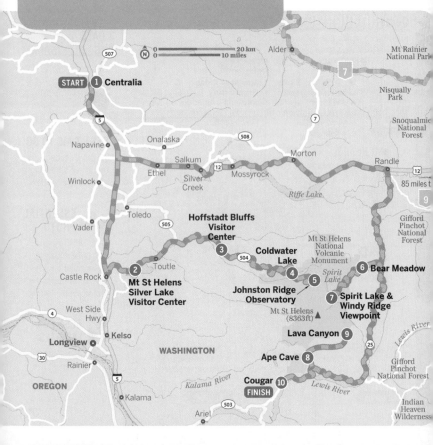

building was taken over by the McMenamins, who restored the brothel to its former glory complete with creaking floorboards, Tiffany lamps and art-deco murals (but without the erstwhile nighttime shenanigans).

 p103

The Drive » Steer south out of Centralia on I-5 for 32 miles to exit 49, where you proceed east on SR-504, aka the Spirit Lake Memorial Hwy.

TRIP HIGHLIGHT

❷ Mt St Helens Silver Lake Visitor Center

Situated 5 miles east of Castle Rock on SR-504,

LINK YOUR TRIP

7 Mt Rainier Scenic Byways

St Helens' taller, potentially more lethal mountain twin is easily accessible via its southeastern Ohanapecosh entrance (p92).

9 Washington Wine Tour

Head east in Randle and continue on to Yakima on the cusp of a sunny valley full of grapes and wineries. Say no more (p105).

MT ST HELENS INSTITUTE

The not-for-profit **Mt St Helens Institute** (www.mshinstitute.org) is one of the most admired educational and conservation groups in the nation. Look out for the institute's expert volunteers at various interpretive sites around the mountain where they organize hikes, talks, films and fundraisers, all related to the volcano and its geology.

the **Silver Lake Visitor Center** (3029 Spirit Lake Memorial Hwy; admission $3; ☺9am-5pm May 1-Sep 30;) is the best introduction to the monument. There's a classic film and various exhibits, including a mock-up of the volcano; duck beneath the cone for displays on the subterranean workings of the mountain. Outside is the mile-long **Silver Lake Wetlands Trail**.

 p103

The Drive » Take the road east along the Toutle River Valley toward the National Volcanic Monument and the blast zone.

❸ Hoffstadt Bluffs Visitor Center

At milepost 27, the impressive wood-and-beam edifice that houses the **Hoffstadt Bluffs Visitor Center** (www.hoffstadtbluffs.com; 15000 Spirit Lake Memorial Hwy; admission free; ☺9:30am-4pm) has a good restaurant – the Fire Mountain Grill – and panoramic views of the Toutle River Valley.

Exhibits inside focus on St Helens' ecology pre-blast, plus there's an outdoor memorial to the 57 people who lost their lives. This is where you can organize **helicopter tours** (per person $149) over the crater.

 p103

The Drive » Continue east on the Spirit Lake Memorial Hwy (504). At milepost 33, a Forest Learning Center runs an interesting film about the eruption. Soon after, you enter the blast zone near the Elk Rock viewpoint.

❹ Coldwater Lake

You're now categorically in the blast zone! Coldwater Lake, 43 miles east of Castle Rock, was created in 1980 when water backed up behind a dam caused by debris brought down by the eruption. The recreation area here (rest rooms, phone, boat launch) is the starting point of the 0.6-mile **Birth of a Lake Trail** (No 246), a paved interpretive hike that seeks to demonstrate the regrowth of vegetation in the area. Look out for beavers and their handiwork.

The Drive >> Follow the increasingly winding Spirit Lake Memorial Hwy (SR-504) through the denuded landscape to the end of the road.

TRIP HIGHLIGHT

⑤ Johnston Ridge Observatory

Situated at the end of SR-504 and looking directly into the mouth of the crater, this famous **observatory** (admission $8; ☺10am-6pm May-Oct) has exhibits that take a more scientific angle than the Silver Lake Visitor Center, depicting the geological events surrounding the 1980 blast and how they advanced the science of volcano forecasting and monitoring. The paved 1-mile round-trip **Eruption Trail** (No 201) offers once-in-a-lifetime views over toward the crater.

The Drive >> Retrace your steps 52 miles to Castle Rock. Go north on I-5 and, at exit 68, east on US 12. In the tiny settlement of Randle, you can refuel with food and gas. Turn right off US 12 onto SR-131, which soon becomes USFS Rd 25. Just past Iron Creek Falls, amid old-growth forest, turn right onto USFS Rd 99.

TRIP HIGHLIGHT

⑥ Bear Meadow

Bear Meadow, just outside the blast zone, is where Gary Rosenquist took his infamous photographs of Mt St Helens erupting on May 18, 1980. The four quick-succession shots which Rosenquist started snapping at 8:32am are reproduced on an interpretive board and show the mountain, 11 miles away, with its northern slopes literally sliding away. Rosenquist, who was camping in the area at the time, was lucky and got out alive, driving north through thick ash. The blast zone stopped less than a mile away from the meadow, as the stands of still healthy trees in the foreground testify.

The Drive >> Two miles further on, you'll enter the blast zone marked by eerie dead trees. Press on past various trailheads to the end of the road.

ANDRE JENNY / ALAMY ©

Hoffstadt Creek Bridge Mt St Helens National Volcanic Monument

TRIP HIGHLIGHT

7 Spirit Lake & Windy Ridge Viewpoint

More remote but less crowded than Johnston Ridge is the harder-to-reach Windy Ridge viewpoint on the mountain's eastern side, accessed via USFS Rd 99. Here visitors get a palpable, if eerie, sense of the destruction that the blast wrought, with felled forests, desolate mountain slopes and the rather surreal sight of lifeless Spirit Lake, once one of the premier resorts in the South Cascades. There are toilets and a snack bar at the viewpoint parking lot, which is often closed until June. Over 350 steps ascend the hillside for close-up views of the crater 5 miles away. A stubbly green carpet covers the ridge slopes in summer as dwarf plants struggle back to life over 30 years later. A few miles down the road you can descend 600ft on the 1.5-mile **Harmony Trail** (No 224) that leads to Spirit Lake.

MT ST HELENS NATIONAL VOLCANIC MONUMENT

Mt St Helens is one of only two National Volcanic Monuments in the nation. The unique park, which measures 110,000 acres, was set aside in 1982 and is mostly comprised of land in the so-called 'blast zone' – the plan being that anything inside the park boundary is to be left to recover as nature intends. The monument, which is closely monitored, acts like a massive outdoor scientific laboratory.

The Drive » Retrace your steps to USFS Rd 25; turn right (south) and drive over Elk Pass and past the Clearwater viewpoint to Pine Creek Work Center, a small information center. Turn west on USFS Rd 90 and drive along the north shore of Swift Reservoir before going right onto USFS Rd 83 and left onto USFS Rd 8303.

- - - - - - - - - - - - -

8 Ape Cave

Ape Cave, on the south flank of Mt St Helens, is a 2-mile-long lava tube formed 2000 years ago by a lava flow that followed a deep watercourse. It's the longest lava tube in the Western Hemisphere. Hikers can walk and scramble the length of Ape Cave on either the 0.8-mile **Lower Ape Cave Trail** or the 1.5-mile **Upper Ape Cave Trail**, which requires a certain amount of scrambling over rock piles and narrower passages. Bring your own light source. Free ranger-led explorations depart from

Apes' Headquarters (8303 Forest Rd; ☉10:30am-5pm Jun-Sep), located at the entrance to the caves, several times daily in the summer.

The Drive » Retrace your route to USFS Rd 83. Turn left and drive to the road's terminus at Lava Canyon.

- - - - - - - - - - - - -

9 Lava Canyon

The geology class continues on St Helens' southeast side. Although the mountain's 1980 lateral blast blew north, the heat of the massive explosion melted its eastern glaciers and created a huge mud flow. Water, boulders and trees came flooding down Muddy Creek, scouring it out and revealing much older lava basalt underneath. This fascinating geological demolition can be seen at Lava Canyon, where a short half-mile interpretive **trail** leads through new-growth

trees to an overlook. To get closer, take a steeper path that zigzags down into the canyon, which you can cross on a bouncy suspension bridge built in 1993. Lava Canyon Falls crashes below. The trail continues further along the Canyon (though it's extremely exposed) to Smith Creek.

The Drive » Track back along USFS Rd 83 to the junction with USFS Rd 90. Turn right (west) and head into the small settlement of Cougar on Yale Lake.

- - - - - - - - - - - - -

10 Cougar

A 'town' with virtually no residents, lowly Cougar (population 120-ish), the nearest settlement to Mt St Helens, was mercifully spared the carnage of the 1980 eruption – though it was temporarily evacuated. Since 1953 it has sat on the shores of Yale Lake, a reservoir created after the construction of the Yale Dam on the Lewis River. It is a good pit stop courtesy of its Lone Fir motel, convenience store (with gas), grill restaurant and peaceful lakeside tranquility. Climbers making a St Helens summit bid often psyche up here.

✕ ⌂ p103

Eating & Sleeping

Centralia ①

✖ Berry Fields   Cafe $

(201 S Pearl St; mains $10) In the culinary
wasteland of Centralia stands an exception to
the rule. This formidable brunch spot situated
in Centralia's biggest antique mall offers
formidable egg concoctions and cinnamon buns
the size of soccer balls.

✖ 🛏 Olympic Club Hotel   Hotel $

(📞360-736-5164; 112 N Tower Ave; bunk/
queen/king $40/60/70; 🛜 🚻) A 'venue hotel'
run by Portland's McMenamin brothers, where
you can eat, sleep, drink, shoot billiards, listen
to music and go to the cinema, all in the same
evening and – more to the point – all without
having to leave the hotel.

Mt St Helens Silver Lake Visitor Center ②

🛏 Blue Heron Inn   B&B $$

(📞360-274-9595; www.blueheroninn.com; Hwy
504; d/ste $170/215; 🛜) A welcome B&B in an
accommodation-lite area, the Blue Heron offers
seven rooms including a Jacuzzi suite in a large
house almost opposite the Silver Lake Visitor
Center on Hwy 504.

Hoffstadt Bluffs Visitor Center ③

✖ Fire Mountain Grill   American $$

(15000 Spirit Lake Memorial Hwy; mains $13-
20; 🕙11am-4pm Thu-Mon) A not untypical
American grill menu is enhanced here by its
unexpectedness (there's nothing else for miles
around) and location (a fine outdoor patio offers
views of the Toutle River and *that* volcano). In
such circumstances those specialty burgers and
10oz steaks start to taste a lot more – well – fiery.

✖ 🛏 Eco Park Resort   Cabin $

(📞360-274-6542; www.ecoparkresort.com;
14000 Spirit Lake Memorial Hwy; campsites &
RV sites $18, yurts $75, cabins $100-110) The
closest full-service accommodations to the
blast zone offers campsites and RV hookups,
basic cabins and rather incongruous Genghis
Khan–style yurts. Shared bathrooms are known
as 'wilderness comfort stations.' Owned by the
family whose Spirit Lake Lodge was swept away
by the 1980 eruption, the resort also features
the **Backwoods Café**, which serves anything
as long as it's beef.

Cougar ⑩

✖ Cougar Grill   American $

(16849 Lewis River Rd; mains $8-12) Zero
competition hasn't left the Cougar Grill resting
on its laurels. On the contrary, this little middle-
of-nowhere abode makes a heavy impression on
passing travelers, itinerants, summiteers and
people who took the wrong turning in Portland.
After savoring the burgers, beer, tacos and
down-country service, most swear they'll be
back.

✖ 🛏 Lone Fir Resort & Café   Motel $

(📞360-238-5120; www.lonefirresort.com;
16806 Lewis River Rd; r $65-85; ❄ 🏊) There's
not a lot to choose from on Mt St Helens'
south side in the noncamping genre, so thank
your lucky stars that this place, in the rather
lonesome settlement of Cougar, backs up its RV
park with a pleasantly sited motel, cafe (pizzas
and burgers, mainly) and swimming pool.
Rustic's the word.

Yakima Valley Home to wines
served at the White House

Washington Wine Tour

9

From the mellow Bordeaux reds of the sunny Yakima Valley to the big, bold flavors of pastoral Walla Walla, Washington wines are as luscious as the landscapes surrounding them.

TRIP HIGHLIGHTS

25 miles

Rattlesnake Hills
Gorgeous bucolic terroir of easy-drinking Bordeaux reds

139 miles

Walla Walla
Where wine, scenery and great food come together

START
Yakima

③

②

Sunnyside

Grandview

⑤

⑧
FINISH

Toppenish
Quirky cowboy town decorated in intriguing murals

21 miles

Red Mountain
Sip renowned vintages on patios overlooking sagebrush-covered hills

72 miles

3 DAYS
140 MILES/225KM

GREAT FOR...

BEST TIME TO GO
April to October for weather and flowers.

 ESSENTIAL PHOTO

Terra Blanca – capture hills covered in orchards and grapevines from the area's grandest villa.

 BEST FOR FOODIES

Walla Walla has the best (and arguably only) concentration of fine eateries.

Washington Wine Tour

Napa? Too crowded. France? Too far away. Fortunately, the Yakima and Walla Walla Valleys have emerged as major winemaking destinations. Come learn about terroir and viticulture, or just dedicate yourself to sampling lush reds and crisp whites in your search for your favorite appellation (you can always spit to manage consumption!). For now this is still an unpretentious, small-town scene with bucolic scenery in all directions, but the wines are nothing less than extraordinary.

❶ Yakima

The town of Yakima is a sprawling, flat mid-century-feeling city that doesn't have much allure, but it's a pleasant enough place to start your trip. The town is home to some of the only bubbles available in this region. Start the day at **Treveri Cellars** (📞509-248-0200; www.trevericellars.com; 225 S 2nd Ave; 🕐noon-6pm Mon-Sat), whose sparkling wines are so good, they're served at the White House.

🍴 🛏 p111

The Drive » From I-82 E, take exit 50 toward Toppenish. Turn right on Buena Way off the exit and continue about 3 miles to 1st St, the main drag of downtown Toppenish.

TRIP HIGHLIGHT

❷ Toppenish

Toppenish makes up for its lack of wineries with its kooky personality. The antique, distinctly Wild West brick and timber buildings are further beautified by some 70 **murals** within the downtown area. Scenes include Native Americans, cowboys and early settlers as well as artistic hat-tipping to the majority Latino population. Country-and-western music is pumped via loudspeaker into the streets. While here, stop into the **American Hop Museum** (www. americanhopmuseum.org; 22 S B St; admission $3; ⊘10am-4pm May-Sep) to think about beer for awhile, and the **Yakama Indian Nation Cultural Center** (www.yakamamuseum.com; 280 Buster Rd; adult/child $6/4; ⊘8am-5pm Mon-Fri, 9am-5pm Sat & Sun) to see crafts from the area's original artists.

The Drive » Go back toward I-82 E but instead of getting on the freeway, cross over it. Cross the Yakima Valley Hwy, then at the crossroads turn left (this is still Buena Way). Take the third right on Highland Rd, up a hill through orchards to Bonair Winery.

TRIP HIGHLIGHT

❸ Rattlesnake Hills

Lazing next to the tiny town of Zillah, the warm, rolling Rattlesnake Hills grow thick with grapevines and apple orchards. Nary a rattlesnake has been found in recent memory but you will find plenty of smooth and delicious Bordeaux reds at any of the dozen or so wineries. Start at wonderfully welcoming **Bonair Winery** (☎509-829-6027; www.bonairwine.com; 500 S Bonair Rd, Zillah; ⊘10am-5pm), one of the oldest in the area, where you're heartily encouraged to picnic on the lawn overlooking the pond – or grab a table in front of the buttery-yellow chateau for tapas.

Just north of Bonair, **Silver Lake Winery** (☎509-829-6235; www.silverlakewinery.com; 1500 Vintage Rd, Zillah; ⊘10am-5pm Apr-Nov, 11am-4pm Thu-Mon Dec-Mar) sits at the top of a hill overlooking the whole valley, making it a prime location for weddings and fancy-schmancy events.

The Drive » You can choose to take I-82 E to exit 80 (about 30 miles) to get to Prosser or take the Yakima Valley Hwy, which leads more slowly through scenic farmlands. With this second option, the Yakima Valley

LINK YOUR TRIP

1 Mountains to Sound Greenway

Drive 36 miles from Yakima to Ellensburg via the Yakima River Valley (p37).

12 Lewis & Clark Trail

From Pasco, you can head west through the Yakima Valley or east to Walla Walla (p129).

DETOUR: YAKAMA SCENIC BYWAY

Start: ❷ Toppenish

This byway leads 63 miles down Hwy 97 from Toppenish to Maryhill (which is on a couple of other Trips, see p191 and p131). You'll pass through native Yakama country and up through the desolate Simcoe Mountains. Highlights between them include the **Greek Orthodox St John the Forerunner Monastery** (www.stjohnmonastery.org; 5 Timmer Lane, Goldendale; ☉9am-2pm & 4-6pm) and **Goldendale Observatory State Park** (www.parks.wa.gov; 1602 Observatory Dr, Goldendale; entry $10; ☉2-5pm & 8pm-midnight Wed-Sun Apr-Oct, shorter hours winter).

Hwy turns into Wine Country Rd at Grandview, which parallels I-82 and on to Prosser.

---

❹ Prosser

The historic center of Prosser is a small grid of brick buildings worthy of a 1950s-era movie set – it's a choice stop for lunch or the night. Stop in at picture-book pretty **Chinook Wines** (www.chinookwines.com; Wine Country Rd; ☉tastings noon-5pm Sat & Sun May-Oct), with a flower-filled yard and picnic area. The winery has been in operation since 1983 and is known for its classy Chardonnay and Sauvignon Blanc. It's just off Wine Country Rd to the east out of town.

Prosser sprawls less scenically across I-82, where you'll find **Vintner's Village**, a collection of excellent wineries in flat, housing-community-like surroundings. **Maison**

Bleue (☎509-378-6527; www.mbwines.com; 357 Port Ave, Studio D; ☉by appointment) is a standout here and has been making critics hurrah about its Rhône-style Syrah. If appointment-making isn't on your agenda, stop at **Airfield Estates** (☎509-786-7401; www.airfieldwines.com; 560 Merlot Dr; ☉11am-5pm), known for its esteemed whites including a zesty, easy-to-love unoaked Chardonnay.

✖ p111

The Drive » Back on I-82 East, another 17 miles of highway brings you to Benton City and the Red Mountain AVA.

Take exit 96 then turn left on SR-224, veering left again when the road forks.

- - - - - - - - - - - -

TRIP HIGHLIGHT

❺ Red Mountain

Red Mountain, just next to Benton City, is the tiniest American Viticultural Area (AVA) in the state, coveted for its vintages brought to perfection on sun-drenched slopes. It's a California-esque landscape here of hills covered in vineyards, golden grass and sagebrush. Meander up N Sunset Rd, making your first stop at humble **Cooper Wine Company** (☎509-588-2667; www.cooperwinecompany.com; 35306 N Sunset Rd; ☉noon-5pm Fri-Mon), whose L'Inizio Bordeaux blend is anything but boring. Next, sample the highly regarded Bordeaux blends at **Hedges Family Estate** (☎509-588-3105; www.hedgesfamilyestate.com; 53511 N Sunset Rd; ☉11am-5pm Sat & Sun Apr-Nov) in a French-inspired mansion; then drive up further to **Taptiel Estate** (☎509-588-4460; www.taptiel.com; 20206 E 583 PR NE; ☉11am-5pm Fri-

CHOCOLATE CHERRIES

When you get to Prosser, be sure to stop at the **Chukar Cherries** store. It has amazing chocolate-covered cherries – not like those gooey ones you get in a box at Christmas; these are really great. Some of them even have wine flavors.

Wine grapes

Sun Apr-Nov), where you'll find delicious Syrah and Cabernet Sauvignons to sip over views of the valley.

Last, take a detour to the grandest estate on this trip, **Terra Blanca** (☎509-588-6082; www. terrablanca.com; 34715 N DeMoss Rd; ☺11am-6pm), on N DeMoss Rd, which runs parallel to N Sunset Rd toward Benton. Try

the reds and dessert wines in the castle-like tasting room or out on the terrace overlooking manicured gardens, a pond, the valley and mountains.

The Drive 》 Go back out to your friend I-82, take the I-182 exit toward Richland then take exit 3. Turn right on Queensgate Dr and an immediate left onto Columbia Park Trail, then another left onto Tulip Lane.

- - - - - - - - -

⑥ Richland, Kennewick & Pasco

Next stop? The Tri-Cities: Richland, Kennewick and Pasco. Nicknamed the Tri-Windies for the pushy gusts of wind that scoot you into the tasting rooms, the trio of towns is home to another batch of wineries just off the freeway, among them

DETOUR: WAITSBURG

Start: ❽ Walla Walla

Twenty-one miles north on US 12 from Walla Walla and 51 miles east on Hwy 124 from Pasco, isolated and bucolic Waitsburg has become the unlikely location of a burgeoning restaurant and bar scene. Within the historic brick buildings of the few wide streets you'll find worth-the-drive Southern fare at **Whoopemup Hollow Cafe** (120 Main St; ⏱5-10pm Wed-Thu, 11:30am-2pm Sat & Sun) or kick back and sip superb cocktails with tapas at **Jimgermanbar** (119 Main St; tapas $4-14; ⏱5pm-late Thu-Mon).

Barnard Griffin (📞509-627-0266; www.barnardgriffin.com; 878 Tulip Lane, Richland; ⏱10am-6pm) in Richland. You don't have to ask if they've won any awards; the medals are practically used as decor.

✗ ⍾ p111

The Drive » Get ready for a change of scenery and wine style. Take US 12 south then east about an hour to the Walla Walla Valley.

- - - - - - - - - - -

❼ West Walla Walla

About 11 miles before you get to Walla Walla you'll find **L'Ecole No 41** (📞509-525-0940; www.lecole.com; 41 Lowden School Rd, Lowden; ⏱10am-5pm). The building alone, an early-1900s schoolhouse, is worth a visit, but the Syrah and Bordeaux earn an easy 'A' among wine-lovers.

Back on the road about another mile toward Walla Walla is **Waterbrook Wine** (📞509-

522-1262; www.waterbrook.com; 10518 W US 12; ⏱10am-6pm Mon-Thu, to 8pm Fri-Sat) with an afternoon-devouring outdoor patio by a pond and authentic, mouthwatering tacos available on Fridays and Saturdays. Imbibe a long selection of wines in the fresh air.

The Drive » Continue east on US 12 into central Walla Walla. The center of town is at Main St and 2nd Ave.

- - - - - - - - - - -

TRIP HIGHLIGHT

❽ Walla Walla

Walla Walla, more than any Washington town, has fermented the ingredients to support a burgeoning wine culture, including a historic Main Street, a handsome college, a warm summer climate and a growing clutch of wine-loving restaurants. If it's time to let the peddle off the metal for a day or two, this is where to do it. The

downtown area has lots of tasting rooms. A good one if you're on a stroll is **Otis Kenyan** (📞509-525-3505; www.otiskenyonwine.com; 23 E Main St; ⏱11am-5pm Thu-Mon) – ask about their quirky story.

✗ ⍾ p111

The Drive » Take Hwy 125 south out of town and turn right on Old Milton Hwy. You'll soon find yourself passing numerous orchards and wineries.

- - - - - - - - - - -

❾ South Walla Walla

The southern part of the Walla Walla wine-growing region is the most scenic, with wineries off the highway and tucked back in apple orchards or within their own vineyards. Fabulous wines are served in a low-key garden patio and tasting room (actually a part of the owner's home) at **Dusted Valley Wines** (📞509-525-1337; www.dustedvalley.com; 1248 Old Milton Hwy; ⏱noon-5pm Thu-Mon Apr-Nov). Just down the road is the not-to-miss **Amavi Cellars** (📞509-525-3541; www.amavicellars.com; 3796 Peppers Bridge Rd; ⏱10am-4pm), whose wines make headlines in the viticulture world. Indulge in their addictive Syrah and Cabernet Sauvignon on the classy yet comfortable outdoor patio, admire the view out to the Blue Mountains and toast to the end of your tour.

Eating & Sleeping

Yakima ❶

✗ Greystone   Fusion $$$

(☎509-248-9801; www.greystonedining.com; 5
N Front St; mains $22-39; ⏰from 6pm Mon-Sat)
Housed in one of the city's original saloons at
the base of the century-old Lund Building, this is
considered to be the city's premier Northwest-
cuisine venue.

🛏 Birchfield Manor   Hotel $$

(☎509-452-1960; www.birchfieldmanor.com;
2018 Birchfield Rd; r $119-159) Locals love the
on-site restaurant; travelers love the early-
20th-century rooms.

🛏 Ledgestone Hotel   Hotel $$

(☎509-453-3151; www.ledgestonehotel.com;
107 North Fair Ave; ste from $109; ❄ @ 🛜)
It looks like a bland chain hotel but all rooms
are stylish one-bedroom suites with mini
kitchens, lounge areas, bathrooms and separate
bedrooms.

Prosser ❹

✗ Bern's Tavern   Bar $

(☎509-786-1422; 618 6th St; mains $8-10;
⏰9am-10pm Sun-Thu, to 2am Fri-Sat) An
antique wooden bar, friendly service, down-
home burgers and enough funky kitsch to make
hipsters smile.

✗ Wine O'Clock   Wine Bar $$

(548 Cabernet Ct, Vintner's Village; pizzatas from
$9; ⏰noon-8pm Fri-Sat, 11am-6pm Sun) Chic
wine bar with a patio serving pizzatas, cheese
plates and light meals to nibble alongside wines
from the Bunnel Family Cellar winery.

Richland, Kennewick & Pasco ❻

✗ Taverna   Fusion $$

(☎509-628-0020; Tagaris Winery, 844 Tulip
Lane, Richland; mains $9-28; ⏰noon-4pm daily,
5-10pm Mon-Sat) The sophisticated dining room

is impressive, but on a pretty day the patio
rules. The seasonal menu includes beautifully
plated seafood and wood-fired pizzas.

🛏 Clover Island Inn   Hotel $

(☎509-586-0541; www.hotelkennewick.com;
435 Clover Island Dr, Kennewick; r from $89;
❄ 🛜 🏊) This unique establishment boasts 152
rooms, its own boat dock and panoramic views
from the top-floor Crow's Nest Restaurant.

Walla Walla ❽

✗ Brasserie 4   French $$$

(☎509-529-2011; 4 E Main St; mains $15-25;
⏰closed Sun & Mon) Cool, minimalist place
where the wait staff know their wines and the
Gallic-inspired food is more than just a few
pretentious names on the menu.

✗ Saffron Mediterranean
Kitchen   Mediterranean $$$

(☎509-525-2112; www.saffronmediterranean
kitchen.com; 125 W Alder St; mains $15-27;
⏰2-10pm, to 9pm winter) Saffron takes
seasonal, local ingredients and turns them into
pure gold. Think: pheasant, ricotta gnocchi,
amazing flatbreads and intelligently paired
wines. The ambience is intimate with a North
African–feeling decor.

🛏 Inn at Abeja   Inn $$$

(☎509-522-1234; www.abeja.net; 2014
Mill Creek Rd; r $215-285) Located on a
picturesque farm in the rolling foothills of the
Blue Mountains, the inn is remote and private,
with gorgeously appointed suites located in
century-old buildings. The best part: Abeja is
also a winery.

🛏 Marcus Whitman Hotel   Hotel $$$

(☎866-826-9422; www.marcuswhitmanhotel.
com; 6 W Rose St; r $124-219) The most elegant
sleeping option in town, with its stately historic
exterior and richly decorated interior.

Mt Shuksan *Be inspired by picture-perfect scenery*

Mt Baker & Lummi Island

10

From seascape to snow in just 84 miles, this journey takes you from one of Puget Sound's lesser known islands to Mt Baker, the white sentinel that frames every northwest Washington vista.

TRIP HIGHLIGHTS

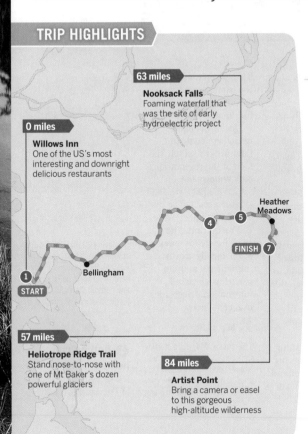

63 miles

Nooksack Falls
Foaming waterfall that was the site of early hydroelectric project

0 miles

Willows Inn
One of the US's most interesting and downright delicious restaurants

Heather Meadows

4

5

FINISH **7**

Bellingham

1

START

57 miles

Heliotrope Ridge Trail
Stand nose-to-nose with one of Mt Baker's dozen powerful glaciers

84 miles

Artist Point
Bring a camera or easel to this gorgeous high-altitude wilderness

---

1–2 DAYS
84 MILES/135KM

GREAT FOR...

BEST TIME TO GO

Mid-July to September, when the top section of the road is snow-free and open.

 ESSENTIAL PHOTO

Mt Shuksan with Picture Lake in the foreground.

 BEST FOR HIKING

Heliotrope Ridge Trail from forest to meadow to glacier in 7.4 scenery-packed miles.

113

10 Mt Baker & Lummi Island

The 57-mile Mt Baker Scenic Byway that winds east from metropolitan Bellingham to the other-worldly flower meadows of Artist Point is one of the Northwest's most magic-invoking drives, replete with moss-draped forests and gurgling creeks. Affix Lummi Island onto the start with its slow-motion traffic and feisty insularity, and you've got pretty much every facet the Pacific Northwest has to offer.

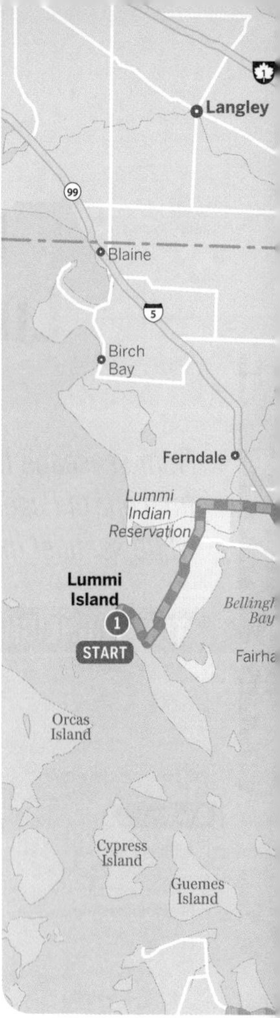

TRIP HIGHLIGHT

❶ Lummi Island

Not technically one of the San Juan Islands but with them in spirit, Lummi acts as a bucolic buffer to the fast-spreading tentacles of American outlet-mall culture that plagues the I-5. A slender green finger of land measuring approximately 9 miles long by 2 miles wide, and supporting a population of just under 1000, this tranquil dose of rural realism is home to the world's only reef-net salmon fishing operation, a pioneering agritourism project and an unhurried tempo of life best epitomized by the island's maximum speed limit – a tortoise-like 25mph.

One of the main reasons to come to Lummi is to sample the food at the reservations-only **Willows Inn** (☎360-758-2620; www.willows-inn.com; tasting menu $135; ⏰dinner Wed-Thu) restaurant. The chefs forage for many of the locally grown ingredients, and the place has garnered international accolades in recent years.

✕ ⌂ p119

The Drive ›› If you're starting from the Willows Inn, take the island's loop road to Lummi's small ferry terminal on the east shore. The five-minute crossing runs every 20 minutes (hourly at weekends) to Gooseberry Point on the mainland. From here, head north on Haxton Rd and right on Slater Rd to join I-5. Forge several miles south and exit to Bellingham.

❷ Bellingham

Imagine a slightly less-eccentric slice of Portland, Oregon,

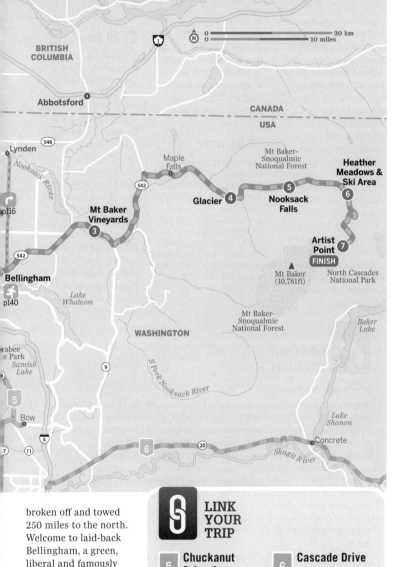

broken off and towed 250 miles to the north. Welcome to laid-back Bellingham, a green, liberal and famously livable settlement that has taken the libertine, nothing-is-too-weird ethos of Oregon's 'City of Roses' and given it a peculiarly Washingtonian twist.

LINK YOUR TRIP

5 Chuckanut Drive & Whidbey Island

If you enjoyed Lummi Island, veer off along Chuckanut Drive for more pastoral scenery (p69).

6 Cascade Drive

You'll find plenty more Cascade giants starting in Everett (p79), 60 miles south down I-5.

Mild in both manners and weather, the 'city of subdued excitement,' as a local mayor once dubbed it, is historically four different towns – Fairhaven, Sehome, Whatcom and Bellingham – that amalgamated into a single metro area in the late 19th century. Despite vestiges of an ugly industrial past along the waterfront, and a flirtation with out-of-town 1980s mall development directed mainly toward bargain-hunting Canadians, Bellingham's downtown has been revitalized in recent years with intra-urban trails, independent food coops, fine brunch spots and – in genteel Fairhaven – a rejuvenated historic district. It's an ideal place to stretch your legs (p140).

 p119

The Drive ›› The Mt Baker Scenic Byway officially begins at exit 255 of I-5 on Sunset Dr, which, within a mile, becomes the Mt Baker Hwy. The road quickly escapes the scattered Bellingham suburbs and dips into the surprisingly pastoral landscape of the Baker foothills. At the Hannegan Rd intersection you can detour north to the town of Lynden.

❸ Mt Baker Vineyards

Wrong side of the Cascade Mountains for grape-growing, you're thinking. Think again! The **Mt Baker Vineyards & Winery** (www.mountbakervineyards. com; 4298 Mt Baker Hwy; ⏱noon-5pm Thu-Sun) is a star player in the Puget Sound AVA (American Viticultural Area), where a cool, wet, year-round climate favors the sowing of mainly white grape varietals such as Siegerrebe and Madeleine Angevine. It's been in operation

---

↱ DETOUR: GO DUTCH

Start: ❷ Bellingham

Washington state has an interesting stash of small towns that harbor a palpable European influence. Leavenworth, in the Eastern Cascades, draws in thousands of tourists annually with an authentic Bavarian look (not to mention its beer and sausages); Poulsbo, near Seattle, has a detectable Norwegian flavor. Lynden, meanwhile, located a few miles north of the Mt Baker Scenic Byway in the agricultural lowlands of the Nooksack Valley, is unmistakably Dutch.

First settled in the 1850s, the area received its first wave of Dutch settlers in the early 1900s – a steady trickle of Calvinist farmers who arrived from the Netherlands via brief stopovers in the Midwest. United by raspberries (the town produces 60% of the US crop), they formed a Christian Reform Church and set up mixed farms on the kind of flat pastoral fields that would have had Van Gogh grasping for his paint palette.

As well as competing for the prize of 'cleanest town in the US,' Lynden also excels in historical preservation. Handsome Front St includes a 72ft windmill, a mall with a canal, various Dutch eateries and the inspired **Lynden Pioneer Museum** (www.lyndenpioneermuseum.com; 217 Front St; admission $7; ⏱10am-4pm Mon-Sat), which eloquently catalogs the pioneer experience.

Rumor has it that people from as far away as California plan pie sorties to **Lynden Dutch Bakery** (421 Front St; ⏱7am-4pm Mon-Thu, to 5pm Fri & Sat) a few doors down. Try the split-pea soup or humungous rhubarb and raspberry pie.

Lummi Island

since 1982, longer than many of the trendy 'nouveau' Walla Walla places. Let curiosity get the better of you and hit its understated tasting room.

The Drive » The well-signposted Scenic Byway (SR-542) tracks the North Fork of the Nooksack River from where it splits near Denning. Ignore various turnoffs in the small settlements of Kendall and Maple Falls, and continue due east. Maple Falls is your last potential gas stop until you return (in 66 miles).

`TRIP HIGHLIGHT`

❹ Glacier

A tiny service center and the last proper settlement before Mt Baker, Glacier is basically a ranger station, two restaurants, a ski shop and a small store. This is where SR-542 enters the Mt Baker-Snoqualmie National Forest. Consequently, many of Mt Baker's best trails start near here. A highlight is the 7.4-mile out-and-back **Heliotrope Ridge Trail**, which begins 8 miles down unpaved USFS Rd 39, 1 mile east of Glacier. The trail takes hikers from thick old-growth

117

forest to flower-filled meadows and, ultimately, a breathtaking Coleman Glacier overlook. At the 2-mile point, the path for the Coleman Glacier ascent of Mt Baker branches to the left. Call into the excellent ranger station for maps, trail information and forest passes ($5).

 p119

The Drive ⟩⟩ You're now in the Mt Baker-Snoqualmie National Forest, where the trees tell a different story: tall moss-covered behemoths that look like ghostly old men sporting green beards. Keep straight on the highway for 6 miles to the Wells Creek Rd. Turn right here and follow the forest road for half a mile to a parking area and the Nooksack Falls viewpoint.

TRIP HIGHLIGHT

❺ Nooksack Falls

Powerful Nooksack Falls drop 175ft into a deep gorge. This was the site of one of America's oldest hydropower facilities, built in 1906 and abandoned in 1997. Sharp-eyed movie nerds will recognize it as one of the hunting scenes in the 1978 film, *The Deer Hunter*.

The Drive ⟩⟩ Rejoin the Scenic Byway and continue east paralleling the Nooksack River. Beyond milepost 48, the road leaves the river valley and starts to climb via a series of switchbacks. Mt Shuksan soon comes into view and at the road's 52 milepost you'll spy the Mt Baker Ski Area's White Salmon Day Lodge on the left.

❻ Heather Meadows & Ski Area

Receiving record-breaking annual snowfall and enjoying one of the longest seasons in the US, the **Mt Baker Ski Area** (www.mtbaker.us) prides itself in being the classic 'nonresort' ski area and a rustic antidote to Whistler in Canada. While luxury facilities are thin on the ground, the fast, adrenaline-fueled terrain has garnered many dedicated admirers. It was also one of the first North American ski locations to accommodate and encourage snowboarders.

There are two day lodges, both equipped with restaurants/cafeterias: the Cascadian-flavored **White Salmon Day Lodge** at milepost 52 and the **Heather Meadows Day Lodge**, 4 miles higher up.

In high summer, **Picture Lake** is the object of most people's affections. The view of Mt Shuksan reflected in its iridescent waters is a Facebook staple. You can wander for a half-mile around its shore taking follow-up snaps, or drive 1 mile further up to the **Heather Meadows Visitor Center** and plenty more trailheads.

The Drive ⟩⟩ Stay right when the road forks at Picture Lake. The last 3 miles (mileposts 55 to 58) of the byway are only open from around mid-July to September and subject to a $5 fee. The road terminates at a parking lot at Artist Point (5140ft).

TRIP HIGHLIGHT

❼ Artist Point

A picnic spot extraordinaire surrounded by what is perhaps the best high-altitude wilderness area in the US that is accessible by road, Artist Point at 5140ft is *high* – so high that in 2011 it remained snowed-in all year. Various hikes fan out from here overlooked by the dual seductresses of Mt Baker and Mt Shuksan. Some are appropriate for families and most are snow-free by mid-July.

The interpretive **Artist Ridge Trail** is an easy 1-mile loop through heather and berry fields with the craggy peaks of Baker and Shuksan scowling in the background. Another option is the half-mile **Fire and Ice Trail** adjacent to the Heather Meadows Visitors Center, which explores a valley punctuated by undersized mountain hemlock; or the 7.5-mile **Chain Lakes Loop** that starts at the Artist Point parking lot before dropping down to pass a half-dozen icy lakes surrounded by huckleberry meadows.

Eating & Sleeping

Lummi Island ❶

🗙 🛏 Willows Inn　　Boutique Hotel $$$
(☎360-758-2620; www.willows-inn.com; 2579 West Shore Dr; r $140-300; ❄ 🛜) Of Lummi's two accommodation options, this 100-year-old beauty reigns supreme with a variety of compact but cozy rooms poised above the Rosario Strait. It also has a creative and internationally lauded restaurant, where pretty much all the ingredients are hauled from nearby Nettles Farm or the island's unique reef-net fishing operation.

Bellingham ❷

🗙 Mount Bakery　　Creperie, Brunch $
(www.mountbakery.com; 309 West Champion St; brunch $6-12; ❂8am-3:30pm) This is where you go on Sunday mornings with a copy of the *New York Times* for Belgian waffles, crepes and organic eggs done any way you like. On weekends everyone with a bike in Bellingham seems to end up here swapping two-wheeled tales.

🗙 Pepper Sisters　　Southwestern $$
(www.peppersisters.com; 1055 N State St; mains $11-15; ❂ from 5pm Tue-Sun, closed Mon; 🚼) People travel from far and wide to visit this cult restaurant with its bright turquoise booths. The food is hard to categorize: call it American Southwestern cuisine with a Northwestern twist. Try the cilantro-and-pesto quesadillas or blue corn rellenos.

🛏 Hotel Bellwether　　Boutique Hotel $$
(☎360-392-3100; www.hotelbellwether.com; 1 Bellwether Way; r $165-284, lighthouse from $398; ❄ 🛜) Bellingham's finest and most charismatic hotel is positioned on a redeveloped part of the waterfront and offers views over toward the whale-like hump of Lummi Island. Billing itself as a European hotel, the Bellwether advertises 66 luxury individually crafted rooms. Its crowning glory is the celebrated 900-sq-ft lighthouse condominium, an old converted three-story lighthouse with a wonderful private lookout.

Glacier ❹

🗙 Il Caffe Rifugio　　Cafe $$
(www.ilcafferifugio.com; 5415 Mt Baker Hwy; ❂Thu-Sun) Just when you thought you were entering the wilderness, a little bit of Portland floats out to meet you. If you assumed your first glimpse of Baker was serendipitous, check out rural Denning where this Euro-centric cafe-restaurant offers big-city quality with field-to-plate freshness. Curry chicken and tortellini Alfredo? Ease on those brakes!

🗙 Milano's Restaurant & Deli　　Italian $$
(www.milanorestaurant.us; 9990 Mt Baker Hwy; dinner $16-20) In common with much of the Mt Baker area, Milano's doesn't win any 'wows' for its fancy interior decor. But when the pasta's al dente, the bread's oven-fresh and you've got an appetite that's been turned ravenous by successive bouts of white-knuckle snowboarding, who's complaining?

🛏 Inn at Mt Baker　　B&B $$
(☎360-599-1359; www.theinnatmtbaker.com; 8174 Mt Baker Hwy; r $155-165) When Mt Baker breaks through the clouds, the views from this rural B&B are unsurpassable. Situated just west of Glacier, uncluttered rooms and ample skylights give this place a light, airy feel. Breakfast is taken on a spectacular deck – weather permitting in the summer. When it gets stormy you can enjoy comfortable rocking chairs and a cozy communal reading room.

Kootenay Lake *A jewel-like fjord framed by mountains*

International Selkirk Loop

11

Covering two American states and one Canadian province, and juxtaposing splendiferous scenery with (frankly) oddball towns, the Selkirk is the great unsung byway of the Pacific Northwest.

TRIP HIGHLIGHTS

148 miles

Kootenay Lake Ferry
The world's longest free ferry ride is also a scene-stealer

97 miles

Columbia Brewery
Creston's bastion of Kokanee beer offers tours and samples

174 miles

Nelson
Canada's little contrarian has preserved its Victorian buildings and charm

Tiger

Newport
START/ FINISH

Sandpoint
Adventure town on Lake Pend Oreille with a cult outdoors following

30 miles

3 DAYS
280 MILES/450KM

GREAT FOR...

BEST TIME TO GO
May to October for sun-dappled lake views.

ESSENTIAL PHOTO
Anything with the turquoise waters of Kootenay Lake in it.

BEST FOR ROADSIDE ATTRACTIONS
The Glass House, an unbreakable cultural icon made completely out of glass bottles.

121

ALL CANADA PHOTOS / ALAMY ©

11 International Selkirk Loop

Borders are arbitrary in the Selkirks, a more remote and geologically older antidote to the Rockies, where curious roadside attractions verge on the esoteric and the word 'clamorous' means the occasional moose blocking your views of so-clear-you-can-drink-it Kootenay Lake. Pack your passport, shake the crowds and plunge into this wildly scenic binational loop through the forgotten corners of Washington, Idaho and British Columbia.

❶ Newport

Newport, a Washington state lavender-growing and logging town, faces off against Oldtown (the town's original incarnation) which sits across the state line in Idaho. The visitors center is situated next to the **Pend Oreille County Historical Museum** (www.pocmuseum.org; 402 S Washington Ave; donation accepted; ⏰10am-4pm May-Oct), housed in a 1908 train depot and filled with local farming and railway paraphernalia.

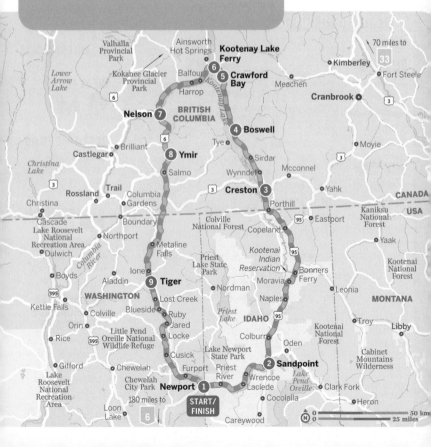

Both look out onto carefully manicured Centennial Plaza that sits majestically at the head of Washington Ave (US 2), your ticket out of town.

The Drive » Follow US 2 east on the north bank of the Pend Oreille River through the town of Priest River to Sandpoint.

TRIP HIGHLIGHT

② Sandpoint

Within 45 minutes of leaving Washington at Newport you hit one of the Northwest's rarest jewels: Sandpoint, Idaho, whose 7500 souls make up the largest US town on the loop. Squeezed between the downhill runs of Schweitzer Mountain and the deep

LINK YOUR TRIP

6 Cascade Drive

Drive west via Spokane and I-90 to the next spectacular mountain range, the volcano-punctuated, snow-enveloped Cascades (p77).

33 Circling the Rockies

Since you brought your passport all this way, you might as well use it further north in what they call the *real* Rockies (p337).

CRESTON VALLEY WILDLIFE AREA

Nature lovers and birders should detour 6 miles (10km) west of Creston to the **Creston Valley Wildlife Area** (www.crestonwildlife.ca), part of the region's most important wildlife corridor. Walk the boardwalks and spot osprey, tundra swans, pelicans or great blue herons from the two birding towers, or sign up for an hour-long guided canoe paddle through the wetlands. Dawn and dusk are the best times to spot wildlife, including the occasional moose chomping in the shadows. Don't miss the very sweet 'turtle crossing' road sign.

---

waters of Lake Pend Oreille, Sandpoint is the most discovered 'undiscovered' town in the nation (countless magazines list it on their 'hidden jewel' lists). Budget a couple of hours to stroll the bars, restaurants and shops of 1st Ave and sup *vino* in the **Pend D'Oreille Winery** (www.powine.com; 220 Cedar St; ⊘10am-6pm Mon-Thu, to 7pm Fri-Sat, noon-5pm Sun), which also offers tours of its *très français* production process.

Sandpoint is right on Lake Pend Oreille ('hanging from the ears,' pronounced 'ponderay'), and the white sand and jet-skis of City Beach are the closest the Idaho Panhandle ever gets to Miami. Bring a swimsuit and preferably some kind of boat.

 p127

The Drive » Hwy 15 heads to Bonner's Ferry, originally built on stilts at the site of a

---

gold rush river crossing, and continues north past ranches, Christmas-tree farms and the world's largest hop farm at Elk Mountain. Branch onto SR-1 and cross into Canada at the Porthill–Rykerts border crossing, where you join Canadian Hwy 21.

TRIP HIGHLIGHT

③ Creston

Creston advertises its premier business with a statue of a 7ft Sasquatch (Bigfoot) making off with a six-pack. Fear not; this is the home of the **Columbia Brewery** (📞250-428-9344; 1220 Erikson St; tours $5; ⊘9:30am-4:30pm Mon-Fri mid-May–mid-Oct), conjurers of the Kokanee and Kootenay brands. The brewery allows tours (four daily) and visits to the sample room. It may not be the most knockout pint in the region but, hey, free beer, dude!

Creston's other pulls are fruit (apples and cherries dominate) and

ALL CANADA PHOTOS / ALAMY ©

murals (local artists have instituted an art walk and mural tour). The downtown's art deco–heavy architecture is interrupted by two grain elevators – the only two city-center silos left in Canada, apparently.

✗ p127

The Drive » The jewel-like fjord of Kootenay Lake bursts into view a few miles outside Creston, a 90-mile slice of turquoise framed by the peaks of the Selkirk and Purcell ranges, whose waters are pure enough to drink. This section is the most scenic of the entire drive and is a favorite of motorcyclists who brave the curves until Boswell.

---

④ Boswell

The wackiest sight on the eastern shore is without doubt Boswell's **Glass House** (Hwy 3A, Boswell, BC; admission CAN$8; ☺8am-8pm Jul & Aug, 9am-5pm May-Jun & Sep-Oct). With a mortuarist's sense of humor, funeral director David H Brown decided to build his dream retirement home out of used embalming-fluid bottles, half a million of them in total (and, more incredibly, then persuaded his wife this was a good idea). The result is a whimsy of turrets, towers, bridges

and even a garden shed, all made from recycled bottles. Brown then topped this off with an interior decorated with fearless 1970s panache and a small army of garden gnomes. No, it ain't pretty, but it is weird.

🛏 p127

The Drive » Keep on lake-hugging Hwy 3A to Crawford Bay.

---

⑤ Crawford Bay

Wizards and muggles (nonwizards) with a penchant for Harry Potter will find empathy

in Crawford Bay on Kootenay Lake at **North Woven Broom** (www. northwovenbroom.com; Hwy 3A, Crawford Bay, BC; ⏲9am-5pm Mar–mid-Oct; 🚗), maker of traditional brooms since 1975. One can only assume that orders have gone through the roof since the late 1990s when the word 'Quidditch' (a fictional sport in the Potter books that is played on broomsticks) entered the language. Numerous US colleges, including Harvard, now compete in real-life Quidditch cups and the workshop's owners once made 50 Nimbus 2000s (Harry Potter's prized broomstick) for a Vancouver book launch. The workshop's feathery golden hues and musky broomcorn fragrance are surprisingly beguiling, almost sensual, and there's something comforting about its almost total lack of modernity. While you're here, check out the glassblowers, blacksmith's forge and weavers' studio across the road.

The Drive » The highway runs out 3 miles (5km) west of Crawford Bay, and it's time for the ferry.

TRIP HIGHLIGHT

❻ Kootenay Lake Ferry

Bridges are overrated. Go slow on the world's longest free ferry ride, courtesy of the Canadian Government and the Kootenay Lake Ferry. The scenic crossing departs every hour or so and offers 40 minutes of superb lake views before docking at Balfour, some 20 miles (32km) northeast of Nelson. If you have some time to kill before departure, drive south from the ferry terminal for

BORDER CROSSING

Since new border regulations were introduced in June 2009, you now need a passport, enhanced driving license or NEXUS card to travel between the US and Canada. Returning to the US you can claim up to $400 of goods without duty after 48 hours or $750 after seven days.

3 miles (5km) to a turnout that marks a section of Pilot Bay Provincial Park, a shoreline haven punctuated with walking trails and the charming white clapboard 1907 **Pilot Bay lighthouse.**

The Drive 》》 At the ferry landing, take SR-31 alongside Kootenay Lake's West Arm to Nelson.

- - - - - - - - - -

TRIP HIGHLIGHT

7 Nelson

Nelson has always flirted with contrarianism. It kept its early-20th-century boomtown buildings when everyone else was tearing theirs down, and it welcomed US Vietnam-era draft dodgers with open arms when their own country sought to prosecute them.

Outdoorsy, alternative and organic, the historic former mining town has a tangible Victorian air, and is considered by many to be the most interesting arty-farty hangout east of Vancouver. Pick up a free architectural walking tour pamphlet to track down the most interesting of the town's 360 heritage buildings, or stroll the waterfront pathway 1.2 miles (2km) to the beaches of Lakeside Park, returning on the restored century-old 'Streetcar No 23.'

Fight your way past Baker St's sitar music and 'positive energy generators' and you'll find the town's most interesting shopping, with local fashions running the gamut from hemp to Gore-Tex.

✕ ⌂ p127

The Drive 》》 Leaving Nelson in your rear-view mirror, the final day's drive takes you south along Hwy 6, past remote, forested (and slightly odd) communities.

- - - - - - - - - -

8 Ymir

The oddest of the odd is historic Ymir (pronounced 'why-mur,' though grinning locals may well try to persuade you the name stands for 'Why Am I Here?'), weirdly named after a figure from Norse mythology, though its history has more to do with gold mining rather than Icelandic giants. Boomtown Ymir – founded as Quartz Creek in 1897 – once listed 10,000 inhabitants. Now there's little more than two hotels and a store. Connoisseurs of the unusual should pop in to the **Hotel Ymir** (www.hotelymir.com; 7104 1st Ave; r $39), a 1916 flophouse that stands frozen in time. Try to imagine a Western saloon-style boarding house run by Bela Lugosi and you'll get an idea of the vibe here.

The Drive 》》 After completing your US border formalities at the sleepy Nelway–Metaline border crossing, continue straight down the Washington SR-31 through the town of Metaline Falls to the Tiger junction.

- - - - - - - - - -

9 Tiger

The fiercely named ex-town of Tiger has been reduced to one last remnant, the 1912 clapboard **Tiger Store** (390372 Hwy 20; ⏲10am-5pm Thu-Mon May-Sep), which functions as a gift shop, cafe, information center and museum of the milling/railway town that once was. Glued to the junction of highways 31 and 20, it serves as a welcome apparition on this final part of the loop, aka the Pend Oreille Scenic Byway.

The Drive 》》 From Tiger, Hwy 20 parallels the Pend Oreille River past bison herds and the log mills of the Kalispell Indian Reservation back to Newport.

Eating & Sleeping

Sandpoint ②

🍴🛏 Lodge at
Sandpoint Boutique Hotel **$$**

(📞208-263-2211; www.lodgeatsandpoint.com;
41 Lakeshore Dr, Sagle; d/ste $169/199; ❄🛜)
Stealing the best lakeside location on the
south shores of Lake Pend Oreille, at the exit
to Long Bridge (2 miles south of Sandpoint),
this modern lodge might have been invented
with the term rustic-chic in mind. A 30-room
capacity keeps things intimate, while plush
features such as a restaurant, gym and adjacent
beach justify the 'boutique' billing.

Creston ③

🍴 Retro Cafe French **$**

(www.retrocafe.ca; 1431 NW Blvd; crepes
CAN$5.75; ⏲7am-5pm Mon-Fri, to 3pm Sat) A
French mirage in southeast British Columbia
(BC), 'retro' will probably be the last thing on
your mind as you scour the hand-scrawled
blackboard and tuck into *très délicieux* crepes.

🍴 Valley View Motel Motel **$**

(📞250-428-2336; www.valleyviewmotel.info;
216 Valley View Dr; d CAN$73-83; ❄🛜) In
the motel-ville of Creston, this could be your
best bet on a view-splayed hillside. It's clean,
comfortable, safe and quiet.

Boswell ④

🛏 Destiny Bay Resort Resort **$$$**

(📞250-223-8234; www.destinybay.com; 11935
Hwy 3A, Boswell, BC; r CAN$255-275; ⏲May-
Oct) Alright, so it's expensive, but the rates
at this superbly romantic lakeshore hideaway
include a four-course dinner and buffet
breakfast. Rooms are in waterfront cottages
or a main lodge, and there's a fairy-tale private
beach with lakeside sauna, fire pit and kayaks.

Nelson ⑦

🍴 All Seasons
Café International, Fusion **$$$**

(📞250-352-0101; www.allseasonscafe.com;
620 Herridge Lane; mains CAN$17-30) The most
widely lauded of Nelson's fine restaurants has
a romantic hideaway patio. The seasonally
changing menu pairs locally sourced produce
and global influences to create 'Left Coast
Inland Cuisine' – think artisanal BC cheeses
with Armenian flatbread and fig chutney.

🍴 Library Lounge American **$$**

(📞250-352-5331; www.humehotel.com;
422 Vernon St; ⏲11am-midnight) For liquid
refreshment head for the historic 1898 Hume
Hotel, pull up a pew in the Library Lounge and
order a pint of organic Liplock or Wild Honey ale,
brewed right in town at the Nelson Brewery. The
food is traditional American (burgers, chicken
wings) with some hard-to-ignore dessert
displays.

🛏 Cloudside Inn B&B **$$**

(📞250-352-3226; www.cloudside.ca; 408
Victoria St; s/d/tr CAN$105/109/139) This
contemporary-styled B&B is a good choice if
you prefer your Victorian-era B&Bs fresh rather
than frilly. Global travelers will find a kindred
spirit in the peripatetic British owners, whose
continent-spanning travel photos line the
hallways.

🍴🛏 Hume Hotel Historic Hotel **$$**

(📞250-352-5331; www.humehotel.com; 422
Vernon St; s/d CAN$99/109; ❄🛜) The Hume's
first incarnation in 1898 was with an eye-
catching rooftop cupola. Since then it has gone
through the standard trajectory of embattled
North American hotels: 1920s art deco rebuild,
1970s neglect, 1980s salvation and 2000s retro
refit and heritage status. Today it's back to its
peak with a spa, wood-paneled interior, and four
different eating and drinking joints.

Lewis & Clark monument, Seaside
America's greatest explorers

END OF THE TRAIL

Classic Trip

On the Trail of Lewis & Clark

12

Follow the Columbia River on this historic drive that marks the climax of Lewis and Clark's cross-continental 1805 journey as they stumbled toward the Pacific and instant immortality.

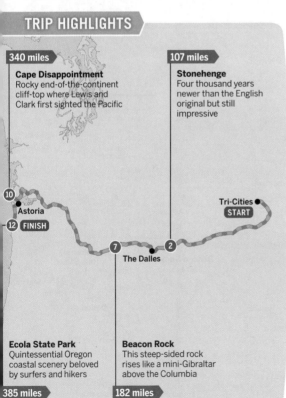

TRIP HIGHLIGHTS

340 miles

Cape Disappointment
Rocky end-of-the-continent cliff-top where Lewis and Clark first sighted the Pacific

107 miles

Stonehenge
Four thousand years newer than the English original but still impressive

Astoria

FINISH

Tri-Cities ●
START

The Dalles

Ecola State Park
Quintessential Oregon coastal scenery beloved by surfers and hikers

385 miles

Beacon Rock
This steep-sided rock rises like a mini-Gibraltar above the Columbia

182 miles

**3–4 DAYS
385 MILES/620 KM**

GREAT FOR...

BEST TIME TO GO

Year-round – if you don't mind frequent rain, the Columbia river valley is always open.

ESSENTIAL PHOTO

Indian Beach, Ecola State Park; the Oregon coast personified.

BEST FOR HISTORY

The Lewis & Clark Interpretive Center in Cape Disappointment State Park.

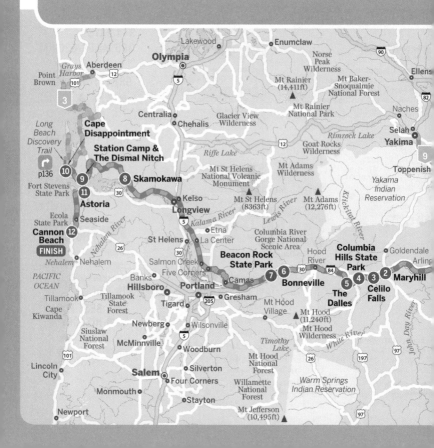

Classic Trip

12 On the Trail of Lewis & Clark

It would take most people their combined annual leave to follow the Lewis and Clark trek in its entirety from St Louis, MO, to Cape Disappointment. Focusing on the final segment, this trip documents the contradictory mix of crippling exhaustion and building excitement that the two explorers felt as they struggled, car-less and weather-beaten, along the Columbia River on their way to completing the greatest overland trek in American history.

❶ Tri-Cities

This trip's start point has a weighty historical significance. The arrival of Lewis and Clark and the Corps of Discovery at the confluence of the Snake and Columbia Rivers on 16 October, 1805, marked a milestone achievement on their quest to map a river route to the Pacific. After a greeting by 200 Indians singing and drumming in a half circle, the band camped at this spot for two days, trading clothing for dried salmon. The

Sacajawea Interpretive Center (📞509-545-2361; Sacajawea State Park, Pasco, WA; admission free; ⏱10am-5pm late Mar-Nov 1; ♿), situated at the river confluence 5 miles southeast of present-day Pasco, relates the story of the expedition through the eyes of Sacajawea, the Shoshone Native American guide and interpreter the Corps had recruited in North Dakota.

✕ p137

The Drive » Head south on I-82 before switching east at the Columbia River on SR-14, aka the Lewis & Clark Hwy. Here, in dusty sagebrush country, you'll pass a couple of minor sites – Wallula Gap, where the Corps first spotted Mt Hood, and the volcanic bluff of Hat Rock, first named by William Clark.

TRIP HIGHLIGHT

❷ Maryhill

Conceived by great Northwest entrepreneur and roadbuilder Sam Hill, the **Maryhill Museum of Art** (www. maryhillmuseum.org; 35 Maryhill Museum Dr, Goldendale, WA; adult/child/senior $9/3/8; ⏱10am-5pm Mar 15-Nov 15) occupies a mansion atop a bluff overlooking the Columbia River. Its eclectic art collection is enhanced by a small Lewis and Clark display, while its peaceful gardens are perfect for a classy picnic punctuated by exotic peacock cries. Interpretive signs point you to fine views down the Columbia Gorge to the riverside spot (now a state park) where Meriwether Lewis and William Clark camped on 21 October, 1805. The park is just one of several along this trip where you can pitch a tent within a few hundred yards of the Corps' original camp.

Another of Hill's creations – a life-sized unruined replica of **Stonehenge** – lies 2 miles to the east.

The Drive » Continue west from Maryhill on SR-14 for 5 miles to the site of the now submerged Celilo Falls.

Potholes Reservoir

Columbia River

ASHINGTON

yside

Richland

Yakima River

82

Tri-Cities ❶

iview

START

97

Lake Wallula

Umatilla

84

Hermiston

84

OREGON

Ukiah

395

0 ——— 50 km
0 ——— 25 miles

LINK YOUR TRIP

9 Washington Wine Tour

After all that Lewis and Clark history you'll need a glass of wine. Break off in the Tri-Cities (p109) for some relaxed quaffing opportunities.

3 Graveyard of the Pacific Tour

Lewis and Clark survived, but others didn't. Find out about the tumultuous maritime history of southwest Washington's coast (p53).

Classic Trip

❸ Celilo Falls

A vivid imagination can be as important as sunscreen when following the 'Trail.' One example of this is the turnout 5 miles west of Maryhill that overlooks what was once the Indian salmon fishing center of Celilo Falls. The explorers spent two days here in late October 1805, lowering their canoes down the crashing falls on elk-skin ropes. A century and a half later the rising waters of the dammed Columbia drowned the falls – which were the sixth-most voluminous in the world – destroying a centuries-old Native American fishing site and rendering much of Clark's description of the region unrecognizable.

The Drive ›› Head west on SR-14, paralleling the mighty Columbia, for another 15 miles.

❹ Columbia Hills State Park

Indian tribes like the Nez Perce, Clatsop and Walla Walla were essential to the success of the Lewis and Clark expedition, supplying them not only with food but also horses and guides. One

of the best places to view tangible traces of the region's Native American heritage is the Temani Pesh-wa (Written on Rocks) Trail at **Columbia Hills State Park** (www. parks.wa.gov; Hwy 14, Mile 85, WA; pictograph tours 10am Fri & Sat Apr-Oct), which highlights the region's best petroglyphs. Reserve a spot in advance on the free guided tours on Friday and Saturday at 10am to view the famous but fragile pictograph of the god Tsagaglal (She Who Watches). The park is also a popular site for rock climbers and windsurfers.

The Drive ›› Two miles west of Horsethief Lake, turn south onto US-197, which takes you across the Columbia River into The Dalles in Oregon. Two miles upriver sits The Dalles Dam, which completely submerged the once-magnificent Celilo Falls and rapids on its completion in 1957.

❺ The Dalles

Once the urban neighbor of the formidable Celilo Falls, The Dalles' image is more mundane these days. The local economy focuses on cherry-growing, computer technology and outdoor recreation. Notwithstanding, the town hosts one of the best Lewis and Clark–related museums along this stretch of the Columbia, sited in the **Columbia Gorge**

Discovery Center (www. gorgediscovery.org; 5000 Discovery Dr; adult/child/senior $9/5/7; ⊙9am-5pm; ♿) on the western edge of the city. Displays detail the 30 tons of equipment the Corps dragged across the continent and the animals they had to kill to survive (including 190 dogs and a ferret). Kids will get a kick from dressing up in Lewis and Clark period costume.

✕ ⊨ p137

The Drive ›› You can continue west from The Dalles on either side of the Columbia (the expedition traveled straight down the middle by canoe) via SR-14 (Washington), or the slower, more scenic SR-30 (Oregon). En route, look for the views down to macabre Memaloose Island, once a burial site for Native Americans who left their dead here in canoes of cedar.

❻ Bonneville

There are two Bonnevilles: Bonneville, Oregon, and North Bonneville, Washington. At this stage in their trip, Lewis and Clark were flea-infested and half-starved from a diet of dog meat and starchy potatolike wapto roots. Fortunately, 21st-century Bonneville – which is famous for its Depression-era dam completed in 1938 – has some tastier culinary offerings to contemplate.

⊨ p137

The Drive ›› Just west of North Bonneville on SR-14 lies Beacon Rock State Park.

TRIP HIGHLIGHT

❼ Beacon Rock State Park

On November 2, 1805, a day after passing modern Bonneville, Clark wrote about a remarkable 848ft-tall monolith he called Beaten Rock, changing the name on his return to **Beacon Rock**. Just over a century later, Henry Biddle bought the rock for the bargain price of $1 (!) and you can still hike his snaking 1-mile trail to the top of the former lava plug in **Beacon Rock State Park** (www.parks.wa.gov; ☼8am–dusk). As you enjoy the wonderful views, ponder the fact that you have effectively climbed up the *inside* of an ancient volcano. For the Corps, the rock brought a momentous discovery, for it was here that the excited duo first noticed the tide, proving at last that they were finally nearing their goal of crossing the American continent.

The Drive ›› Your next stop along SR-14 should be the fantastic views of the flood-carved gorge and its impressive cascades from the Cape Horn overview. From here, it's a straight shot on I-5 to Kelso and then over the Lewis & Clark Bridge to parallel the Columbia River westward on SR-4.

HISTORIC PARK

The so-called **Lewis & Clark National & State Historical Parks** (www.nps.gov/lewi; admission $3) combines 10 different historical sites clustered around the mouth of the Columbia River, each of which relate to important facts about the Corps of Discovery and its historic mission to map the American West. It was formed through the amalgamation of various state parks and Historic Sites in 2004, and is run jointly by the National Park Service and the states of Washington and Oregon. Highlights include Cape Disappointment, Fort Clatsop and the 6.5-mile Fort to Sea trail linking Clatsop and the ocean at Sunset Beach.

❽ Skamokawa

For most of their trip down the Columbia River, Lewis and Clark traveled not on foot but by canoe. There's nowhere better to paddle in the Corps' canoe wake than at the **Skamokawa Center** (www.skamokawakayak.com; 1391 Rte 4, Skamokawa, WA; 5-7hr tour $115), which offers one- or two-day kayak tours to Grays Bay or Pillar Rock, where Clark wrote 'Great joy in camp we are in view of the Ocian, this great Pacific Octean which we been So long anxious to See.'

The Drive ›› Continue on SR-4 northwest out of Skamokawa. In Naselle, go southwest on SR-401.

❾ Station Camp & Dismal Nitch

Just east of the Astoria-Megler Bridge on the north bank of the Columbia River, a turnout marks Dismal Nitch, where the drenched duo were stuck in a pounding weeklong storm that Clark described as 'the most disagreeable time I have ever experienced.' The Corps finally managed to make camp at Station Camp, 3 miles further west, now an innocuous highway pullout, where they stayed for 10 days while the two leaders, no doubt sick of each other by now, separately explored the headlands around Cape Disappointment.

The Drive ›› You're nearly there! Contain your excitement as you breeze the last few miles west along Highway 101 to Ilwaco and the inappropriately named Cape Disappointment.

Classic Trip

WHY THIS IS A CLASSIC TRIP
BRENDAN SAINSBURY, AUTHOR

This retracing of the Corps of Discovery's transcontinental wilderness odyssey is as close as it gets to an American pilgrimage. Lewis and Clark were, without doubt, America's greatest explorers and the nation wouldn't be the same today without them. Meticulous, curious, brave and groundbreaking, they also came in peace; only one small incident on their return journey with the Blackfeet Indians marred the charitable spirit of the Corps' grail-like quest.

Top: Cape Disappoinment
Left: Beacon Rock
Right: Fort Clatsop, Astoria

DANITA DELIMONT / GETTY IMAGES ©

GARY WEATHERS / GETTY IMAGES ©

RUSS BISHOP / ALAMY ©

⑩ Cape Disappointment

Disappointment is probably the last thing you're likely to be feeling as you pull into blustery cliff-top **Cape Disappointment State Park** (Hwy 100; ⊙6:30am-dusk). Find time to make the short ascent of Mackenzie Hill in Clark's footprints and catch your first true sight of the Pacific. You can almost hear his protracted sigh of relief over two centuries later.

Located on a high bluff inside the park not far from the Washington town of Ilwaco, the sequentially laid-out **Lewis & Clark Interpretive Center** (☎360-642-3029; Hwy 100; adult/youth $5/2.50; ⊙10am-5pm) faithfully recounts the Corps of Discovery's cross-continental journey using a level of detail the journal-writing explorers would have been proud of. Anally retentive information includes everything from how to use an octant to what kind of underpants Lewis wore! A succinct 20-minute film backs up the permanent exhibits. Phone ahead and you can also tour the impressive end-of-continent **North Head Lighthouse** (tours $2.50) nearby.

135

The Drive » From Ilwaco, take Highway 101 back east to the 4.1-mile long Astoria-Megler Bridge, the longest continuous truss bridge in the US. On the other side lies Astoria in Oregon, the oldest US-founded settlement west of the Mississippi.

- - - - - - - - - - - - -

⓫ Astoria

After the first truly democratic ballot in US history (in which a woman and a black slave both voted), the party elected to make their winter bivouac across the Columbia River in present-day Oregon. A replica of the original **Fort Clatsop** (adult/child $3/free; ⊙9am-6pm Jun-Aug, to 5pm Sep-May), where the Corps spent a miserable winter in 1805–06, lies 5 miles south of Astoria. Also on-site are trails, a visitors center and buckskin-clad rangers who wander the camp between mid-June and Labor Day sewing moccasins (the Corps stockpiled an impressive 340 pairs for their return trip), tanning leather and firing their muskets.

✕ ⊨ p137

The Drive » From Fort Clatsop, take Highway 101, aka the Oregon Coast Hwy, south through the town of Seaside to Cannon Beach.

- - - - - - - - - - - - -

TRIP HIGHLIGHT

⓬ Cannon Beach

Mission accomplished – or was it? Curiosity (and hunger) got the better of the Corps in early 1806 when news of a huge beached whale ('that monstrous fish') lured Clark and Sacagawea from a salt factory they had set up near the present-day town of Seaside down through what is now Ecola State Park to Cannon Beach.

Ecola State Park is the Oregon you may have already visited in your dreams: sea stacks, crashing surf, hidden beaches and gorgeous pristine forest. Crisscrossed by paths, it lies 1.5 miles north of Cannon Beach, the high-end 'antiresort' resort so beloved by Portlanders.

Clark found the whale near **Haystack Rock**, a 295ft sea stack that's the most spectacular landmark on the Oregon coast and accessible from the beach. After bartering with the Tillamook tribe, he staggered away with 300lb of whale blubber – a feast for the half-starved Corps of Discovery.

✕ ⊨ p137

DETOUR:
LONG BEACH DISCOVERY TRAIL

Start: ⓾ Cape Disappointment

Soon after arriving in 'Station Camp,' the indefatigable Clark, determined to find a better winter bivouac, set out with several companions to continue the hike west along a broad sandy peninsula, coming to a halt near present-day 26th St in Long Beach, where Clark dipped his toe in the Pacific and carved his name on a cedar tree for posterity. The route of this historic three-day trudge has been recreated in the Long Beach Discovery Trail, a footpath which runs from the small town of Ilwaco, adjacent to Cape Disappointment, to Clark's 26th St turnaround. Officially inaugurated in September 2009, the trail has incorporated some dramatic life-sized sculptures along its 8.2-mile length. One depicts a giant gray whale skeleton, another recalls Clark's recorded sighting of a washed-up sea sturgeon, while a third recreates in bronze the original cedar tree (long since uprooted by a Pacific storm).

Eating & Sleeping

Tri-Cities ❶

✖ Atomic Ale Brewpub & Eatery Pub $

(www.atomicalebrewpub.com; 1015 Lee Blvd; pizzas $9-12; ⊘ closed Sun) Hanford-inspired 'gallows humor' pervades this cheery microbrewery, well known for its wood-fired specialty pizzas and locally crafted Atomic Amber. Real intellectuals grab an Oppenheimer Oatmeal Stout.

The Dalles ❺

✖ Baldwin Saloon American $$

(☎541-296-5666; www.baldwinsaloon.com; 205 Court St; lunch/dinner mains from $10/20; ⊘11am-10pm Mon-Sat) The Baldwin is more about atmosphere than the food (burgers and decadent desserts). The saloon is a one-time bar, brothel, steamboat office and coffin storage warehouse that's been in business since 1876.

⊨ Celilo Inn Boutique Motel $$

(☎541-769-0001; www.celiloinn.com; 3550 East 2nd St; d from $119; ❄ 🤖 ⊠) Overlooking The Dalles Dam on the Columbia River, the Celilo is a sort of upmarket motel whose plushness suggests regular refurbs.

Bonneville ❻

⊨ Bonneville Hot Springs Resort & Spa Hotel $$$

(☎866-459-1678; www.bonnevilleresort.com; 1252 E Cascade Dr, North Bonneville, WA; r $159-289) Recover from the rigors of the trail at this luxurious hotel, pool and spa complex a mile or two east of Beacon Rock. If this had been here in 1805, a knackered Lewis would have probably plumped for the restorative eucalyptus wrap.

Astoria ⓫

✖ T Paul's Urban Café International $$

(www.tpaulsurbancafe.com; 1119 Commercial St; mains $9-16; ⊘9am-9pm Mon-Thu, to 10pm Fri & Sat, 11am-4pm Sun) Cooks up formidable lunchtime quesadillas served with nachos and a homemade salsa dip.

✖⊨ Commodore Hotel Boutique Hotel $$

(☎503-325-4747; www.commodoreastoria.com; 258 14th St; d with shared/private bath from $89/149; @ 🤖) This early-20th-century wonder reopened in 2009 after 45 years as a pigeon coop. The birds and moths have been replaced by a stylish set of European-style rooms and suites. Don't miss the 14th Street Coffee House next door with its fine java and neo-industrial decor.

⊨ Hotel Elliott Historic Hotel $$

(☎503-325-2222; www.hotelelliott.com; 357 12th St; d/ste $99/189; ❄ 🤖) In the oldest part of the oldest town west in the Pacific Northwest is the elegant Elliot, a period piece that has clawed its way up to boutique standard without losing its historical significance.

Cannon Beach ⓬

✖ Newman's French, Italian $$$

(☎503-436-1151; www.newmansat988.com; 988 S Hemlock St; mains $19-28; ⊘dinner Tue-Sun) Fuse the world's two greatest cuisines (Italian and French) to create a regionally lauded fine-dining experience in this historic beach house turned restaurant.

⊨ Cannon Beach Hotel Historic Hotel $$

(☎503-436-1392; www.cannonbeachhotel.com; 1116 S Hemlock St; d $140-255; @ 🤖) Classy joint with small but meticulously turned-out rooms in a historic wooden Craftsman-style building dating from 1914. A downstairs lounge and cafe/bistro add to the charm.

STRETCH
YOUR LEGS
SEATTLE

Start/Finish King Street Station/Seattle Center

Distance 2 miles

Duration 3½ hours

Successive mayors have tried hard to alleviate Seattle's car chaos, and – hills and drizzly rain aside – this is now a good city for walking. Strategically placed coffee bars provide liquid fuel for urban hikers.

Take this walk on Trips

King Street Station

The start/finish point of the Empire Builder train to Chicago and mid-point for the Cascades and Coast Starlight services, Seattle's main station was designed to imitate St Mark's bell tower in Venice. Now dwarfed by loftier towers, it was the tallest structure in Seattle upon its completion in 1906. It lay neglected until the late 2000s when restoration work revealed a once-grandiose interior.

The Walk » From the station entrance, head quite literally around the corner onto S Jackson St.

Zeitgeist Coffee

Start this walk the way Seattleites start each day: with a latte. You'll find chain coffee shops on every corner, but **Zeitgeist Coffee** (www.zeitgeistcoffee.com; 171 S Jackson St; ⏲6am-7pm Mon-Fri, 8am-7pm Sat-Sun), in a converted warehouse, is a great place to hang out with the hip crowd.

The Walk » Go west on S Jackson St and right on 1st Ave S, admiring the redbrick Victorian buildings.

Pioneer Square

Seattle was born in the muddy shores of Elliott Bay and reborn here post the catastrophic 1889 fire. The handsome redbrick buildings remain, built in a style known as Richardson Romanesque in the 1890s. Yesler Way was America's original 'Skid Row,' so named as they used to skid logs down the thoroughfare toward the harbor.

The Walk » Walk north on 1st Ave into the modern downtown core.

Seattle Art Museum

Seattle isn't just a meeting ground for Gore-Tex-wearing adventurers planning sorties into the surrounding mountains. There's culture here too. The **Seattle Art Museum** (www.seattleartmuseum.org; 1300 1st Ave; adult/student/child $13/7/free; ⏲10am-5pm Tue-Sun, to 9pm Thu-Fri) is the best place to start. The collections span multiple genres from modern Warhol to Northwestern totem poles.

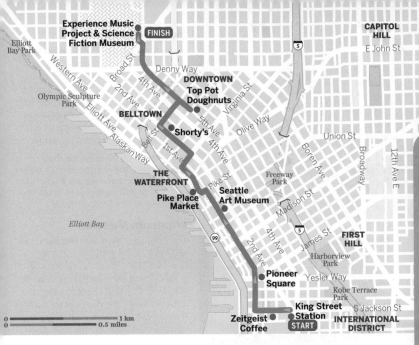

The Walk >> Continue north on 1st Ave two blocks to Pike Place Market.

Pike Place Market

The soul of the city is encased in 105-year-old **Pike Place Market** (www.pikeplacemarket.org; 1501 Pike Pl). You'll need an early start if you want to spend more time dodging flying fish and less time dodging hordes of people. Locals love it for its fresh flowers, produce and seafood; for out-of-towners, its big neon sign is a quintessential Seattle photo op.

The Walk >> Exit the north end of Pike Pl and you're in Belltown.

Shorty's

An early pulpit for grunge music, Belltown, north of downtown, has gone upscale since the 1990s with new condo developments and huddles of restaurants. A standout is **Shorty's** (www.shortydog.com; 2222 2nd Ave), a cross between a pinball arcade and a dive-bar.

The Walk >> Turn right on Bell St and right again on 5th Ave.

Top Pot Doughnuts

Inhabiting an old car showroom, **Top Pot Doughnuts** (2124 5th Ave; ⊘6am-7pm Mon-Fri, 7am-7pm Sat-Sun) has done for doughnuts what Champagne did for wine. The coffee isn't bad either.

The Walk >> Walk along 5th Ave to the intersection with Denny Way. Hang a left and you'll see the Seattle Center and Space Needle in front of you.

Experience Music Project & Science Fiction Museum

It's hard to miss the huge, crazily colorful building at the foot of the Space Needle. That would be the **Experience Music Project & Science Fiction Museum** (www.empsfm.org; 325 5th Ave N; adult/child $20/14; ⊘10am-7pm), a fun place to immerse yourself in rock and roll and/or sci-fi for one admission price.

The Walk >> To get back to the start simply catch bus 131 ($2.25) from Broad St and 2nd Ave which drops you in South Jackson St near King Street Station.

STRETCH
YOUR LEGS
BELLINGHAM

Start/Finish Hotel Bellwether/Village Books

Distance 4 miles

Duration 3½ hours

Despite a rusty ring of old dockyards along its waterfront and modern malls clustered around the interstate, Bellingham's downtown is refreshingly walkable these days, with intra-urban trails, traffic-calmed streets and, in genteel Fairhaven, a rejuvenated historic district.

Take this walk on Trips

Hotel Bellwether

Kick off outside the **Hotel Bellwether** (☎360-392-3100; www.hotelbellwether.com; 1 Bellwether Way), on a redeveloped part of the waterfront with water-hugging paths and views toward the whale-like hump of Lummi Island. The adjacent marina is a good place to ogle at other people's multimillion-dollar yachts.

The Walk ≫ From the marina, walk down Bellwether Way onto Roeder Ave; turn right and then left, crossing the railway tracks onto W Holly St. Cut up through the Maritime Heritage Park toward the distinctive redbrick of Whatcom City Hall.

Whatcom Museum

The revamped **Whatcom Museum** (www.whatcommuseum.org; 121 Prospect St; adult/concession $10/8; ⊙noon-5pm Tue-Sun; ♿) is spread over three buildings: historic Whatcom City Hall (built in 1892), the adjacent Syre Education Center and the innovative Lightcatcher building, which incorporates a spectacular 37ft glass wall. A rich array of exhibits includes historical material, Northwest art and Native American basket weaving.

The Walk ≫ From the Lightcatcher building, head one block along Commercial Ave to the junction of W Champion St.

Mt Baker Theatre

With its minaretlike tower and elaborate interior, the grand **Mt Baker Theatre** (www.mountbakertheatre.com; 106 N Commercial St), built in 1925, harks back to an era when form was as important as function. Showcasing everything from live music to plays, the theater regularly draws in quirky national talent.

The Walk ≫ Cross W Champion St and walk the half block to W Magnolia St. Turn left and continue two blocks to the corner of Railroad Ave, Bellingham's traffic-calmed, bike-friendly main thoroughfare. Numerous one-of-a-kind shops and cheap eating joints will detain you here.

Mallards

The start (or end) point of many a Bellingham date night, lurid **Mallards** (www.mallardicecream.com; 1323 Railroad Ave;

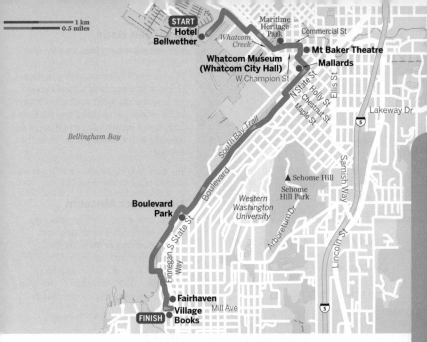

⏱10am-11pm Sun-Thu, 11am-11pm Fri & Sat) is a 1950s-style ice-cream parlor with a zillion flavors – many of them weirdly exotic. Come here before or after a show and try the vanilla-and-pepper or green-tea varieties – all organic, of course!

The Walk ≫ Continue south on Railroad Ave, stopping for a microbrew in the Boundary Bay Brewery & Bistro, if you wish. At the T-junction with E Maple St, hang left and proceed half a block to the start of the South Bay Trail.

Boulevard Park

The epitome of Bellingham's waterside rejuvenation, this park – accessed via a footbridge over the railway line – is cherished by locals for its San Juan Island views and sunsets. There's an outdoor theater and chic outlet of Woods Coffee, the sustainable local roasters. The **South Bay Trail**, which bisects the park, travels out on a boardwalk over the water before swinging back to land on the cusp of Fairhaven.

The Walk ≫ Cross the railway, go right on 10th St and you're quickly in Fairhaven.

Fairhaven

Bellingham's history is enshrined in the Fairhaven district, once a separate city founded in the 1880s but later amalgamated with its big brother to the north. These days Fairhaven's handsome cluster of redbrick buildings have been reincarnated as specialty shops, European-style cafes and off-beat art galleries. A map/brochure gives the rundown of every building.

The Walk ≫ Make your way over to the corner of Mill Ave and 11th St.

Village Books

Bellingham has long nurtured bookish inclinations and sports almost a dozen bookstores. Ruling the roost is **Village Books** (www.villagebooks.com; 1210 11th St), a sprawling community resource with the popular Colophon Cafe next door.

The Walk ≫ To return to the start, take bus 401 from Fairhaven to Bellingham station (on Railroad Ave). Change here onto bus 4 and get off at the Holly St/Broadway St junction for Bellwether Way.

STRETCH YOUR LEGS
LEAVENWORTH

Start/Finish München Haus

Distance 2 miles

Duration 1½ hours

Beer, sausages, nutcrackers, gabled Bavarian hotels and even some leafy forest – there aren't many places where you can enjoy such a condensed exposé of German culture in the US. Get out of your car and say guten tag to Leavenworth.

Take this walk on Trip

München Haus

Sizzling **München Haus** (www.munchen haus.com; 709 Front St; snacks from $6; ⏰11am-11pm) is 100% alfresco, meaning the hot German sausages and pretzels served up here are essential stomach-warmers in the winter, while the Bavarian brews and casual beer garden atmosphere do a good job of cooling you down in the summer.

The Walk >> Exit München Haus, turn right and wander half a block down Front St.

Nutcracker Museum

If you have a penchant for obscure, highly specialized museums, stop by the **Nutcracker Museum** (www.nutcrackermuseum.com; 735 Front St; admission $2.50; ⏰2-5pm; 🚻), which exhibits more than 6000 nutcrackers (see p82). There's a souvenir shop downstairs.

The Walk >> Cross the road to the park.

Front Street Park

A feature sadly absent in most American small towns is the good old main square. Leavenworth likes to be different, furnishing the strip facing Front St with lawns, an elegant bandstand, elaborate flower displays and a maypole. Numerous festivals enliven the space year-round and it is the centerpiece of the Christmas Lights Festival.

The Walk >> Keep straight on Front St to the intersection with 10th St.

Icicle Brewery

One of Washington's newest brewpubs, **Icicle Brewery** (www.iciclebrewing.com; 935 Front St) opened in 2010 with a funky outdoor patio and a modern-rustic interior (the tasting room) that's hard to resist. Pop in to sample the Khaos (the homebrewed beer, not the atmosphere, which is relaxed). Brewery tour are offered on Saturdays at noon.

The Walk >> Cut down 10th St (Festhallen Strasse) for one block and turn right on Commercial St (Markt Strasse).

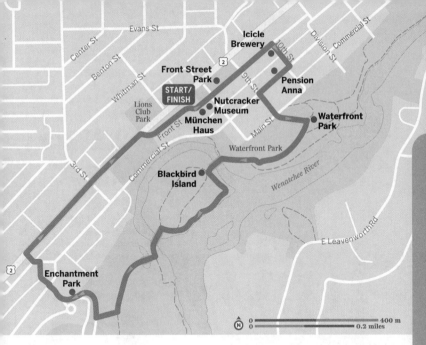

Pension Anna

For Leavenworth's most quintessentially Bavarian architectural creation, stop by to admire **Pension Anna** (☏509-548-6273; www.pensionanna.com; 926 Commercial St; r $149-230, chapel ste $239-330; ℙ). Examine the gabled roof, timbered balconies and geranium-filled flower boxes, and – should you decide to stay – slip inside to see the hand-painted Austrian furniture. The onion-domed St Joseph's chapel is let out as a luxury hotel suite.

The Walk ❯❯ Turn left on 9th St (Alpen Strasse) and follow the slope down into the trees, lured by the melodious tinkle of the Wenatchee River. Suddenly this urban stroll has gone rural.

Waterfront Park

Tucked out of view but surprisingly close, this green area provides access to the Wenatchee River. Follow the leafy domain from 9th St to catch a glimpse of Sleeping Lady Mountain, ringed by a border of green foliage. Interpretive signs furnish the route and help explain the local plant and animal life.

In summer, people launch inner tubes from the riverbanks. In winter, it's an informal cross-country skiing park.

The Walk ❯❯ Follow the path through the trees and cross the footbridge onto Blackbird Island.

Blackbird Island

You're just as likely to spot an osprey as a blackbird on this small bird-filled nodule of land formed by a silt vacuum from a mill pond in the 1930s.

The Walk ❯❯ Take the left fork and follow the main trail alongside the river to a second footbridge. Cross it and proceed to the lawns and sports grounds of Enchantment Park.

Enchantment Park

Connected by Enchantment Bridge to Blackbird Island, this park has various trailheads, a playground and rest rooms. Take the steep path up the grassy knoll and through the residential quarter to return to the main drag (US 2).

The Walk ❯❯ Turn right and stroll past the gabled hotels to the start point.

Oregon Trips

LAID-BACK OREGON CONCEDES ONLY ONE INTERSTATE HIGHWAY to those with a misplaced sense of urgency. The real joy in Oregon is lazily criss-crossing the state along back roads and scenic byways. And boy, are they scenic. The Cascades are dense with natural wonders, including mountains, waterfalls, forests and hot springs. The Oregon coast offers a completely different experience, with miles and miles of coastal highway stringing together charming seaside towns.

If sparsely populated Oregon still feels too busy for you, head to the remote eastern part of the state. In the land of fossils and pioneer relics, you can't help but think, 'Where am I, and what have they done with all the towns?'

Columbia River Gorge Old highway (Trip 16)
DESIGN PICS / CRAIG TUTTLE / GETTY IMAGES ©

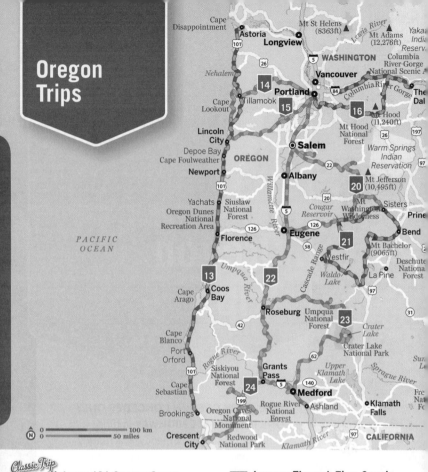

Oregon Trips

Classic Trip

13 Highway 101 Oregon Coast 7 Days
Diversions include whale-watching, lighthouses and seafood. (p149)

14 Three Capes Loop 2 Days
Detour off Hwy 101 through Capes Meares, Lookout and Kiwanda. (p163)

15 Willamette Valley Wine Tour 2 Days
Pinot Noir is the star at Oregon's answer to the Napa Valley. (p171)

Classic Trip

16 Columbia River Gorge & Mt Hood 3 Days
See two of Oregon's best features. (p179)

17 Journey Through Time Scenic Byway 3 Days
Dig deep into Oregon's history – millions of years deep. (p189)

18 Blue Mountains Loop 3 Days
Head off the beaten track into pioneer days. (p197)

19 Hells Canyon Scenic Byway 4 Days
Spectacular vistas await in the remote northeast corner of Oregon. (p205)

20 To Bend & Back 5 Days
Outdoorsy Bend surrounds itself with opportunities for fun. (p213)

 DON'T MISS

Cape Perpetua

The best coast view isn't on the highway; drive to the top of Cape Perpetua for dizzying vistas on Trip **13**

Kennedy School

Roam the halls of this former Portland school where you can spend the night, drink in the cafeteria and watch movies in the gym on Trip **22**

Thomas Condon Paleontology Center

Get a fascinating lesson in history and paleontology on Trip **17**

Golden State Heritage Site

Not all ghost towns are in remote locations. This abandoned mining town is amazingly located right off I-5 on Trip **23**

Oregon Caves National Monument

After showing off with waterfalls and mountains, nature goes underground at the 'Marble Halls of Oregon.' Check them out on Trip **24**

Cape Sebastian *Wind past dramatic ocean views*

Classic Trip

Highway 101 Oregon Coast

13

Routes like Highway 101 are the reason the road trip was invented. It meanders the length of the Oregon coast past sandy beaches, colorful tide pools and nearly a dozen lighthouses.

TRIP HIGHLIGHTS

1 mile

Astoria
Cute Victorian town at the mouth of the Columbia

161 miles

Cape Perpetua
Hands-down the best views on the Oregon Coast

134 miles

Newport
Tide pools and two lighthouses make this a coastal favorite

283 miles

Port Orford
Hike Humbug Mountain and meet some prehistoric creatures

START
1
Tillamook
9
11
Florence
Coos Bay
17
Brookings
FINISH

7 DAYS
340 MILES/547KM

GREAT FOR...

BEST TIME TO GO

Visit July to October, when the weather is more cooperative.

 ESSENTIAL PHOTO

The life-size T-rex outside Prehistoric Gardens.

 BEST HIKING

Cape Perpetua offers several breathtaking hikes.

Classic Trip

13 Highway 101 Oregon Coast

Scenic, two-lane Highway 101 follows hundreds of miles of shoreline punctuated with charming seaside towns, exhilarating hikes and ocean views that remind you're on the edge of the continent. In this trip, it's not about getting from point A to point B. Instead, the route itself is the destination. And everyone from nature lovers to gourmands to families can find their dream vacation along this exceptional coastal route.

TRIP HIGHLIGHT

① Astoria

We begin our coastal trek in the northwestern corner of the state, where the Columbia River meets the Pacific Ocean. Ever-so-slightly inland, Astoria doesn't rely on beach proximity for its character. It has a rich history, including being a stop on the Lewis and Clark trail (p136). Because of its location, it also has a unique maritime history, which you can explore at the **Columbia River Maritime Museum** (www.crmm.org; 1792 Marine Dr; adult/child $12/5; ◷9:30am-5pm).

Astoria has been the location of several Hollywood movies, making it a virtual Hollywood by the sea: it's best known as the setting for cult hit *The Goonies*. Fans can peek at the **Goonies House** (368 38th St) and the **Clatsop County Jail** (732 Duane St).

✕ 🛏 p160

The Drive » Head south on Highway 101 14.5 miles to Gearhart.

② Gearhart

Check your tide table and head to the beach; Gearhart is famous for its razor clamming at low tide. All you need are boots, a shovel or a clam gun, a cut-resistant glove, a license (available in Gearhart) and a bucket for your catch. Watch your fingers – the name razor clam is well earned. Boiling up a batch will likely result in the most memorable meal of your trip. For information on where, when and how to clam, visit the **Oregon Department of Fish & Wildlife website** (www.dfw.state.or.us); it's a maze of a site, so just Google 'ODFW clamming.'

The Drive » Don't get too comfortable yet: Seaside is just 2.4 miles further down the coast.

③ Seaside

Oregon's biggest and busiest resort town delivers exactly what you'd expect from a town called Seaside, which is wholesome,

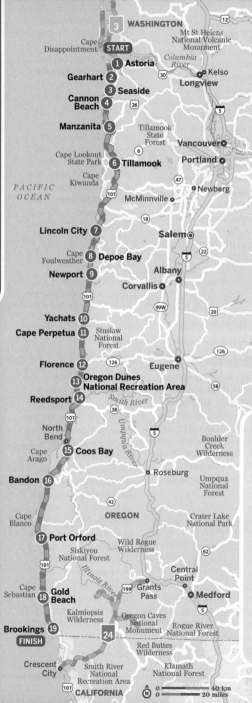

Coney Island-esque fun. The 2-mile boardwalk – known as 'the Prom' – is a kaleidoscope of seaside kitsch, with surrey rentals, video arcades, fudge, elephant ears, caramel apples, saltwater taffy and more. It's also where you'll find the **Seaside Aquarium** (www.seasideaquarium.com; 200 N Promenade; adult/child $8/4; ⏰9am-7pm;). Open since 1937, the privately owned aquarium isn't much more than a few fish tanks, a touch pool and a small indoor seal tank where you can feed the splashy critters, but it's a fun stop for inquisitive kids.

✕ p160

The Drive » Leave the beach behind for a bit as you veer inland for the 8.8-mile drive to Cannon Beach.

🔗 LINK YOUR TRIP

3 Graveyard of the Pacific Tour

Continue your coastal adventure with this trip that starts in Astoria and heads north into Washington (p53).

24 Caves of Highway 199

Pop down to Crescent City, CA, for a short but lovely trip east that delivers you back to I-5 (p247).

Classic Trip

❹ Cannon Beach

Charming Cannon Beach is one of the most popular beach resorts on the Oregon coast. The wide sandy beach stretches for miles, and you'll find great photo opportunities and tide-pooling possibilities at glorious **Haystack Rock**, the third-tallest sea stack in the world. (What's a sea stack, you might ask? It's a vertical rock formation – in this case, one that's shaped like a haystack.) For the area's best coastal hiking, head immediately north of town to **Ecola State Park** (www.oregonstateparks.org; day-use $3), where you can hike to secluded beaches.

✗ ⛵ p160

The Drive ❯❯ Follow the coast 14.4 miles through Oswald West State Park to reach your next stop.

❺ Manzanita

One of the more laid-back beach resorts on Oregon's coast is the hamlet of Manzanita – much smaller and far less hyped than Cannon Beach. You can relax on the white-sand beaches, or, if you're feeling more ambitious, hike on nearby **Neahkahnie Mountain**, where high cliffs rise dramatically above the Pacific's pounding waves. It's a 3.8-mile climb to the top, but the views are worth it: on a clear day, you can see 50 miles out to sea.

The Drive ❯❯ Drive 27 miles from Nehalem Bay to Tillamook Bay to reach inland Tillamook.

❻ Tillamook

Not all coastal towns are built on seafood and sand. Tillamook has an entirely different claim to fame: cheese. Thousands stop annually at the **Tillamook Cheese Visitors Centre** (4175 N US 101; ⏰8am-8pm) for free samples. You might choose to skip the dairy altogether and head to one of two interesting museums: the **Pioneer Museum** (www.tcpm.org; 2106 2nd St; adult/child $4/1; ⏰10am-4pm Tue-Sun) has antique toys, a great taxidermy room (check out the polar bear) and a basement full of pioneer artifacts. And just south of town, the **Tillamook Naval Air Museum** (www.tillamookair.com; 6030 Hangar Rd; adult/child $9/5; ⏰9am-5pm) has a large collection of fighter planes and a 7-acre blimp hangar.

The Drive ❯❯ South of Tillamook, Highway 101 follows the Nestucca River through pastureland and logged-off mountains 44 miles to Lincoln City.

❼ Lincoln City

The sprawling modern beach resort of Lincoln City serves as the region's principal commercial center. In addition to gas and groceries, the town does offer a unique enticement to stop: from mid-October to late May volunteers from the Visitor and Convention Bureau hide brightly colored glass floats – which have been hand-blown by local artisans – along the beaches, making a memorable souvenir for the resourceful and diligent vacationer.

✗ p160

THREE CAPES LOOP

South of the town of Tillamook, Highway 101 veers inland from the coast. An exhilarating alternative route is the slow, winding and sometimes bumpy Three Capes Loop (p163), which hugs the shoreline for 30 miles and offers the chance to go clamming (p168). En route you'll traverse Cape Meares, Cape Lookout and Cape Kiwanda – three stunning headlands that you'd otherwise miss entirely.

The Drive » It's back to the coast for the 12-mile drive south to Depoe Bay.

- - - - - - - - - -

8 Depoe Bay

Though edged by modern timeshare condominiums, Depoe Bay still retains some original coastal charm. It lays claim to having the 'world's smallest navigable harbor' and being the 'world's whale-watching capital' – pretty big talk for such a pint-sized town. Whale-watching and charter fishing are the main attractions in the area, though 5 miles south of town there is the **Devil's Punchbowl**, an impressive collapsed sea cave that churns with waves and offers good tide pools nearby.

The Drive » Another 12.8 miles brings you to the lively tourist city of Newport.

- - - - - - - - - -

TRIP HIGHLIGHT

9 Newport

Don your marine-biologist cap and head to **Yaquina Head Outstanding Natural Area** (750 Lighthouse Dr; entry $5; ☉dawn-dusk), a giant spit of land that protrudes nearly a mile into the ocean. This headland is home to some of the best touch pools on the Oregon coast. You'll also get a good look at the tallest lighthouse in

YAQUINA HEAD LIGHTHOUSE

If Yaquina Head Lighthouse in Newport, Oregon, seems a little creepier than a lighthouse ought, that's because it was featured in the 2002 Naomi Watts film *The Ring*. Built in 1873, it was originally called Cape Foulweather Lighthouse, but in the movie it was known as the Moesko Island Lighthouse. (The lighthouse was also in the 1977 masterpiece *Nancy Drew: Pirate's Cove*.)

Oregon, **Yaquina Head Lighthouse** (not to be confused with **Yaquina Bay Lighthouse**, 3 miles south).

Also worth a stop: the cutting-edge **Oregon Coast Aquarium** (www.aquarium.org; 2820 SE Ferry Slip Rd; adult/child 3-12 $19/12; ☉9am-6pm; ⊞). The seals and sea otters are cute as can be, and the jellyfish room is a near psychedelic experience. But what really knocks this place off the charts is the deep-sea exhibit that lets you walk through a Plexiglas tunnel through sharks, rays and other fish.

✕ ⊨ p160

The Drive » Another 24 miles to Yachats along the edge of the Siuslaw National Forest.

- - - - - - - - - -

10 Yachats

One of the Oregon coast's best-kept secrets is the friendly little town of Yachats (ya-*hots*), which kicks off about 20 miles of spectacular shoreline. This entire area was once a series of volcanic intrusions that resisted

the pummeling of the Pacific long enough to rise as oceanside peaks and promontories. Acres of tide pools are home to starfish, sea anemones and sea lions.

Fourteen miles south of town, picturesque **Heceta Head Lighthouse** (92072 Hwy 101, South Yachats) is one of the most photographed lighthouses on the Oregon coast. You can't see it from the highway, but you can park at **Heceta Head State Park** (day use $5) for great views from afar, as well as a trail leading past the former **lightkeeper's quarters** (now a bed and breakfast – see listings) and up to the lighthouse.

✕ ⊨ p161

The Drive » Just 3 miles down the coast is dramatic Cape Perpetua.

- - - - - - - - - -

TRIP HIGHLIGHT

11 Cape Perpetua

Whatever you do, don't miss the spectacular scenery of the **Cape**

Classic Trip

Perpetua Scenic Area (day-use $5), just 3 miles south of Yachats. You could easily spend a day or two exploring trails that take you through moss-laden, old-growth forests to rocky beaches, tide pools and blasting marine geysers.

At the very least, drive up to the **Cape Perpetua Overlook** for a colossal coastal view from 800ft above sea level – the highest point on the coast. While you're up there, check out the historic **West Shelter** observation point built by the Civilian Conservation Corps in 1933.

If you have more time to spend, stop at the **visitors center** (⏰10am-5:30pm daily summer, 10am-4pm Wed-Mon off-season) to plan your day. High points include **Devil's Churn**, where waves shoot up a 30ft inlet to explode against the narrowing sides of the channel, and the **Giant Spruce Trail**, which leads to a 500-year-old Sitka spruce with a 10ft diameter.

The Drive ❱❱ It's 22 miles to Florence, but only 12 to the Sea Lion Caves.

---

⑫ Florence

Looking for a good, old-fashioned roadside attraction? North of Florence is the **Sea Lion Caves** (www.sealioncaves.com; adult/child $12/8; ⏰8:30am-6pm; 👶), an enormous sea grotto that's home to hundreds of groaning sea lions. Open to the public since the 1930s, the cave is accessed by an elevator that descends 208ft to the sea lions' stinky lair.

Here's the deal: it can be fascinating, but you might feel a little taken when you realize the view is exactly the same as what was on the monitor up in the gift shop – and there's not even free fudge samples down there. But if money's no object, you'll enjoy watching the sea lions cavort, especially if you have kids in tow.

🍴 p161

The Drive ❱❱ The Oregon Dunes start just south of Florence and continue for the next 50 miles.

WHY THIS IS A CLASSIC TRIP
MARIELLA KRAUSE, AUTHOR

Meandering your way down Oregon's coastline is the epitome of a carefree vacation. There are no major cities, no hustle, no bustle – just miles of ocean on one side of the road and miles of hiking on the other. My personal favorite part of the trip? Spending the night at Heceta Head Lighthouse and waking up to a seven-course breakfast, followed by hiking at Cape Perpetua.

Left: Heceta Head Lighthouse
Right: Elk at Ecola State Park

CRAIG TUTTLE / CORBIS ©

Classic Trip

13 Oregon Dunes National Recreation Area

As you drive south you start to notice something altogether different: sand. Lots of it. Stretching 50 miles, the **Oregon Dunes** are the largest expanse of oceanfront sand dunes in the US. Sometimes topping heights of 500ft, these mountains of sand undulate inland up to 3 miles. Hikers and birdwatchers stick to the peaceful northern half of the dunes, and the southern half is dominated by dune buggies and dirt bikes.

At Mile 200.8, the **Oregon Dunes Overlook** is the easiest place to take a gander if you're just passing through. To learn more about trails and off-road vehicles, visit the **Oregon Dunes NRA Visitors Center** (855 Highway Ave,

Reedsport; ⊘8am-4:30pm). For the area's biggest dunes, the 6-mile **John Dellenbeck Trail** (at Mile 222.6) loops through a wilderness of massive sand peaks.

The Drive » Reedsport is about halfway into the dunes area, about 22 miles south of Florence.

14 Reedsport

Reedsport's location in the middle of the Oregon Dunes makes it an ideal base for exploring the region. Check out the **Umpqua Lighthouse State Park**, offering summer tours of a local 1894 **lighthouse** (adult/child $3/2; ⊘10am-4pm May-Oct, varies rest of year). Opposite is a whale-watching platform, and a nearby nature trail rings freshwater **Lake Marie**, which is popular for swimming.

Want to see how Oregon's largest land mammal spends its free time? Three miles east of town on Hwy 38, you can spy a herd of about 120 Roosevelt elk meandering about at the **Dean Creek Elk Viewing Area**.

The Drive » Enjoy the sand for another 27.5 miles, as you reach Coos Bay and the end of the dunes.

15 Coos Bay

The no-nonsense city of Coos Bay and its modest neighbor North Bend make up the largest urban area on the Oregon coast. Coos Bay was once the largest timber port in the world. The logs are long gone, but tourists are slowly taking their places.

In a historic art-deco building downtown, the **Coos Art Museum** (www. coosart.org; 235 Anderson Ave; adult/child $5/2; ⊘10am-4pm Tue-Fri, 1-4pm Sat) provides a hub for the region's art culture with rotating exhibits from the museum's permanent collection.

Cape Arago Hwy leads 14 miles southwest of town to **Cape Arago State Park** (www. oregonstateparks.org), where grassy picnic grounds make for great perches over a pounding sea. The park protects some of the best tide pools on the Oregon coast and is well worth the short detour.

The Drive » Highway 101 heads inland for a bit then gets back to the coast 24 miles later at Bandon.

16 Bandon

Optimistically touted as Bandon-by-the-Sea, this little town sits

WHALE-WATCHING

Each year, gray whales undertake one of the longest migrations of any animal on earth, swimming from the Bering Strait and Chukchi Sea to Baja California – and back. Look for them migrating south in winter (mid-December through mid-January) and north in spring (March through June).

happily at the bay of the Coquille River, with an Old Town district that's been gentrified into a picturesque harborside shopping location that offers pleasant strolling and window-shopping.

Along the beach, ledges of stone rise out of the surf to provide shelter for seals, sea lions and myriad forms of life in tide pools. One of the coast's most interesting rock formations is the much-photographed **Face Rock**, a huge monolith with some uncanny facial features that does indeed look like a woman with her head thrown back – giving rise to a requisite Native American legend.

The Drive » Follow the coastline another 24 miles south to Port Orford. This part of the drive isn't much to look at, but not to worry: there's more scenery to come.

TRIP HIGHLIGHT

17 Port Orford

Perched on a grassy headland, the hamlet of Port Orford is located in one of the most scenic stretches of coastal highway, and there are stellar views even from the center of town. If you're feeling ambitious, take the 3-mile trail up **Humbug Mountain** (38745 Hwy 101), which takes you up, up, up past streams and through prehistoric-looking landscapes to

the top, where you'll be treated to dramatic views of Cape Sebastian and the Pacific.

Speaking of prehistoric scenery: your kids will scream at the sight of a tyrannosaurus rex 12 miles south of town in front of **Prehistoric Gardens** (36848 US 101; adult/child $10/8; ⊙9am-6pm; 🅿). Life-size replicas of the extinct beasties are set in a lush, first-growth temperate rain forest; the huge ferns and trees set the right mood for going back in time.

✕ 🛏 p161

The Drive » The scenery starts to pick up again, with unusual rock formations lining the 28-mile drive to Gold Beach.

18 Gold Beach

Next you'll pass through the tourist hub of Gold Beach, where you can take a jet boat excursion up the scenic **Rogue River**. But the real treat

lies 13 miles south of town, when you enter the 12-mile stretch of coastal splendor known as the **Samuel Boardman State Scenic Corridor**, featuring giant stands of Sitka spruce, natural rock bridges, tide pools and loads of hiking trails.

Along the highway are well over a dozen roadside turnouts and picnic areas, with short trails leading to secluded beaches and dramatic viewpoints. A 30-second walk from the parking area to the viewing platform at **Natural Bridge Viewpoint** (Mile 346) offers a glorious photo op of rock arches – the remnants of collapsed sea caves – after which you can decide whether you want to commit to the hike down to **China Beach**.

✕ 🛏 p161

The Drive » It's just 34 miles to the California border, and 28 to Brookings.

CRAIG TUTTLE / CORBIS ©

⑲ Brookings

Your last stop on the Oregon coast is Brookings. With some of the warmest temperatures on the coast, Brookings is a leader in Easter lily-bulb production; in July, fields south of town are filled with bright colors and a heavy scent. In May and June you'll also find magnificent displays of flowers at the hilly, 30-acre **Azalea Park** (Azalea Park Rd).

History buffs take note: Brookings has the unique distinction of being the location of the only WWII aerial bombing on the US mainland. In 1942, a Japanese seaplane succeeded in bombing nearby forests with the intent to burn them, but they failed to ignite. The Japanese pilot, Nobuo Fujita, returned to Brookings 20 years later and presented the city with a peace offering: his family's 400-year-old samurai sword, which is now displayed at the **Chetco Community Public Library** (405 Alder St).

✕ 🛏 p161

Bandon Beach Rock formations at low tide

Classic Trip

Eating & Sleeping

Astoria ❶

✕ Wet Dog Café — Brewpub $$
(www.wetdogcafe.com; 144 11th St; mains $9-14; ⊙lunch & dinner, to 2am Fri & Sat) For casual dining there's no beating this large, quirky pub, which brews its own beer with names such as Poop Deck Porter and Bitter Bitch IPA.

🛏 Hotel Elliott — Hotel $$
(☎503-325-2222; www.hotelelliott.com; 357 12th St; d $149-189; ☻❄☎) Standard rooms have charming period elegance at this historic hotel. For more space, get a suite (the 'presidential' boasts two bedrooms, two baths, a grand piano and a rooftop deck).

Seaside ❸

✕ Bell Buoy — Seafood $$
(☎503-738-6348; 1800 S Roosevelt Dr; mains $8-18; ⊙11:30am-7:30pm, closed Tue & Wed winter) Best known as a seafood store, this down-to-earth, family-run establishment has an attached seafood restaurant serving outstanding fish and chips, chowder and more.

Cannon Beach ❹

✕ Lumberyard — American $$
(☎503-436-0285; www.thelumberyardgrill. com; 264 3rd St; mains $11-20; ⊙lunch & dinner Thu-Mon; 👪) This family-friendly eatery has something for everyone, including seven kinds of burgers, rotisserie specialties, pot pies, sandwiches, pizzas and steaks.

🛏 Blue Gull Inn — Motel $$
(☎800-507-2714; www.haystacklodgings. com; 487 S Hemlock St; d $59-219; ☻☎) These are some of the more affordable rooms

in town, with comfortable atmosphere and toned-down decor, except for the colorful Mexican headboards and serapes on the beds. Kitchenettes available.

Lincoln City ❼

✕ Blackfish Café — Northwestern $$$
(☎541-996-1007; www.blackfishcafe.com; 2733 NW US 101; mains $15-23; ⊙lunch & dinner Wed-Mon) This is one of the coast's best restaurants, specializing in cutting-edge cuisine highlighting fresh seafood and seasonal vegetables. Reserve ahead for simple but delicious Northwest-inspired dishes.

Newport ❾

✕ Rogue Ales Public House — Pub $$
(☎541-265-3188; www.rogue.com; 748 SW Bay Blvd; mains $8-22; ⊙11am-1am) Don't miss out on microbrews, best quaffed at outdoor tables or seated inside at the big wooden bar. There's an expansive food menu, too.

🛏 Newport Belle — B&B $$
(☎541-867-6290; www.newportbelle.com; South Beach Marina; d $150-165; ☻) For a unique stay there's no beating this sternwheeler B&B – likely the only one of its kind. The five small but shipshape rooms have private baths and water views, while the common spaces are wonderful for relaxing.

🛏 Beverly Beach State Park — Campground $
(☎877-444-6777; www.oregonstateparks. org; Hwy 101; tents $17-21, yurts $40) With campsites, heated yurts and a long, wide beach lying just across the highway, this is the perfect base for ocean exploration. It's 7 miles north of Newport.

Yachats ⑩

✖ Green Salmon Coffee House
Coffeehouse $

(☎541-547-3077; 220 US 101; snacks under $7; ☻breakfast & lunch Tue-Sun; 🖉) Queue up at the counter for spectacularly tasty breakfast items including pastries, lox bagels and fair-trade coffee. This cafe is a popular local hangout, and they earn bonus points for their focus on organic ingredients and sustainable practices.

🛏 Heceta Head Lighthouse
B&B $$

(☎541-547-3416, 866-547-3696; www.hecetalighthouse.com; 92072 Hwy 101 S; r $133-315) Bunking in the former lightkeeper's quarter is a treat – especially given this B&B's exquisitely private setting. A seven-course gourmet breakfast will leave you stuffed.

Florence ⑫

✖ Waterfront Depot
Northwestern $$

(☎541-902-9100; www.thewaterfrontdepot.com; 1252 Bay St; mains $11-15; ☻4-10pm) Come early to snag one of the few waterfront tables, then enjoy your jambalaya pasta or crab-encrusted halibut. There are excellent small plates too if you want to try a bit of everything, and desserts are spectacular. Reserve ahead.

Port Orford ⑰

✖ Red Fish
Northwestern $$

(☎541-336-2200; www.wix.com/lenabree/redfish; 517 Jefferson St; lunch $8-12, dinner $24-29; ☻11am-9pm, from 9am Sat & Sun) Turning Port Orford on its sleepy head is this slick seaview restaurant that offers breakfast, lunch and dinner. Prices are reasonable, despite the fancy Northwest cuisine menu. Reserve ahead.

🛏 Wildspring Guest Habitat
Luxury Cabins $$$

(☎866-333-9453; www.wildspring.com; 92978 Cemetery Loop; d $198-306; ☻@☎) A few acres of wooded serenity greet you at this quiet retreat. Five luxury cabin suites, with elegant furniture, radiant-floor heating and slate showers, make for a very comfortable and romantic getaway. Breakfast included.

🛏 Cape Blanco State Park
Campground $

(☎541-332-6774, 800-452-5687; www.oregonstateparks.org; tent & RV sites/cabins $20/39) At the other end of the spectrum is this campground located on a high, sheltered rocky headland with beach access and great views of the lighthouse. Showers, flush toilets and boat ramp available.

Gold Beach ⑱

✖ Patti's Rollin 'n Dough Bistro
American $$

(☎541-247-4438; 94257 N Bank Rogue Rd; mains $9-15; ☻breakfast & lunch Tue-Sun) This tiny bistro has a limited breakfast and lunch menu, but what's there really counts. Chef Patti Joyce has studied at the Culinary Institute of America, and it shows. Reservations recommended.

🛏 Ireland's Rustic Lodges
Lodge, Cabins $$

(☎541-247-7718; www.irelandsrusticlodges.com; 29346 Ellensburg Ave; d $80-220; ☎) A wide variety of accommodations awaits you at this woodsy place. There are suites, rustic cabins, beach houses and even RV sites. A glorious garden sits in front while beach views are out back.

Brookings ⑲

✖ Mattie's Pancake & Omelette
American $

(☎541-469-7211; 15975 Hwy 101; mains $7-13; ☻breakfast & lunch Mon-Sat) This casual breakfast and lunch spot offers 20 kinds of omelettes along with pancakes (chocolate chip!) – no surprise given its name. Sandwiches and salads for lunch.

🛏 Harris Beach State Park
Camping $

(☎541-469-2021, 800-452-5687; www.oregonstateparks.org; tents/yurts $20/39) The area's best (make that only) coastal camping. Camp beachside or sleep in a yurt. Showers, flush toilets and coin laundry available.

Cape Meares Hike through spruce forest for top views

Three Capes Loop

14

Whether you're coming from Portland or detouring off Highway 101, the dramatic, ever-changing scenery from forested Cape Meares to sandstone Cape Kiwanda is worth slowing down for.

TRIP HIGHLIGHTS

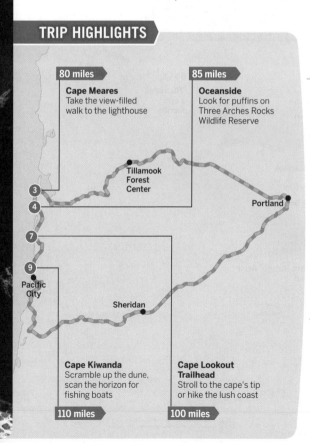

80 miles

Cape Meares
Take the view-filled walk to the lighthouse

85 miles

Oceanside
Look for puffins on Three Arches Rocks Wildlife Reserve

Tillamook Forest Center

Portland

3

4

7

9

Pacific City

Sheridan

Cape Kiwanda
Scramble up the dune, scan the horizon for fishing boats

110 miles

Cape Lookout Trailhead
Stroll to the cape's tip or hike the lush coast

100 miles

2 DAYS
176 MILES/283KM

GREAT FOR...

BEST TIME TO GO

May to October to avoid chilling wind and rain.

 ESSENTIAL PHOTO

Capture the lens of the Cape Lookout Lighthouse contrasting with the steel sea.

 BEST BEACH

Cape Kiwanda has endless sands and a dune to climb.

14 Three Capes Loop

Cape Meares, Cape Lookout and Cape Kiwanda are some of the coast's most stunning headlands, strung together on a slow, winding and sometimes bumpy 30-mile alternative to US 101. If you start from Portland you'll drive through towering forests and salmon-filled river country to complete a loop. But however you tackle this trip, strap on your boots for walks through spruce groves and over dunes to basalt and sandstone precipices.

❶ Tillamook Forest Center

Learn about the stretch of forest between Portland and the sea at the **Tillamook Forest Center** (www.tillamookforestcenter.org; 45500 Hwy 6; admission free; 🕙 10am-4pm Oct-May, 10am-5pm Wed-Sun Jun-Sep), 51 miles from Portland. The interpretive center focuses on the history of wildfire in the region via hands-on exhibits, a 40ft replica fire tower to climb and a suspension bridge over an incredibly scenic part of

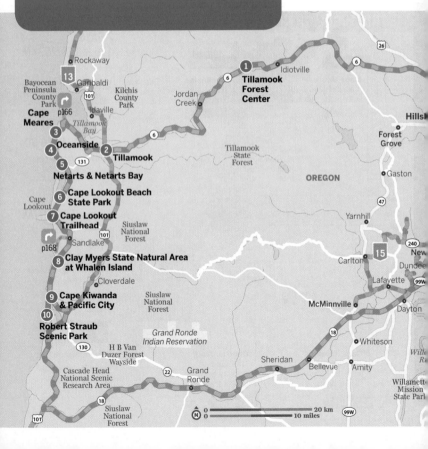

the Wilson River; the film *Legacy of Fire* is worth watching. Also enjoy over 20 miles of hiking on the **Wilson River Trail** that wends along this powerful, Douglas fir- and maple-lined river renowned for its steelhead fishing. It's a 2-mile walk to Wilson Falls where you can splash through rapids moving around big boulders – look for signs of beavers and listen for kingfishers.

The Drive » Head 22 miles west to Tillamook through the scenic Tillamook State Forest.

② Tillamook

Best known for its huge cheese industry, Tillamook is a nondescript town that's worth a stop to down some dairy. Two miles north of town is the famed **Tillamook Cheese Visitors Center** (www.tillamookcheese.com; 4175 N US 101; ⊙8am-8pm), which produces more than 100 million pounds of the product every year. Line up for free cheese samples, lick down an ice-cream cone or peek into the factory floor assembly line; there's a cafe too. Aircraft lovers should stop at the gargantuan **Tillamook Naval Air Museum** (www.tillamookair.com; 6030 Hangar Rd; adult/child $9/5; ⊙9am-5pm) 2 miles south of town on the way toward the next stop.

✕ p169

The Drive » Hwy 6 turns into Hwy 131 Scenic Route as it heads west. Shortly after the

Tillamook Naval Air Museum take the right signposted for Cape Meares. Drive a mile around the Tillamook Estuary then uphill 2 miles to the cape.

TRIP HIGHLIGHT

③ Cape Meares

The first trailhead of Cape Meares has two trails through luxurious spruce forest: a 2.1-mile trail down to rocky **Meares Beach** or a quarter-mile stroll to **Big Spruce**, heralded as the largest Sitka spruce in Oregon (it's 144ft tall and 15.5ft in diameter). A half-mile further driving down Hwy 131 leads you to a second, much more developed parking area with paved paths to the perhaps-haunted 1889 **Cape Meares Lighthouse** (www.capemeareslighthouse.org; ⊙11am-4pm Apr-Oct); there are many viewpoints and information panels along the quarter-mile walk. A shorter dirt path leads to the impressive **Octopus**

LINK YOUR TRIP

13 Highway 101 Oregon Coast

Hwy 101 leads straight into Tillamook. Follow this trip's directions from there (p149).

15 Willamette Valley Wine Tour

Follow the directions from Robert Straub Scenic Park toward Portland and you'll hit McMinnville. From here you can follow the Willamette Valley Wine Tour (p171).

DETOUR:
BAYOCEAN PENINSULA COUNTY PARK

Start: ❷ **Tillamook**

At a humble fork in the road, where Hwy 131 veers left toward Cape Meares, turn right to Bayocean Peninsula County Park and follow the road about 2 miles. Today you'd hardly guess that this was once the site of a very swanky planned resort community built in 1906. In 1914 the town had 2000 residents even though access was by steamship. The residents built a jetty in 1917 to ease the often-rough boat landings. Within a few years, shifting currents caused by the jetty made the beach begin to disappear; the townspeople extended the jetty and the problem amplified with more and more structures getting devoured by the ocean. By the late 1930s most of the remaining houses were abandoned and in 1953 the post office closed. In 1971 the last building, a car garage, crumbled into the sea. Today a commemorative sign is all that is left. It's a beautiful, isolated sandy stretch great for hiking along the beach and birdwatching.

Tree, a legendary eight-limbed spruce that mystifies science.

The Drive » Descend 3 miles down the cape then turn right to Oceanside.

TRIP HIGHLIGHT

❹ Oceanside

This tiny village of cozy beach houses perched over a long, flat white-sand beach is the most charming on this route and a great stop for lunch, dinner or overnight. The **Three Arches Rocks Wildlife Reserve** can be seen at the far right if you're facing the ocean. With binoculars you'll be able to see the orange beaks and yellow head tufts of tufted puffins, one of this coast's most recognizable birds, out on these towering rocks. Picnic or fly kites on the beach, search for agates

in the winter months or just chill out in the seaside vibe.

 p169

The Drive » Turn left onto Hwy 131 again and drive 2 miles to Netarts.

----

❺ Netarts & Netarts Bay

Take a sharp turn on Happy Camp Rd to reach a small parking lot for a pretty stretch of white beach protected by a wide, flat sandbar island. Or you can continue on Hwy 131 another quarter mile to Crab Ave on the left that goes into 'town,' which is a couple of ramshackle motels and deli markets. It's not the most scenic stop but it may be easier to park here than the more popular beaches on busy weekends.

p169

The Drive » Follow the Scenic Route signs that lead to a road veering left that winds along Netarts Bay, known for its clamming. After a few miles you'll rejoin Hwy 131 to Cape Lookout.

----

❻ Cape Lookout State Park

Besides great camping, there are several trails that fan out from this lovely, protected, white sand beach area. Take the 2.3-mile (one-way) North Trail through lush forest and over cliffs to the summit of Cape Lookout, or the 2.4-mile (one-way) Cape Trail that goes through coastal rainforest to a panoramic lookout on the cape. Otherwise, try the easier 1.8-mile (one-way) South Trail over to a secluded beach off the cape.

p169

GERHARD ZWERGER-SCHONER / IMAGEBROKER ©

Netarts Bay

The Drive » Climb a little over a mile uphill then drive another 1.5 miles along the cape to the Cape Lookout Trailhead.

- - - - - - - - - - - - -

TRIP HIGHLIGHT

7 Cape Lookout Trailhead

You can access the same trails (at different points) that are found at Cape Lookout Beach State Park from here. If you're

after a short stroll, take the trail to the far left of the parking lot then walk straight at the first junction about 300ft along. In half a mile you'll be rewarded with a viewpoint – on a clear, sunny day you can see all the way to Cape Kiwanda.

The Drive » After descending about 5 miles from Cape Lookout you'll pass inland dunes on your right, a popular

ATV spot. At the next junction turn right and continue about 4 miles.

- - - - - - - - - - - - -

8 Clay Myers State Natural Area at Whalen Island

Whalen Island is a virtually untouched, wildlife-filled, wooded island that's surrounded by the Sand Creek Estuary. A trail makes a

167

CLAMMING

If you're around Netarts Bay at a minus tide you're likely to see groups of rubber-booted, bucket-wielding foragers combing the beach. Want to get in on the clamming action? First, everyone 14 and older needs a $7 shellfish license available at sporting good stores (there are a few in Tillamook) or get one at the Oregon **Department of Fish & Wildlife** (www.dfw.state.or.us/MRP/shellfish/regulations.asp) website, where you can also check the regulations, limits and seasonal closures. Cockles, little necks, gaper clams and other species are all present but razor clams are the real prize. In all cases, show up about an hour before the lowest tide with a bucket, shovel and/or a clam gun, look for small holes in the sand then dig fast!

relatively flat but truly gorgeous 1.4-mile loop from the parking lot through low forest to fringing white-sand beaches. Wildlife that may be spotted here includes deer, otter, bear and (gulp!) cougar. It also has some of the best tent camping on this trip but given the animal life, you probably don't want to leave out any food.

 p169

The Drive ≫ Go south 7 miles on Hwy 131 along the coast till the road veers inland at Cape Kiwanda.

TRIP HIGHLIGHT

❾ Cape Kiwanda & Pacific City

The best beach of the Three Capes sits in front of tiny Pacific City, south of the towering sandstone, dune-covered Cape Kiwanda. Wide and lush with sand space to spare, you can hike the cape via the dune (under a quarter mile but straight up). Back on the beach, Dory fishermen haul their boats in or out from the beach around

6am and sunset when the weather is calm. You can buy fish from them or order it at many local restaurants.

 p169

The Drive ≫ Head south through Pacific City then turn right at the first crossroads.

---

❿ Robert Straub Scenic Park

You can access the wild and rugged part of Cape Kiwanda Beach via this little park at the Nestucca Sand Spit, where the legendary – and Chinook salmon-friendly – Little Nestucca River meets the sea. The beach here is less protected and thus is windier and has stronger surf and currents. You can find shelter from the elements in the grass-covered dunes.

The Drive ≫ Go back toward Pacific City, follow the signs for Highway 101 and then to Portland via Hwy 18.

↱ DETOUR: SANDLAKE

Start: ❼ **Cape Lookout Trailhead**

About 2 miles before Whalen Island is a turnoff leading to Sandlake, a spit of land that's home to 1076 acres of sand dunes. Folks from all over the Pacific Northwest come here to camp, drink beer and tool around in their ATVs. You can join the fun watching the spills and thrills or, if that doesn't sound good, plug your ears and race back to the highway.

Eating & Sleeping

Tillamook ❷

✕ Pacific Seafood   Seafood $

(☎503-377-2323; 5150 Oyster Dr, Bay City; ⏱10am-8pm) Casual restaurant where you can check out the lightning-fast assembly-line processing of oysters; it's about 6 miles north of Tillamook in Bay City.

Oceanside ❹

✕ Roseanna's Cafe   International $$

(☎503-842-7351; 1490 Pacific Ave; mains $7-22; ⏱7am-8pm Sun-Thu, 7am-9pm Fri & Sat) All round the best place to eat on this route. Choose from pastas, seafood and veggie options served in a sailor-shabby-chic seaside setting with a touch of elegance.

✕ Brewin' In The Wind   Cafe $

(1505 Pacific Ave; mains $6-15; ⏱7am-7pm) Inviting, cozy nook to grab a coffee, homemade baked goods, soups and good burgers.

⛺ Oceanfront Cabins   Cabins $

(☎888-845-8475; www.oceanfrontcabins. com; 1610 Pacific Ave; cabins $70-125; 🛖) Basic cabins, some with kitchens, steps from the beach.

Netarts & Netarts Bay ❺

✕ Schooner   Seafood/American $$

(2065 Netarts Boat Basin Rd; mains $13-28; ⏱11:30am-8pm Mon-Thu, 9am-9pm Fri, 7am-9pm Sat & Sun) Wonderful bay views from the glass enclosed eating area make the cocktails, locally sourced meals (oysters, fish, beef and more) even better.

Cape Lookout State Park ❻

⛺ Cape Lookout State
Park Campground   Campground $

(☎800-452-5687; www.reserveamerica.com; tent/RV sites $19/24, cabins $76) Thirty-eight

full-hookups, 173 tent sites, 13 yurts ($36) and six cabins are available at this beachside beauty of a campground. Book early.

Clay Meyers State Natural Area at Whalen Island ❽

⛺ Whalen Island,
Tillamook County Park   Campground $

(☎May-Oct 503-965-6085, Oct-Apr 503-322-3522; www.co.tillamook.or.us/gov/Parks/Campgrounds.htm; sites $10-20) There are 34 adorable wooded campsites steps from the beach; there are no hookups but they do have a dump site.

Cape Kiwanda & Pacific City ❾

✕ Delicate Palate   Fusion $$$

(☎503-965-6464; 35280 Brooten Rd; mains $26-32; ⏱4-9pm Wed-Sun) The foodie's splurge for this stretch of coast. Dine on specialties like Asian seafood bouillabaisse and oven roasted rack of lamb in huckleberry red wine reduction sauce. It also has a bar with a more basic menu and outdoor seating.

✕ The Grateful Bread   Cafe & Bakery $

(34805 Brooten Rd; mains $9-12; ⏱8am-3pm Thu-Mon) Start with heaping portions of fresh and delicious soups, salads, tacos, Dory-caught fish, veggie and meat dishes then finish with fabulous fresh breads, cookies, desserts and maybe a souvenir tie-dyed T-shirt.

⛺ Pelican Pub & Brewery   American $$

(Cape Kiwanda; mains $12-32; ⏱8am-10pm Sun-Thu, 8am-11pm Sat & Sun) The food is only OK but a good beer selection and setting, with tables inches from the sand, make it worth a stop.

⛺ Inn at Cape Kiwanda   Hotel $$$

(☎888-965-7001; www.yourlittlebeachtown. com/inn; 33105 Cape Kiwanda Dr; r $163-262; 📶🛖) A classy and popular place that offers luxurious seaview rooms, balconies and a location to die for.

Stoller Vineyards Sustainable, well-heralded wines

Willamette Valley Wine Tour

15

Country roads lead through Pinot Noir–covered hills to small wineries with fresh, bucolic views and renowned vintages.

TRIP HIGHLIGHTS

14 miles

Carlton
Charming small town with tasting rooms and eateries

8 miles

Brick House Vineyards
A quintessential Oregon winery complete with compost heaps and friendly dogs

③

④

• Newberg
START/ FINISH

⑥

Lafayette •

⑤

McMinnville
Find food and wine action in the historic downtown

22 miles

Domaine Drouhin Oregon
The majestic setting and wines offer a whiff of France

33 miles

**2 DAYS
50 MILES/80KM**

GREAT FOR...

BEST TIME TO GO
April to August for sunshine on green hills.

ESSENTIAL PHOTO
Domaine Drouhin Oregon: take a picture of Pinot Noir vines with a view of the valley.

BEST SCENERY
Stop 6 through stop 8: take in the hillside beauty of the Dundee Hills appellation.

DANITA DELIMONT STOCK / AWL IMAGES ©

15 | Willamette Valley Wine Tour

Oregon's Willamette Valley stretches over 100 miles from Eugene to Portland and more than 200 wineries lie within its six subappellations. Most of these are approachable, family-run operations dedicated to producing small quantities of high-quality Pinot Noir and sometimes other varietals. Organic, sustainable practices are the norm. This trip takes in the top half of the valley where you'll find the greatest concentration of wineries amid scenic farmlands.

1 Newberg

The gateway to the Willamette Valley wine country was founded as a Quaker settlement and ironically was 'dry' for most of its early history. It's the biggest town in the area (population 23,312) and the one whose historic architecture has been most surrounded and overwhelmed by strip malls and fast-food joints. Still, it's a convenient place to stay and start your trip.

✕ ⍞ p177

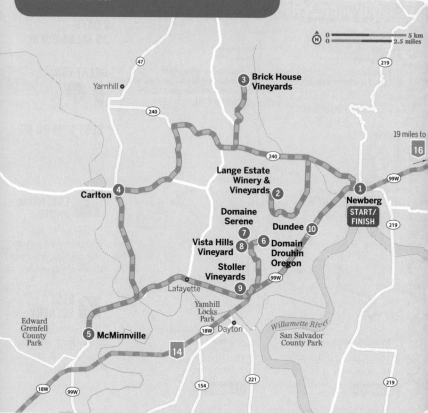

The Drive » Take Hwy 240 west where the landscape quickly turns into the beautiful vineyard-covered countryside you came here for. Turn right on Red Hills Rd and follow the signs up to Lange, 3.5 miles from the turn-off. The last half is on a well-maintained gravel road.

- - - - - - - - - - -

② Lange Estate Winery & Vineyards

Your first tasting is at the **Lange Estate Winery & Vineyards** (📞503-538-6476; www.langewinery.com; 18380 NE Buena Vista Dr, Dundee; tasting free; ⏰11am-5pm daily), founded by one of the valley's earlier families. Here you'll find all the makings of an authentic Willamette Valley winery: gorgeous views, good wines and shaggy dogs. It's very much a family affair and they're known for their good-value Pinot Noir called Three Hills Cuvee.

LINK YOUR TRIP

16 **Columbia River Gorge & Mt Hood**

Head back through Portland and east on Historic Highway 30 (p179).

14 **Three Capes Loop**

Take the loop backwards by driving to Pacific City from Hwy 99W (p163).

TOP TIP: MARK YOUR CALENDAR

Many Willamette Valley wineries are open for tastings only on certain days of the week (usually Wednesday through Sunday or just the weekend) while others offer visits by appointment only. But on Memorial Day and Thanksgiving Day weekends, nearly all of the valley's wineries open their doors to the public – no reservations required. These are widely publicized and very busy weekends. Inside tip: most wineries also open their doors on the weekends prior to these...for those in the know.

The Drive » Head back down to Hwy 240, turn left, drive about 3 miles and turn right at Ribbon Ridge Rd. After about 2.5 miles, turn right on Lewis Rogers Lane to Brick House Vineyards.

- - - - - - - - - - -

TRIP HIGHLIGHT

③ Brick House Vineyards

Lying within the Ribbon Ridge appellation, **Brick House Vineyards** (📞503-538-5136; www.brickhousewines.com; 18200 Lewis Rogers Lane, Newberg; tasting fee $10; ⏰1-4pm Sat & by appointment) is another classically Oregonian winery. Brick House's owner, Doug Tunnel, is a former CBS foreign correspondent and an Oregon native. He's also one of the state's pioneers in organic farming. And the winery is great. Drive up and dogs come out to greet you. Stand in the barn and look out over the vines and the compost piles

and you'll get a sense of the unpretentious charm that makes the Willamette Valley so special. The winery itself occupies a converted barn and the Pinot Noir, Chardonnay and Gamay Noir poured here are as fine as the experience is fresh.

The Drive » Go back down Ribbon Ridge Rd and turn right on Hwy 240. After about 2 miles turn left onto Stag Hollow Rd, then right on Carlton–Chehalem Creek Rd, which eventually turns into Carlton's Main St.

- - - - - - - - - - -

TRIP HIGHLIGHT

④ Carlton

It's hard to come up with a better descriptive word for Carlton than 'adorable.' Just a few streets wide, the town is made up almost entirely of pretty, historic buildings that house an impressive number of tasting rooms, great restaurants, antique shops, a jam maker and a fabulous French-style bakery. You won't find a better stop for lunch, and it's also a lovely place to stay overnight. If you're here on a Friday or Saturday, head to the particularly well-respected **Scott Paul Wines** (☎503-852-7300; www.scottpaul.com; 128 S Pine St, Carlton; tasting fee $5; ⏱11am-4pm Fri & Sat, by appointment Wed-Sat), which only produces Pinot Noirs. Whenever you're here, be sure to wander around town aimlessly to turn up plenty of delicious surprises.

✖️ 🛏️ p177

The Drive » Go south on Tualatin Valley Hwy 47. After about 4.5 miles turn right on Hwy 19 which goes right into downtown McMinnville.

- - - - - - - - - - - - -

TRIP HIGHLIGHT

❺ McMinnville

At the heart of the region's wine industry lies McMinnville. Stay within its historic, red-brick downtown district and you'll find older buildings, art galleries, boutiques and fine restaurants, along with a small-town feel as kids play on sidewalks and tourists stroll up and down the main artery of 3rd St; head outside this area and this image is dimmed by modern housing communities and shopping areas. It's a great place to stay, eat and end your tour of the wine region.

As you'd expect, there are also several wineries and tasting rooms that you can easily find by taking a stroll around downtown. The most special is **Eyrie Vineyards** (☎503-472-6315; www.eyrievineyards.com; 935 NE 10th St; tasting fee $5; ⏱tasting room noon-5pm Wed-Sun). The owner here, David 'Papa Pinot' Lett, planted the region's first vines (including the first Pinot Gris in the USA) in 1965 and the first wines were produced in 1970. Today David's son, Jason, runs the operation.

✖️ 🛏️ p177

The Drive » Head northeast on Hwy 99W. After 8 miles turn left at OR 18W/SE Dayton Bypass then take an immediate right onto NE MacDougall Rd. After half a mile turn left on NE Breyman Orchards Rd and follow the signs to Domaine Drouhin.

- - - - - - - - - - - - -

TRIP HIGHLIGHT

❻ Domaine Drouhin Oregon

You may be on day two at this point and it's time for a little more glamour. Owned by renowned Burgundy producer Maison Joseph Drouhin, **Domaine Drouhin Oregon** (☎503-864-2700; www.domainedrouhin.com; 6750 Breyman Orchards Rd, Dayton; tasting fee $10; ⏱tasting room 11am-4pm Wed-Sun) is famed as much for its history as it is for its Pinot Noir. The winery

owes its existence in part to the 1979 Gault Millau 'Wine Olympics', a blind tasting held in France. In the competition, McMinnville's Eyrie Vineyards placed in the top 10, holding its own against France's most esteemed Pinots, including one from the respected Maison Joseph Drouhin. This stoked Drouhin's already existing

DANITA DELIMONT STOCK / AWL IMAGES ©

Newberg A winemaker uses nitrogen to push Pinot Noir from a barrel

interest in the Willamette Valley (Drouhin first visited the valley in 1961), and he soon decided it was time to extend the family's operation. In 1988 he opened Domaine Drouhin Oregon under the management of his daughter, winemaker Véronique Drouhin. She still makes the wine and the top picks are named after her three children.

Today the winery is one of the most elegant and scenically located in the valley and the wines, which are made from grapes planted in the French style with vines close together, have a distinct old-world touch.

The Drive >> Go straight out the driveway across Breyman Orchards Rd (don't turn) and follow the signs for Domaine Serene.

- - - - - - - - - -

⑦ Domaine Serene

Domaine Serene
(☎503-864-4600; www. domaineserene.com; 6555 NE Hilltop Lane, Dayton; tasting fee $15; ☺ tasting room 11am-4pm Wed-Mon) is one of the Willamette Valley's best-known wineries heralded, as would be expected, for its Pinot Noir. It's a grand, modern

TOP TIP: SPIT & DRIVE

Some words of advice: when tasting wine, learn to spit. That bucket is there for a reason. Spitting will actually mark you as a pro rather than an amateur.

place with a stunning wine cellar and lovely views over the rolling hills and vineyards that sweep across the valley. Along with Pinot Noir, the winery produces highly regarded Chardonnays and a Syrah, which it makes from grapes grown in Washington State's Walla Walla region. You can go with the standard tasting-room-only wine tasting or tour the entire winery, including the cellar, as part of the VIP tour – that, however, will cost you extra.

The Drive › Turn right out of the driveway and don't blink or you'll miss Vista Hills Vineyard, your next stop.

⑧ Vista Hills Vineyard

A short hop down the road is **Vista Hills Vineyard** (☏503-864-3200; www.vistahillsvineyard.com; 6475 Hilltop Lane, Dayton; tasting fee $10; ⊙noon-5pm Wed-Sun) with wonderful views from the cozy Treehouse Tasting Room that's literally up in the trees. This

unpretentious place offers a unique approach to wine making: Vista Hills' wines (Pinot Noir and a delicious fruity Pinot Gris) are made in several different facilities around the valley using Vista Hills grapes. The subtleties of vintages, in other words, are determined by more than just the weather. Another unique trait: 10% of its profits go to a foundation created by the owners to offer financial support to students pursuing higher education. It should come as no surprise that sustainability is one of the winery's core values.

The Drive › Go back down Breyman Orchards Rd and turn right at NE MacDougall Rd. Stoller Vinyards is about a mile along.

⑨ Stoller Vineyards

On the site of what was once the biggest turkey farm in Oregon, **Stoller Vineyards** (☏503-864-3404; www.stollervineyards.com; 16161 NE McDougall Rd, Dayton; tasting fee $10; ⊙tasting room 11am-5pm Sat & Sun) is one of

the most ecologically sustainable wineries in the country, if not the world. The winery building holds the US Green Building Council's gold-level certification for Leadership in Energy and Environmental Design, plus the architecture (that looks like a cross between a grain elevator and a barn – but prettier) is true to the site's history. It produces well-heralded Pinot Noirs and Chardonnays.

The Drive › Backtrack east on NE MacDougall Rd, drive a little over a mile then turn right onto Hwy 99W. You'll be in central Dundee in under 4 miles.

⑩ Dundee

Dundee is the hub of the Dundee Hills, the Willamette Valley's preeminent subappellation, where you've already visited three superb wineries. Now it's time to see what the region can produce for lunch and chances are you won't be disappointed. Although Dundee isn't the most scenic of the region's towns, it's pleasant enough with a few parks and early 20th-century homes. The real draw, however, is that it's teeming with fabulous restaurants.

✕ ⊨ p177

Eating & Sleeping

Newberg ❶

✖ Painted Lady   Northwestern $$$

(☎503-538-3850; www.thepaintedladyrestaurant
.com; 201 S College St; prix fixe $60-100; ☺dinner
Wed-Sun) Local, organic and seasonal ingredients
are emphasized in the four-course menu, served
in an 1890s Victorian house.

🛏 Allison Inn & Spa   Resort $$$

(☎503-554-2525, 877-294-2525; www.
theallison.com; 2525 Allison Lane; d from $295;
☺❄🛜🏊) Spacious, plush rooms, relaxing
soaking tubs, an excellent restaurant, gorgeous
stone landscaping, their own vineyard nearby,
and they're eco-friendly to boot.

Carlton ❹

✖ Horseradish   Cheese & Wine Bar $$

(211 West Main St; meals $7-12; ☺noon-3pm
Mon-Thu, noon-10pm Fri & Sat, 1-5pm Sun)
Gourmet meals, cheese plates and a wine bar.
Hosts live music on Friday and Saturday nights.

🛏 Brookside Inn
On Abbey Road   B&B $$$

(☎503-852-4433; www.brooksideinn-oregon.
com; 8243 NE Abbey Rd; r $180-350) Luxurious
nine-room guesthouse in the heart of wine
country.

🛏 Casa Della Valle   B&B $

(☎503-852-0189, www.airbnb.com; 819 South
Pine Rd; d $65-75) Like a museum of tasteful
early-20th-century bric-a-brac, super friendly
and right in town.

McMinnville ❺

✖ Nick's Italian Cafe   Italian $$

(☎503-434-4471; www.nicksitaliancafe.com;
521 NE 3rd St; mains $12-26; ☺11:30am-2:30pm
& 5-9pm Mon-Fri, 5-9pm Sat, noon-8pm Sun)
Going strong for over 30 years, Nick's has
excellent wood-fired pizza and Italian fare that's
a favorite with local wine makers.

✖ Joel Palmer House   Northwestern $$$

(☎503-864-2995; www.joelpalmerhouse.com;
600 Ferry St, Dayton; mains $29-37; ☺5-9pm
Tue-Sat) Fine dining; the chef, a fun guy,
specializes in mushrooms.

✖ Thistle   Northwestern $$

(☎503-472-9623; www.thistlerestaurant.com;
228 NE Evans St; mains $18-20; ☺dinner Tue-
Sat) The locally inspired, organic menu changes
daily; portions are small, well-created and truly
delicious.

🛏 McMenamins Hotel Oregon   Hotel $

(☎503-472-8427, 888-472-8427; www.
mcmenamins.com; 310 NE Evans St; d $50-110;
☺❄🛜) Expect eccentricities like eclectic
artwork on all the walls; most of the classic old
rooms share bathrooms, which are kept in good
order.

🛏 Joseph Mattey House B&B   B&B $$

(☎503-434-5058; www.josephmatteyhouse.
com; 10221 NE Mattey Lane; d $150-175;
☺❄🛜) An 1892 Queen Anne Victorian
farmhouse featuring country-style atmosphere,
charming old details and four comfortable
rooms with quilts and lace.

Dundee ❾

✖ Recipe   Mediterranean $$

(www.recipenewbergor.com; 115 N Washington
St; lunch $7-16, dinner $16-23; ☺11:30am-9pm
Tue-Sat) Adorably cozy space serving perfectly
made French- and Italian- inspired stews,
steaks and pastas, as well as their house-made
charcuterie.

🛏 Black Walnut Inn & Vineyard   Inn $$$

(☎503-429-4114, 866-429-4114; www.
blackwalnut-inn.com; 9600 NE Worden Hill Rd; r
$295-425) One of the Willamette Valley's most
luxurious lodgings.

Multnomah Falls The highest
waterfall in Oregon

Classic Trip

Columbia River Gorge & Mt Hood

16

Towering waterfalls, excellent hiking, hot springs, fruit farms – what else could you want from a long weekend? Add shimmering lakes and snow-capped Mt Hood, and the diversity becomes surreal.

TRIP HIGHLIGHTS

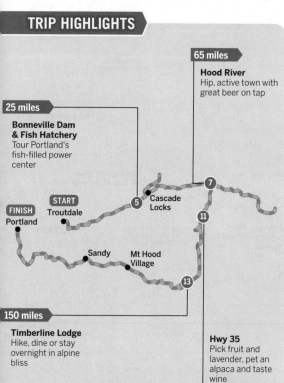

65 miles

Hood River
Hip, active town with great beer on tap

25 miles

Bonneville Dam & Fish Hatchery
Tour Portland's fish-filled power center

START Troutdale

FINISH Portland

5 Cascade Locks

7

11

Sandy   Mt Hood Village

13

150 miles

Timberline Lodge
Hike, dine or stay overnight in alpine bliss

Hwy 35
Pick fruit and lavender, pet an alpaca and taste wine

125 miles

3 DAYS
215 MILES/346KM

GREAT FOR...

BEST TIME TO GO

May to October: fruit is in season, everything is lush and all roads are open.

ESSENTIAL PHOTO

Multnomah Falls – get a top-to-bottom shot of one of the country's highest cascades.

BEST FOR VIEWS

Enjoy a panorama of the lushest part of the Columbia Gorge from Vista House.

179

16 Columbia River Gorge & Mt Hood

Few places symbolize the grandeur of the Pacific Northwest like the Columbia River Gorge and Mt Hood. Start along this massive cleft in the Cascade Range that measures up to 4000ft deep and is graced by 77 waterfalls. Meanwhile, great white Mt Hood peeks out from behind in all its 11,240ft glory. As you drive up the mountain from the gorge you'll be treated to a fertile foodie heaven of fruit farms and vineyards.

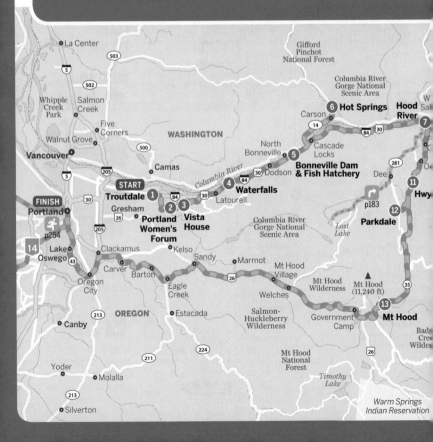

❶ Troutdale

Although the metal arch over Troutdale (erected in 2010) isn't the official entrée to the Historic Route 30 (which starts a few miles west from here), this is the logical place to turn off the I-84 from Portland and begin a journey into Columbia Gorge's moss-covered wonderland. Troutdale's center is adorably early-20th-century and a pleasant place to stretch your legs before the drive.

🛏 p187

The Drive » Continue through town then turn right (inland) after the bridge, following the signs for Historic Route 30 toward Corbett. The road follows the forested Sandy River before veering left.

❷ Portland Women's Forum

Pull into this parking lot for your first view of the Columbia Gorge. This spot was once the site of the Chanticleer Hotel, built in 1912. It was here, in 1913, that the plans were made for building Hwy 30, which would become Oregon's first modern paved road. Unfortunately the hotel burned down in 1931 but the panoramas are as splendid as ever.

The Drive » Turn left from the parking lot, drive along the ridge and watch as Hwy 30 turns into classic Columbia Gorge country, with increasing mossy lushness.

❸ Vista House

Built between 1916 and 1918, this stone roadside rotunda sits atop Crown Point, 733ft above the Columbia River, and offers magnificent 180-degree views. From the outside, the building looks like it only houses a small information center, but there's a worthwhile historical **museum** (admission free; ◷10am-4pm) and gift shop hidden down a staircase underground. Weather permitting, you can also go upstairs to the fabulous outdoor viewing deck.

The Drive » Take a right directly out of the parking lot and head downhill as the road winds along the old highway and its stone barriers into increasing greenery.

❹ Waterfalls

Welcome to a land so lush and vibrantly green that it looks more like something described in a fantasy novel than reality. This 9-mile section of Hwy 30 could easily be nicknamed 'Waterfall Alley' for the excessive number of

🔗 LINK YOUR TRIP

17 Journey Through Time Scenic Byway

From The Dalles, it's about 30 miles east along Hwy 84 and the Columbia River Gorge to Maryhill (p191).

14 Three Capes Loop

Head back through Portland and go west on Hwy 26 toward the coast (p163).

Classic Trip

spectacular cascades tumbling over mossy basalt cliffs. The falls are at their gushiest in spring. If you're into hiking you could easily spend a day or two exploring this area, or you can take short walks to the easier access places. **Multnomah Falls**

is the highest in Oregon and the busiest stop – you'll find more peace and quiet around the lesser-known spots.

The Drive » Keep heading east on Hwy 30 till it merges with I-84 shortly after Ainsworth State Park. After a few miles, take exit 40 toward Bonneville Dam.

TRIP HIGHLIGHT

5 Bonneville Dam & Fish Hatchery

Upon its completion in 1938, Bonneville

became the first dam on the Columbia River, permanently altering one of the continent's mightiest rivers, as well as one of the world's most important salmon runs. It's worth stopping here to check out the **visitors center** (☎541-374-8820; admission free; ☺9am-5pm) that has good exhibits, free tours to the powerhouse throughout the day and a theater showing videos of the dam's history; the underwater viewing room into the fish ladder is a highlight. Afterwards, stroll the nearby fish hatchery, making sure to visit the gargantuan 10ft-long sturgeon named Herman.

The Drive » Get back on I-84 and drive about 3.5 miles upstream to exit 44, which leads you to the Bridge of the Gods (toll $1 each way) into Washington State. Turn east on Hwy 14.

6 Hot Springs

Feel like a nice warm soak to ease your car-stiff bum? **Carson Hot Spring Resort** (☎509-427-8292; www.carsonhotspringresort.com; 372 St Martin Rd, Carson; mineral baths $20; ☺spa 8am-7pm) is hardly fancy, but its modesty is its finest feature; the first-come, first-served mineral baths are a true escape from any kind of hype. To get there, turn left on

---

TOP WATERFALLS

The following are all off Hwy 30, listed from west to east.

Latourell Falls (249ft) The first major waterfall as you come east on Hwy 30. Hike 10 minutes to reach it, or go a mile to the top.

Bridal Veil Falls (140ft) Two-tiered falls reached via an easy half-mile walk. A separate wheelchair-accessible trail passes through a meadow.

Wahkeena Falls (242ft) Hike up the Wahkeena Trail, join Trail No 441 and head down to Multnomah Falls. Return via the road for the 5-mile loop.

Multnomah Falls (642ft) The gorge's top attraction. Trail No 411 leads to the top (1 mile). Continue up foresty Multnomah Creek and the top of Larch Mountain (another 7 miles).

Oneonta Falls (75ft) Located within the lovely half-mile Oneonta Gorge. Carefully scamper over log jams and wade in water up to waist-high. Fun and worth it!

Horsetail Falls (176ft) Just east of Oneonta Gorge. A 4.5-mile loop begins here, passing through Ponytail Falls and Triple Falls. Walk a half-mile east on Hwy 30 (passing the Oneonta Gorge) to return.

Elowah Falls (289ft) More isolated but pretty falls located about a mile off the highway. Hike to the top, then take a 0.7-mile side trail to McCord Creek Falls (2.5 miles round-trip).

DETOUR: LOST LAKE

Start: 7 Hood River

For a classic Mt Hood photo op, detour 25 miles south of Hood River to the spectacular Lost Lake. Flanked by forest, this stunning blue body of mountain water frames the white cone of Mt Hood like a perfect postcard. Along with fabulous views, the detour offers respite from the heat when the gorge gets too hot. To get there from Hood River, take Hwy 281 to Dee and follow the signs. Allow at least half a day for the excursion.

Wind River Rd from Hwy 14, then take a right on Hot Springs Ave.

For a more luxurious experience, head to **Bonneville Hot Springs Resort & Spa** (☎866-459-1678; www.bonnevilleresort.com; 1252 E Cascade Dr, North Bonneville; pool day use Mon-Thu $15, Fri-Sun $25), which has an elegant 25m indoor pool filled with mineral water, plus indoor and outdoor Jacuzzis. Look for the entrance road ('Hot Springs Way') across from the Washington Bonneville Dam visitor center road.

🛏 p187

The Drive 》 Backtrack over the Bridge of the Gods, then head east on I-84.

TRIP HIGHLIGHT

7 Hood River

Your next stop is the windy riverside town of Hood River, one of the world's top windsurfing and kiteboarding destinations. It's also one very attractive town, thanks to its old homes

and stunning setting on the Columbia River. Plus Mt Hood, with its hiking trails and ski runs, is only a stone's throw away. It should come as no surprise that Hood River has a youthful, adrenaline-hungry population and a main drag packed with good restaurants, boutique shops and adventure sports stores.

🍴 🛏 p187

The Drive 》 Get back on I-84 E for around 10 miles, then take exit 69 to Mosier. This links you back up with Historic Route 30 for another incredibly scenic 9 miles.

---

8 Rowena Crest

The summit of this portion of Historic Route 30 has a parking lot with views over the Columbia Gorge, which at this point is losing its lushness to windy, barren hillsides and steep, stratified cliff faces. Here there are two hiking trails: the walk to **Tom McCall Point**

Trail (3 miles round-trip) will get you glimpses over the rolling hills of the plateau and Mt Adams, while the easier **Rowena Plateau Trail** (2.5 miles round-trip) is a particular good spot for May wildflowers and leads to the waterfowl-filled **Rowena Pond**.

The Drive 》 Historic Route 30 winds down the hill back to river level. Follow the signs to the Columbia Gorge Discovery Center.

---

9 Columbia Gorge Discovery Center

The informative **Columbia Gorge Discovery Center** (☎541-296-8600; www.gorgediscovery.org; 5000 Discovery Dr; adult/child $8/4; ◷9am-5pm) covers the history of the gorge from its creation by cataclysmic floods, through its Native American inhabitants, to the early pioneers, settlers and eventual damming of the river. Whether you're a gorge fanatic or a first-time visitor, the center will undoubtedly increase

Classic Trip

WHY THIS IS A CLASSIC TRIP
CELESTE BRASH, AUTHOR

Few routes take in this much beauty in so small a space – not only that but all this starts only a half-hour from downtown Portland! The waterfall strip of the Columbia Gorge is one of the most beautiful places I know, and Mt Hood's sharp snowy peak is symbolic of the region. The hiking is phenomenal, the people you meet are down to earth, and you can pick fruit and drink fabulous beer and wine.

Top: Mount Hood Railroad
Left: Crown Point
Right: Bonneville Dam

BOB POOL / GETTY IMAGES ©

JOHN ELK III / ALAMY ©

your appreciation for one of the Pacific Northwest's most amazing natural landscapes.

The Drive » Go back out to Historic Route 30 or I-84 (they run parallel to each other from here but Historic Route 30 is more scenic), east a couple of miles to The Dalles.

❿ The Dalles

Though steadfastly unglamorous, The Dalles offers decent camping and hiking, and the fierce winds are excellent for windsurfing and kiteboarding. Sights here include the fascinating **Fort Dalles Museum** (☎541-296-4547; www. fortdallesmuseum.org; 500 W 15th St; adult/child $5/1; ◷10am-4pm); it's Oregon's oldest museum and is full of historical items. Built in 1957, **The Dalles Dam & Lock** produces enough electricity to power a city of a million inhabitants. **The Dalles Dam Visitors Center** (☎541-296-9778; Clodfelter Way; ◷9am-5pm Jun-Sep) contains the expected homage to hydroelectricity, along with a fish cam to view migratory salmon – it's east on the frontage road from exit 87 off I-84.

🛏 p187

The Drive » From here you'll backtrack on Historic Route 30 or I-84 (the faster option) to Hood River. Take exit 64 and follow the signs for Hwy 35, which leads inland toward Mt Hood.

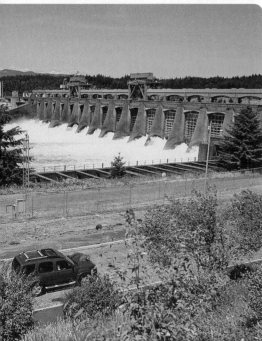

BUDDY MAYS / ALAMY ©

Classic Trip

⓫ Highway 35

The first 16.5 miles of Hwy 35 to Parkdale is the first leg of the 'Fruit Loop,' named for all its agriculture. Wind along scenic fertile lands, easy-to-spot family fruit stands, U-pick orchards, lavender fields, alpaca farms and winery tasting rooms. There are blossoms in spring, berries in summer, and apples and pears in fall – with plenty of festivals and celebrations throughout the seasons (except for winter). It's a good way to sample the area's agricultural bounties while appreciating the local scenery too – try not to get in an accident from ogling the larger-than-life Mt Hood when it's in view.

The Drive » Enjoy the scenery of endless orchards and vineyards, and stop whenever you feel the whim – there are over 30 businesses to choose from!

⓬ Parkdale

Your ascent ends at the little town of Parkdale, a great stop for lunch.

MOUNT HOOD RAILROAD

If you're tired of the road, the **Mount Hood Railroad** (www.mthoodrr.com) also starts here and runs scenically up a similar route to Hwy 35, past the towns of Odell and Dee before its terminus in Parkdale. The views are spectacular, the cars are beautifully restored and the food is memorable. You can also choose to go on special train excursions that include wine tasting and visits to museums.

You can also visit the tiny **Hutson Museum** (4967 Baseline Dr; admission $1; ☺ limited hours Apr-Oct) in a country-perfect red farmhouse. It has displays of rocks and minerals, Native American artifacts and local memorabilia – plus a garden of native plants.

 p187

The Drive » Return to Hwy 35 and follow it south for 27 miles around grand, white-capped Mt Hood to Hwy 26.

⓭ Mt Hood

At 11,240ft, Mt Hood is the highest peak in Oregon. Its pyramid shape makes it peek out from behind many hills, ever enhancing the view. The best place to enjoy this alpine world is **Timberline Lodge** (☎503-272-3158, snow report 503-222-2211; www.timberlinelodge. com; lift tickets adult/child $56/36), a handsome wooden gem from the 1930s, offering glorious shelter and refreshments to both guests and nonguests (and yes, some exterior shots of *The Shining* were filmed here). In summer, wildflowers bloom on the mountainsides and hidden ponds shimmer in blue, making for some unforgettable hikes; in winter, downhill and cross-country skiing dominates people's minds and bodies.

From here there's also convenient access to the **Pacific Crest Trail** (PCT). Whether you hike 2 miles or 12 miles along the PCT, the views of Mt Hood are incredible. The trail is easy to find – follow the signs to the right of the lodge.

p187

The Drive » Continuing about 6 miles northwest down Hwy 26, you'll come to the town of Government Camp. From here it's another 56 miles through forest-clad villages and eventually suburban sprawl to Portland, where the trip ends.

Eating & Sleeping

Troutdale ❶

🛏 McMenamins Edgefield   Hotel $

(📞503-492-3086; www.mcmenamins.com; 2126 SW Halsey St; dm $35, r $58-120; 🚗) Not just a great hotel: there's also a golf course, brewery, restaurant, movie theater, live music and gardens.

Hot Springs ❻

🛏 Bonneville Hot Springs Resort & Spa   Hotel $$$

(📞866-459-1678; www.bonnevilleresort.com; 1252 E Cascade Dr, North Bonneville; d from $200; ❄ @ 🛜 🏊) Offers grand, stylish rooms, fine dining and full spa services.

🛏 Carson Hot Springs Resort   Hotel $

(📞509-427-8292; www.carsonhotspringresort.com; 372 St Martin Rd, Carson; r from $80) Locally loved but rustic resort.

Hood River ❼

🍴 Celilo Restaurant & Bar   Northwestern $$

(📞541-386-5710; www.celilorestaurant.com; 16 Oak St; mains $16-21; 🕐lunch & dinner) A modern and beautiful restaurant that uses quality, sustainable ingredients.

🍴 Double Mountain Brewery   Pub $

(www.doublemountainbrewery.com; 8 4th St; sandwiches $6.50-9, pizzas $14-20; 🕐11:30am-11pm Sun-Thu, to midnight Fri & Sat) Step into this small brewpub for a tasty sandwich or excellent brick-oven pizza. Limited menu, but the food is great and the beer even better.

🛏 Columbia Gorge Hotel   Hotel $$$

(📞541-386-5566; www.columbiagorgehotel.com; 4000 Westcliff Dr; d $209-289; ❄ @ 🛜) A historic Spanish-style hotel, set high on a cliff above the Columbia River.

🛏 Inn of the White Salmon   Inn $

(📞509-493-2335; www.innofthewhitesalmon.com; 172 West Jewett Blvd; dm $25, d $90-135; ❄ 🛜) Over the bridge in White Salmon is this pleasant and contemporary 16-room inn with comfortable guest rooms in different styles.

The Dalles ❿

🛏 Celilo Inn   Boutique Motel $$

(📞541-769-0001; www.celiloinn.com; 3550 E 2nd St; d $109-240; ❄ @ 🛜 🏊) A slick and trendy spot with gorgeous contemporary rooms, many offering views of The Dalles' bridge and dam.

Parkdale ⓬

🍴 Apple Valley BBQ   Barbecue $$

(4956 Baseline Dr; lunch $7-12, dinner $12-20; 🕐11am-8pm Wed-Sun) Barbecue ribs, pulled pork, burgers, salads and homemade pie in a 1950s flashback setting.

Mt Hood ⓭

🛏 Timberline Lodge   Lodge $$

(📞503-272-3311; www.timberlinelodge.com; d $110-290; 🛜 🏊) More a community treasure than a hotel, this gorgeous historic lodge offers a variety of rooms, from bunk rooms that sleep up to 10 to luxury suites. Fine cuisine with a Northwestern emphasis is offered at the elegant **Cascade Dining Room** (mains $22-34), with great views and atmosphere.

Government Camp

🍴 Ice Axe Grill   Brewpub $$

(www.iceaxegrill.com; 87304 E Government Camp Loop; mains $12-18; 🕐11:30am-9pm Sun-Thu, till 10pm Fri & Sat) Offers a friendly, family-style atmosphere and pub fare including good pizzas, shepherd's pie and gorgonzola-and-pepper bacon burgers.

Painted Hills Sunset emphasizes the colors of these striking hills

Journey Through Time Scenic Byway

17

An epic drive across windswept plains, desolate badlands and forested mountain passes. Visit ghost towns and fossil beds, gold-mining sites and small-town museums.

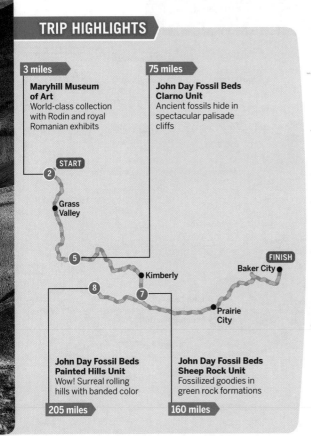

3 miles

Maryhill Museum of Art
World-class collection with Rodin and royal Romanian exhibits

75 miles

John Day Fossil Beds Clarno Unit
Ancient fossils hide in spectacular palisade cliffs

START
2

Grass Valley

5

FINISH
Baker City

Kimberly

8

7

Prairie City

John Day Fossil Beds Painted Hills Unit
Wow! Surreal rolling hills with banded color

205 miles

John Day Fossil Beds Sheep Rock Unit
Fossilized goodies in green rock formations

160 miles

**3 DAYS
363 MILES/584KM**

GREAT FOR...

BEST TIME TO GO
June to September for warm temperatures and less rain.

ESSENTIAL PHOTO

John Day Fossil Beds Painted Hills Unit – the love-child of a *National Geographic* spread and a Mark Rothko painting.

BEST FOR HISTORY

The Thomas Condon Paleontology Center.

189

17 Journey Through Time Scenic Byway

Unless you count the futuristic-looking windmills around the town of Wasco, a more precise name for this state scenic byway would be Journey *Back* in Time Scenic Byway. From the moment you leave Hwy 84 it's truly a time warp: ghost towns lie off the roadside, fossils expose millions of years of history, and even the restaurants and hotels make you feel you've driven into decades past.

❶ Stonehenge

Although it's not part of the official byway, the perfect place to kick off your time travel is at the full-scale replica of **Stonehenge** (admission free; ⏰7am-10pm), on the Washington side of the Columbia River, just east of Hwy 97. Built by eccentric businessman Sam Hill as a memorial to the 13 men in Klickitat County killed in WWI, the site is a completed version of the Salisbury Plain monument, although its detractors

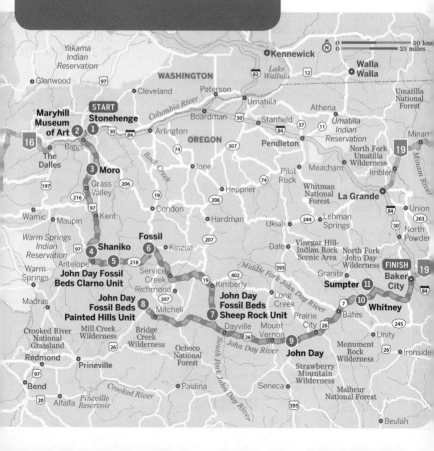

argue that the keystone is incorrectly aligned with the stars.

The Drive » Turn left on Hwy 14 and drive about four miles to the Maryhill Museum of Art.

TRIP HIGHLIGHT

❷ Maryhill Museum of Art

The spectacular **Maryhill Museum of Art** (www.maryhillmuseum.org; 35 Maryhill Museum Dr, Goldendale, WA; adult/child/senior $9/3/8; ⏰9am-5pm Mar 15-Nov 15; ♿), set in a mansion on a bluff above the Columbia River, was another Sam Hill project. Among its eclectic exhibits is a noteworthy collection of Rodin sculptures, a room full of decadent objects once belonging to

LINK YOUR TRIP

16 Columbia River Gorge & Mt Hood

From The Dalles it's only about 30 miles east along Hwy 84 and the Columbia River Gorge to Maryhill (p179).

19 Hells Canyon Scenic Byway

The Hells Canyon Scenic Byway begins in Baker City right where this trip ends so they link up perfectly (p205).

Queen Marie of Romania and Native American artifacts.

The Drive » Make a right on Hwy 14 then another right two miles later onto Hwy 97, which takes you over the Columbia River via the Sam Hill Memorial Bridge. The scenic byway officially begins in the town of Biggs. From here it's about 20 miles to the next stop past grassy hills, wind farms and homesteads.

❸ Moro

In Moro you'll find **Sherman County Historical Museum** (www.shermanmuseum.org; 200 Dewey St, Moro; adult/student $3/1; ⏰10am-5pm May 1-Oct 31; ♿). For a small-town museum it has some surprisingly interesting exhibits, including on the history of wheat production, Native Americans and rural living in the days of old. The town is also home to a handful of antique shops that are worth a browse.

The Drive » South on Hwy 97 you'll be treated to breathtaking views of several volcanoes in the distance, including Mt Hood, Mt Jefferson and Mt Adams. Continue on 35 miles through the near-deserted towns of Grass Valley and Kent.

❹ Shaniko

This wee ghost town (population 26) was once the wool-shipping center of the US. Its decrepit old buildings make for exceptional photo ops, and its architectural

grand dame, the Shaniko Hotel, is one of the finer historic buildings in eastern Oregon. (It was recently refurbished but was closed and up for sale when we passed.) A few shops and a tiny museum are open through summer.

The Drive » Continue south on Hwy 218. About a mile out the road narrows and winds as it descends through sagebrush-covered hills to the minuscule settlement of Antelope. Turn east here onto Hwy 218 and drive about 16 miles to the next stop.

TRIP HIGHLIGHT

❺ John Day Fossil Beds Clarno Unit

Dramatically eroded Palisade Cliffs mark your arrival at the John Day Fossil Beds Clarno Unit, your first stop in the **John Day Fossil Beds National Monument** (www.nps.gov/joda; admission free; ⏰all units daylight hours year-round; ♿) trilogy. The short trails and fossil remains plunge you into a time more than 40 million years ago, when the region was subtropical forest. Wander the half-mile Geologic Time Trail to the Trail of Fossils, and you'll see boulder-sized fossils of logs, seeds and other remains from the ancient forest. The quarter-mile Arch Trail leads to a natural arch in the striking Palisade Cliffs.

The Drive » Continue 18 miles northeast to Fossil.

WITOLD SKRYPCZAK / GETTY IMAGES ©

6 Fossil

The town of Fossil (population 370) is aptly named given that it's in the middle of paleontology heaven. It's a good stop for lunch and you can browse the town's very small **Fossil Museum** (cnr Adams St & 4th St; admission by donation; ⏰9am-4pm Mon, 1-4pm Wed-Sun) or dig for fossils in the town's **public digging area** ($5 per person for up to two handfuls). You're pretty much guaranteed to find something and there's usually someone around to help explain what you've dug up.

The Drive ››› Head 20 miles southeast on Hwy 19 to the tiny Service Creek (population 2), an old stagecoach stop which today consists of a recommended inn and a rafting-put-in-cum-campground on the John Day River. It's exceptionally scenic along the river valley for the next 40 miles to the next stop.

✗ ⛏ p195

TRIP HIGHLIGHT

7 John Day Fossil Beds Sheep Rock Unit

The rust-colored walls of the river canyon narrow and then open up again before reaching the spectacular John Day Fossil Beds Sheep Rock Unit. Continue 3 miles south to the **Thomas Condon Paleontology Center** (32651 Hwy 19, Sheep Rock Unit; admission free; ⏰9am-5:30pm, reduced hours in winter; ♿). This is where everything comes together. With giant murals and exhibits of fossilized skulls, skeletons, leaves, nuts and branches, the center brings to life the region's history.

After filling your head with paleontology, drive across the highway to the historic **Cant Ranch House** (Hwy 19, Sheep

Shaniko A ghost town with great photo opportunities

Rock Unit; admission free; ⊙9am-5:30pm, reduced hours in winter; (♿)), perfect for a picnic or snack on the wooden tables overlooking the John Day River. Then backtrack the 3 miles (north) to the **Blue Basin Area** parking lot at the Sheep Rock Unit. Hike the 0.6-mile Island in Time Trail and/or the 3-mile Blue Basin Overlook Trail. The former passes replicas of large mammal fossils and ends in a massive amphitheater of towering greenish pinnacles. The latter leads around and above the amphitheater.

The Drive >> From Hwy 19 turn west onto Hwy 26, from where it's 36 miles to Mitchell. At 25 miles check out the tree on the north side of the road covered with shoes. It's been there as long as anyone can remember – string a pair up for good luck. From Mitchell it's another 10 miles to the Painted Hills Unit.

- - - - - - - - - - - -

TRIP HIGHLIGHT

❽ John Day Fossil Beds Painted Hills Unit

This is a detour off the official byway but it's arguably the most striking unit of the John Day Fossil Beds, so you won't want to miss it.

The goal is to see the low-slung, colorfully banded Painted Hills at sunset, when the evening light emphasizes the ochres, blacks, beiges and yellows of the eroded hillsides; an honorable reason to stay overnight in Mitchell. At the site, choose from four trails including the 0.5-mile Painted Hills Overlook and Trail (the most picturesque of the area) and the Painted Cove Trail that takes you via boardwalk around a hill (5 to 10 minutes) to see the area's popcorn-textured claystone up close.

The Drive >> Backtrack east along Hwy 26 and pass the Hwy 19 junction to Picture Gorge, a canyon hemmed in by stone pillars known as Picture Gorge Basalts. Two miles along is the Mascall Formation Overlook, where you'll get spectacular views of the John Day River, Strawberry Mountains, Picture Gorge and Mascall and Rattlesnake formations. It's another 36 miles to John Day.

 p195

9 John Day

After so many small towns, the one-stoplight town of John Day (population 1821) feels like a metropolis. Make your way to the outstanding **Kam Wah Chung State Heritage Site** (250 NW Canton St, John Day; admission free; 9am-5pm May-Oct;), which served as an apothecary, community center, temple and general store for Chinese gold miners and settlers from the late 19th century until the 1940s. Today it's a widely acclaimed museum featuring the history of the building and the region's Chinese past.

The Drive >> Drive east past stop-for-the-night-worthy Prairie City into the lush, conifer-clad Blue Mountains. Up the first grade, pull off at the Strawberry Mountain Overlook for views of the John Day River Valley and the Strawberry Mountains. Continue northeast over Dixie Pass (elevation 5280ft), swing left onto Hwy 7, cross Tipton Summit (elevation 5124ft) and you'll drop into a lovely valley.

 p195

10 Whitney

This isolated and unsignposted prairie settlement, a ghost town in the best sense of the word, was once a busy logging town and the primary stop on the Sumpter Valley Railroad. Its sagging wooden buildings, which lie on either side of a short dirt road that branches south from Hwy 7, are certainly worth a stop. Find it between mile marker 15 and 16.

The Drive >> About 9 miles east turn left on Sumpter Valley Hwy, then drive another 3 miles or so to Sumpter.

11 Sumpter

Once home to 3500 people, the town today is a sleepy cluster of Old West buildings huddled along a dusty main drag. The official attraction is the **Sumpter Valley Dredge**, a massive relic of gold-mining engineering sitting beside the river. The dredge's 72-bucket 'digging ladder' extracted some 9 tons of gold. Once you return from here to Hwy 7, it's 26 miles to the Eastern Oregon hub of Baker City (see p210).

> ✓ **TOP TIP: SHORT CUT TO MITCHELL**
>
> Taking Hwy 207 from Service Creek 30 miles to Mitchell will shave about 50 miles off your route and also saves you from having to backtrack east along Hwy 26 – but you'll miss some exceptional scenery along the John Day River.

ROCK ART

If you're heading east through Picture Gorge (on Hwy 26), at the far end you'll see a sign on the left and a gravel parking area big enough for about two cars. There's a little footpath from the pullout. Walk down the footpath and then hang onto the rock wall on your left, lean around and you'll see some red pictographs. They're really cool. And you can't hurt them because you can't reach them.

Eating & Sleeping

Fossil ❻

✖ Big Timber Family Restaurant
American $$

(☎541-763-4328; 540 1st St, Fossil; mains $5-20; ☺7am-7pm Sun-Thu, 7am-8pm Fri & Sat; ⊞) Down-home restaurant with big breakfasts, burgers and country-style dinners.

Service Creek

⊨ Service Creek Lodge
Guesthouse $

(☎541-468-3331; www.servicecreeklodge.com; 38686 Hwy 19; d $75-95; ⊜✳🖰) This fine lodge has six awesome, comfortable rooms with country quilts, plus a restaurant and rafting services. Rates include breakfast.

⊨ Donnelly Service Creek River Access Park
Campground $

(Hwy 207 near Hwy 19, Service Creek; sites $5) Bare-bones riverside campground popular with rafters. Pit toilets, no water.

John Day Fossil Beds Painted Hills Unit (Mitchell) ❽

✖ Bridge Creek Cafe
American $

(☎541-462-3434; 208 Hwy 26, Mitchell; mains $5-9; ☺6am-3pm Sun-Fri; ⊞) Petite diner with homemade pie and the usual country cooking.

✖ Little Pine Cafe
American $

(☎541-462-3532; www.littlepinecafe.com; 100 E Main St, Mitchell; mains $8-15; ☺11:30am-7:30pm Tue-Sun; ⊞) Fabulous country diner with burgers, sandwiches, soups and ice-cream pancakes.

⊨ Historic Oregon Hotel
Hotel $

(☎541-462-3027; www.theoregonhotel.net; 104 E Main St, Mitchell; dm $15, r $39-89; 🖰⊞) Historic 13-room hotel with kitschy, comfy rooms, each with its own theme; dorm room available.

John Day ❾

⊨ Dreamers Lodge
Motel $

(☎541-575-0526, 800-654-2849; 144 N Canyon Blvd, John Day; r $65-69; 🖰) Friendly, immaculately kept 1960s-era motel with spacious rooms, coffee makers, mini-fridges and decor that's brilliantly outdated.

✖ Snaffle Bit
International $$

(830 S Canyon City Blvd; mains $8-23; ☺11:30am-9pm Wed-Fri, 4-9pm Sat) John Day's best hamburgers are at this no-nonsense restaurant with a nice fountain patio. Also on the menu are salads, pasta, Mexican specialties and decent margaritas.

✖ Outpost
International $

(www.gooutpost.com; 201 W Main St; mains $7-17; ☺6am-9pm) There's something for everyone at this Western-style joint. And breakfast too! Good atmosphere with rustic decor.

Prairie City

✖ Chuck's Little Diner
American $

(☎541-820-4353; 142 Front St, Prairie City; mains $6-9; ☺6am-2pm Wed-Sun) With its Formica-top bar, tarnished chrome bar stools, friendly staff and greasy breakfast classics, this is a diner par excellence.

⊨ Hotel Prairie
Hotel $$

(☎541-820-4800; www.prairiecityoregon.com/prairie-city-oregon-hotel-prairie.html; 112 Front St; d $75-135; ⊜✳🖰) A historic 1905 hotel with nine suites, most with private bath.

⊨ Strawberry Mountain Inn B&B
B&B $$

(☎800-545-6913; www.strawberrymountaininn.com; 710 NE Front St; d $95-125; ⊜✳🖰) East of Prairie City near the Strawberry Mountain Wilderness, this beautiful B&B offers five romantic rooms, most with private bath, and great meadow views.

Elkhorn Mountains Head off the beaten path and into rural splendor

Blue Mountains Loop

18

From Oregon Trail wagon stops to million-acre forests and rodeo towns, this loop shows off Eastern Oregon's rural variety.

TRIP HIGHLIGHTS

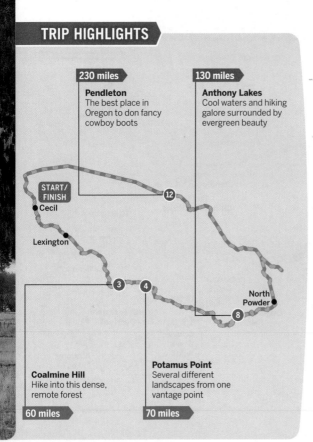

230 miles

Pendleton
The best place in Oregon to don fancy cowboy boots

130 miles

Anthony Lakes
Cool waters and hiking galore surrounded by evergreen beauty

START/FINISH
Cecil

Lexington

3 **4**

North Powder

8

12

Coalmine Hill
Hike into this dense, remote forest

60 miles

Potamus Point
Several different landscapes from one vantage point

70 miles

3 DAYS
240 MILES/386KM

BEST FOR...

BEST TIME TO GO
June to September, the only time all the roads are open!

ESSENTIAL PHOTO
Potamus Point – capture a panorama of a Wild West quilt of color.

BEST FOR HISTORY
Look for 100-year old Oregon Trail wagon ruts at the Oregon Trail Interpretive Center.

18 Blue Mountains Loop

This trip takes you way off the beaten path through country that feels as if the pioneer days never ended. Start in the grain kingdoms of Morrow County before heading up and up into deep, remote, wildlife-filled forests. Just as you start craving a real cup of coffee you'll descend back to civilization via the good 'ole cow-poking towns of Union and La Grande to lively, Western-chic Pendleton.

1 Cecil

Turn onto Hwy 74 from the Columbia River Gorge and stratified river country is quickly replaced by grassy fields and hillside tracts of space-age windmills. The first town you come to is the sheep and grain farming hamlet of Cecil, which was founded in the late 1800s when William Cecil stopped here on the Oregon Trail to fix his wagon and ended up opening a wagon repair shop. Take Cecil's one road to the left off

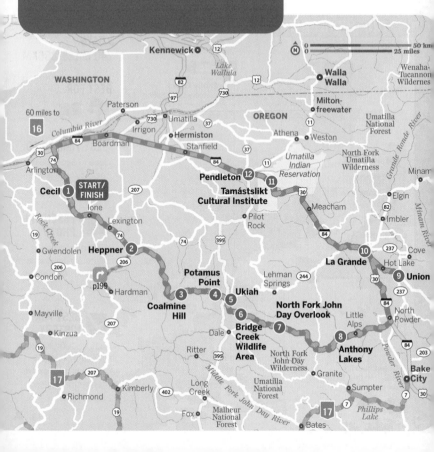

Hwy 74 to check out the ancient **Cecil Store**, a photogenic Old West–style building with a ghost town feel to it.

The Drive » Continue down Hwy 74 through the grain elevator dominated towns of Morgan (a ghost town), Ione and Lexington. The scenery here is the highlight: picture-perfect homesteads and grazing horses along a meandering creek bed.

- - - - - - - - - -

❷ Heppner

Welcome to the big smoke (although 'spoke' may be more fitting) of Morrow County. Heppner has a massive grain elevator, a small grid of wide streets and a few stately brick buildings. The town's pride and joy is the majestic **Historic Morrow County Courthouse**

LINK YOUR TRIP

16 Columbia River Gorge & Mt Hood

It's about 60 miles east along Hwy 84 from The Dalles to the turn-off for Hwy 74 (p179).

17 Journey Through Time Scenic Byway

From Baker City take the mountainous half of this route via Ukiah or I-84 to Pendleton to create a loop (p189).

(☎541-676-9061; 100 Court St) built in 1903 and still in use, making it one of the oldest continuously used courthouses in the state. It's also said to be haunted, perhaps by the 275 people who lost their lives in the 1903 Heppner Flood. Call if you want a tour.

Another worthwhile stop is the **Morrow County Museum** (444 N Main St; admission $3; ⌚1-5pm Tue-Fri & 11am-3pm Sat Mar-Oct), where you'll find a collection of pioneer and rural artifacts. Then, before you hit the road again, check in at the **US Forest Service Ranger Station** (117 S Main St; ⌚7am-3pm) for maps, trail and road information.

The Drive » Main St leads into Hwy 206/207. After about a mile turn left toward Willow Creek Reservoir on Hwy 53. From here it's 24 miles to Cutsforth Park where the Umatilla National Forest officially starts. It's another 2 miles from here to Coalmine Hill.

✕ ⌷ p203

DETOUR: HARDMAN

Start: ❷ Heppner

Once a stagecoach stop named 'Rawdog,' Hardman's demise began in the late 1880s when Heppner was chosen as the location for the train stop. The town's last business closed in 1968 and today it's one of the region's most scenic ghost towns. The most attractive building is the renovated dance hall.

It's a 40-mile round trip drive south from Heppner along Hwy 207.

- - - - - - -

TRIP HIGHLIGHT

❸ Coalmine Hill

The best way to explore the pine and fir tree loveliness of the 1.4-million-acre **Umatilla National Forest** is on foot. Stop at the **Coalmine Hill Trailhead** to tackle the 2.5-mile one-way **Bald Mountain Trail** where you'll be rewarded with a view over Butter Creek. At about 1.25 miles you'll pass **Gibson Cave**, which provided shelter to Native American families long ago. During the 1930s Great Depression, a man named Gibson lived here and became known as a modern caveman.

The Drive » Head south on NF-270 a little over a mile then turn right on NF-021/Western Raite Lane/Western Rt Rd. Continue 6 miles before hanging a right on Arbuckle Mt Rd/NF-180. Continue to follow Arbuckle Mt Rd for about 2.5 miles. Turn right on NF-030 then right onto NF-5316 5 miles on, then right 1.5 miles later on NF-360.

TOP TIP: NAVIGATING FOREST ROADS

It's easy to get lost in this tangle of forest roads, so make sure you fill up your tank in Heppner, bring plenty of water, snacks and emergency supplies, let the Ranger Station know where you're going and keep meticulous track of the route you've taken so that in a worst case scenario you can at least backtrack. Cell phone reception and GPS coverage are iffy at best so don't expect to rely on anything besides your wits.

TRIP HIGHLIGHT

❹ Potamus Point

This is the best viewpoint of the trip, looking over North Fork John Day River. In winter herds of elk can be seen from here but unfortunately the road is closed at this time. In the summer months, enjoy the vistas of mountain ponds and unusual rock formations.

The Drive » Backtrack to NF-030 then take a quick right onto NF- 5316. After around 6 miles turn right on NF-053. After 10 miles this turns into OR-244 E/Ukiah-Hilgard Hwy and a little over a mile later you'll be back to civilization in Ukiah.

❺ Ukiah

Nestled within the Camas Prairie, this tiny town is surrounded by rolling grasslands and cut by clear Camas Creek. It's the low, flat heart of the Blue Mountains and a pleasant place for a leg stretch, but there's not much on offer besides the small supply shop.

The Drive » Travel west on OR-244 W/Main St/Ukiah-Hilgard Hwy a little over a mile, then turn right at Granite/Ukiah Rd 52 and travel four miles. The entrance to the wildlife area is on the right side of the road.

❻ Bridge Creek Wildlife Area

This protected area is known mostly as a wintering ground for elk, but in summer (the only time of year it's accessible without specialty equipment – plus you need a permit to enter between December 1 and April 30) you'll see plenty of birdlife, including mountain bluebirds and horned larks. For a bit of exercise, take the 1/8-mile-long Ron Bridges Memorial Trail for views over Bridge Creek Flats. The trailhead is on the right, one mile after the wilderness area on Granite/Ukiah Rd 52.

The Drive » Drive nine miles east on Granite-Ukiah Rd 52.

❼ North Fork John Day Overlook

Pull over for spectacular views (when it's clear) over the patchwork of color of the John Day Wilderness to the north, the majestic Strawberry Mountains to the south and the river-filled Bridge Creek Flats to the southeast. If it's early or late in season you may be able to spot elk.

The Drive » Continue east on Granite-Ukiah Rd 52 then turn left on NF-73. Drive around 16 miles then turn right toward NF-300/172 and follow the signs to Anthony Lakes.

TRIP HIGHLIGHT

❽ Anthony Lakes

Known for its powdery winter skiing, Anthony Lakes is also a trove of excellent hiking in summer with alpine landscapes, five lakes and craggy granite peaks. Anthony Lake is the only lake accessible by car, and it's also the biggest and most crowded. Better, take the one-mile hike to Black Lake, which is smaller and just as beautiful, to find serious tranquility. Find the trailhead at the Anthony Lakes Campground.

Pendleton Round-Up

The Drive » Head back to NF-73 and turn right into Anthony Lake Rd that eventually turns into Anthony Lakes Hwy. After about 9 miles of winding downhill through pines, turn left on Ellis Rd/Ermey Davis Rd then take the first right on River Lane. This will lead you onto OR-237 N/La Grande-Baker Hwy toward Union.

 p203

❾ Union

One of Eastern Oregon's most likeable, unpretentious towns, Victorian-era, brick-solid Union is like a smaller, cuter version of La Grande and is a quieter place to spend the night if you're ready for a stop. While you're here, learn more about cowboys then and now at the **Union County Museum** (333 South Main St; admission $4; ☺9am-4pm Mon-Sat, May-Oct).

The Drive » Get back on the La Grande-Baker Hwy. In about 13 miles you'll see the first exit for La Grande.

 p203

❿ La Grande

Apart from its pleasant historic area downtown, La Grande is really just a stop for food, gas and lodging. Thirteen miles west of town, however, is the **Oregon Trail**

Interpretive Center (I-84 exit 248; $5 Northwest Forest Pass required for parking; ☺8am-8pm Memorial Day-Labor Day), a great place for a visceral feeling of what it was like for Oregon Pioneers crossing the Blue Mountains. Paths wind through the forest to ruts left by pioneer wagons – still visible after 150 years. Find the center on well-marked roads from freeway exit 248.

The Drive » Continue on I-84 towards Pendleton. About 25 miles along you'll find yourself descending Emigrant Hill on a 6% downgrade. Stop at the Cabbage Hill Viewpoint to experience something akin to looking down from the heavens. Just before Pendleton, take exit 216 to the Tamástslikt Cultural Center.

✗ p203

⓫ Tamástslikt Cultural Institute

You've learned all about the pioneers so now it's time to delve into the cultures that were here long before covered wagons. State-of-the-art exhibits weave voices, memories and artifacts through an evolving history of the region at this grand **cultural center** (www.tamastslikt.org; 72789 Hwy 331; adult/child $8/6; ☺9am-5pm, closed Sun Nov-Mar).

The Drive » Get back onto I-84 W. In about 2.5 miles you'll see the first exit for Pendleton.

TRIP HIGHLIGHT

⓬ Pendleton

Eastern Oregon's largest city, 'wild and woolly' Pendleton is a handsome old town famous for its wool shirts and rowdy, big-name rodeo, the **Pendleton Round-Up** (1205 SW Court Ave; ☺mid-Sep). The town has managed to retain a glint of its cow-poking past, though in the past few years at least one small boutique winery has popped up, not to mention art galleries and antique shops.

Take a free tour of **Pendleton Woolen Mills** (www.pendleton-usa.com; 1307 SE Court Pl; ☺8am-6pm Mon-Sat, 9am-5pm Sun, tours at 9am, 11am, 1:30pm & 3pm Mon-Fri), which has been weaving blankets for more than 100 years, and is especially known for Native American designs.

The Drive » From here it's about 70 miles to the Hwy 74 turnoff to Cecil where the loop began.

✗ p203

Eating & Sleeping

Heppner ❷

✘ Howe's About Pizza   Pizza $$

(📞541-676-5210; 111 Court St; pizzas from $12; 🕙10am-8pm Mon-Sat) Get delicious handmade pizzas and homemade ice cream at this little hole-in-the-wall near the courthouse. Take-out orders welcome.

🛏 Northwestern Motel & RV Park   Motel $

(📞541-676-9167; www.heppnerlodging.com; 389 N Main St; r from $58; ❋🛜) Kitschy outside with red-and-white paint, green shamrocks and garden gnomes a go-go, the clean, stylish rooms are a big surprise. Each one has a theme, including cowboy, zebra and oriental.

Anthony Lakes ❽

🛏 Anthony Lakes Campground   Campground $

(📞800-452-5687; www.reserveamerica.com; sites from $8; 🕙Jul-Sep) A gorgeous but busy campground right on the lake with views of the Elkhorn Mountains. There are nearly 40 tent and trailer sites but no RV hookups or dump stations.

Union ❾

🛏 Union Hotel   Hotel $

(📞541-562-6135; www.thehistoricunionhotel. com; 326 N Main St; d $65-119; ❋🛜) All 16 rooms at this historic, atmospheric hotel are decorated individually and three come with a kitchenette. One room with outside bath is $45.

La Grande ❿

✘ Ten Depot Street   American $$

(📞541-963-8766; www.tendepotstreet.com; 10 Depot St; mains $11-25; 🕙5-10pm Mon-Sat) This longtime local favorite offers something

for everyone, including a few surprises such as Thai salad and an emu burger. Classy, old atmosphere, with a good selection of microbrews available.

Pendleton ⓬

✘ Hamley's Steakhouse   American $$

(📞541-278-1100; www.thehamleysteakhouse. com; 8 SE Court Ave; mains $10-34; 🕙5-9pm Sun-Thu, till 10pm Fri & Sat) This 150-seat steakhouse has been gorgeously done up with wood floors, stone accents and tin ceilings. Hamley's empire also includes a Western shop, art gallery, cafe and wine cellar.

✘ Prodigal Son Brewery   Brewpub $

(www.prodigalsonbrewery.com; 230 SE Court Ave; mains $8-12; 🕙11am-11pm Mon-Sat, noon-9pm Sun) Pendleton's only brewery-pub has eight creatively named beers on tap such as the tempting 'Fatted Calf Sacrificial Stout.' A great-quality pub menu offers Ploughman plates, fish 'n' chips, a couple of sandwiches, burgers and truly fantastic onion rings.

🛏 Working Girls Old Hotel   Hotel $

(📞541-276-0730; www.pendletonunderground tours.org; 21 SW Emigrant Ave; d $75-95; ❋❋) Run by Pendleton Underground Tours (who run walking tours of town), this one-time bordello offers four pretty, antique-filled rooms in Victorian style, along with one three-room suite. There's a kitchen and dining room for guests to share.

🛏 Pendleton House B&B   B&B $$

(📞541-276-8581, 800-700-8581; www. pendletonhousebnb.com; 311 N Main St; d $100-140; ◉❋🛜) This pink 1917 Italian Renaissance mansion's details are amazing, with original furniture, wallpaper and even drapes. Be prepared to get to know your neighbors, however – the five beautiful rooms (two with half-baths) share one full bath.

Imnaha Canyon The dramatic views just keep getting better

Hells Canyon Scenic Byway

19

North America's deepest river gorge is more than just scorching temperatures and desolate landscapes. You'll find both, but you'll also find forested ridge tops, peaceful river valleys and hamlets.

TRIP HIGHLIGHTS

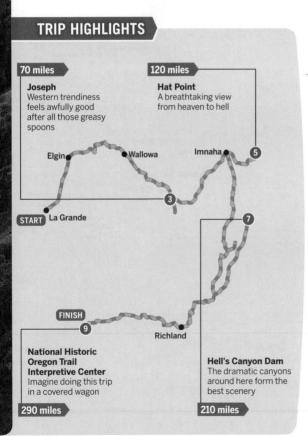

70 miles

Joseph
Western trendiness feels awfully good after all those greasy spoons

120 miles

Hat Point
A breathtaking view from heaven to hell

Elgin ● ● Wallowa

Imnaha ● **5**

3

START La Grande

7

FINISH
9

Richland

National Historic Oregon Trail Interpretive Center
Imagine doing this trip in a covered wagon

290 miles

Hell's Canyon Dam
The dramatic canyons around here form the best scenery

210 miles

---

4 DAYS
270 MILES/434KM

GREAT FOR...

BEST TIME TO GO

June to September – the road from Imnaha to Halfway is closed at other times.

 ESSENTIAL PHOTO

Capture the majesty of an 8000ft rise from river to peak at Hat Point.

 BEST DAY

Exploring the vistas and valleys of Hells Canyon, stops 6 to 9.

205

DENNIS FRATES / ALAMY ©

19 Hells Canyon Scenic Byway

In this remote corner of Oregon, at the foot of the Seven Devils Mountains, lies one of the Pacific Northwest's most spectacular sights: Hells Canyon, measuring 8043ft deep from peak to river. The few roads that access the canyon and the mountains above offer spectacular vistas but are only open in summer months, once the snows have melted and temperatures soar.

❶ La Grande

The Oregon Trail crossed this valley, and pioneers rested here before traversing the challenging Blue Mountains. La Grande is the best place in the region to stock up on provisions (trail mix? sunscreen? water?) before driving into the boondocks. Despite the number of services and the few blocks of historical brick architecture, the city isn't that memorable.

✕ ⨭ p211

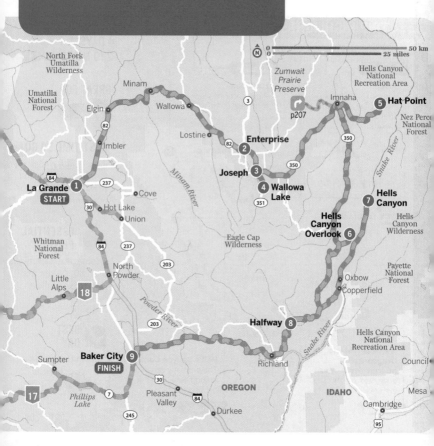

The Drive >> Take I-82 east and you'll soon be in farmlands hemmed in by mountains. After the tiny town of Minam, the road veers right to run along the Minam River through a beautiful, slim valley with pine-covered hillsides. You'll eventually drive through the small settlements of Wallowa and Lostine.

❷ Enterprise

Unlike nearby Joseph (which has arguably become *too* cute), Enterprise maintains its good-old small-town atmosphere. In fact, its downtown – two blocks of handsome buildings – is lonesome at times. It's a good, economical place to rest for the night and get any gear you may realize you need after all (fish hooks? bug spray?).

LINK YOUR TRIP

17 **Journey Through Time Scenic Byway**

It's a seamless link: start in Baker City, where the Journey Through Time Scenic Byway ends (p189).

18 **Blue Mountains Loop**

From La Grande, drive south 25 miles on Hwy 84 to North Powder or northwest toward Pendleton to hook up with this varied circuit (p197).

DETOUR: ZUMWAIT PRAIRIE PRESERVE

Start: ❺ Hat Point

If you have a high-clearance vehicle and three to five hours to spare, detour up to Zumwait Prairie Preserve. Owned by the Nature Conservancy, this 51-sq-mile preserve is the largest remaining grassland of its kind in the US. Several trails meander through the prairie, which is home to a vast number of hawks and eagles. To get there, take the dirt Camp Creek Rd, which departs Little Sheep Creek Hwy about 1 mile south of Imnaha.

The **Wallowa Mountains Visitor Center** (☎541-426-5546; www.fs.fed.us/r6/w-w; 88401 Hwy 82; ⏰8am-6pm Mon-Sat; 🛗) is an invaluable place to stock up on information about Hells Canyon and surrounding areas. Since it burned down in 2010, the center has been temporarily relocated to the **Wallowa County Chamber of Commerce** (115 Tejaka St) – but it will probably reopen at its previous highwayside location at some point.

✕ 🛏 p211

The Drive >> Joseph is only 6 miles down I-62.

TRIP HIGHLIGHT

❸ Joseph

If ever there was a trendy eastern Oregon town, it's Joseph. You can see its wealth right on the brick sidewalks, where well-groomed planter boxes and huge bronze statues

sit proudly on every downtown corner. In fact, Joseph is noted for its cast-bronze sculptures, thanks in part to **Valley Bronze** (☎541-432-7445; www.valleybronze.com; 18 S Main St). Foundry tours are $15 per person. You can also vist the **Wallowa County Museum** (☎541-432-6095; 110 S Main St; adult/child $2.50/free; ⏰10am-5pm Memorial Day-late Sep), housed in an 1888 bank building and notable for its displays on pioneer and Nez Perce histories.

✕ 🛏 p211

The Drive >> Drive 6 miles south on Wallowa Lake Rd (Hwy 351).

❹ Wallowa Lake

Over 5 miles long and glacially formed, Wallowa Lake sits at the foot of the Wallowa Mountains, dominated at its southern end by 9617ft Chief Joseph Mountain.

Giant old-growth conifers tower over a grassy beach area here, and families lounge in the sun, fish and otherwise frolic away the summer afternoons. A major trailhead starts at the south end of Wallowa Lake Rd. One popular trail from here is the 6-mile one-way jaunt to the gorgeous **Aneroid Lake**.

 p211

The Drive ›› Backtrack to Joseph then take Hwy 350 east. After leaving Joseph, the road passes a highway sign that tellingly reads 'Open Range Next 23 Miles,' then meets up with Little Sheep Creek, which it follows all the way to Imnaha.

TRIP HIGHLIGHT

⑤ Hat Point

Now it's time to leave civilization behind. Get an early start for the 30-mile drive to **Imnaha**, one of the most isolated towns in the US. You may want to stay the night here (if you didn't in Joseph or Enterprise), see p211, before tackling the route ahead.

The area around Imnaha has some of the most dramatic scenery of the trip. A 24-mile gravel road leads to Hat Point (elevation 6982ft) from Imnaha. The good news: only the first 5 or 6 miles are steep. The road follows a spectacular forested ridge, offering stunning views along the way. Be sure to stop at

the **Granny View Vista** pullout. By the time you get to Hat Point, you'll wonder if the views could get any better. They do. Atop Hat Point stands the 82ft **Hat Point lookout tower**, a fire lookout offering dizzying 360-degree views of the Seven Devils, the Wallowas and Hells Canyon itself. And, yes, you can climb to the top. Without a doubt, this is one of the grandest views in the Pacific Northwest. In summer, the road is usually passable for all passenger cars.

The Drive ›› Head back to Imnaha and follow the gravel Upper Imnaha Rd south to USFS Rd 39 (also called Wallowa Mountain Loop Rd). This is a dusty, scenic drive along the Imnaha River Valley. If you wish to avoid the dust, backtrack along Little Sheep Creek Hwy to USFS Rd 39 and swing left.

⑥ Hells Canyon Overlook

Whichever route you take, after joining USFS Rd 39, continue southeast until the turnoff for the Hells Canyon Overlook. This is the *only* overlook into Hells Canyon that's accessible by paved road, so take advantage of it. Although you don't get the same 360-degree views as from Hat Point, it's a marvelous vista nonetheless.

The Drive ›› This southern end of USFS Rd 39 is bucolic, with meadows and old farmhouses flanking the river. When you reach Hwy 86, turn left toward Copperfield and Oxbow.

TRIP HIGHLIGHT

⑦ Hells Canyon

At Copperfield, you'll reach the Snake River and officially be at the

Hells Canyon White-water rafting trips venture into otherwise inaccessible areas

very bottom of Hells Canyon. Down here, it's hot, hot, hot, and the canyon has absolutely no problem living up to its name. Cross the Snake River into Idaho and turn onto Idaho's Forest Rd 454 (also called Hells Canyon Dam Rd), which eventually dead-ends at Hells Canyon Dam. Here you will find the **Hells Canyon Visitor Center** (☎541-785-3395; Hells Canyon Dam, FR 454; ⏰8am-4pm summer only; ♿), which is a must if you need hiking trail information. The **Stud Creek Trail** begins immediately below the visitors center and passes some great spots to relax above the river and ponder the immensity of your surroundings.

North of Hells Canyon Dam and the visitors center, the Snake River returns to its natural flowing self, descending through epic scenery and roaring rapids. You can float those rapids by signing on with **Hells Canyon Adventures** (☎541-785-3352; www.hellscanyonadventures.com; 4200 Hells Canyon Dam Rd, Oxbow), which offers

**TOP TIP:
OLLOKOT
CAMPGROUND**

One of our favorite spots to go is Ollokot Campground, not that we camp there, but because it's so beautiful in there with the river and the trees. It's just off the Wallowa Mountain Loop Rd (USFS Rd 39), about an hour or so from Imnaha.

rafting and jet-boat trips into an otherwise inaccessible area. If there's time for a hike, tackle the 4.5-mile (out and back) **Allison Creek Trail**, which you'll pass about 12 miles north of Oxbow (10 miles before the dam); it has a total elevation gain of about 1200ft up Allison Creek Canyon.

🛏 p211

The Drive » From Hells Canyon, return by way of Hwy 86 to Halfway.

8 Halfway

Halfway is an idyllic little town lying on the southern edge of the Wallowa Mountains and surrounded by beautiful meadows dotted with old barns and hay fields. It's also a friendly spot with just enough tourist services to make it a decent base to explore the Hells Canyon Dam area. The

Pine Ranger Station (☎541-742-7511; 38470 Pine Town Lane; ☺7:30-11:45am & 12:30-4:30pm Mon-Thu, to 3:30pm Fri) is 1 mile south of Halfway and acts as the region's tourist information.

The **Pine Valley Museum** (☎541-742-5346; admission by donation; ☺10am-4pm Sat & Sun summer) is located right in the middle of town and has a few of the region's old photos and relics. It's open on weekdays and by request for a $5 fee.

🛏 p211

The Drive » You're way more than halfway there! It's 54 miles through pastoral countryside to the end of the trail at Baker City.

TRIP HIGHLIGHT

9 Baker City

In the gold-rush days, Baker City was the largest metropolis between Salt Lake City

and Portland, and a heady mix of miners, cowboys, shopkeepers and loggers kept the city's many saloons, brothels and gaming halls boisterously alive. Today the city's wide downtown streets and historical architecture recall its rich bygone days.

To remind yourself how easy your modern road trip is, stop in at the evocative **National Historic Oregon Trail Interpretive Center** (☎541-523-1843; www.oregontrail.blm.gov; 22267 Hwy 86; adult/senior $5/3.50; ☺9am-6pm Apr-Oct, to 4pm Nov-Mar; ♿), one of the best museums in the state. Lying atop a hill 7 miles east of town along Hwy 86, the center contains interactive displays, artifacts and films that brilliantly illustrate the day-to-day realities of the pioneers who crossed this region in the 1800s. Outside you can stroll on the 4-mile interpretive path and spot the actual Oregon Trail.

🛏 p211

Eating & Sleeping

La Grande ❶

✖ Mt Emily Ale House   Pub $$
(www.mtemilyalehouse.com; 1202 Adams Ave; mains $8-15; ☺11:30am-close Tue-Fri, 4:30pm-close Sat) Attractive brewery-restaurant serving burgers, salads, gourmet pizzas and craft ales.

⨺ Hot Lake Springs   Hotel $$
(☎541-963-4685; www.hotlakesprings.com; 66172 Hwy 203; d $150-350; ❄🛜) Eight miles southeast of La Grande is this grand historic old building with 22 big, beautiful suites.

Enterprise ❷

✖ Terminal Gravity Brewing   Brewpub $
(☎541-426-0158; 803 School St; mains $7-11; ☺11am-10pm Wed-Sat, 4-9pm Sun & Mon) One of Oregon's best breweries with outdoor tables and pastas, salads, burgers and sandwiches.

⨺ Ponderosa Motel   Motel $
(☎541-426-3186; www.ponderosamotel.hotels. officelive.com; 102 E Greenwood St; d $70-80; ❄🛜) Right in downtown with an attractive wood-and-stone facade.

Joseph ❸

✖ Embers Brewhouse   Brewpub $
(☎541-432-2739; 206 N Main St; mains $8-15; ☺7am-9pm Sun-Thu, to 10pm Fri & Sat; 🍴) Serves pizza, sandwiches, salads and microbrews. Fabulous front deck.

⨺ Bronze Antler B&B   B&B $$
(☎541-432-0230; www.bronzeantler.com; 309 S Main St; r $129-259) This restored Craftsman-style bungalow offers four elegant rooms.

Wallowa Lake ❹

✖ Vali's Alpine Restaurant   Hungarian $$
(☎541-432-5691; 59811 Wallowa Lake Hwy; mains $11-15; ☺5pm & 7pm seatings Wed-Sun

Memorial Day-Labor Day, Sat & Sun only rest of year) Hungarian specialties are all excellent here. No credit cards; reservations are required.

⨺ Wallowa Lake
State Park   Campground $
(☎541-432-4185; 72214 Marina Lane; tent/RV sites $20/25, yurts $38) This popular lakeside state park offers more than 200 campsites, along with two yurts.

Imnaha

✖ Imnaha Store & Tavern   Tavern $$
(☎541-577-3111; 71300 Lower Imnaha Rd; mains $6-17.50; ☺9am-9pm) This store, restaurant and tavern stocks minimal supplies but has a reliable bar menu and offers tent sites ($5).

⨺ Imnaha River Inn   B&B $$
(☎541-577-6002; www.imnahariverinn.com; Lower Imnaha Rd; r $120-130) Gorgeous log-sided B&B with comfy, themed rooms.

Hells Canyon ❼

⨺ Hells Canyon B&B   B&B $
(☎541-785-3373; www.hells-canyon-bed-and-breakfast.com; 49922 Homestead Rd, Oxbow; r $70) Friendly B&B with modest rooms and a deck overlooking Hells Canyon Reservoir.

Halfway ❽

⨺ Pine Valley Lodge   Lodge $$
(☎541-742-2027; www.pvlodge.com; 163 N Main St; d incl breakfast $85-140; ❄🛜) Halfway's fanciest accommodation, with seven very comfortable rooms in three buildings.

Baker City ❾

⨺ Geiser Grand Hotel   Hotel $$
(☎541-523-1889; www.geisergrand.com; 1996 Main St; r $105-165) Baker City's downtown landmark and fanciest lodgings.

Deschutes River *Take advantage of ridiculously good weather*

To Bend & Back

You may be tempted to make a beeline for Bend – with its sunshine, microbrews and amazing array of outdoor activities – but take time to enjoy the spectacular stop-offs along the way.

TRIP HIGHLIGHTS

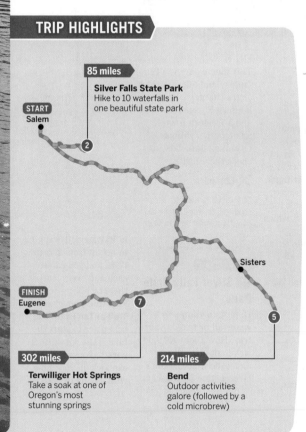

85 miles

Silver Falls State Park
Hike to 10 waterfalls in one beautiful state park

START
Salem

Sisters

FINISH
Eugene

302 miles

Terwilliger Hot Springs
Take a soak at one of Oregon's most stunning springs

214 miles

Bend
Outdoor activities galore (followed by a cold microbrew)

5 DAYS
280 MILES/450KM

GREAT FOR...

BEST TIME TO GO
April to October, though there's always something to do.

ESSENTIAL PHOTO
Lower South Falls in Silver Falls State Park.

BEST MUSEUM
Bend's High Desert Museum offers great insight into the area.

20 | To Bend & Back

Pack your snowshoes, swimsuit, hiking boots, daypack and kayak: you'll need them all in Bend. This high desert town enjoys glorious weather and blue skies 250 days a year – not to mention microbreweries and a quirky character for when you're ready to have fun. Along the drive to Bend, you'll experience waterfalls, hot springs and miles and miles of forest, making this an ideal trip for the outdoor adventurer.

① Salem

Your trip begins in the state capital, just an hour south of Portland. Before setting off on your journey, stop for a little pioneer history at the **Willamette Heritage Center** (www.missionmill.org; 1313 Mill St SE; adult/child $6/3; ◷10am-5pm Mon-Sat), which includes two homes, a parsonage, a Presbyterian church and a mill, all looking much like they did in the 1840s and '50s.

If you've got kids in tow, thrill them with a stop in the **Enchanted Forest** (www.enchantedforest.com; 8462 Enchanted Way SE, Turner; adult/child $10/9; 🚗), 7 miles south of Salem.

This theme park is a fun fantasyland offering rides (extra charge), a haunted house, a European village and a Western town, among other things. Opening hours vary, so check the website.

✕ 🛏 p219

The Drive » Head 10 miles southeast on Hwy 22, then take Hwy 214 10 miles west to Silver Falls.

TRIP HIGHLIGHT

② Silver Falls State Park

Hoping to glimpse a waterfall or two on your trip? How about 10? And we're not just talking along the way; Oregon's largest state park packs in 10 waterfalls ranging in height from 27ft to 177ft, and you can see each and every one of them by hiking an 8-mile loop trail known as the **Trail of Ten Falls**. The best place to start the hike is the South Falls parking lot, where you can kick off your hike with a bang by walking

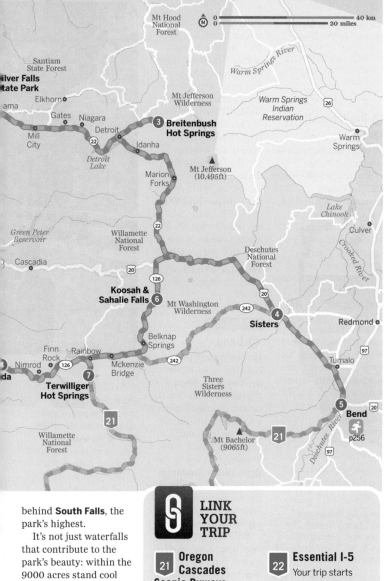

behind **South Falls**, the park's highest.

It's not just waterfalls that contribute to the park's beauty: within the 9000 acres stand cool forests of Douglas fir, western hemlock, big leaf maples and cedars, with ferns, Oregon grape and salmonberry covering the forest floor.

LINK YOUR TRIP

21 Oregon Cascades Scenic Byways

This trip also takes you to Bend via different routes; mix and match to build your dream itinerary (p221).

22 Essential I-5

Your trip starts and ends along this major thoroughfare, and you can pick it up going in either direction (p231).

The Drive ›› Head back to Santiam Hwy/Hwy 22 and continue west for 40 miles, then strike north for 10 miles on Breitenbush Rd, just past Detroit Lake.

- - - - - - - - - - -

❸ Breitenbush Hot Springs

Set above the Breitenbush River on a 154-acre reserve inside Willamette National Forest, Breitenbush Hot Springs is as Oregon as it gets. Along with a fantastically relaxing soak, you'll get a solid dose of earthy Oregonian mellowness. Hot mineral water burbles out of several springs at a scorching 180°F to 200°F (82°C to 93°C) and is cooled to prime soaking temperatures with water from the river. There are seven pools in all. Three overlook a pretty meadow and one of these is a silent pool. Another four pools are arranged in order of temperature, from 100°F to 107°F (37°C to 41°C). Elsewhere, a sauna sits over an open spring and is entirely heated by the steam.

The Drive ›› Head back to Hwy 22 and drive south. This scenic stretch of road will meet up with Hwy 20, and then it's 26 more miles to Sisters.

- - - - - - - - - - -

❹ Sisters

Looking like a movie set for a spaghetti Western, Sisters was once a stagecoach stop and trade town for loggers and ranchers. Today, it's a bustling tourist destination whose main street is lined with boutiques, art galleries and eateries housed in Western-facade buildings.

There's nothing specific here that you have to see – unless you're in town for the **Sisters Rodeo** (www. sistersrodeo.com) in June or the **Outdoor Quilt Show** (www.sistersoutdoorquiltshow. org) in July – but it's still a cute town to mosey around in for a while.

The Drive ›› From Sisters it's a quick 20-minute hop down to Bend.

- - - - - - - - - - -

TRIP HIGHLIGHT

❺ Bend

Hip, outdoorsy, and enjoying ridiculously good weather, Bend is the darling of the high desert. You could spend a week here hiking, paddling, climbing, mountain biking – the list goes on. Stop by the **Bend Visitor Center** (750 NW Lava Rd; ☺9am-5pm Mon-Fri, 10am-4pm Sat, plus 10am-4pm Sun summer) to explore your options.

With the lovely Deschutes River carving its way through the heart of the city, Bend also offers an attractive downtown full of boutiques, galleries and dining options, which you can explore on our walking tour (p256).

DAVID L MOORE-OR / ALAMY ©

To learn more about the area, don't miss the superb – and rather extensive – **High Desert Museum** (www. highdesertmuseum.org; 59800 S US 97; adult/child $15/9; ☺9am-5pm, 10am-4pm winter), which covers everything from Native American culture to live animal displays on 135 acres of pine forest.

✕ ⊨ p219

The Drive ›› Take Hwy 20 north, curving back through Sisters, then go south where Hwy 126/McKenzie Hwy splits off. Look for the turnoff to the Koosah & Sahalie Falls about 5 miles later.

Goodpasture Bridge Oregon's second-longest wooden bridge

6 Koosah & Sahalie Falls

Right off the roadside of McKenzie Hwy are two of Oregon's most impressive waterfalls. The McKenzie River plunges 120ft over Sahalie Falls – the more dramatic of the two – and after a good snowmelt it drenches everything around it in mist as it roars into the frothy pool below.

Only 0.3 miles downstream, Koosah Falls measures 90ft and is wider and easier going than its upstream neighbor. The stretch of the McKenzie River between the falls is utterly spectacular, with roaring cascades that tumble over basalt boulders, through massive logjams and into deep, dark pools.

The Drive >> Keep following Hwy 126 another 24 miles and turn left on Aufderheide Rd. Continue on for 8 miles more.

TRIP HIGHLIGHT

7 Terwilliger Hot Springs

Also known as Cougar Hot Springs for its proximity to Cougar Reservoir, this wildly popular hot springs near Terwilliger Reservoir is known for its beautiful setting among the trees in the Willamette National Forest. You can read about it in more detail on p228, but since it's just a short distance off this route we wanted to make sure you didn't miss it.

The Drive >> Keep following Hwy 126 another 19 miles to the town of Vida.

8 Vida

Oregon is known for its wooden bridges, and right along your route in Vida is the state's second-longest, **Goodpasture**

217

FIRE ON MT WASHINGTON

About a mile after you join Hwy 20, the lush greenery dwindles and the trees start to look like a weird art project involving charred toothpicks. This is the handiwork of a pair of wildfires – the Bear Butte Fire and the Booth Fire – that joined together in the summer of 2003 to become the B&B Complex Fire, burning over 90,000 acres of the Cascades.

It's hard not to want to stare at the devastation. But keep your eyes on the road for now, because you can pull over at the **Mt Washington Viewpoint**, between Miles 84 and 85. Here you'll find dramatic views of the mountains and seven interpretive signs that give you the full picture.

Bridge. A wooden truss bridge, it's painted white and looks almost like a small-town church – albeit a 237ft-long church that straddles a river. It's right on the highway, so you can stop for a picture (it is a rather good-looking bridge) or just point and say, 'Oooooh,' as you whiz past. Look for it on the left after Mile 26.

The Drive » Stay on the highway, but not for long – Leaburg is the next town over and just under 7 miles away.

to investigate, located on the grounds of the **River Run Gallery** (42827 McKenzie Hwy). The gallery is open by appointment, but even if it's closed you can wander the grounds and check out large-scale metal sculptures and other structures, including a stained-glass gazebo, a churchless steeple, and a fantastical Cinderella-style pumpkin carriage.

The Drive » You're in the home stretch: just 22.5 more miles to Eugene.

⑨ Leaburg

Leaburg could easily be one of those towns you pass along the way without giving a second thought to, except right on the roadside is some amazing outdoor art that demands you pull over

Where to start? For great fun and a quintessential introduction to Eugene's peculiar vitality, try to time your visit with the **Saturday Market** (www.eugenesaturdaymarket.org), held each Saturday from April through mid-November. Otherwise, wander the **5th St Public Market** (www.5stmarket.com; 296 E 5th Ave; ☺10am-7pm Mon-Sat, 11am-5pm Sun), an old mill that now anchors several dozen restaurants, cafes and boutique stores.

To wrap up your trip with a bit of culture, stop by the **Jordan Schnitzer Museum of Art** (http://jsma.uoregon.edu; 1430 Johnson Lane; adult/child $5/free; ☺11am-5pm Tue-Sun, to 8pm Wed). This renowned museum offers a 13,000-piece rotating permanent collection with an Asian art specialty. Highlights include a 10-panel Korean folding screen and a standing Thai Buddha in gold leaf.

✗ 🛏 p219

⑩ Eugene

It's back to civilization in dynamic and liberal Eugene, full of energetic college students, pretty riverside parks and a plethora of restaurant choices.

Eating & Sleeping

Salem ❶

✗ Word of Mouth Bistro
American $

(☏503-930-4285; 140 17th St NE; mains $8-11; ☺breakfast & lunch) This excellent bistro should be on any food-lover's agenda. Breakfast treats include crème brûlée, French toast and asparagus-brie omelettes. Sandwiches and burgers rule at lunch.

✗ Wild Pear
American $

(☏503 378-7515; 372 State St; mains $7-12; ☺10am-5pm Mon-Sat) Popular deli serving a little bit of everything – fish tacos, Greek wraps, pizzas, even Vietnamese *pho*. They want everyone to leave happy, and it seems to be working.

🛏 Grand Hotel
Hotel $$

(☏877-540-7800; www.grandhotelsalem.com; 201 Liberty St SE; d from $129; ✳@🛜♒) Salem's best lodgings are downtown next to the conference center. The stylish, modern rooms have sitting areas, and breakfast is included.

Bend ❺

✗ Victorian Café
Breakfast $$

(☏541-382-6411; 1404 NW Galveston Ave; mains $8-14; ☺breakfast & lunch) Bend's best breakfast spot is especially awesome for its eggs Benedict (nine kinds). It's also good for sandwiches, burgers and salads.

✗ Pine Tavern
American $$

(www.pinetavern.com; 967 NW Brooks St; mains $13-34; ☺lunch & dinner) Everyone should find something here, from smoked-salmon salad to house meatloaf to rib-eye steak. There's an excellent back patio.

🛏 Old St Francis School
Hotel $$

(☏541-382-5174; www.mcmenamins.com; 700 NW Bond St; d $135-185; ⊖✳🛜) The McMenamin brothers gave this former school colorful new life as a whimsical, 19-room hotel. Enjoy a Turkish soaking tub, on-site brewpub and movie theater.

🛏 Mill Inn
Inn $$

(☏541-389-9198, 877-748-1200; www.millinn. com; 642 NW Colorado Ave; d $80-160; ⊖🛜) A 10-room boutique hotel with colorful, classy rooms – full breakfast included. One dorm room is available for $30 per bed.

Eugene ❿

✗ 5th Street Public Market
Fast Food $

(www.5stmarket.com; 296 E 5th Ave; ☺10am-7pm Mon-Sat, 11am-5pm Sun) Italian? Mexican? Burgers? Options abound in this cheery market that anchors several dozen restaurants, cafes and stores around a pretty central courtyard.

✗ Café Zenon
American $$

(☏541-684-4000; www.zenoncafe.com; 898 Pearl St; dinner mains $17-24; ☺11am-10pm Mon-Fri, from 9am Sat, 9am-2pm & 5-10pm Sun) This downtown restaurant serves European-inspired main dishes – but it's the salads, appetizers and especially desserts that keep folks coming back.

🛏 C'est La Vie Inn
B&B $$

(☏541-302-3014; www.cestlavieinn.com; 1006 Taylor St; d $140-170; ⊖✳@🛜) This gorgeous, restored Victorian house is a neighborhood show-stopper full of lovely details. Beautiful antique furniture fills the living and dining rooms, while three rooms and a suite offer comfort and luxury.

🛏 Campbell House
Inn $$

(☏541-343-1119; www.campbellhouse. com; 252 Pearl St; d incl breakfast $129-349; ⊖✳@🛜) A large inn with 18 rooms and lovely common spaces that's well located on a hill in an upscale neighborhood; breakfast buffet included.

South Sister *Stratovolcanoes tower over the landscape*

Classic Trip

Oregon Cascades Scenic Byways

21

Oregon's Central Cascades are a bonanza of natural wonder. Scenic byways pack in lush forests, thundering waterfalls, snow-capped mountains, high desert and lakes galore.

TRIP HIGHLIGHTS

178 miles

Terwilliger Hot Springs
A series of hot pools in a gorgeous natural setting

139 miles

Dee Wright Observatory
A Civilian Conservation Corps project offering spectacular views

• Sisters

⑧

⑨

⑫

• Bend

Mt Bachelor

START/ FINISH
Westfir

④

Salt Creek Falls
Right off the road is the second-highest waterfall in Oregon

26 miles

152 miles

Proxy Falls
Sheer veils of water tumble over columnar basalt

---

4 DAYS
240 MILES/386KM

GREAT FOR...

BEST TIME TO GO

Go June through September to avoid seasonal road closures.

 ESSENTIAL PHOTO

Salt Creek Falls, the second-highest waterfall in Oregon.

 BEST HOT SPRINGS

Terwilliger Hot Springs at Cougar Reservoir.

21 Oregon Cascades Scenic Byways

The region around Oregon's Central Cascades is, without a doubt, some of the most spectacular terrain in the entire state. But one scenic byway just isn't enough to see it all. Here you have our version of an Oregon sampler platter: a loop that brings together several of the best roads to create a majestic route full of the state's best features.

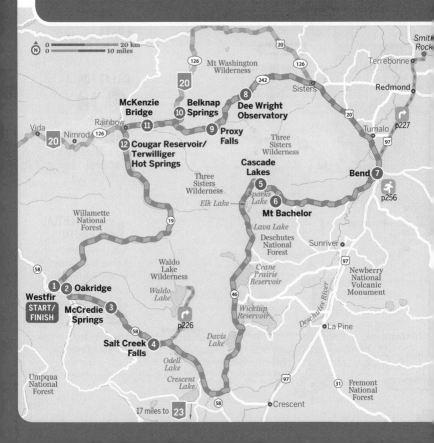

1 Westfir

Before you spend several days enjoying abundant natural wonders, start with a quick photo op of an entirely man-made one: Oregon's longest covered bridge, the 180ft **Office Bridge**. Built in 1944, the bridge features a covered walkway to enable pedestrians to share the way with logging trucks crossing the Willamette River.

If you plan to do some exploring or mountain biking in the area, pick up a map of the Willamette National Forest at the **Middle Fork Ranger District** (46375 Hwy 58; ⏰8am-4:30pm Mon-Fri, plus Sat in summer).

🛏 p229

LINK YOUR TRIP

To Bend & Back
20 One trip isn't enough to cover the Cascades; this complementary route offers alternate paths through the same countryside (p213).

Crater Lake Circuit
23 Crater Lake is a must-see, and it's just south of the Cascades. Take Hwy 97 south from Bend to join this route (p239).

The Drive » Oakridge is just a few miles to the east on either Hwy 58 or Westfir–Oakridge Rd.

2 Oakridge

Oakridge is one of Oregon's mountain biking meccas. There are hundreds of miles of trails around town, ranging from short, easy loops to challenging single-track routes. For novice riders, the **Warrior Fitness Trail** is a mostly flat 12-mile loop. The **Larison Creek Trail** is a challenging ride through old-growth forests, and the 16-mile **Alpine Trail** is considered the 'crown jewel' of the local trails for its 7-mile downhill stretch. **Oregon Adventures** (📞541-968-5397; www.oregon-adventures.com; 47921 Hwy 58) offers shuttles to the top so you can skip the climb; they also offer bike-tour packages.

🛏 p229

The Drive » From Oakridge, Hwy 58 climbs steadily up the Cascade Range's densely forested western slope. Your next stop is about 10 miles east of Oakridge; park on the right just past Mile Marker 45.

3 McCredie Hot Springs

Because **McCredie Hot Springs** (admission free; ⏰dawn-dusk) lies just off the highway, it's a very popular spot for everyone from mountain bikers fresh off the trails near Oakridge to truckers plying Hwy 58. Despite this, it's worth a stop if only because it's the site of one of the largest – and hottest – thermal pools in Oregon. If you can hit it early in the morning or late in the evening midweek, you could have the place to yourself.

There are five pools in all: two upper pools that are often dangerously hot (as in don't-even-dip-your-foot-in hot), two warm riverside pools and one smaller, murkier but usually perfectly heated pool tucked back into the trees. **Salt Creek** rushes past only steps from the springs and is ideal for splashing down with icy water.

The Drive » Keep heading east another 12 miles and pull off the highway at the signed parking lot.

TRIP HIGHLIGHT

4 Salt Creek Falls

At 286ft, this monster of a waterfall is Oregon's second highest. After a good snowmelt, this aqueous behemoth really roars, making for one of the most spectacular sights on the trip. Walk from the parking lot to the viewpoint and there below, in a massive basalt amphitheater hidden by the towering trees, 50,000 gallons of water pour every minute over a cliff into a giant, dark, tumultuous pool. Be sure to hike

Classic Trip

WHY THIS IS A CLASSIC TRIP
MARIELLA KRAUSE, AUTHOR

This trip doesn't promise something for everyone; the Central Cascades' appeal is intoxicatingly single-minded. It epitomizes Oregon's outdoorsy aesthetic, and it's perfect for the road-tripper who wants to hike for hours, find hidden waterfalls, swim in crystal-clear lakes, see entire forests whizzing by the car window, and strip down at the end of a long day to jump into a natural hot spring.

Top: McKenzie River
Left: Dee Wright Observatory
Right: Salt Creek Falls

DOCBOBNY / DREAMSTIME ©

the short trail downhill toward the bottom of the falls. It's lined with rhododendrons that put on a colorful show in springtime, and the views of the falls on the way down are stunning.

Salt Creek Falls is also the starting point for some excellent short hikes, including a 1.5-mile jaunt to **Diamond Creek Falls** and a 4.75-mile hike to **Vivian Lake**.

The Drive » Continue along Hwy 58 until you reach the Cascade Lakes Scenic Byway (Hwy 46), which winds its way north through numerous tiny lakes and up to Mt Bachelor. This road is closed from November to May; as an alternative, follow Hwy 97 to Bend.

----

5 Cascade Lakes

We could get all scientific and explain how lava from nearby volcanoes created the lakes around this area, or we could just tell you that Hwy 46 isn't called the Cascade Lakes Scenic Byway for nothing. The road winds past lake after beautiful lake – **Davis Lake**, **Crane Prairie Reservoir**, **Lava Lake**, **Elk Lake** – all worth a stop. Most have outstanding camping, trout fishing, boating and invigorating swimming ('invigorating' being a euphemism for *cold*).

We love **Sparks Lake** for its scenic beauty set against the backdrop of Mt Bachelor, and it's perfect for peaceful

Classic Trip

paddling. If you find yourself without a boat, **Wanderlust Tours** (☎800-862-2862; www.wanderlusttours.com; half-day tour $55) can hook you up with a guided canoe or kayak tour.

📖 p229

The Drive » Mt Bachelor is just a few miles past Sparks Lake. If Hwy 46 is closed for the season, you can backtrack from Bend to reach Mt Bachelor.

- - - - - - - - - - - - - -

⑥ Mt Bachelor

Glorious Mt Bachelor (9065ft) provides Oregon's best skiing. Here, Central Oregon's cold, continental air meets up with the warm, wet Pacific air. The result is tons of fairly

dry snow and plenty of sunshine, and with 370in of snow a year, the season begins in November and can last until May.

At **Mt Bachelor Ski Resort** (www.mtbachelor.com; adult lift tickets $53-73), rentals are available at the base of the lifts. Mt Bachelor grooms about 35 miles of cross-country trails, though the day pass (weekends and holidays $17, weekdays $14) may prompt skiers to check out the free trails at **Dutchman Flat Sno-Park**, just past the turnoff for Mt Bachelor on Hwy 46.

The Drive » Ready to add a little civilization to your rugged outdoor adventure? Head east to Bend, which is just 22 miles away.

- - - - - - - - - - - - - -

⑦ Bend

Sporting gear is *de rigueur* in a town where you can go rock-climbing

in the morning, hike through lava caves in the afternoon, and stand-up paddleboard yourself into the sunset. Plus, you'll probably be enjoying all that activity in great weather, as the area gets more than 250 days of sunshine each year (don't forget the sunscreen!).

Find out what downtown has to offer with our walking tour (p256). And be sure to check out the excellent **High Desert Museum** (www.highdesertmuseum.org; 59800 S US 97; adult/child $15/9; ⏱9am-5pm, 10am-4pm winter; ♿). It charts the exploration and settlement of the West, but it's no slog through history. The fascinating Native American exhibit shows off several wigwams-worth of impressive artifacts, and live animal exhibits and living history are sure to be hits with the kids.

✕ 📖 p229

The Drive » Head north to Sisters (p216), then drive northwest along Hwy 242. This is part of the McKenzie Pass–Santiam Pass Scenic Byway – closed during the winter months. Your next stop is 15 miles from Sisters.

- - - - - - - - - - - - - -

TRIP HIGHLIGHT

⑧ Dee Wright Observatory

Perched on a giant mound of lava rock, built entirely of lava rock, in the middle

---

DETOUR: WALDO LAKE

Start: ④ Salt Creek Falls

There's no shortage of lakes in the area, but lovely Waldo Lake stands out for its amazing clarity. Because it's at the crest of the Cascades, water doesn't flow into it from other sources; the only water that enters it is rainfall and snowfall, making it one of the purest bodies of water in the world. In fact, it's so clear that objects in the water are visible 100ft below the surface. You can swim in the summer months (it's too cold in the winter), and if you're feeling ambitious after playing 'I Spy' on the lakebed, you can hike the **Waldo Lake Trail**, a 22-mile loop that circumnavigates the lake.

Newberry National Volcanic Monument

of a field of lava rock, stands the historic Dee Wright Observatory. The structure, built in 1935 by Franklin D Roosevelt's Civilian Conservation Corps, offers spectacular views in all directions. The observatory windows, called 'lava tubes', were placed to highlight all the prominent Cascade peaks that can be seen from the summit, including Mt Washington, Mt Jefferson, North Sister, Middle Sister and a host of others.

The Drive » Head west on Hwy 242 to Mile Marker 64 and look for the well-signed Proxy Falls trailhead.

- - - - - - - - - - -

TRIP HIGHLIGHT

⑨ Proxy Falls

With all the waterfalls around the Central Cascades – hundreds of them in Oregon alone – it's easy to feel like 'You've seen one, you've seen 'em all.' Not so fast. Grab your camera and see if you're not at least a little impressed by photogenic Proxy Falls. If there were a beauty contest for waterfalls, Proxy would certainly be in the running, scattering into sheer veils down a mossy wall of columnar basalt. It's not even like the falls make you work for it: it's an easy 1.3-mile loop from the parking area. If you want to save the best for last, take the path in the opposite direction from what the sign suggests so you hit Upper Proxy Falls first and you can build up to the even better Lower Proxy Falls.

The Drive » Nine miles from the falls, turn right on Hwy 126 (McKenzie Hwy); Belknap is just 1.4 miles away.

DETOUR: SMITH ROCK

Start: ⑦ **Bend**

Best known for its glorious rock climbing, **Smith Rock State Park** (www.oregonstateparks.org; 9241 NE Crooked River Dr, Terrebonne; day use $5) boasts rust-colored 800ft cliffs that tower over the pretty Crooked River, just 25 miles north of Bend. Nonclimbers can enjoy miles of hiking trails, some of which involve a little rock scrambling.

227

Classic Trip

⑩ Belknap Hot Springs

Although nudity is the norm at most hot springs, Belknap is the sort of hot spring you can take your grandmother to and neither of you will feel out of place. Two giant swimming pools filled with 103°F (40°C) mineral water provide optimum soaking conditions in a family environment. The McKenzie River rushes by below, trees tower over everything and, as far as we could tell, everyone still has a good time. An excellent alternative to camping, the resort has rooms for nearly all budgets.

🛏 p229

The Drive ⟫ Head southwest on Hwy 126 for 6 miles to get to your next stop.

⑪ McKenzie Bridge

Although from the road it looks like there is nothing but trees, there's actually plenty to do around here, including fishing on the McKenzie River and hiking on the nearby **McKenzie River National**

BLAST FROM THE PAST

The Cascades are a region of immense volcanic importance. Lava fields can be seen from McKenzie Pass and along Hwy 46. Road cuts expose gray ash flows. Stratovolcanoes like South Sister and Mt Bachelor and shield volcanoes like Mt Washington tower over the landscape. Although it's not instantly obvious when you drive to the center of **Newberry National Volcanic Monument** (39 miles south of Bend), you're actually inside the caldera of a 500-sq-mile volcano. What could be stranger than that? It's still active.

Recreation Trail. To learn more about all your recreational options, stop at the **McKenzie River Ranger Station** (57600 McKenzie Hwy, McKenzie Bridge; ⊙8am-4:30pm, reduced hrs winter), about 2 miles east of town. The rangers are fonts of information, plus you can find anything you ever wanted to know about the McKenzie River trail, including maps and books.

🛏 p229

The Drive ⟫ West of McKenzie Bridge, turn left on Hwy 19 (aka Aufderheide Memorial Drive) just past Rainbow. After almost 8 miles, you'll come to the parking lot from which you'll take a 0.25-mile trail through old-growth forest.

⊘ TRIP HIGHLIGHT

⑫ Cougar Reservoir/ Terwilliger Hot Springs

In a picturesque canyon in the Willamette

National Forest is one of the state's most stunning hot springs. From a fern-shrouded hole, scorching water spills into a pool that maintains a steady minimum temperature of 108°F (42°C). The water then cascades into three successive pools, each one cooler than the one above it. Sitting there staring up at the trees is an utterly sublime experience. After hiking back to the car, you can even jump into Cougar Reservoir from the rocky shore below the parking lot.

The Drive ⟫ Continue down Hwy 19 back to Westfir.

Eating & Sleeping

Westfir ①

🛏 Westfir Lodge B&B $

(📞541-782-3103; www.westfirlodge.com; 47365 1st St; r $85-105) Lovely B&B chock-full of antiques. Baths are private but most are outside the room. Full English breakfast included. Cheesecake served most evenings.

Oakridge ②

🛏 Oakridge Motel Motel $

(📞541-782-2432; www.theoakridgemotel.com; 48197 Hwy 58; r $45) With a log exterior and wooden walls inside, this otherwise run-of-the-mill motel is slightly more interesting than some others.

Cascade Lakes ⑤

🛏 Cultus Lake Resort Motel $

(📞541-408-1560; www.cultuslakeresort. com; Hwy 46; cabins per night $85-155) Offers 23 homey cabins with a two-night minimum; week-only from July 4 to September 1. Book well ahead. There's a restaurant, too.

🛏 Sparks Lake Campground Campground $

(Hwy 46; campsites free; 🕐Jul-Sep) It's one of the most scenically situated campgrounds on the entire route, with views of Mt Bachelor and meadows. Pit toilets available; no water.

Bend ⑦

✖ Blacksmith Steakhouse $$$

(📞541-318-0588; www.bendblacksmith.com; 211 NW Greenwood Ave; mains $16-35; 🕐4:30-10pm) This renowned restaurant offers cowboy comfort food with a twist – such as gourmet meat loaf or grilled tenderloin with melted blue cheese – plus a full bar serving creative cocktails.

✖ Victorian Café Breakfast $$

(📞541-382-6411; 1404 NW Galveston Ave; mains $8-14; 🕐breakfast & lunch) One of Bend's best breakfast spots, Victorian Café is especially awesome for its eggs Benedict (nine kinds). It's also good for sandwiches, burgers and salads.

✖ Deschutes Brewery Brewpub $$

(📞541-382-9242; www.deschutesbrewery.com; 1044 NW Bond St; dinner mains $11-18; 🕐11am-11pm Mon-Thu, to midnight Fri & Sat, to 10pm Sun) Bend's first microbrewery gregariously serves up plenty of food and handcrafted beers.

🛏 McMenamins Old St Francis School Hotel $$

(📞541-382-5174; www.mcmenamins.com; 700 NW Bond St; d $135-185; 😊❊📶) The McMenamin brothers do it again with this old schoolhouse remodeled into a classy 19-room hotel. A restaurant-pub, three other bars and a movie theater keep you entertained.

Belknap Hot Springs ⑩

🛏 Belknap Hot Springs Resort Resort $$

(📞541-822-3512; www.belknaphotsprings. com; Hwy 126 near Hwy 242; campsites $25-35, r $100-185, cabins $60-400, day use only $7-12) In addition to soaking, the resort boasts an 18-room lodge, 14 private cabins and 15 tent sites, so it's affordable for nearly all budgets.

McKenzie Bridge ⑪

🛏 Cedarwood Lodge Cabins $$

(📞541-822-3351; www.cedarwoodlodge.com; 56535 McKenzie Hwy; cabins $105-185; closed winter) Ensconce yourself in one of eight rustic, comfortable, fully equipped cabins set above the McKenzie River.

Ashland's Elizabethan Stage
Shakespeare's plays draw crowds

Essential I-5 **22**

Taking the direct route? That doesn't mean you have to miss out on Oregon's road-trip staples. Right off the I-5 lie pioneer history, covered bridges, even a little Shakespeare.

TRIP HIGHLIGHTS

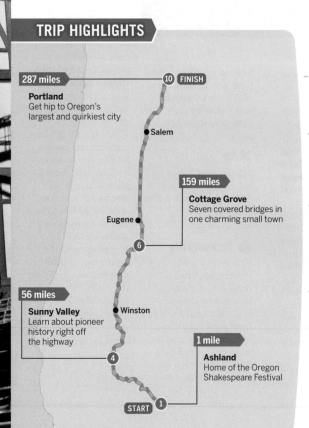

287 miles

Portland
Get hip to Oregon's largest and quirkiest city

10 FINISH

● Salem

159 miles

Cottage Grove
Seven covered bridges in one charming small town

Eugene ●

6

56 miles

Sunny Valley
Learn about pioneer history right off the highway

● Winston

4

1 mile

Ashland
Home of the Oregon Shakespeare Festival

START 1

1–2 DAYS
300 MILES/483KM

GREAT FOR...

BEST TIME TO GO

March through October, when everything is open.

 ESSENTIAL PHOTO

Any of the covered bridges of Cottage Grove.

 BEST FOR CULTURE

A night of theater at Ashland's Shakespeare Festival.

LEE FOSTER / ALAMY ©

231

22 | Essential I-5

The word 'interstate' seldom evokes a road-tripper's dream itinerary, but I-5 will dash those preconceived notions. Oregon's major thoroughfare takes you through mountains, farmland and forests, and there's plenty to see and do along the way — provided you know which exits to take. Just off the highway, you'll find historical sites, roadside attractions and more. It's also the jumping-off place for many of Oregon's backroad gems.

TRIP HIGHLIGHT

❶ Ashland

Prithee, fair traveler, begin thine trip in Ashland, and get thee to the box office, for the players of the **Oregon Shakespeare Festival** (☏541-482-4331 www. osfashland.org; 15 S Pioneer St; tickets $20-96) do strut and fret upon three stages each year from February through October. Back in the Victorian era, Ashland was known for its sulfurous mineral springs that smell not unlike rotten eggs. But now the festival's 10 productions are Ashland's primary claim to fame and draw visitors from all over. The whole town gets in on the act, with nods to the bard found at every turn. For more on Ashland see p258.

✗ 🛏 p237

The Drive » From Ashland, head north on I-5 and take exit 30, then go west on OR-238 for 6 miles.

❷ Jacksonville

This former gold-prospecting town is the oldest settlement in southern Oregon and a National Historic Landmark. Small but endearing, the town's main drag, California St, is lined with well-preserved brick-and- wood buildings dating from the 1880s. But the best place to get in touch with local history is to wander the 32-acre **Jacksonville Cemetery**, at the top of Cemetery Rd, which you access at East E St and N Oregon St, where historic pioneer gravesites chronicle wars, epidemics and other untimely deaths.

The Drive » Take Oregon St north and it will meet up with I-5 in Gold Hill. The well-signed Vortex is a bit over 4 miles north of town on Sardine Creek Rd.

❸ Gold Hill

Some attractions will suck you in more than others, but Gold Hill's **Oregon Vortex** (www. oregonvortex.com; 4303 Sardine Creek L Fork Rd; adult/child/under 6 $9.75/$/free; ⏰9am-4pm Mar-Oct) has gravitational pull on its side, luring visitors with its unexplained phenomena: how did that broom stand up on its own? What made that water run uphill? Detractors will try to explain away the mysterious events that have drawn crowds since the 1930s, but it just sounds like, 'Blah, blah, physics, blah.' Isn't it more fun to just believe?

The Drive » Backtrack to I-5 and go north 27 miles to exit 71. Sunny Valley is right off the highway.

TRIP HIGHLIGHT

4 Sunny Valley

Sunny Valley serves as a quick, convenient stop for a little Oregon pioneer history. Visible from the highway, you could mistake it for a Western-themed rest stop, thanks mostly to the **Applegate Trail Interpretive Center** (www.rogueweb.com/interpretive; 500 Sunny Valley Loop; admission $5.95; ☉10am-5pm daily Jun-Oct, reduced hrs off-season, closed Dec 1-Mar 15), an excellent little museum gussied up like a spaghetti-western storefront, where history is brought to life with taxidermy and sound effects.

If the museum's closed, you can still check out the **covered bridge** that crosses **Grave Creek** and the namesake

🔗 LINK YOUR TRIP

21 Oregon Cascades Scenic Byways

From Eugene, drive 42 miles east to Westfir to kick off a tour of some of the state's most beautiful scenery (p221).

23 Crater Lake Circuit

Hop off at Medford for an inland loop that includes the serene and mysterious Crater Lake (p239).

grave itself, belonging to one Martha Crowley, a pioneer girl who died of typhoid fever on the Applegate wagon train.

The Drive » Get back on I-5 and travel 71 miles to exit 112. Take Hwy 99 N for just under 9 miles.

⑤ Winston

Tiny Winston itself isn't much of a drawcard, but 10 miles southwest is where you'll find the **Wildlife Safari** (www.wildlifesafari.net; I-5 exit 119; adult/child $18/12; ⊙9am-5pm; 🚗) – an animal attraction you don't even have to get out of your car for. Here you can drive around a 600-acre park dotted with inquisitive ostriches, camels, giraffes, lions, tigers and bears (oh, my!) among other exotic animals, then hop right back on the highway and keep driving.

The Drive » Follow OR-42 north to I-5, then travel 48 miles north to get to Cottage Grove. To get to the Mosby Creek bridges, go east on Main St, pass under I-5, then continue 2.5 miles on Mosby Creek Rd and turn left on Layng Rd to access trailhead parking.

ROBIN LOZNAK / ZUMA PRESS / CORBIS / GETTY IMAGES ©

TRIP HIGHLIGHT

⑥ Cottage Grove

With seven covered bridges around town, Cottage Grove has rightfully earned its nickname of the Covered Bridge Capital of Oregon. But the most famous bridge here is a small, open-top railroad trestle that had a cameo at the beginning of the movie *Stand By Me*, when the four pre-teen boys set off on their journey into the woods. The rails have been paved over, and the **Mosby Creek Trestle Bridge** is now part of the **Row River Trail**, easily accessible for hikers, bikers and film buffs. It's also kind of a two-fer, as it crosses the creek just a couple hundred feet from Lane County's oldest covered bridge, the photogenic **Mosby Creek Bridge** built in 1920.

The Drive » Take Mosby Creek Rd back to I-5, then travel north 17.5 miles and take exit 192 for Eugene.

Wildlife Safari An emu gets up close in this drive-though park

❼ Eugene

Fun-loving Eugene is full of youthful energy, liberal politics and alternative lifestylers, making it a vibrant stop along your I-5 travels. Here you'll find a great art scene, exceptionally fine restaurants, boisterous festivals, miles of riverside paths and several lovely parks. A hike up wooded **Skinner Butte**, directly north of downtown, provides good orientation and a bit of exercise (though you can drive up if you're feeling lazy).

If you want to get a dose of history while you're at it, stop at the **Museum of Natural and Cultural History** (http://natural-history.uoregon.edu; 1680 E 15th Ave; adult/child $3/2, free Wed; ⏰11am-5pm Wed-Sun). Housed in a replica of a Native American longhouse, this museum contains good displays on Native American artifacts and fossils.

✕ 🛏 p237

The Drive 》》 Get back on I-5 and travel north 66 miles to the capital of Oregon.

DETOUR: SILVER FALLS STATE PARK

Start: ⑧ Salem

Sure, most of Oregon's 100-plus waterfalls are tucked away in the mountains, but that doesn't mean you have to take a whole separate trip. You can see 10 of them just 22 miles east of Salem at **Silver Falls State Park** (day use $5). Take an 8-mile loop to see them all, or skip straight to the tallest, 177ft **South Falls**. See also p214.

⑧ Salem

As long as you're driving across the Beaver State, be sure to stop by and pay homage – perhaps even sing a few bars of 'Oregon, My Oregon' – at the **Oregon State Capitol** (www.leg.state.or.us; 900 Court St; ☺8am-5pm Mon-Fri). The third Oregon capitol building (the first two burned down) is a sleek, deco-style structure faced with gray Vermont marble. The most notable features of the capitol are four Works Progress Administration–era murals lining the rotunda. Check the schedule – you might be able to catch a free tour.

The Drive ≫ Take I-5 north another 20 miles, then take exit 278 toward Aurora.

⑨ Aurora

Originally built as a religious commune, the town of Aurora still has a common purpose, but now it's antique shops galore (rather than the Golden Rule–based teachings of founder Wilhelm Keil). Dozens of shops line the main streets with offerings that range from rustic to quirky to garage-sale-esque.

If you like your antiques big and chunky instead of dainty and fragile, then make your way immediately to the awesome **Aurora Mills Agricultural Salvage Yard** (www.auroramills. com; 14971 First St NE; ☺10am-5pm Tue-Sun). An enormous, two-story building houses a cornucopia of vintage signs, architectural elements and dazzling miscellany that has the ability to both inspire and overwhelm.

The Drive ≫ Aurora is practically a suburb of Portland, so hop back on I-5 and drive 25 miles to reach downtown and your final destination.

TRIP HIGHLIGHT

⑩ Portland

Stay for more than 10 minutes and you're bound to feel like you've ended up in an episode of *Portlandia* at some point. Quirky, friendly, laid-back – but with a slightly disproportionate number of hipsters sporting bushy beards and skinny jeans – Portland is a must-do on any I-5 itinerary. Stop a while to experience some of the best food, art, beer and music the Pacific Northwest has to offer.

If you didn't book a room at the McMenamin brothers' **Kennedy School** (☎503-249-3983; 5736 NE 33rd Ave), you should at least pop into this former elementary school that's now a hotel, brewpub and movie theater. Wander the halls to check out their colorful collection of mosaics, collages and other cool artworks.

Be sure to poke around the hip boutiques, cafes, bars, bike shops and bookstores along three eastside streets: N Mississippi Ave, NE Alberta St and SE Hawthorne Blvd. Then head downtown and use our walking tour (p254) to discover some of downtown's best stop-offs.

✕ ⛱ p237

Eating & Sleeping

Ashland ❶

✕ Morning Glory   Cafe $

(☎541-488-8636; 1149 Siskiyou Blvd; breakfast $9-12; ⊙8am-1:30pm) This colorful, casual cafe located in a former house is one of Ashland's best breakfast joints, with creative dishes like the crave-worthy Moroccan oatmeal. For lunch there's soup, salad and sandwiches.

✕ Standing Stone
Brewing   Brewery-Restaurant $$

(☎541-482-2448; www.standingstonebrewing. com; 101 Oak St; mains $9-16; ⊙lunch & dinner) Popular brewery-restaurant with burgers, salads, wood-fired pizzas and fancier dinner choices like steaks and seafood; there's also a half-dozen microbrews.

⍔ Palm Motel   Motel $$

(☎800-691-2360; www.palmcottages.com; 1065 Siskiyou Blvd; $103-239; ⛫) A lovably retro, renovated 1940s motor court with a pool and pleasant outdoor seating areas. The smallest rooms are tiny; upgrade if your budget allows.

⍔ Country Willows   B&B $$$

(☎800-945-5697; www.countrywillowsinn. com; 1313 Clay St; d $140-260; ⊜❋@⛆⛫) Feels like the country, but it's only minutes from downtown. This luxurious B&B has nine rooms, plus suites and a cottage, all of which come with a gourmet breakfast.

Eugene ❼

✕ McMenamins
North Bank   American $$

(☎541-343-5622; 22 Club Rd; mains $8-17; ⊙11am-11pm Sun-Thu, to midnight Fri & Sat) Gloriously located on the banks of the mighty Willamette, this pub-restaurant has some of the best views in Eugene as well as the quirky style the McMenamin brothers are known for.

✕ Beppe & Gianni's Trattoria Italian $$

(☎541-683-6661; www.beppeandgiannis. net; 1646 E 19th Ave; mains $14-20; ⊙dinner) One of Eugene's most beloved restaurants: homemade pastas are the real deal here, and the desserts are excellent. Reservations only for groups of eight or more; otherwise, expect a wait.

⍔ C'est La Vie Inn   B&B $$

(☎541-302-3014; www.cestlavieinn.com; 1006 Taylor St; d $140-170, ste $260; ⊜❋@⛆) The unique architecture of this Queen Anne Victorian built in the late 1800s makes it a neighborhood stunner, and the rooms are sumptuously decorated with (tasteful) period details and claw-foot tubs.

Portland ❿

✕ Little Big Burger   Burgers $

(☎503-274-9008; www.littlebigburger.com; 122 NW 10th Ave; mains $4-8; ⊙11am-10pm) Tiny space, tiny burgers. Grab a seat at the counter or at one of the handful of tables in this bright, cheery joint for mini-burgers (including veggie) made from prime ingredients. Wash it down with a side of truffle fries and a can of craft beer.

⍔ Ace Hotel   Boutique Hotel $$

(☎503-228-2277; www.acehotel.com; 1022 SW Stark St; from $105; ⊜❋@) Currently Portland's trendiest place to sleep is this unique downtown hotel fusing industrial, retro and minimalist styles.

⍔ Kennedy School   Hotel $$

(☎503-249-3983, 888-249-3983; www. mcmenamins.com; 5736 NE 33rd Ave; d $115-145; ⊜⛆) Sleep in a classroom, drink in detention hall or eat in the cafeteria of this former school. We can hardly imagine a hotel more fun than this one.

Crater Lake Still waters reflect mountains, like a giant mirror

Crater Lake Circuit

23

Make it a day trip or stay a week – serene, mystical Crater Lake is one of Oregon's most enticing destinations. The best route takes you on a heavily forested, waterfall-studded loop.

TRIP HIGHLIGHTS

199 miles

Toketee Falls
Two tiers flow dramatically over columnar basalt

95 miles

Crater Lake
Clear, blue, serene – this famous lake is like no other

6

● Roseburg

4

3

● Medford

● Ashland

START/
FINISH

Prospect
Take a short hike to the Avenue of Giant Boulders

57 miles

1–3 DAYS
365 MILES/587KM

GREAT FOR...

BEST TIME TO GO
Late May to mid-October when all the roads are open.

 ESSENTIAL PHOTO
No surprise here: Crater Lake.

 BEST WATERFALL
Two-tiered Toketee Falls is our favorite.

23 Crater Lake Circuit

The star attraction of this trip is Crater Lake, considered by many to be the most beautiful spot in all of Oregon. The sight of the still, clear and ridiculously blue water that fills an ancient volcanic caldera is worth the trip alone, but the drive there is lined with beautiful hikes, dramatic waterfalls and natural hot springs, all right off the highway.

❶ Ashland

A favorite base for day trips to Crater Lake, Ashland is bursting at the seams with lovely places to sleep and eat (though you'll want to book your hotel rooms far in advance during the busy summer months). Home of the **Oregon Shakespeare Festival**, it has more culture than most towns its size, and is just far enough off the highway to resist becoming a chain-motel mecca.

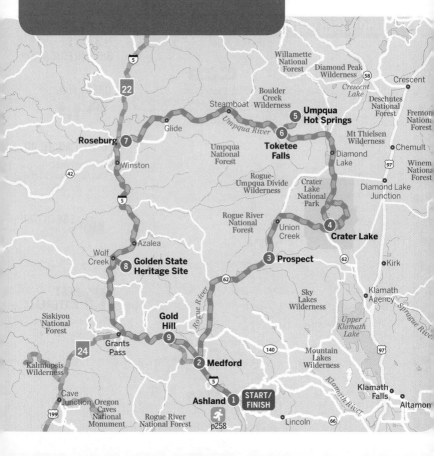

It's not just Shakespeare that makes Ashland the cultural heart of Southern Oregon. If you like contemporary art, check out the **Schneider Museum of Art** (www. sou.edu/sma; 1250 Siskiyou Blvd; suggested donation $5; ⏰10am-4pm Mon-Sat).

Ashland's historic downtown and lovely **Lithia Park** make it a dandy place to spend some time before or after your journey to Crater Lake. Check out our walking tour on p258 for an easy orientation.

 p245

The Drive ⟩⟩ Medford is 13 miles north of Ashland on I-5.

- - - - - - - - - - - -

② Medford

Southern Oregon's largest metropolis is where you hop off I-5 for your

LINK YOUR TRIP

24 Caves of Highway 199

Go from forest to caves to beach with this trip that starts in Grants Pass, between Medford and Roseburg (p247).

22 Essential I-5

Join up with this tour of Oregon's major thoroughfare at Ashland, Medford or Roseburg (p231).

trek out to Crater Lake, and it can also serve as a suitable base of operations if you want a cheap, convenient place to bunk down for the night.

On your way out, check out the **Table Rocks**, impressive 800ft mesas that speak of the area's volcanic past and are home to unique plant and animal species. Flowery spring is the best time for hiking to the flat tops, which were revered Native American sites. After TouVelle State Park, fork either left to reach the trailhead to Lower Table Rock (3.5-mile round-trip hike) or right for Upper Table Rock (2.5-mile round-trip hike).

 p245

The Drive ⟩⟩ The drive along Hwy 62 isn't much until after Shady Cove, when urban sprawl stops and forest begins. Your next stop is 45 miles northwest in Prospect.

- - - - - - - - - - - - -

TRIP HIGHLIGHT

③ Prospect

No wonder they changed the name of Mill Creek Falls Scenic Area – that implies you're just going to see another waterfall (not that there's anything wrong with that). But the real treat at **Prospect State Scenic Viewpoint** is hiking down to the **Avenue of Giant Boulders**, where the Rogue River crashes dramatically through huge chunks

of rock and a little bit of scrambling offers the most rewarding views.

Take the trail from the southernmost of two parking lots on Mill Creek Dr. Keep left to get to the boulders or right for a short hike to two viewpoints for **Mill Creek Falls** and **Barr Creek Falls**. If you've got one more falls-sighting left in you, take the short hike from the upper parking lot to the lovely **Pearsony Falls**.

The Drive ⟩⟩ Follow Hwy 62 for another 28 miles to get to the park turnoff at Munson Valley Rd.

- - - - - - - - - - - -

TRIP HIGHLIGHT

④ Crater Lake

This is it: the main highlight and reason for being of this entire trip is Oregon's most beautiful body of water, **Crater Lake** (www.nps.gov/ crla; admission per vehicle $10, good for 7 days). This amazingly blue lake is filled with some of the clearest, purest water you can imagine – you can easily peer a hundred feet down – and sits inside a 6-mile-wide caldera created when Mt Mazama erupted nearly 8000 years ago. Protruding from the water and adding to the drama of the landscape is **Wizard Island**, a volcanic cinder cone topped by its own mini crater called Witches Cauldron.

Get the overview with the 33-mile **Rim Drive** (open June to mid-October),

JIM LUNDGREN / ALAMY ©

which offers over 30 viewpoints as it winds around the edge of Crater Lake. The gloriously still waters reflect surrounding mountain peaks like a giant dark-blue mirror, making for spectacular photographs and breathtaking panoramas.

You can also camp, ski or hike in the surrounding old-growth forests. The popular and steep mile-long **Cleetwood Cove Trail**, at the north end of the crater, provides the only water access at the cove. Or get up close with a two-hour **boat tour** (adult/child $32/22; ⏰10am-3pm Jul-mid-Sep).

✗ 🛏 p245

The Drive » Head north on Hwy 138 for 41 miles and turn right on Rd 34.

- - - - - - - - - -

❺ Umpqua Hot Springs

Set on a mountainside overlooking the North Umpqua River, Umpqua Hot Springs is one of Oregon's most splendid hot springs, with a little bit of height-induced adrenaline thanks to the position atop a rocky bluff.

Toketee Falls

Springs are known for soothing weary muscles, so earn your soak at Umpqua by starting with a hike – it is in a national forest, after all – where you'll be treated to lush, old-growth forest and waterfalls punctuating the landscape. Half a mile from the parking lot is the scenic, 79-mile **North Umpqua Trail**.

The Drive » The turnout for Toketee Falls is right on Hwy 138, 2 miles past the Umpqua turnoff.

- - - - - - - - - - -

TRIP HIGHLIGHT

❻ Toketee Falls

More than half a dozen waterfalls line this section of the Rogue-Umpqua Scenic Byway, but the one that truly demands a stop is the stunning, two-tiered Toketee Falls. The falls' first tier drops 40ft into an upper pool behind a cliff of columnar basalt, then crashes another 80ft down the rock columns into yet another gorgeous, green-blue pool below. One tiny disclaimer: although the hike is just 0.4 miles, there's a staircase of 200 steps down to the

TOP TIP: VISITING CRATER LAKE

Crater Lake's popular south entrance is open year-round and provides access to Rim Village and Mazama Village, as well as the park headquarters at the Steel Visitors Center. In winter you can only go up to the lake's rim and back down the same way; no other roads are plowed. The north entrance is only open from early June to late October, depending on snowfall.

viewpoint, so climbing back up to your car is a bit of a workout.

The Drive >> From here, the scenery tapers back down to normal as you leave the Umpqua National Forest, but it's just one more hour back to Roseburg.

------

7 Roseburg

Sprawling Roseburg lies in a valley near the confluence of the South and North Umpqua Rivers. The city is mostly a cheap, modern sleepover for travelers headed elsewhere (such as Crater Lake), but it does have a cute, historic downtown area and is surrounded by award-winning wineries.

Don't miss the excellent **Douglas County Museum** (www.co.douglas.or.us/museum; I-5 exit 123; adult/child $5/free; ☻10am-5pm Tue-Sat; 🚹), which displays the area's cultural and natural histories.

Especially interesting are the railroad derailment photos and history of wine exhibit. Kids have an interactive area and live snakes to look at.

 p245

The Drive >> Go south on I-5 for 47 miles and take the Wolf Creek exit. Follow Old State Highway 99 to curve back under the interstate. Golden is 3.2 miles east on Coyote Creek Rd.

------

8 Golden State Heritage Site

Not ready to return to civilization quite yet? Stop off in the ghost town of **Golden**, population zero. A former mining town that had over 100 residents in the mid-1800s, Golden was built on the banks of Coyote Creek when gold was discovered there.

A handful of structures remain, as well as some newfangled interpretive signs

that tell the tale of a curiously devout community that eschewed drinking and dancing, all giving a fascinating glimpse of what life was like back then. The weathered wooden buildings include a residence, the general store/post office, and a classic country church. Fun fact: the town was once used as a location for the long-running Western TV series *Gunsmoke*.

The Drive >> Go south another 45 miles on I-5 and take exit 43. The Oregon Vortex is 4.2 miles north of the access road.

------

9 Gold Hill

Just outside the town of Gold Hill lies the **Oregon Vortex** (www.oregonvortex.com; 4303 Sardine Creek L Fork Rd; adult/child/6 and under $9.75/7/free; ☻9am-4pm Mar-Oct) where the laws of physics don't seem to apply – or is it all just an optical illusion created by skewed buildings on steep hillsides? However you see it, the place is definitely bizarre: objects roll uphill, a person's height changes depending on where they stand, and brooms stand up on their own... or so it seems.

Eating & Sleeping

Ashland ❶

✖ Morning Glory
Cafe $

(☎541-488-8636; 1149 Siskiyou Blvd; breakfast $9-12; ⏰8am-1:30pm) There's bound to be something that will make you happy on their extensive menu full of creative dishes. Expect a long wait for weekend brunch.

✖ Dragonfly Cafe
Cafe $$

(☎541-488-4855; www.dragonflyashland. com; 241 Hargadine St; dinner mains $14-22; ⏰8am-3pm, dinner from 5pm) Tucked away on a side street, Dragonfly is an under-the-radar treat. They serve inventive, Latin-Asian fusion breakfast, lunch and dinner, and the twinkle-lit patio is lovely in summer.

⎸ Columbia Hotel
Hotel $$

(☎541-482-3726, 800-718-2530; www. columbiahotel.com; 262-1/2 E Main St; d $89-149; ⊛✳@⧼) The Columbia is a fabulously located 'European-style' hotel – which means most rooms share a bath. It's the best deal in downtown Ashland, with 24 quaint vintage rooms.

Medford ❷

✖ Organic Natural Cafe
American $

(☎541-245-9802; 226 E Main St; mains under $10; ⏰7am-7pm Mon-Sat; ✎) The theme here is all about local, organic, vegan and gluten-free. In addition to panini-style sandwiches and burgers, there's a salad bar, fresh juices and fruit smoothies.

✖ Porters
American $$

(☎541-857-1910; www.porterstrainstation. com; 147 N Front St; mains $18-30; ⏰dinner) This gorgeous, Craftsman-style restaurant is decked out in dark-wood booths and boasts an awesome patio next to the train tracks. Steak, seafood and pasta dishes dominate the menu.

Crater Lake ❹

✖ Crater Lake Lodge Dining Room
Northwestern $$$

(☎541-594-2255/3217; mains $27-36; ⏰7am-9pm) Try for a table with a lake view; either way, you'll feast on Northwest cuisine like blue cheese halibut and baked citrus duck. Dinner reservations recommended.

⎸ Crater Lake Lodge
Lodge $$$

(☎541-594-2255, 888-774-2728; www. craterlakelodges.com; d $164-290; ⊛) Open late May to mid-October, this grand old lodge has 71 simple but comfortable rooms (no TV or telephones) – but it's the common areas that are most impressive, with large stone fireplaces, rustic leather sofas and a spectacular view of Crater Lake from the outside patio.

⎸ Cabins at Mazama Village
Cabin $$

(☎541-830-8700, 888-774-2728; www. craterlakelodges.com; d $138, tent/RV site $21/$27; ⊛) Also open late May to mid-October, these attractive four-plexes offer 40 additional in-park rooms. They're 7 miles from Crater Lake, with a small grocery store and gas pump nearby. There are also 200 campsites available mid-June through September.

Roseburg ❼

✖ McMenamins Roseburg Station Pub
American $

(☎541-672-1934; 700 SE Sheridan St; mains $8-12; ⏰lunch & dinner, till midnight Fri & Sat) Pure McMenamins style, which means colorful, whimsical and fun. Burgers, sandwiches and salads (finished with a microbrew) are the rule at this cozy pub-restaurant.

Oregon Caves National Monument
Climb, twist and wriggle through

Caves of Highway 199

24

Short but scenic, Hwy 199 strings together a hit parade of natural wonders, from wildflower-covered mountain trails to marble caves and redwood forests, culminating in the Pacific Coast.

TRIP HIGHLIGHTS

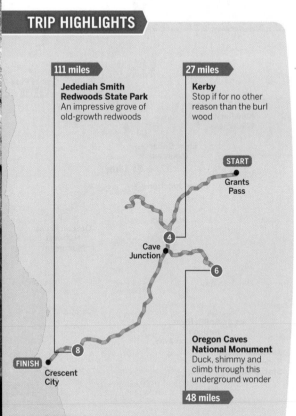

111 miles

Jedediah Smith Redwoods State Park
An impressive grove of old-growth redwoods

27 miles

Kerby
Stop if for no other reason than the burl wood

 START
Grants Pass

4
Cave Junction

6

 FINISH
Crescent City

8

Oregon Caves National Monument
Duck, shimmy and climb through this underground wonder

48 miles

2 DAYS
154 MILES/248KM

 GREAT FOR...

BEST TIME TO GO
April through October, when the caves are open.

ESSENTIAL PHOTO
You, on the banks of the scenic Smith River.

BEST BOTANY LESSON
Check out the carnivorous *Darlingtonia* plant.

JAMES STEINBERG / GETTY IMAGES ©

247

24

Caves of Highway 199

Think Highway 199 is just a convenient connector from the interstate to the coast and Highway 101? Well, you could buzz through it in a couple of hours and think, 'My, what pretty trees we passed.' But take your time and you'll discover an amazing amount of natural diversity all conveniently packaged into one compact area. Prepare to picnic, hike, climb, swim and explore all along the Redwood Highway.

1 Grants Pass

As a modern and not particularly scenic city, Grants Pass isn't a huge tourist destination, but its location on the banks of the Rogue River makes it a portal to adventure. White-water rafting, fine fishing and jet-boat excursions are the biggest attractions, and there's also good camping and hiking in the area. If you're here on a Saturday between mid-March and Thanksgiving, be sure to check out the **Outdoors**

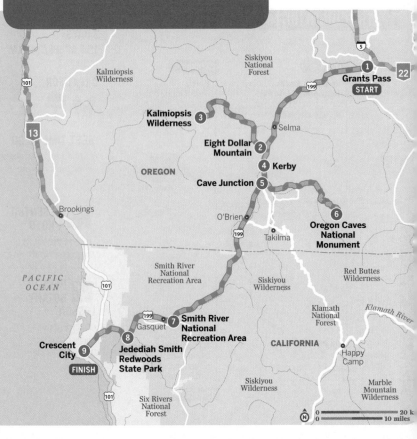

Growers' Market (4th & F Sts; ⏱9am-1pm Sat), a farmers and craft market that draws the city together.

Since the theme of this trip is caves, be sure to stop by the **Visitors' Center** (1995 NW Vine Street) and snap a picture with the local caveman statue for posterity.

 p253

The Drive › Take Hwy 199 24 miles west and turn right on Eight Dollar Rd, just 3.5 miles past Selma. The trailheads mentioned below are less than a mile from the turnout.

② Eight Dollar Mountain

If you think seeing some rare, carnivorous plants would just about make your trip, you've come to the right place. This area

LINK YOUR TRIP

13 Highway 101 Oregon Coast

From Crescent City, drive north to Brookings to kick off your Oregon coastal adventure (p149).

22 Essential I-5

Grants Pass is right on this major thoroughfare that gets you where you're going and has some fun along the way (p231).

is one of the only places on earth where you'll find the *Darlingtonia californica* (also called the Pitcher Plant, the Cobra Lily and 'that little plant that eats bugs'). Beautiful and deadly (but not to us), this lily-like plant gobbles up insects and digests them. The **Eight Dollar Mountain Boardwalk Trail** offers easy viewing of the *Darlingtonia* with a gentle stroll on a boardwalk trail – or if you refuse to be coddled, opt for the still-not-that-strenuous one-mile hike that overlooks the Illinois River.

The Drive › Continue west on USFS Rd 4201 (Eight Dollar Rd). It's 16 long, winding miles from the boardwalk, taking a little over an hour to navigate.

③ Kalmiopsis Wilderness

One of Oregon's largest wilderness areas, the remote Kalmiopsis Wilderness is famous for its rare plant life. About 150 million years ago, the area was separated from North America by a wide gulf and vegetation evolved on its own, so by the time the mountains fused to the continent the plant life was very different from that of the mainland. These unique plant species are showcased on the steep, 0.75-mile hike to **Babyfoot**

Lake. In addition to the carnivorous *Darlingtonia*, the pink-flowered *Kalmiopsis leachiana* and rare Port Orford cedar are found almost nowhere else on earth.

The Drive › Backtrack to US 199. Turn right and go 2.7 miles south to Kerby.

TRIP HIGHLIGHT

④ Kerby

With a population of just 400 – and sometimes listed as a ghost town – tiny Kerby still has a surprising amount going for it. First of all, there's the **Kerbyville Museum** (24195 US 199; adult/child $5/2; ⏱11am-3pm Tue-Sat, noon-3pm Sun Apr-Oct), which is located in an 1880s pioneer home and offers insight into pioneer life and Native American history.

And for real roadside fun, try the whimsical **It's a Burl Gallery** (www.itsaburl.com; 24025 US 199; ⏱8am-5pm), which looks like a hobbit home right on the highway. Part gallery, part attraction, it features fantastical carvings, driftwood sculptures and elaborate treehouses. At the very least, stop by and admire their garden gallery.

 p253

The Drive › Go 2.4 short miles south on US 199 to the town of Cave Junction.

FRANK SITEMAN / GETTY IMAGES ©

❺ Cave Junction

Relatively bustling among towns along US 199, Cave Junction is the jumping-off point for the **Oregon Caves National Monument**. The local terroir – taking advantage of both coastal and inland climates – lends itself nicely to Pinot Noir and Chardonnay, which you can sample at several local wineries.

While you're out here in the middle of nowhere, be on the lookout for lions, leopards, tigers, and jaguars – you can actually spot all of those and more at **Great Cats World Park** (www. greatcatsworldpark.com; 27919 Redwood Hwy; adult/ child $14/10; ⊙10am-6pm in summer, reduced schedule off-season; 🚻). Especially popular among kids and cat lovers, this interactive, 10-acre park features more than 30 trained cats, which, although big enough to eat your head, will merely lick their chops at you.

❌ 🛏 p253

The Drive » Drive southeast on OR-46 for 19 miles.

TRIP HIGHLIGHT

❻ Oregon Caves National Monument

The 'Marble Halls of Oregon' are the highlight of any US 199 trip. During your spelunking adventure at

Oregon Caves National Monument (📞541-592-2100; www.nps.gov/orca; adult/ child $8.50/6; ⊙9am-6pm Jun-Sep, varies rest of year), expect to climb, twist, duck and wiggle your way through the 3 miles of passages and stairs during the 90-minute tour. Your reward is myriad cave formations, such as cave popcorn, pearls, moonmilk, classic pipe organs, columns and stalactites.

Guided tours run at least hourly – half-hourly in July and August. Dress warmly, wear good shoes and be prepared to get dripped on. For safety reasons, children less than 42in tall are not allowed on tours.

A handful of short nature trails surround the area, such as the 0.75-mile **Cliff Nature Trail** and the 3.3-mile **Big Tree Trail**, which loops through old-growth forest to a huge Douglas fir.

❌ 🛏 p253

The Drive » Backtrack to US 199 and head south. After about 15 minutes you'll cross the state line into California. The Smith River Information Center is 34 miles southwest of Cave Junction.

❼ Smith River National Recreation Area

For about 16 miles, **Smith River** weaves back and forth alongside the Redwood Highway,

Jedediah Smith Redwoods State Park

TREETOP TREK

Why settle for a motel when you can sleep in a treehouse? The **Out 'n' About Treesort** (☎541-592-2208; www.treehouses.com; 300 Page Creek Rd, Takilma; treehouse $130-280) near Cave Junction in Takilma offers 16 different kinds of treehouses that sleep between two and six guests. If your fear of heights or their booked-up rooms (reservations are crucial) are keeping you from a treetop sleepover, consider stopping by for a ride on a **zip-line** (☎541-592-2207) or a **horseback trail ride** (☎541-592-2208; 2-hr ride $80)

making this stretch of the **Six Rivers National Forest** the prettiest part of the drive. In summer you can stop off for a swim in the clear, emerald waters; in winter you can try to land a trophy-sized salmon or steelhead (or at least something modest for dinner).

Short, easy and right off the highway, the 2-mile **Myrtle Creek Trail** (US 199 & South Fork Rd) is a popular hike that's lush and green. As you traipse through wildflowers, ferns, cedars and red alder, look for unusual species that will bring out the botany enthusiast in you.

To learn more about the area, stop by **Smith River Information Center** (☎707-457-3131; 10600 US 199, Gasquet; ☻8am-4:30pm Mon-Fri).

The Drive ⟫ Drive 9.6 miles west on US 199 to get to the Hiouchi Information Center.

TRIP HIGHLIGHT

❽ Jedediah Smith Redwoods State Park

Tree-huggers can find plenty to hug in this forest filled with centuries-old redwoods, spruce, hemlock and Douglas firs – and with 20 miles of hiking and nature trails, there's a lot to explore, even if you choose not to canoodle. **Jedediah Smith Redwoods State Park** (information center at 1440 US 199; ☻sunrise-sunset) is a blissfully undeveloped spot full of old-growth redwoods, which can grow up to 300 feet tall. The park's best scenery can be found at **Stout Grove**. To get there, go south on South Fork Rd. After half a mile, turn right on Douglas Park Rd then continue onto the narrow, unpaved Howland Hill Rd for one of the best redwood routes anywhere.

The Drive ⟫ Go 4.5 miles west to the junction of Hwy 101, then take 101 south 4.5 more miles into Crescent City.

❾ Crescent City

You've made it! After nonstop trees, mountains and rivers, you get a change of pace when US 199 dead-ends at the Pacific Ocean. Slightly scruffy Crescent City is hardly the crown jewel of the Pacific Coast, but **Beachfront Park** (Howe Dr between B & H Sts) is a great harborside beach for families, with picnic tables, a bicycle trail and no waves.

The **Battery Point Lighthouse & Museum** (☎707-464-3089; south end of A St; admission $3; ☻10am-4pm Wed-Sun Apr-Sep) offers tours, but only at low tide, and only April through September. But if you luck out (call first) you'll see the keeper's quarters and over 150 years of artifacts, plus a spectacular ocean view from the top.

Nearby, you can hike through the wetlands at the 5000-acre **Tolowa Dunes State Park** to find sand dunes, beaches strewn with driftwood, two lakes and more than 250 species of birds.

✕ ⮡ p253

Eating & Sleeping

Grants Pass ❶

✕ Laughing Clam   Pub-restaurant $$

(☎541-479-1110; 121 SW G St; mains $8-22; ☺lunch & dinner Mon-Sat) Exotic dishes like the cosmic Cajun catfish sandwich and magic mushroom burger are served up at this neon-lit, brick-walled eatery. More standard things like fish 'n' chips, pasta and jambalaya are also available, along with a few rotating microbrews.

⌂ Buona Sera Inn   Motel $

(☎541-476-4260; www.buonaserainn.com; 1001 NE 6th St; d $65-105; 🐾📶) An Argentine/French-Lebanese couple have lovingly renovated this old motel into a comfortable, even slightly luxurious place with 14 country-style rooms. All have quality linens and boast a fridge and microwave; some come with a kitchenette.

Kerby ❹

⌂ Kerbyville Inn   Inn $

(☎541-592-4689; www.bridgeviewwine.com/kerbyvilleinn.php; 24304 Redwood Hwy; $59-105) There's one queen room and four suites, two of which have spa tubs and all of which include continental breakfast. The owners are super-friendly and, since they also own Bridgeview Vineyards, free wine tasting is included.

Cave Junction ❺

✕ Wild River Brewing & Pizza Co   Pizza $$

(☎541-592-3556; www.wildriverbrewing.com; 249 Redwood Hwy; pizza $7-25; ☺lunch & dinner) Fill up on pizza, burgers, sandwiches and microbrews. There are large family tables inside, but if it's sunny, the back deck (overlooking a creek) is the place to be.

⌂ Country Hills Resort   Campground, Cabin $

(☎541-592-3406; www.countryhillsresort.com; 7901 Caves Hwy; tent/RV sites $16/22, d $54-58, cabins $75-95) A friendly, rustic place, this resort has five comfortable country-style rooms and six cabins that come with kitchenettes.

Oregon Caves National Monument ❻

⌂ Oregon Caves Chateau   Hotel $$

(☎541-592-3400, 877-245-9022; www.oregoncaveschateau.com; 20000 Caves Highway, Cave Junction; d $99-155; ☺May-Oct) A stone's throw from the cave's entrance, this six-story lodge has 23 simple, vintage rooms with huge windows facing the forest. Have dinner in the dining room or a snack in the Caves Cafe.

Crescent City ❿

✕ Good Harvest Cafe   Cafe $

(☎707-465-6028; 700 Northcrest Dr at Hwy 101; ☺breakfast and lunch; 📶) The hands-down best place to eat in Crescent City serves big salads, homemade soups, smoothies, sandwiches, omelettes, beer and lots for vegetarians. Too bad it's closed at dinner.

⌂ Anna Wulf Bed & Breakfast   B&B $$

(☎707-464-5340; www.annawulfhousebedandbreakfast.com; 622 J St; rooms/suites $100/$150) Nice, Victorian-style B&B built in 1896. It's not as frilly inside as the lavender exterior would predict. The Honeymoon Suite has an inviting clawfoot tub.

⌂ Crescent Beach Motel   Motel $$

(☎707-464-5436; www.crescentbeachmotel.com; 1455 US Highway 101 S; d $107-130) Simple, dated rooms, but they're clean, and when you see the view you won't care: the beach is right outside your back patio door.

STRETCH
YOUR LEGS
PORTLAND

Start/Finish Stumptown Coffee

Distance 2 miles

Duration Three hours

With green spaces galore, the world's largest independent bookstore, art, handcrafted beer, a vibrant food culture and a livability rating that's off the charts, Portland is made for walking. This route takes you to the highlights of downtown.

Take this walk on Trips

Coffee & Doughnuts

Start with coffee at **Stumptown Coffee** (128 SW 3rd Ave; ☺6am-9pm Mon-Fri, 7am-9pm Sat, 7am-8pm Sun), roasting its own beans since 1999. A minute's walk away is **Voodoo Doughnut** (www.voodoodoughnut. com; 22 SW 3rd Ave; ☺24hr), which bakes quirky treats – go for the bacon maple bar or the 'voodoo doll' filled with raspberry jelly 'blood.'

The Walk » Head toward the waterfront on pedestrian-only SW Ankeny St.

Saturday Market & Tom McCall Waterfront Park

Victorian-era architecture and the lovely **Skidmore Fountain** give the area beneath the Burnside Bridge near-European flair. Hit it on a weekend to catch the chaotic **Saturday Market** (www. portlandsaturdaymarket.com; SW Ankeny St & Naito Pkwy; ☺10am-5pm Sat, 11am-4:30pm Sun Mar-Dec), an outdoor crafts fair with yummy food carts. From here you can explore the Tom McCall Waterfront Park along the Willamette River.

The Walk » Walk north under the Burnside Bridge through the park, then turn left on NW Couch St and right into NW 3rd Ave.

Chinatown

The ornate **Chinatown Gates** (cnr NW 4th Ave & W Burnside St) define the southern edge of Portland's so-called Chinatown – but you'll be lucky to find any Chinese people here at all. The main attraction is the **Classical Chinese Gardens** (www. portlandchinesegarden.org; NW 3rd Ave & NW Everett St; adult/child $8.50/6.50; ☺10am-6pm), a one-block haven of tranquility, ponds and manicured greenery.

The Walk » Make your way west on NW Davis St to NW 8th Ave.

Museum of Contemporary Craft

The **Museum of Contemporary Craft** (www.museumofcontemporarycraft.org; 724 NW Davis St; adult/child $4/3; ☺11am-6pm

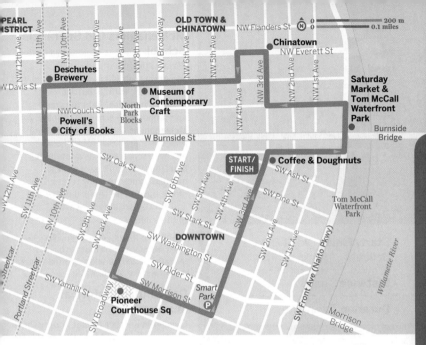

Tue-Sun, to 8pm Thu;) hosts some of the best exhibits you'll find anywhere in Portland, generally featuring fine crafts from artists throughout the Pacific Northwest. Several other top-notch galleries can be found on this block.

The Walk » Continue up NW Davis St to NW 11th Ave.

Deschutes Brewery

Since walking makes you thirsty and you're in Beervana (a group is lobbying to make this Portland's official name), it's high time for a pint and/or lunch. Grab a table under the arches framing the restaurant at **Deschutes Brewery** (www.deschutesbrewery.com; 210 NW 11th Ave; ⏱11am-11pm Mon-Thu, to midnight Fri & Sat).

The Walk » Walk west on NW 11th Ave one block to find yourself in the Pearl District's upmarket shopping area.

Powell's City of Books

Powell's City of Books (☎503-228-4651; www.powells.com; 1005 W Burnside St; ⏱9am-11pm;) is, until someone proves otherwise, the world's largest independent bookstore. Find a whole, awe-inspiring city block of new and used titles and prepare to get lost.

The Walk » Cross W Burnside St then turn left on SW Stark St and right on SW Broadway St to SW Morrison St.

Pioneer Courthouse Square

End your walk in the heart of downtown Portland. This brick plaza is nicknamed 'Portland's living room' and is the most visited public space in the city. When it isn't full of hacky-sack players, sunbathers or office workers lunching, the square hosts concerts, festivals, rallies, farmers markets – and even summer Friday-night movies, **Flicks on the Bricks** (www.pioneercourthousesquare.org/calendar). Around the square is an endless array of shopping, restaurants and food carts.

The Walk » Head east one block down SW Morrison St, turn left on SW 3rd Ave and in five blocks you'll be back at Stumptown Coffee.

STRETCH YOUR LEGS
BEND

Start/Finish Old St Francis School

Distance 2 miles

Duration Two hours

Pretty, compact and occasionally even a little sleepy, downtown Bend has a friendly, laid-back vibe and a small-town feel. Discover public art, quirky businesses, bustling brewpubs and local history in this 2-mile tour of downtown.

Take this walk on Trips

McMenamins Old St Francis School

Former students would hardly recognize their old parochial school today, with its quirky murals, fantastical light fixtures and pronounced sense of whimsy. **McMenamins Old St Francis School** (www.mcmenamins.com; 700 NW Bond St) has been repurposed as a fun-loving hotel, but you don't have to be an overnight guest to enjoy recess. The movie theater, brewpub, outdoor bar and Turkish soaking pool are all open to the public.

The Walk » From the front doors of the school, go left and follow Bond St two short blocks southwest to Idaho Ave, where you'll find the next stop between Bond St and Wall St.

Des Chutes Historical Museum

Located in another former grade-school building, the **Des Chutes Historical Museum** (www.deschuteshistory.org; 129 Northwest Idaho Ave; adult/youth $5/$2; ◷10am-4:30pm Tue-Sat) has plenty to teach you about local history, showing off historical photos and artifacts that illuminate the lives of pioneers, Native Americans, loggers and everyday citizens.

The Walk » Cross Wall St to admire the historic Trinity Episcopal Church. Head northeast on Wall St then go left on Louisiana Ave to Drake Park.

Drake Park

Nature's never far away in Bend; if you can't hit the trails, slopes or river, Drake Park provides a quick fix right downtown. The Deschutes River flows through the park, slowing briefly to form scenic Mirror Pond. Grab a bench, spread a picnic, feed the geese or stroll the paths of this pretty, tree-lined park surrounded by some of Bend's nicest Craftsman homes. If you're lucky, you might catch a performance of **Shakespeare in the Park** (www.shakespearebend.com).

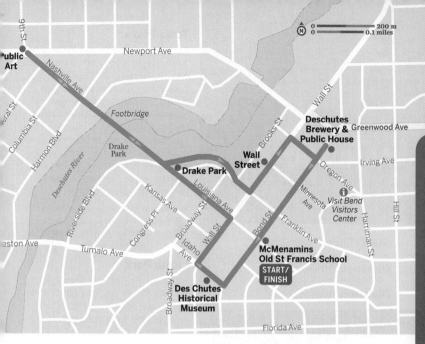

The Walk ›› Cross the pedestrian bridge and continue on Nashville Ave for three blocks.

Public Art

In the roundabout at the intersection of Newport Ave and Nashville Ave is a metal horse sculpture called *Bueno Homage to the Buckaroo*. It's all part of the **Roundabout Art Route** (www.roundaboutartroute.com), which has beautified 20 local roundabouts with large-scale sculptures. This is the only one that's walking distance from downtown, but it might inspire you to jump in your car and visit them all.

The Walk ›› Double back across the river over the pedestrian bridge, turning left on the path that follows Riverside Blvd. When the path ends, continue onto Franklin Ave and turn left on Wall St one block later.

Wall Street

Bend's charming downtown is epitomized in the stretch of Wall Street between Franklin Ave and Oregon Ave. Wander in and out of stores and boutiques and check out the historic **Tower Theatre** (835 NW Wall St), built in 1940. Be sure to stop and indulge your sweet tooth (as well as any children you may have in tow) at **Powell's Sweet Shop** (818 NW Wall St; 🚻).

The Walk ›› Go right on Oregon Ave and left on Bond St, another street with lots of shops to explore; the brewery will be half a block down on your right.

Deschutes Brewery & Public House

The **Deschutes Brewery** (1044 NW Bond St; ⊙ from 11am Mon-Sun) is just one stop on the 'Bend Ale Trail,' a group of 9 local microbreweries that will help you reach 'beervana.' The best way to experience their extensive beer menu? The six-beer sampler – though even choosing just six can be difficult. The food is no afterthought: they serve a wide range of way-better-than-pub grub.

The Walk ›› Follow Bond St south to return to your starting point.

STRETCH YOUR LEGS ASHLAND

Start/Finish Town Plaza

Distance 2 miles

Duration Two hours

With a historic downtown right on the edges of a beautifully designed park, Ashland's best assets are all within easy walking distance of each other – including the ever-popular Oregon Shakespeare Festival.

Take this walk on Trips

Town Plaza

People have been 'taking the waters' in Ashland ever since a lithia-water spring was discovered in 1907; early visitors flocked here to enjoy its supposed health benefits. Sample the coveted mineral water at the **Lithia Fountain** on the Town Plaza, or just enjoy watching unsuspecting tourists take a drink and quickly spit it out: the water tastes and smells like rotten eggs, and just to enhance the experience, it's also carbonated.

The Walk » Right behind the plaza is the northern tip of Lithia Park. Head south to explore the 1.4-mile stretch of greenery; because it's so narrow, it's hard to get lost.

Lithia Park

Listed on the National Register of Historic Places, fetching Lithia Park has been around since 1892. The 93-acre park got a dramatic upgrade in 1914, thanks to the hiring of Golden Gate Park's John McLaren as landscape architect. Today the park includes fountains, a Japanese garden, tennis courts, a duck pond and a band shell – not to mention miles of tree-lined trails. Enjoy colorful blossoms in spring, lush greenery in summer and dazzling, changing colors in fall.

The Walk » When you're done exploring the park, head back to the plaza and turn right on E Main St. One short block later, turn right on Pioneer St.

Shakespeare Theatres

Even if you don't have tickets to the **Oregon Shakespeare Festival** (☏541-482-4331; www.osfashland.org; 15 S Pioneer St) you can still join the fun during festival season. Plan ahead to catch a **backstage tour** (◷10am Tue-Sun; adult/child 6-17 $13/9) that takes you behind the scenes of their three stages, including the outdoor Elizabethan stage. For something more spur-of-the-moment, there are free, half-hour **Green Shows** (Jun–mid-Oct) in the festival courtyard before each night's performance.

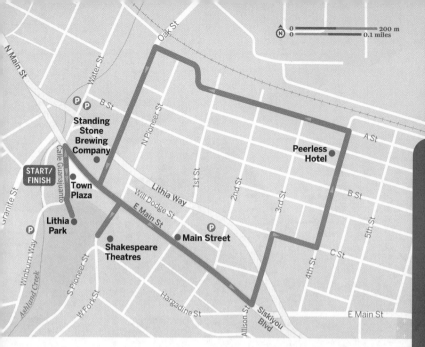

The Walk » Make your way back to Main St and turn right again to explore the historic downtown.

Main Street

The few blocks of Main St between Oak St and N 3rd St are the heart of town, and they're lined with historical buildings that have been turned into shops, cafes and boutiques. The 1910 **Columbia Hotel** (262 E Main St) is Ashland's oldest hotel and it contains the oldest phone booth in Oregon, complete with pressed-tin ceiling.

The Walk » Keep heading east until you reach N 3rd St, then turn left. Turn right on C St, then left on N 4th St. You'll pass a mishmash of commercial buildings as you head toward the old railyard area.

Peerless Hotel

Built in 1900, the **Peerless Hotel** (265 Fourth St) started as a modest boarding house for railroad workers with 10 rooms and one bath. The building was restored (and baths added) in 1994, and part of the process included uncovering and restoring the photogenic, 10ft-tall Coca-Cola sign painted on the exterior brick walls back in 1915.

The Walk » Head west along A St to make your way through the historic railroad district. Turn left on Oak St and get ready for refreshments.

Standing Stone Brewing Company

Sure, there's the craft microbrew made right on the premises. And, yes, there's the sampler tray that lets you try six at once. But **Standing Stone Brewing Company** (101 Oak St; ⊘11:30am-9pm; 🏃) is about more than just beer: the varied menu offers everything from nachos to Thai curry to wild salmon, and there's a kids' menu with lots of non-beer drink options. There's even live music on the back patio during the summer.

The Walk » Just south is the Town Plaza where you began the walk.

British Columbia Trips

FOLLOW WINDING ROADS INTO THE DEEP FORESTS of northern Vancouver Island, where bald eagles soar and black bears munch dandelions on the roadside. Hop through the Gulf Islands, visiting galleries and beaches and watching for orca. Or point your wheels north toward Whistler where dramatic glazed mountaintops scrape the sky. Then coast back down to explore dynamic Vancouver or quaint Victoria.

Healthy living reaches its zenith in British Columbia (BC). You'll eat well, drink well and play well. From islands to glaciers to world-class vineyards, this region beckons for road trips and doesn't disappoint.

British Columbia Trips

To Skagway
(530 km)
ALASKA
Ketchikan

37

USA
CANADA

Dixon
Interance

Prince
Rupert

Terrace

Houston

16

Babine
Lake

Stuart
Lake

Rose
Point

usset

Kitimat

Vanderh

Haida
Gwaii

31

Skidegate

Heroute Strait

Naniku
Lake

Ootsa
Lake

Natalkuz
Lake

Coast Mountains

Gardner Canal

Tetachuck
Lake

Tweedsmuir
Provincial
Park

Estevan
Group

Juan
Perez
Sound

Harvey
Islands

Réserve de Parc
National et Site
Patrimonial Haïda
de Gwaii Haanas

Don
Peninsula

Burke Channel

Charlotte
Lake

Cape
St James

Queens
Sound

Queen
Charlotte
Sound

Fitz Hugh
Sound

Smith
Sound

BRITISH
COLUMBIA

Scott
Islands

Seymour Inlet

Homathk
Icefield

PACIFIC
OCEAN

Cape
Scott

Port
Hardy

Port
McNeill

Brooks
Peninsula

Vancouver
Island

Nootka
Sound

Tofino

29

19

Campbell
River

Strathcona
Provincial
Park

Nanai
Lak
Cowic

4

Pacific Rim
National Park

Cape
Flattery

N 0   200 km
   0   100 miles

Vancouver & the Fraser Valley
25 **2 Days**

Brave suspension bridges and relive pioneer life in a dramatic mountain valley. (p265)

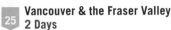

Classic Trip
Sea to Sky Highway 1–2 Days
26 Go from coastal towns to snowy peaks with classic BC sights and views en route. (p273)

A Strait Hop 2–3 Days
27 Features some of BC's largest trees, contemporary fishing villages and an awe-inspiring ferry ride. (p283)

Southern Vancouver Island Tour
28 **4–5 Days**

Time slows down with mellow island-hopping, artsy villages and dramatic beaches. (p293)

Vancouver Island's Remote North
29 **2–3 Days**

Endless sand, old-growth forest, whales, bears and plenty of Native culture. (p301)

Classic Trip
Okanagan Valley Wine Tour
30 **2 Days**

Overflowing fruit stands, award-winning vineyards and amazing cuisine next to a shimmering lake. (p309)

DON'T MISS

Native Culture

With state-of-the-art museums, art galleries, totem poles and modern communities, Native culture is accessible on Trips 26 29 31

Local Refreshments

In-house roasted coffee, local breweries, countless wineries and unique cideries will tempt your taste buds on Trips 27 28 30

Dramatic Beaches

Long Beach with its endless sand, remote Botanical Beach and forested China Beach await on Trips 27 28 29

Ancient Forests

Looking up at the towering old-growth trees in Cathedral Grove, Goldstream Provincial Park and Capilano will leave you dizzy on Trips 27 29 25

Wildlife

While never a sure bet, you have a chance to spot a bear, a bald eagle or a pod of whales on Trips 26 29 32 33

---

31 **Haida Gwaii Adventure 2 Days**
Experience remote wilderness and fascinating Native culture on these edge-of-the-earth islands. (p319)

Classic Trip

32 **Up the Inside Passage 4 Days**
Travel aboard a scenic ferry to far-flung coastlines and gold-rush boom towns. (p327)

33 **Circling the Rockies 3 Days**
See iconic mountain scenery and wildlife at its greatest. (p337)

Stanley Park An urban oasis that's bigger than New York's Central Park

Vancouver & the Fraser Valley

25

This tour has something for everyone – parks, beaches, mountains, vineyards, hot springs and a big dollop of history, starting with an exploration of the coveted seaside city of Vancouver.

TRIP HIGHLIGHTS

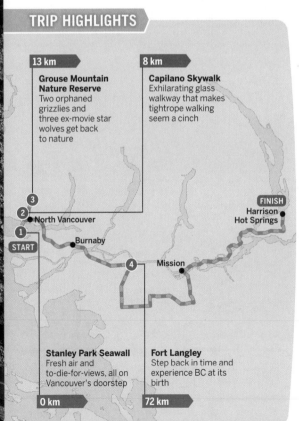

13 km

Grouse Mountain Nature Reserve
Two orphaned grizzlies and three ex-movie star wolves get back to nature

8 km

Capilano Skywalk
Exhilarating glass walkway that makes tightrope walking seem a cinch

③
② ● North Vancouver
①
START ● Burnaby

④ ● Mission

FINISH
Harrison Hot Springs ●

Stanley Park Seawall
Fresh air and to-die-for-views, all on Vancouver's doorstep

0 km

Fort Langley
Step back in time and experience BC at its birth

72 km

**2 DAYS
124 MILES/198KM**

GREAT FOR...

BEST TIME TO GO

June to September for warm days and plenty of ripened fruit.

 ESSENTIAL PHOTO

A picture of friends wobbling over the Capilano Suspension Bridge is iconic.

BEST FOR FAMILIES

Fort Langley offers family fun for all ages. And you might strike it rich at the gold panning!

25 Vancouver & the Fraser Valley

As you step out onto the swinging Capilano Suspension Bridge, get eyed up by a grizzly bear atop Grouse Mountain or watch your children practicing their bartering skills for wolverine skins at Fort Langley, you might wonder what happened to the promised pretty valley drive. But don't worry – it's there. With dramatic mountains rising up on either side, a tour along the Fraser River is as action-packed as it is scenic.

TRIP HIGHLIGHT

❶ Stanley Park

Just steps from downtown Vancouver but seemingly worlds away, Stanley Park is an urban oasis, covered in a quarter of a million trees that tower as high as 249ft (67m). Bigger than New York's Central Park, this 1000-acre peninsula is a favorite hangout for locals, who walk, run or cycle around the 5.5 mile (8.8km) super-scenic **seawall** that circles the outer edge

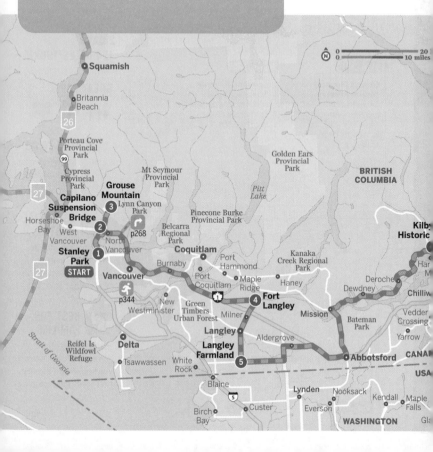

of the park. The path offers amazing views of Burrard Inlet and passes impressive totem poles, squat Brockton Point Lighthouse and log-strewn Third Beach, where you can take a dip. Also watch for **Siwash Rock** standing sentry off the western shore. Meaning 'he is standing up,' it was named after a traditional Native legend that purports it's a man transformed into stone; the hole in the rock is where he kept his fishing tackle.

Looking out across palm-tree fringed English Bay, Second Beach has a heated outdoor **swimming pool** (⊙May-Sep) that is suitable for families. From here, a long sandy beach stretches south along Beach Avenue. On the park's eastern shore you'll find a fantastic **water park** (⊙10am-6pm Jun-Sep) that will keep your kids happily squealing for hours.

Also in the park is the ever-popular **Vancouver Aquarium** (☎604-659-3474; www.vanaqua.org; adult/child CAN$21/13; ⊙9:30am-5pm Sep-Jun, to 7pm Jul & Aug), a non-profit conservation centre that's home to penguins, beluga whales, dolphins, reef sharks and other aquatic life.

🛏 ✕ p271

The Drive ≫ Head north over Stanley Park Causeway and the beautiful Lions Gate Bridge to North Vancouver. Head east on Marine Drive for a block and turn left onto Capilano Rd, heading north for 1.5 miles (2.5km).

TRIP HIGHLIGHT

❷ Capilano Suspension Bridge

Not for the faint of heart, **Capilano Suspension Bridge** (☎604-985-7474; www.capbridge.com; 3735 Capilano Rd; adult/child CAN$31.95/12; ⊙8:30am-8pm Jun-Aug, reduced off-season) is the world's longest (460ft/140m) and highest (230ft/70m) suspension bridge, swaying gently over the roiling waters of Capilano Canyon. As you gingerly cross, try to remember that the steel cables you are gripping are embedded in huge concrete blocks on either side. The region's most popular attraction – hence the summertime crowds – the grounds here include rainforest walks, totem poles and some smaller bridges strung between the trees that offer a lovely squirrel's eye forest walk. You can also try your bravery on the **Skywalk**, a 20in (51cm) wide glass

LINK YOUR TRIP

27 **A Strait Hop**
Hop on the ferry at Horseshoe Bay, just west of North Vancouver (p283).

26 **Sea to Sky Highway**
Head northwest from Vancouver, rather than east, and wind your way up into the mountains (p273).

LOCAL KNOWLEDGE: LORD STANLEY'S PARK

When Governor General Lord Stanley officially dedicated Stanley Park in 1888, a spectator to the ceremony wrote: 'Lord Stanley threw his arms to the heavens, as though embracing within them the whole of one thousand areas of primeval forest, and dedicated it to the use and enjoyment of peoples of all colors, creeds and customs, for all time.'

walkway secured with horizontal bars to a granite cliff face and suspended 300ft (91m) over the canyon floor. Deep breath...

The Drive » Continue north on Capilano Rd. This turns into Nancy Greene Way, which ends at the next stop.

TRIP HIGHLIGHT

❸ Grouse Mountain

One of the region's most popular outdoor hangouts, **Grouse Mountain** (www.grousemountain.com; 6400 Nancy Greene Way; adult/child CAN$40/14, plus Eye of the Wind adult/child CAN$50/14; ⏰9am-10pm) rises 4039ft (1231m) against north Vancouver's skyline. In summer, Skyride gondola tickets to the top include access to lumberjack shows, alpine hiking trails and a **wildlife refuge** that's home to orphaned grizzly bears and timber wolves. A couple of extra dollars gets you a ticket onto an open chairlift that takes you up to 4100ft (1250m)

above sea level (children must be 3.3ft/1m tall). You can also brave the two-hour, five-line circuit zip-line course (CAN$110 including Skyride) or the Eye of the Wind tour which takes you to the top of a 20-story wind turbine tower for spectacular 360° views. In winter, Grouse is also a magnet for skiers and snowboarders.

The Drive » Return south down Nancy Greene Way and Capilano Rd, taking a left onto Edgemont Blvd which leads to

Hwy 1. Head east through the trees, following the highway through Burnaby, crossing Burrard Inlet over the Second Narrows Bridge and then the Fraser River over the impressive, 10-lane Port Mann Bridge. Continue on Hwy 1, exiting at 88 Ave East and following the signs to the next stop. This drive takes just under an hour.

TRIP HIGHLIGHT

❹ Fort Langley

Little Fort Langley's tree-lined streets and 19th-century storefronts make it one of the Lower Mainland's most picturesque historic villages. Its main historic highlight is the evocative **Fort Langley National Historic Site** (www.pc.gc.ca/fortlangley; 23433 Mavis Ave; adult/child CAN$7.80/3.90; ⏰9am-5pm Jul & Aug, seasonal variations; 🚹), perhaps the region's most important old-school landmark.

DETOUR: LYNN CANYON PARK

Start: ❷ Capilano Suspension Bridge

A free alternative to Capilano, **Lynn Canyon** (www.lynncanyon.ca; Park Rd; ⏰7am-9pm May-Aug, seasonal variations) is a verdant park with its own slightly smaller suspension bridge. There are also plenty of excellent hiking trails and some great tree-hugging picnic spots. Check out the park's **Ecology Centre** (www.dnv.org/ecology; 3663 Park Rd; admission CAN$2; ⏰10am-5pm Jun-Sep, seasonal variations) for displays on the area's rich biodiversity. To find the park, head east on Hwy 1 from Capilano Rd and turn left on Lynn Valley Rd.

IAN COOK / GETTY IMAGES ©

Fraser Valley

A fortified trading post since 1827, this is where James Douglas announced the creation of British Columbia in 1858, giving the site a legitimate claim to being the province's birthplace. Chat with costumed re-enactors knitting, working on beaver pelts or sweeping their pioneer home. Also open to explore are re-created artisan workshops and a gold-panning area that's very popular with kids (they also enjoy charging around the wooden battlements and dressing up in clothes from the era). And when you need a rest, sample baking and lunchtime meals from the 1800s in the cafe. This is an ideal place for families and anyone who wants to see history in action.

Be sure to check the fort's website before you arrive: there's a wide array of events that bring the past back to life, including a summertime evening campfire program that will take you right back to the pioneer days of the 1800s.

✗ 🛏 p271

The Drive » Head south out of the village on Glover Rd, crossing Hwy 1 and then taking a slight left so that you're travelling south on 216th Street. The next stop is just past 16th Ave.

- - - - - - - - - - - - - - - -

⑤ Langley Farmland

The vine-covered grounds of **Domaine de Chaberton** (📞604-530-1736; www.domainedechaberton.com; 1064 216 St; ⏲10am-6pm Mon-Sat, 11am-6pm Sun) are the Fraser Valley's oldest winery operation, here since 1991. The French-influenced, 55-acre (22-hectare) vineyard specializes in cool-climate whites: its subtle, Riesling-style Bacchus is dangerously easy to drink too much of on a languid sunny afternoon. There's also a handy bistro here if you need to soak up your overindulgence with a hearty meal.

From here, head south and right on 4th St to the charming **Vista D'oro** (📞604-514-3539; www.vistadoro.com; 346 208th St; ⏲11am-5pm Thu-Sun), a working farmstead where you can load up on fresh pears, plums, apples and stripy heirloom tomatoes. There's also a smorgasbord of exotic potted treats in the little farm shop. Sample preserves such as piquant mango lime salsa and sweet rhubarb and vanilla jam. Also pick up a bottle of the unusual fig wine or the port-style walnut wine made from nuts grown just outside the shop.

The Fraser Valley is home to countless farms, producing everything from tulips to cheese. Many accept visitors, give tours and sell their wares in farm shops. If you're keen to visit some more, go to www.circlefarmtour.com for details.

The Drive » Return north up 216th St and hang a right on North Bluff Rd. Continue east for four blocks and turn left onto 248th St which takes you north to the Fraser Hwy. Head east, following signs for Abbotsford, and then north on the Abbotsford Mission Hwy. This takes you over the Fraser River to Hwy 7. Turn right and follow the road along the river, through farmland and past rambling homesteads. This drive is approximately 1½ hrs, with plenty of produce stops en route. Turn right onto School Rd and then right again onto Kilby Rd.

TOP TIP: TRAFFIC REPORTS

Traffic over the Lions Gate Bridge and along Hwy 1 can be heavy enough to bring you to a standstill at times. Check the **Drive BC** website (www.drivebc.ca) for traffic, construction and incident reports.

⑥ Kilby Historic Site

The clocks turn back to the 1920s when you enter **Kilby Historic Site** (☎604-796-9576; www.kilby.ca; 215 Kilby Rd; adult/child CAN$9/7; ⏰11am-5pm May-Sep, 11am-4pm Thu-Mon Apr, Sep & Oct), all that remains of the once thriving Harrison Mills community. Join a tour led by costumed interpreters as you explore the general

store, hotel, post office and working farm, complete with friendly farm animals. You may even get a chance to try your hand at making traditional ice cream.

The Drive » Return to Hwy 7 and carry on east, passing through farmland and hazelnut orchards. Turn left on Hwy 9, which takes you to Harrison.

⑦ Harrison Hot Springs

Set on the edge of Harrison Lake with views to forest-carpeted mountains, **Harrison Hot Springs** (www.tourismharrison.com) is a resort town that draws both locals and visitors to its sandy beach, warm lagoon and lakeside promenade. While the lake itself is glacier-fed, two hot springs bubble at the southern end of the lake and the warm water can be enjoyed year round at the town's upscale resort (guests only) or the indoor public pool (☎604-796-2244; cnr Hot Springs Rd & Esplanade; adult/child CAN$8.50/6.25; ⏰9am-8pm).

 p271

DETOUR: HOPE

Start: ⑦ Harrison Hot Springs

Hope's nickname is the 'Chainsaw Capital' and this rather unusual moniker certainly draws attention. The name was earned by the wooden sculptures peppered throughout the town. Hope is a small community at the eastern edge of the Fraser Valley, set beneath the shadow of the Cascade Mountains. Created with (you guessed it) chainsaws, the 70-plus sculptures are the products of both local and visiting artists. Most depict wildlife, including the Sasquatch who is believed to live in the nearby woods.

If Hope looks oddly familiar to you, you may be dating yourself. The original *Rambo* movie was filmed here in 1982. For a self-guided tour map of the sculptures and *Rambo* locations, visit the visitor centre on the edge of town. To reach Hope, continue east on Hwy 7.

Eating & Sleeping

Stanley Park ❶

✖ Raincity Grill — West Coast $$$

(☎604-685-7337; www.raincitygrill.com;
1193 Denman St; mains lunch/brunch/dinner
CAN$15/18/28) Just outside the park, this
restaurant was sourcing and serving unique BC
ingredients long before it was fashionable. It's
a great showcase for west-coast cuisine: the
CAN$30 three-course tasting menu (served
between 5pm and 6pm) is a bargain and the
weekend brunch is a local legend. Pick up
takeout gourmet fish 'n chips for CAN$10, then
head to English Bay Beach for a picnic.

🛏 Listel Vancouver — Boutique Hotel $$$

(☎604-684-8461, 800-663-5491; www.
thelistelhotel.com; 1300 Robson St; d from
CAN$180) Just blocks from the park and the
beach, this art-filled hotel is a graceful cut above
the other boutique options in town. Attracting a
grown-up gaggle of sophisticates, the mood-lit
rooms are suffused with a relaxing west-coast
ambience and art-deco style. The on-site
O'Doul's resto-bar hosts nightly live jazz.

🛏 Sylvia Hotel — Hotel $$$

(☎604-681-9321; www.sylviahotel.com; 1154
Gilford St; s/ste from CAN$140/215) Generations
of guests keep coming back to this ivy-covered
gem for a dollop of old-world charm. The lobby
of this beachside inn resembles a Bavarian
pension – all stained-glass windows and dark-
wood paneling – and many of the comfortable
rooms have great views. The best are the 12
apartment suites, which include full kitchens.

🛏 Granville Island Hotel — Boutique Hotel $$$

(☎604-683-7373, 800-663-1840; www.
granvilleislandhotel.com; 1253 Johnston St; d from
CAN$170) Seriously comfortable beds await you
here, with the public market, plenty of dining,
shopping and theater options right on your
doorstep. Characterized by contemporary west-
coast decor, the rooms feature exposed wood and
soothing earth tones. There's also a cool rooftop
Jacuzzi, while the on-site brewpub makes its own
distinctive beer (Jamaican Lager recommended).

Fort Langley ❹

✖ Veggie Bob's Growcery Cafe — Vegetarian $

(☎604-888-1223; www.veggiebobs.ca; Glover
Rd; mains CAN$6-10; ☉11am-5pm; 🖉) This
cafe and organic produce shop is overflowing in
a wonderful way. Tidy checked tablecloths and
barrels of apples greet you, along with a hearty
menu of sandwiches, burgers and soups. Try the
Mexi Burger or go for the simple (but amazingly
tasty) aged cheddar, fresh basil and vine tomato
sandwich. It's all organic.

🛏 Fort Langley Guesthouse — B&B $$

(☎604-309-6738; www.fortlangleyguesthouse.
com; 9097 Queen St; r CAN$135-165) Set in a
gabled home in the village, with a pretty garden
and lots of privacy, the two guestrooms here
have period charm. The Honeysuckle Room has
an eating area, a big tub and beautiful wooden
beds. Breakfast includes home baking, local
sausages and fresh fruit.

Harrison Hot Springs ❺

✖ Yukiya Sushi — Japanese $$

(☎604-796-2633; 140 Esplanade Ave; mains
CAN$14-20; ☉11am-8pm) With authentic
Japanese decor and mouth-watering smells
coming from the kitchen, this welcoming
lakeside restaurant bids you to sit down and fill
your belly. You'll want to fill up on the delicious
appetizers like gyoza or edamame, but save
room for the sushi, udon noodles and tempura.

🛏 Harrison Hot Springs Resort — Hotel $$$

(☎866-626-8822; www.harrisonresort.com;
100 Esplanade Ave; r CAN$135-165) This fabled
resort exudes peace. Open since 1886, it has
an art-deco flair and impeccable service.
The five hot spring pools are set in an inner
courtyard complete with trees and fairy lights.
There is also a divine-smelling spa, numerous
restaurants and a concierge who can arrange
everything from fishing trips to golf.

Sea to Sky Highway *Views range from majestic to jaw-dropping*

Classic Trip

Sea to Sky Highway

26

The coastal scenery here is magnificent – as are the deep forests, crashing waterfalls and lofty mountains. When you can see it all in a day, this tour is almost too good to be true.

TRIP HIGHLIGHTS

132 km — **10** **FINISH**

Squamish Lil'wat Cultural Centre
Native culture revealed through fascinating, interactive exhibits

9

87 km

Brandywine Falls
Your knees will go to jelly as you look over the plummeting water

56 km — **5**

Brackendale Eagle Run
Soaring, hunting and hanging out in the hundreds

● Squamish

3

35 km

Britannia Mine Museum
Grab your hard hat for a look into a mining community

Horseshoe Bay ●
START

1–2 DAYS
82 MILES/132KM

GREAT FOR...

BEST TIME TO GO

November to March has the best snow; June to September offers hiking, plus driving without chains.

 ESSENTIAL PHOTO

Get the ultimate snowy-peak picture from Tantalus Outlook.

 BEST FOR OUTDOOR ENTHUSIASTS

Ski Olympic-style down Mt Whistler.

x

x

273

Classic Trip

Sea to Sky Highway

Drive out of North Vancouver and straight into the wild west coast. This short drive reveals the essence of British Colombia's coast with majestic sea and mountain views, opportunities to get active, wildlife-watching possibilities and a peek into the rich Native American culture and pioneer history that is woven along this highway. There's even freshly roasted, organic coffee en route. How much more 'BC' can you get?

❶ Horseshoe Bay

As clouds and mist drift in across the snowcapped mountains of Howe Sound, standing at the foot of Horseshoe Bay may well make you feel like you've stepped into Middle Earth. Green-forested hills tumble down around the village, which has a small-town, remote vibe that doesn't attest to its proximity to Vancouver. Grab a coffee and some fish 'n chips from one of the many waterfront cafes and watch the bobbing fishing boats from the seaside park. Venture out onto the wharf and breathe in the salty air. This first stop is all about slowing down and taking it all in.

Have a wander through the **Spirit Gallery** (www.spirit-gallery.com; 6408 Bay St; ⏰10am-6pm with seasonal variations), which is filled with classic and contemporary Native American designs. You'll find everything from eye glasses to animal hand-puppets, prints, pewter and carvings.

✕ p281

The Drive ❯❯ Head west on Hwy 99 North which curves around the coast and follows Howe Sound north. You'll be travelling between steep mountainsides, down which waterfalls plummet, and the often misty ocean where islands are perched like sleeping giants. Watch out for Tunnel Point Lookout on the western side of the highway for a vantage point across the sound.

❷ Porteau Cove Provincial Park

Once popular with Native Americans for sturgeon fishing, Porteau Cove is one of the oldest archaeological sites on the Northwest coast. These days it's a haven for divers, with reefs that support countless species of marine life, such as lingcod and octopus. The rocky beach is good for exploring, with plenty of logs to clamber on, and in summer the water is just about warm enough for a very quick dip.

The Drive ❯❯ From here, the sound narrows and as you continue north on Hwy 99, the mountains from the opposite shore begin to loom over you.

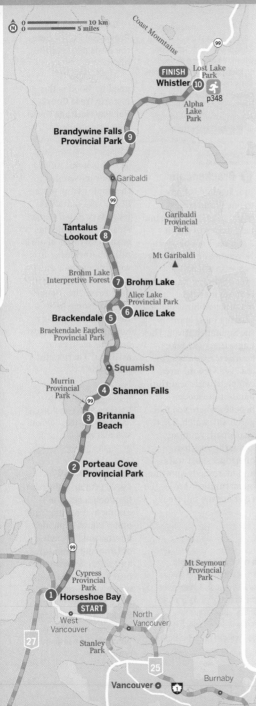

0 10 km
0   5 miles

Coast Mountains

99

FINISH Lost Lake Park
Whistler 10 p348

Alpha Lake Park

Brandywine Falls Provincial Park 9

Garibaldi

99

Garibaldi Provincial Park

Tantalus Lookout 8

Mt Garibaldi ▲

Brohm Lake Interpretive Forest 7 **Brohm Lake**

Alice Lake Provincial Park

Brackendale 5 6 **Alice Lake**

Brackendale Eagles Provincial Park

Squamish

Murrin Provincial Park 4 **Shannon Falls**

99

3 **Britannia Beach**

2 **Porteau Cove Provincial Park**

99

Cypress Provincial Park Mt Seymour Provincial Park

1 **Horseshoe Bay**
START

West Vancouver North Vancouver

Stanley Park

25

Vancouver ○ Burnaby

TRIP HIGHLIGHT

3 Britannia Beach

Operational from 1904 to 1974, the mine at Britannia Beach produced more copper than any other mine in the British empire. Accessible only by boat until 1956, the tight-knit community that grew here was entirely linked to the 150 miles (210km) of mine running through the mountain, but also established a library, a school and even a roller rink.

Today you can don a hard hat and hop on a train that takes you 6ft under into the mines. With hands-on exhibits, gold-panning, an engaging film and entry into the dizzying 20-story mill, the **Britannia Mine Museum** (www. britanniaminemuseum.ca;

LINK YOUR TRIP

25 **Vancouver & the Fraser Valley**

Hwy 99 begins in North Vancouver so it's easy to link these tours (p265).

27 **A Strait Hop**

Trip 27 goes through Horseshoe Bay, the first stop on this tour. You could therefore do the Sea to Sky Highway as a detour (p283).

Britannia Beach; adult/child CAN$21.50/13.50; ⏰9am-5:30pm; 👪) has plenty to keep you (and any kids in tow) busy. You'll need a couple of hours here (see p278).

🍴 p281

The Drive » Continue north on Hwy 99, through the lush green Murrin Provincial Park.

④ Shannon Falls

Torpedoing 1100ft (335m) over the mountaintop, Shannon Falls are the third largest in the province. Alongside these powerful falls is where Squamish Native medicine people trained.

A short, picturesque walk through the woods leads to a viewing platform. You can also hike from here to the peak of the **Stawamus Chief**.

The Drive » Continue north on Hwy 99, past the Stawamus Chief and through Squamish, where you can stop for road snacks (p281), gas and supplies. Carry on down the highway, taking a left on Depot Rd and then left onto Government Rd. The next stop is a few minutes up the road on the right.

⑤ Brackendale

Brackendale is home to one of the largest populations of wintering bald eagles in North America. Visit between November and February to see an almost overwhelming number of these massive, magnificent birds feasting on salmon in the Squamish River. The **Eagle Run** (Government Rd; www.brackendaleeagles. com) is a viewing area complete with beautiful, hand-built wooden benches where you can perch and watch. There's also a path running along the riverbank, offering a short walk and more eagle-spotting opportunities. Across the river are the tall trees of **Brackendale Eagles Provincial Park** where the birds perch in the night.

Also in this neighborhood is the historic **West Coast Railway Heritage Park** (www.wcra.org; 39645 Government Rd; adult/child CAN$15/10; ⏰10am-5pm; 👪). This large, mostly outdoor museum is the final resting place of British Columbia's legendary *Royal Hudson* steam engine and has around 90 other historic railcars, including 10 working engines and cabooses, sleepers and mail cars. Check out the handsome new Roundhouse building, housing the park's most precious trains and artifacts. There's also a kids' zone.

The Drive » From Brackendale, Hwy 99 North leaves the Squamish River and heads into the trees. The next stop is on the right.

⑥ Alice Lake

Delve into an old-growth hemlock forest for hiking and biking trails and a lakeside picnic. Surrounded by a ring of towering mountains and offering two sandy beaches and relatively warm water in summer, **Alice Lake Provincial Park** is a popular spot for a dip, a walk and a picnic on the lakeside lawns.

LOOK FAMILIAR?

The mine at Britannia Beach has been used as a filming location for more than 50 movies and TV shows. *X-Files*, *Smallville*, *Dark Angel* and *Insomnia* are just a few of the names on its list of appearances.

If you carry on to Shannon Falls and have any teens with you, they'll likely experience severe déjà vu. These falls featured in the *Twilight* film *Breaking Dawn*.

THE STAWAMUS CHIEF

This guy is hard to miss. Towering 2300ft (700m) above the waters of Howe Sound, it's the second-largest freestanding granite monolith in the world. The Stawamus Chief and its three peaks have long been considered a sacred place to the Squamish people; they once came here seeking spiritual renewal. It's also the nesting grounds of peregrine falcons, who have increasingly returned to the area.

The views from the top are unbelievable, but getting up there is a challenge. The sheer face of the monolith has become a magnet to rock climbers, while hikers take trails from the eastern side. If you plan to scale the Chief, pick up a map and any supplies in nearby Squamish.

If you want to stretch your legs, the **Four Lakes Trail** (3.75 miles/6km) is a fairly easy hike that does a loop around all four lakes in the park, passing through stands of Douglas fir and western red cedar. Keep your eyes (and your ears) peeled for warblers, Steller's jay and chickadees as well as for box turtles that sometimes sun themselves on the logs at Stump Lake.

The Drive » Continue north along Hwy 99.

7 Brohm Lake

Less developed than Alice Lake Provincial Park, **Brohm Lake Interpretive Forest** has 6.25 miles (10km) of walking trails, many of them easy and flat. The lake is warm enough for a swim in the summer as the sun filters down through the tree-lined shore.

Archaeological digs from this area have unearthed arrowheads and tools from early Native American communities that date back 10,000 years. The area was later the scene of a logging mill and today is home to **Tenderfoot Fish Hatchery** (☺9am-3pm), a facility aimed at replenishing depleted salmon stocks, which fell from around 25,000 in the 1960s to around 1500 in the early 1980s. You can visit the hatchery and take a self-guided tour by following a 2-mile (3km) trail from Brohm Lake.

The Drive » Continue up Hwy 99 just over 2 miles (3km) to the next stop.

8 Tantalus Lookout

This viewpoint looks out across the Tantalus Mountain Range. Tantalus was a character in Greek mythology who gave us the word 'tantalize'; apparently the mountains were named by an explorer who was tempted to climb the range's snowy peaks, but was stuck on the other side of the turbulent Squamish River. In addition to Mt Tantalus, the Greek hero's entire family is here – his wife, Mt Dione, his daughter, Mt Niobe, his son, Mt Pelops, and his grandson, Mt Thyestes.

The Squamish people once used this area to train in hunting and believe that long ago, hunters and their dogs were immortalized here, becoming the soaring mountain range. Those stone hunters must be rather tantalized themselves; the forested slopes of

TOP TIP: GAS STATION?

There is nowhere to fill your tank between North Vancouver and Squamish, a distance of around 29 miles (46km). This is mountain driving so make sure you've got at least half a tank when you set out.

CHRISTOPHER KIMMEL / GETTY IMAGES ©

LOCAL KNOWLEDGE
ANNA GILROY
HISTORICAL
INTERPRETER,
BRITANNIA MINE
MUSEUM

I'm always taken aback by the depth and richness of the social history in Britannia. It was a unique place – an entire community was built around this mine. It's often missed by visitors thinking, 'Yes, this was a copper mine for a while, then it shut down and became a museum,' but so many residents of Britannia come back to tell us about their childhood here and what a fantastic community it was. And still is! Many people still call Britannia home.

Top: A gondola ride over Whistler
Left: Shannon Falls
Right: Village Stroll, Whistler

the mountains are home to grizzly bears, elk, wolverines, wolves and cougars.

The Drive » Follow Hwy 99 14 miles (22km) north through the woods, skirting the edge of Daisy Lake before reaching the next stop on your right.

TRIP HIGHLIGHT

⑨ Brandywine Falls Provincial Park

Surging powerfully over the edge of a volcanic escarpment, **Brandywine Falls** plunge a dramatic 230ft (70m) – a straight shot into the pool below. Follow the easy 10-minute trail through the woods and step out onto the viewing platform, directly over the falls.

From here you can also see **Mt Garibaldi**, the most easily recognizable mountain in the Coast Range. Its distinctive jagged top and color has earned it the name Black Tusk. This mountain is of particular significance to local Native American groups who believe the great Thunderbird landed here. With its supernatural ways, it shot bolts of lightning from its eyes, creating the color and shape of the mountaintop.

A 4.3-mile (7km) looped trail leads further through the park's dense forest and ancient lava beds to Cal-Cheak Suspension Bridge.

Classic Trip

The Drive » Continue north along Hwy 99, passing Creekside Village and carrying on to the main Whistler Village entrance. (It's well signposted and obvious once you see it.)

TRIP HIGHLIGHT

10 Whistler

Nestled in the shade of the formidable Whistler and Blackcomb Mountains, Whistler has long been Vancouver's golden child. Popular in winter for its world-class ski slopes, dogsledding and bobsledding, and in summer for everything from hiking to mountain biking and scream-inducing zip-line runs, Whistler draws fans from around the world. It was named for the furry marmots that fill the area with their loud whistle; in addition to marmots, there are plenty of black bears about.

The site of many of the outdoor events at the 2010 Winter Olympic and Paralympic Games, Whistler has gone and gotten all grown-up. Its centre is filled with an eclectic mix of stores – everything from hot shops to Lululemon and Billabong. You'll also find flash hotels and seemingly countless cafes and restaurants – take a stroll on our walking tour (p348).

Criss-crossed with over 200 runs, the **Whistler-Blackcomb** (www.whistlerblackcomb.com; 3-day lift ticket adult/child/ youth CAN$279/140/237) sister mountains are linked by a 2.75-mile (4.4km) gondola that includes the world's longest unsupported span. Ski season runs late November to April on Whistler and June on Blackcomb. **Ziptrek Ecotours** (www.ziptrek. com; Carleton Lodge, Whistler Village; adult/ child CAN$110/90; year-round;) offers zip-line courses that will have you screaming with gut-quivering pleasure.

While you're here, be sure to take in the dramatic wood-beamed **Squamish Lil'wat**

THE STORY BEGINS...

As you enter the Squamish Lil'wat Cultural Centre, take a look at the carved cedar doors you're passing through. The center's guide map says: 'The right door, with the human face and hands up, represents the Squamish welcoming all visitors into the Centre. The mountains represent our traditional territory. The left door depicts the silver tip grizzly bear – protector of the Lil'wat. The salmon symbolizes sharing. The carving honours a mother bear and cub that walked through the Centre during construction.'

Cultural Centre (www. slcc.ca; 4854 Blackcomb Way; adult/child/youth CAN$18/8/11; 9:30am-5pm), built to resemble a traditional longhouse. This beautiful space is filled with impressive relics, art, images and interactive displays that tell of traditional and contemporary cultures of the Squamish and Lil'wat Nations. Join one of the hourly tours to be greeted with drumming and a welcome song. You'll also be shown traditional weaving techniques and have the chance to create your own cedar rope. Also check out the fantastic gift shop and try contemporary Native American cuisine (such as a bison and wild bear smokey or a salmon bannock burger) at the cafe.

p281

Eating & Sleeping

Horseshoe Bay ❶

✖ The Boathouse   Seafood $$$

(📞604-921-8188; www.boathouserestaurants.
ca; 6695 Nelson Ave; brunch/lunch/dinner
CAN$15/20/28; ⏱11:30am-9:30pm Mon-Sat,
10am-9:30pm Sun; 🚻) With a big, open sea
view that's a necessity in Horseshoe Bay, the
Boathouse is casual in a sophisticated kind of
way. Crisp white tablecloths and oysters on ice
await diners, as does a contemporary seafood
menu with choices like stuffed prawns with
mango salsa and miso-crusted wild halibut.
Arrive before 2pm if you want to partake in the
tasty brunch. There's also a kids' menu.

Britannia Beach ❸

✖ Galileo Coffee Company   Cafe $

(📞604-896-0272; 173 Hwy 99; baked goods
CAN$4; ⏱7am-3pm) Located just south of
Britannia Beach, it's a wonder you can't follow
your nose to this place from Horseshoe Bay.
Inside this unassuming roadside house, coffee is
roasting to perfection. Grab a cup for the road or
sit and savor it with some tummy-pleasing treats.

Squamish

✖ Howe Sound Pub
& Brewing Company   Pub $$

(📞604-892-2603; www.howesound.com;
37801 Cleveland Ave; lunch CAN$12-15) This
rustic brewery has a deck with views of the
Chief (p277), where you can get comfortable
and partake in some yam fries and oatmeal
stout. Or head inside the wood-and-beam pub
for handmade pizzas, eclectic burgers and
sandwiches, and pub favorites like pot pie and
fish 'n chips (battered, of course, with the local
honey pale ale).

Whistler ❿

✖ 21 Steps   Contemporary $$

(📞604-966-2121; www.21steps.ca; St
Andrew's House, Main Village; mains CAN$15-
30; ⏱5:30pm-midnight; 🚻) Attentive staff
is well-versed in the creative, indulgent menu
that will leave you savoring every morsel. The
chef goes that extra mile, caramelizing the
pecans or creating tantalizing sauces. There's
tender meat, fresh seafood, meal-like salads
and amazing pastas. The only difficulty is in
choosing. This place is fairly casual and has a
kids' menu to prove it. Also check out the great
attic bar, a Whistlerite favorite.

🛏 Adara Hotel   Hotel $$

(📞604-905-4009; www.adarahotel.com; 4122
Village Green, Main Village; r CAN$130-160) Skis
and boots and snowboards give a lot of wear
and tear to a hotel and consequently, most
hotels in Whistler have a well-loved feel. But
you won't care, because you'll love the Adara
too. Filled with designer details like fancy
lighting, plush throws, mood acoustics and
iPod docking stations, the rooms feel snug and
comfortable. The beds are cloud-like and the
service is warm.

🛏 Edgewater Lodge   Hotel $$$

(📞604-932-0688, 888-870-9065; www.
edgewater-lodge.com; 8020 Alpine Way;
r CAN$190-230) Hidden in a peninsula
outstretched into Green Lake and surrounded
by old-growth forest, this 12-room lodge is
what 'getting away from it all' is all about. A few
minutes' drive past Whistler on Hwy 99, each
homey room overlooks the water – sit in your
padded window alcove and watch the ospreys
or hit the surface with a kayak rental. There's
also a fabulous restaurant here.

Victoria British Columbia's
charming seaside capital

A Strait Hop

27

BC's forested, multi-fjorded coastline stretches for around 15,000 miles (24,000km). But you don't have to drive that far for a taste of the region's salty, character-packed waterfront communities.

TRIP HIGHLIGHTS

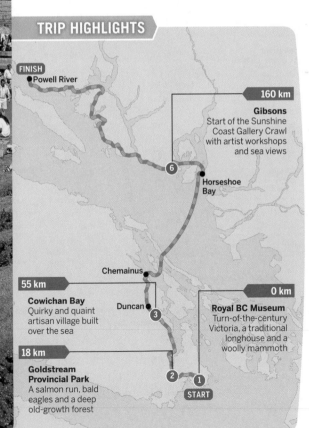

FINISH Powell River

160 km
Gibsons
Start of the Sunshine Coast Gallery Crawl with artist workshops and sea views

Horseshoe Bay

Chemainus

55 km
Cowichan Bay
Quirky and quaint artisan village built over the sea

Duncan

0 km
Royal BC Museum
Turn-of-the-century Victoria, a traditional longhouse and a woolly mammoth

18 km
Goldstream Provincial Park
A salmon run, bald eagles and a deep old-growth forest

START

2–3 DAYS
219 MILES/351KM

GREAT FOR...

BEST TIME TO GO
June to mid-September offers the most sunshine and least rain.

 ESSENTIAL PHOTO
Clouds draped across mountaintops from the Horseshoe Bay ferry.

BEST FOR ART LOVERS
Be inspired by Cowichan Bay's artisan galleries.

27 A Strait Hop

Perhaps it's the way the sunlight reflects across the ever-shifting ocean, or the inevitable forest walks and beachcombing that seem an essential part of life on the coast. Whatever the reason, the towns and villages snuggled up next to the Pacific draw artistic folk from all over the world. It's here that they settle down and create strong communities and beautiful art. Take this leisurely tour for a slice of life on both the mainland and Vancouver Island.

TRIP HIGHLIGHT

1 Victoria

British Columbia's seaside capital city is dripping with colonial architecture and has enough museums, attractions, hotels and restaurants – many showcasing lip-smacking regional ingredients – to keep most visitors happy for an extra night or two. Check out our walking tour (p346) to get you started.

Must-see attractions include the evocative **Royal BC Museum**

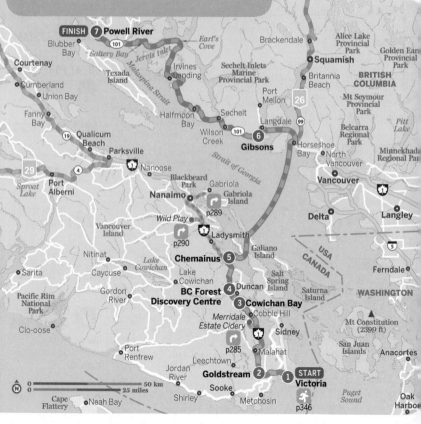

(www.royalbcmuseum.bc.ca; 675 Belleville St; adult/child CAN$21.60/15.75; ⏰10am-5pm). Come eye to beady eye with a woolly mammoth and look for cougars and grizzlies peeking from behind trees. Step aboard Captain Vancouver's ship, enter a First Nations cedar longhouse, and explore a recreated street from the early colonial city, complete with Chinatown, stores and a little movie house. The museum also has an IMAX theater and worthwhile special exhibits.

Also worth visiting is the **Art Gallery of Greater Victoria** (www.aggv.bc.ca; 1040 Moss St; adult/child CAN$13/2.50; ⏰10am-5pm Mon-Sat,

LINK YOUR TRIP

26 Sea to Sky Highway

Join this trip at Horseshoe Bay, making a return trip to Whistler and then carrying on to Gibsons (p273).

29 Vancouver Island's Remote North

From Nanaimo on Vancouver Island, head north to Parksville or catch the ferry between Powell River on the mainland and Courtenay on the island (p301).

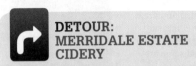

DETOUR: MERRIDALE ESTATE CIDERY

Start ② Goldstream

After leaving Goldstream, head west off the highway onto Cobble Hill Rd. This loops through farmland and wine-growing country. Watch for asparagus farms, llamas, blueberry stalls and vineyards. Stop in at **Merridale Estate Cidery** (www.merridalecider.com; 1230 Merridale Rd, Cobble Hill; ⏰10:30am-4:30pm), an inviting apple-cider producer offering seven varieties as well as a fortified wine and an unusual brandy-distilling operation.

Cobble Hill Rd crosses over the highway and loops east to Cowichan Bay.

to 9pm Thu, noon-5pm Sun), home to one of Canada's best Emily Carr collections. Aside from Carr's swirling nature canvases, you'll find an ever-changing array of scenic temporary exhibitions.

Hop on the **Victoria Harbour Ferry** (www.victoriaharbourferry.com; tickets from CAN$5, tour adult/child CAN$22/10) whose captains get you from A to B, but also give insightful, historical tours. The colorful armada of tiny tugboats stop at numerous docks around the harbor, including the Inner Harbour, Songhees Park and Fisherman's Wharf. Or opt for the full hop-on, hop-off tour.

 p291

The Drive 》 Follow Hwy 1 (which begins its cross-country journey in Victoria) west and into the sometimes narrow, heavily forested Malahat Dr.

TRIP HIGHLIGHT

② Goldstream Provincial Park

Just inside Malahat Dr, the abundantly scenic **Goldstream Provincial Park** (www.goldstreampark.com) drips with ancient, moss-covered cedar trees and a moist carpet of plant life. The short walk through the woods to the **Freeman King Visitor Centre** (⏰9am-4:30pm) is beautiful; once you're there, take in the center's hands-on exhibits about natural history.

Goldstream Provincial Park is known for its chum salmon spawning season (from late October to December), when the water literally bubbles with thousands of struggling fish. Hungry bald eagles also swoop in at this time to feast on the full-grown salmon.

You'll also find great hiking here: marked trails range from tough to easy and some are wheelchair accessible. The visitor center can advise. If you do head off down the trail, remember this is bear and cougar country.

The Drive » From Goldstream, the Malahat climbs north to its summit with a number of gorgeous viewpoints over Brentwood Bay. Continue on Hwy 1, following signs east off the highway for Cowichan Bay.

- - - - - - - - - - - - - - - - -

TRIP HIGHLIGHT

3 Cowichan Bay

With a colorful string of wooden buildings perched on stilts over a mountain-shadowed ocean inlet, Cowichan Bay is well worth the stop. Wander down the pier of the **Maritime Centre** (www.classicboats. org; 1761 Cowichan Bay Rd; admission by donation; ⊘9am-dusk) to peruse some salty boat-building exhibits and intricate models and to get a great view of the harbor. Duck into the many galleries and studios tucked in the bay.

Head to **Mud Room** (www.cowbaymudroom.com; 1725 Cowichan Bay Rd; ⊘9am-6pm) to see potters at work making useable objects like mugs and plates. Look for seaside-themed mugs and the increasingly famous yellow-glazed dragonfly motif pieces.

Gabriola Island

COUGAR!

Weighing in at around 160lbs, cougars are stealth in the extreme. One alone can hunt and a kill a 600lb moose. While they're rarely seen, they can (and do) attack so it pays to be prepared – especially as the majority of the large cats in the region reside on the southern third of Vancouver Island.

Cougars are most active at dusk and dawn and most encounters take place in late spring and summer, however cougars roam and hunt at any time of the day or night and in all seasons. Almost all cougar attacks are on children, so keep your young ones close when you're outside and pick them up immediately if you see a cougar. Hike in groups of two or more and make enough noise to prevent surprising a cougar.

If you come across a cougar, always give it an avenue of escape. Talk to the cougar in a confident voice, face it and remain upright. Do not turn your back on the cougar. Do not run. Try to back away from the cougar slowly. If the cougar appears aggressive, do all you can to enlarge your image. Don't crouch down or try to hide. Pick up sticks or branches and wave them about. Convince the cougar that you are a threat, not prey. And if a cougar does attack, fight back!

Also visit **Spinning Ninny** (www.spinningninny.ca; 1725 Cowichan Bay Rd; ☺9am-6pm). Representing around 20 local artists, this eclectic boutique is a real find, with clothing, jewelry, feltwork, pottery, hats and more. Also worth your attention is Arthur Vickers' **Shipyard Gallery** (www.arthurvickers. com; 1719 Cowichan Bay Rd; ☺ 9am-5pm). Vickers' celebrated carvings and paintings focus on his First Nations lineage and are displayed in an atmospheric gallery.

The artisans are also at work in the bay's kitchens. This is a great place to stop for lunch.

✖ 🍽 p291

The Drive ≫ Return to Hwy 1 and head north a further 7.5 miles (12km).

LOCAL KNOWLEDGE: LOCAL NOSH

We source as much as possible from the [Cowichan] Valley. Our duck and pork comes from farms a few miles away and we also bring in regional seafood: clams from Cortez Island and spot prawns from Samson Narrows. And we have a big selection of wines from local vineyards like Blue Grouse and Cherry Point.

Luke Harms, owner Masthead Restaurant (p291),
Cowichan Bay

❹ BC Forest Discovery Centre

You won't find Tigger in this 100 acres (40 hectares) of woods, but if you want to know more about those giants swaying overhead, stop in at the **BC Forest Discovery Centre** (www. discoveryforest.com; 2892 Drinkwater Rd, Duncan; adult/ child CAN$15/10; ☺ 10am-4:30pm Apr-Nov). Woodland paths lead you among western yews, Garry oaks and 400-year-old fir trees with nesting bald eagles in their branches. Visit a 1920s sawmill and a 1905 wooden schoolhouse, and climb to the top of a wildfire lookout tower. Hop on a historical train for a ride around the grounds and over a trestle and check out the logging trucks from the early 1900s. Visit the indoor exhibit to get the lowdown on contemporary forest management.

The Drive ›› It's a 12.5-mile (20km) journey to the next stop. Continue north on Hwy 1, turning right onto Henry Rd and then left onto Chemainus Rd.

5 Chemainus

The residents of this tree-ringed settlement – a former resource community that had swiftly become a ghost town – began commissioning **murals** on its walls in the 1980s as part of a forward-thinking revitalization project. The paintings – there are now 41 dotted around the town – soon became visitor attractions, triggering the town's rebirth. Among the best are the 54ft-long pioneer-town painting of Chemainus c 1891 on Mill St; the 50ft-long depiction of First Nations faces and totems on Chemainus Rd; and the evocative mural showing the waterfront community as it was in 1948, on Maple St.

Pick up a walking tour map of the murals from the visitor information center or follow the yellow footprints beginning at the Waterwheel Park in the center of town (where there's also a parking lot).

DETOUR: GABRIOLA ISLAND

Start: 5 Chemainus

If you're tempted by those mysterious little islands peeking at you off the coast of Vancouver Island, take the 20-minute **BC Ferries** (www.bcferries.com) service from Nanaimo's Inner Harbour to **Gabriola Island** (www.gabriolaisland.org). Home to dozens of artists plus a healthy smattering of old hippies and 1960s US-draft dodgers, there's a tangible air of quietude to this rustic realm. Pack a picnic and spend the afternoon communing with the natural world in a setting rewardingly divorced from big-city life.

The lower part of the town is rather quiet but the southern end of Willow St is packed with cafes, restaurants and boutique galleries to keep you and your wallet occupied.

The impressive **Chemainus Theatre Festival** (www. chemainustheatrefestival. ca; 9737 Chemainus Rd; tickets from adult/child CAN$34/17) is popular and frequented by Victorians. Check the website to see what's playing.

The Drive ›› Head north on Hwy 1 toward Nanaimo. Follow the signs to Departure Bay and catch a BC Ferry for Langdale on the mainland. This journey across the Strait of Georgia is breathtaking. You'll first need to cross to Horseshoe Bay (one hour, 35 minutes) and then continue on to Langdale (40 minutes). From Langdale, it's a short drive along Hwy 101 to Gibsons.

TRIP HIGHLIGHT

6 Gibsons

Gibsons *feels* cozy. If you didn't know better, you'd think you were on an island – such is the strong community, nearly isolated feel this town exudes. Head straight for the waterfront area – known as **Gibsons Landing** – where you can take in the many bright-painted clapboard buildings that back on to the water's edge, as well as the intriguing artisan stores.

A walk to the town's main wooden jetty leads past a colorful array of houseboats and floating garden plots. You'll also come to the sun-dappled, gently bobbing gallery of **Sa Boothroyd** (www. saboothroyd.com; Government Wharf; ⊙10am-5pm). The artist is often on hand to illuminate her browse-worthy and often humorous works. Although her bigger canvases are suitably pricey, there are lots of original trivets, coasters and tea cozies to tempt you.

 p291

The Drive » Continue along the winding, tree-lined Hwy 101 – expect to glimpse sandy coves winking at you through the forests on your left. The highway leads through Sechelt (where you can stop for supplies) and on along the Malaspina Strait to Earl's Cove. Hop on a BC Ferry across Jervis Inlet to Saltery Bay. This 50-minute trip winds past islands and forested coastline. From Saltery Bay, continue on Hwy 101 along the coast to Powell River.

- - - - - - - - - - - - -

❼ Powell River

Powell River is the Sunshine Coast's most vibrant community. It was founded in the early 1900s when three Minnesota businessmen

DETOUR: WILD PLAY

Start: ❺ Chemainus

Fancy zipping, swinging or jumping from a giant tree? Stop off at **Wild Play** (www.wildplayparks.com; 35 Nanaimo River Rd, Nanaimo; activities from CAN$25; ⏰10am-5:30pm Jun-Aug, shorter hrs Sep-May; 👶) for some woodland adventure on canopy obstacle courses and a daredevil bungee-jump zone.

dammed the river to create a massive hydroelectric power plant. Not long after, a pulp mill was built to take advantage of the surrounding forests and handy deepwater harbor, with the first sheets of paper trundling off its steamy production line in 1912. Within a few years, the mill – still there today, but much reduced in size – had become the world's largest producer of paper newsprint, churning out 275 tons daily.

SUNSHINE COAST GALLERY CRAWL

Along Hwy 101, keep your eyes peeled for a jaunty purple flag or two fluttering in the breeze. These indicate that an artist is at work on the adjoining property. Pick up the *Sunshine Coast Purple Banner* flyer from area visitor centers and galleries to find out where the artists are located. Some are open for drop-in visits – others prefer that you call ahead. The region is studded with arts and crafts creators, working with wood, glass, clay and just about everything else. For further information, check www.suncoastarts.com.

Today there's an active and artsy vibe to this waterfront town and it's great for wandering. Many of Powell River's oldest streets are named after trees and some are still lined with the heritage workers' cottages that kick-started the settlement. The steam-plumed mill is still here, too – although it's shrinking every year and its former grounds are being transformed into parkland. Dip into this history at **Powell River Museum** (www.powell rivermuseum.ca; 4798 Marine Ave; adult/child CAN$2/1 ⏰9am-4:30pm Jun-Aug, 9am-4:30pm Mon-Fri Sep-May), which covers the area's First Nations heritage and its tough pioneer days: check out the photos of early settlers.

If you spend the night in town, catch a film at the quaint **Patricia Theatre** (www.patriciatheatre. com; 5848 Ash Ave; adult/child CAN$9/5.50), Canada's longest-running cinema.

 p291

Eating & Sleeping

Victoria ❶

✕ John's Place · Canadian $$

(723 Pandora Ave; www.johnsplace.ca; mains CAN$7-17) Victoria's best weekend brunch spot, this wood-floored, high-ceilinged heritage room is lined with funky memorabilia. Start off with a basket of addictive house-made bread, but save room for heaping pasta dishes or a Belgian waffle breakfast. And don't leave without trying a thick slab of pie from the case at the front.

⬛ Laurel Point Inn · Hotel $$$

(☎250-386-8721; www.laurelpoint.com; 680 Montreal St; d from CAN$180-300) This large hotel is something of an institution in Victoria. This is where the rich and glamorous stay and where you should head if you want a little pampering. Down duvets, music on demand and divine balcony views all await you. Service is impeccable and it's a short walk to downtown.

Cowichan Bay ❸

✕ Hilary's Artisan Cheese · Deli $$

(☎250-715-0563; www.hilaryscheese.com; 1737 Cowichan Bay Rd; mains CAN$7-16) Grab lunch to go or cozy up beside a fantastic view in this relaxed deli. Dig into thick-cut sandwiches, cheese platters and hearty soups. This is also the place for picnic relishes, jams and cheese.

✕ True Grain Bread · Bakery $

(www.truegrain.ca; 1725 Cowichan Bay Rd) French loaf, sourdough or raisin – whatever your favorite bread, you'll find it here, handcrafted, organic and milled on-site. Homemade crackers and cookies will add to your picnic hamper. Be sure to taste-test the bread of the month. (It was rosemary, garlic and asparagus when we visited!)

✕ Masthead Restaurant · Seafood $$$

(www.themastheadrestaurant.com; 1705 Cowichan Bay Rd; mains CAN$26-30; ⏰5-10pm) In a restored 1868 hotel, this classy place creates seafood treats like prosciutto-wrapped snapper or crusted wild salmon. Enjoy with sterling views and a great Cowichan Valley wine list.

⬛ Dreamweaver · B&B $$

(☎250-748-7688; www.dreamweaver bedandbreakfast.com; 1682 Botwood Lane; d from CAN$135) Perched on the edge of the village, just steps away from the restaurants and galleries, this Victoria-style home welcomes guests with three comfortable, rather floral rooms. The Magnolia Suite, with its canopied bed and giant soaker tub, is made all the lovelier with balcony sea views.

Gibsons ❻

✕ Molly's Reach · Diner $

(☎604-886-9710; 647 School Rd, Gibsons; mains CAN$8-12; ⏰7am-9pm) If you've ever seen an episode of *The Beachcombers*, an iconic Canadian TV show from the '70s, you'll quickly recognize this diner as part of the set. This legendary place dishes up comfort food made fresh from local ingredients, along with mesmerizing views of the marina bristling with boats.

Powell River ❼

✕ Shinglemill Pub & Bistro · Pub $$

(☎604-483-3545; 6233 Powell Pl; mains CAN$12-20; ⏰11am-10pm). Built over the lake on the edge of town, this popular pub knocks out hearty burgers, salads and sandwiches. In addition to the well-known Reubens and Caesars, the menu has more exotic fare like truffle lobster cakes and honey-lime chicken burgers.

⬛ Old Courthouse Inn · Hotel $$

(☎604-483-4000; www.oldcourthouseinn.ca; 6243 Walnut St; r from CAN$100) Built in 1939, the Tudor-style courthouse is now a quaint seaside hotel. The eight rooms have each been lovingly restored with turn-of-the-century furnishings and decor. Stay in the Old Police Station, the Judge's Chambers or the Sheriff's Office.

Sidney *This sunny seaside town is ideal for wandering*

Southern Vancouver Island Tour

28

Begin on the Gulf Islands among uncommon amounts of creativity and tranquility. Then cross through ancient, fern-lined forests to the island's wild west coast.

TRIP HIGHLIGHTS

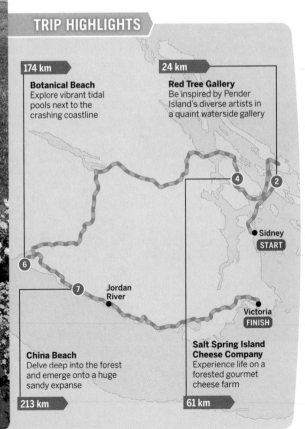

174 km

Botanical Beach
Explore vibrant tidal pools next to the crashing coastline

24 km

Red Tree Gallery
Be inspired by Pender Island's diverse artists in a quaint waterside gallery

Sidney
START

6

7

Jordan River

Victoria
FINISH

China Beach
Delve deep into the forest and emerge onto a huge sandy expanse

213 km

Salt Spring Island Cheese Company
Experience life on a forested gourmet cheese farm

61 km

4–5 DAYS
182 MILES/290KM

GREAT FOR...

BEST TIME TO GO
June to September for frequent ferries, warm weather and possible whale sightings.

ESSENTIAL PHOTO
Botanical Beach's crashing waves.

BEST FOR OUTDOOR ADVENTURERS
Salt Spring Island for biking and hiking, and kayaking in sun-dappled lakes.

293

Southern Vancouver Island Tour

Salty air and the sound of crashing waves – whether you're standing on the deck of a Gulf Island ferry or on the sandy expanse of China Beach, the sea is an essential part of life in this corner of the world. It creates pods of creativity – small islands where artisans practice traditional crafts like pottery and cheese-making. And it shapes the untamed western coastline, with its dramatic beaches backed by dense forests.

❶ Sidney

A short trip north of Victoria, the sunny seaside town of Sidney is ideal for wandering. Along the main street, an almost unseemly number of bookstores jostle for space with boutique shops and cafes. When you reach the water, you'll find the **Seaside Sculpture Walk** (www.sculpturewalk. ca) leading to locally created art, a picturesque pier and amazing island vistas. Watch the sea for seals and herons or

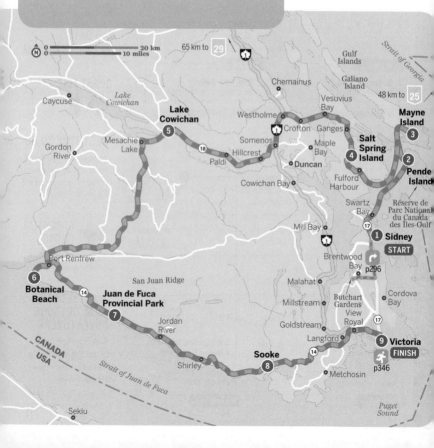

join a whale-watching tour with **Sidney Whale Watching** (📞250-656-7599; www.sidneywhalewatching. com; 2537 Beacon Ave).

While you're at the waterfront, visit the compact but brilliant **Shaw Ocean Discovery Centre** (www.oceandiscovery. ca; 9811 Seaport Place; adult/ child CAN$14/4; 🕙10am-5pm). It opens your eyes to the color and diversity in the neighboring Salish Sea with aquariums, touch pools and plenty of hands-on exhibits. The staff is well-versed and the gift shop is a treasure trove.

🍴 🛏 p299

LINK YOUR TRIP

25 Vancouver & the Fraser Valley

From any of the Gulf Islands, you can catch a ferry to Tsawwassen on the mainland to connect with Hwy 1 into Vancouver or out toward Harrison Hot Springs (p265).

29 Vancouver Island's Remote North

When you reach Hwy 1 after leaving Salt Spring Island, you can carry on north to pick up this even more off-the-beaten-track trip (p301).

The Drive » Follow Hwy 17 (Patricia Bay Hwy) north to its end and the BC Ferry Terminal. Board a boat for a beautiful crossing to Pender Island.

- - - - - - - - - - - - -

TRIP HIGHLIGHT

② Pender Island

As you disembark the ferry onto this small island, you are quickly wrapped in a feeling of quiet and of time forgotten. Narrow roads wind within deep forests where you'll see countless walking trails, quail crossings and confident deer.

Pender is actually two islands – North and South, joined by a small bridge. **Gowland** and **Tilly Point** on South Pender have beach access; head to Tilly Point for tidal pools and views of Mt Baker. Sheltered **Medicine Beach** on the North Island has sand and lots of logs for climbing. While on the beaches, keep your eyes peeled for wildlife – resident bald eagles, seals, sea lions, mink and otters.

Pender is also home to countless artists. Pick up a copy of Pender Island Artists Guide on the ferry or on Pender for a list of all the galleries. A great place to start is the **Red Tree Gallery** (www. retreegallery.ca; 4301 Bedwell Harbour Rd; 🕙10am-5pm) in quaint Hope Bay. This arts cooperative displays the work of over 15 local artists, with everything

from photography to glass art, jewelry, paintings and hand-spun wool.

For locally produced wine, head to tranquil **Morning Bay Vineyard** (www.morningbay.ca; 6621 Harbour Hill Dr; 🕙10am-5pm Wed-Sun). Using grapes from its own terraced vineyard and other vineyards across BC, it produces small batches that are worth trying; the Merlot is particularly excellent.

Also worth a look is **Pender Islands Museum** (www.penderislandmuseum. org; 2408 South Otter Bay Rd; 🕙10am-4pm Jul-Aug, 1-4pm Sat & Sun Apr-Jun & Sep-Oct), housed in an original 1908 farmhouse. Explore the history of the island through recreated rooms, old photos and exhibits.

🍴 🛏 p299

The Drive » Return to the ferry terminal on North Pender and board a ferry through the channel to Mayne Island.

- - - - - - - - - - - - -

③ Mayne Island

As the boat pulls into Mayne Island, you're greeted with colorful wooden houses, quaint communities and lots of deer. Head to **Georgina Point Lighthouse** for water- and mountain-filled views across Active Pass. The water literally bubbles here with the strength of the current. This is a popular spot for eagles to fish and you're

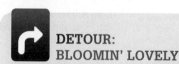

DETOUR: BLOOMIN' LOVELY

Start: ❶ Sidney

Billboards begin advertising it in Washington State. Not far from Sidney, **Butchart Gardens** (www.butchartgardens.com; 800 Benvenuto Ave, Brentwood Bay; adult/child CAN$30/3; ⊙9am-10pm Jun-Sep) is British Columbia's most famous botanical attraction. The century-old gardens, which originated from an attempt to beautify an old cement factory site, have been cleverly planned to ensure there's always something in bloom, no matter what the season. In summer, there's a firework display on Saturdays and in winter the twinkling lights are magical. Look out for seasonal price reductions.

also likely to see (and hear) sea lions resting on nearby rocks.

For a quiet retreat, visit **Japanese Garden** (Dinner Bay Community Park, Dinner Point Rd), dedicated to the many Japanese families who settled on the island from 1900 onward. Once constituting a third of the population, they contributed more than half of the island's farming, milling and fish-preservation work. During WWII the government saw them as a national threat and forced their removal. Few ever returned. The garden contains Japanese elements within a forest – a charcoal pit kiln,

shrines and a peace bell, plus a more traditional Japanese garden.

🍴 p299

The Drive ⟫ Return to the ferry terminal and board a ferry to Fulford Harbour on Salt Spring Island.

- - - - - - - - - - - -

TRIP HIGHLIGHT

❹ Salt Spring Island

When folks from Victoria talk about quitting their job and making jam for a living, chances are they're thinking of moving to Salt Spring. Once a hippie refuge and later a yuppie retreat, it's now home to anyone who wants a quieter life without leaving convenience

behind. The main town of **Ganges** has it all, from grocery stores to galleries. If you're coming from Mayne, it'll feel full-on; it's a wonderful place to explore.

Salt Spring is also home to many an artist. Pick up a **Studio Tour** (www.saltspringstudiotour. com) brochure or visit the website to choose between 33 working studios. With everything from bakers to carvers and winemakers, there'll be something to tempt your curiosity. Stop in at **Waterfront Gallery** (107 Purvis Lane, Ganges; ⊙10am-5pm), which carries the work of over 80 local artists with pottery, tea, glassware, knitwear, candles and birdhouses.

When you're first off the ferry at Fulford Harbour, stop in at **Salt Spring Mercantile** (379 Dukes Rd; ⊙8:30am-6pm), which sells lots of local products like Salish Sea Chocolates (try the cherry with hazelnut!), fresh chutneys and soap.

OFF THE FENCE

Going strong for over 20 years, **Art Off the Fence** (www.art-off-the-fence.com) started as just that – an artist exhibiting her work all over her fence. Each year in mid-July, a handful of artists hang their work on the fence and in the orchard of a Pender property, creating a weekend-long outdoor gallery. Look, shop, enjoy the live music and meet some of the island locals.

ULANA SWITUCHA / ALAMY ©

Ganges Saturday Market on Salt Spring Island Locally made goat cheese

Visit **Salt Spring Island Cheese Company** (www.saltspringcheese.com; 285 Reynolds Rd; ☺10am-5pm) on Weston Creek Farm to meet the goats and sheep that produce milk for the cheese, see it being made, and be awed by the beautiful finale – taste cheeses adorned with lemon slices, flowers and chilies.

Head to **Ruckle Park** for ragged shorelines, gnarly arbutus forests and sun-kissed farmlands. There are trails here for all skill levels as well as a great ocean view for a picnic. **Mt Maxwell** offers a

steep but worthwhile hike and **Cushion Lake** and **St Mary's Lake** are swimming haunts in summer. If you want to explore sans car, visit **Island Escapes** (📞250-537-2553; www.islandescapades.com; 163 Fulford-Ganges Rd) in Ganges to rent kayaks and join excursions, or **Spokespeople** (📞250-653-9088; Fulford Harbour), on the dock, to rent bikes.

✕ 🛏 p299

The Drive » Explore the island's diverse landscape of rolling meadows and dense forest, heading north to Vesuvius Bay where you can board a ferry to Crofton on Vancouver Island.

From the east coast, curve inland along Hwy 18 and the glassy-calm waters of Lake Cowichan.

- - - - - - - - - -

❺ Lake Cowichan

Hop out of the car at Lake Cowichan for a few deep breaths at the ultra-clear, tree-fringed lakefront. This is a perfect spot for swimming or setting out for a hike along the lakeside trails. After the town of Lake Cowichan, it's another 64km (40-mile) stretch (without services) through the heart of the island. You'll encounter cathedral-calm old-growth

MARKET DAY

If you arrive on Salt Spring Island on a summer weekend, the best way to dive into the community is at the thriving **Saturday Market** (www.saltspringmarket .com; Centennial Park, Ganges; 8am-4pm Sat Apr-Oct), where you can tuck into luscious island-grown fruit and piquant cheeses while perusing locally produced arts and crafts.

woodland here where towering spruce and Douglas firs, many more than five centuries old, dominate the landscape.

The Drive » From Lake Cowichan, follow South Shore Rd and then Pacific Marine Rd to Port Renfrew and on to Botanical Beach. Pacific Marine Rd is narrow and winding but takes you through breathtaking forest.

TRIP HIGHLIGHT

⑥ Botanical Beach

Feeling very much like the edge of the earth, it's worth the effort to get to Botanical Beach. Follow the winding road from Port Renfrew and then the sometimes steep forest path down to the beach. Used as a student marine station since 1900, the tidal pools here are rich in life. Look for sea stars, chitons, anemones, gooseneck barnacles, sea palms and purple sea urchins. Surrounded by a windblown coastline and crashing waves, this is also a favorite springtime haunt of orcas and gray whales, as well as a feeding ground for harbor seals.

The rocks here can be slippery and the waves huge; take care and watch the tide.

✗ p299

The Drive » Head south on Hwy 14.

TRIP HIGHLIGHT

⑦ Juan de Fuca Provincial Park

Continue south into the dramatic coastal wilderness of **Juan de Fuca Provincial Park** (www.bcparks.ca). There are several good stop-off points along this rugged stretch, each with memorable views of the rocky, ocean-carved seafront where trees cling for dear life and whales slide past just off the coast. Our favorite is **China Beach**, reached along a fairly gentle, well-maintained trail through dense forest. The prize is a long stretch of windswept sand. **French Beach** is also popular with day-trippers and requires less of a leg-stretch.

The Drive » Continue south along Hwy 14, skirting the coastline to Sooke.

⑧ Sooke

Once considered the middle of nowhere, seaside Sooke is gaining popularity and is a great place to bunk down for the night. For an introduction to the area, stop in at **Sooke Region Museum** (www. sookeregionmuseum.com; 2070 Phillips Rd; admission free; 9am-5pm, closed Mon winter), which has intriguing exhibits on the district's pioneer past, including the tiny Moss Cottage, one of the island's oldest pioneer homes where 'Aunt Tilly' bustles about her chores.

🛏 p299

The Drive » From Sooke, follow Hwy 14 (Sooke Rd) east, all the way to Trans-Canada Hwy 1. Join the eastbound traffic which will lead you on to nearby Victoria.

⑨ Victoria

The provincial capital is vibrant, charming and very walkable. The picturesque Inner Harbour, magnetic boutique shopping and belly-thrilling cuisine make it understandably popular. Add an outgoing university crowd, strong arts community and a hefty royal family fan club, and you get an interesting, diverse population. Explore all it has to offer on our walking tour (p346).

✗ 🛏 p299

Eating & Sleeping

Sidney ❶

✕ Toast   Cafe $

(☎250-665-6234; 2400 Bevan Ave; mains CAN$4-10; ⏰7:30am-5pm Mon-Sat; 🖶) This is hands-down Sidney's most welcoming cafe with expertly made coffees, a mean breakfast smoothie and heartily topped bagels.

🛏 Cottage At Kildara   Cottage $$$

(☎250-857-3303; www.freshviewevents.com/ accommodations.htm; 11293 Chalet Rd; r per night/week CAN$295/1350; 🚗) Nestled in an English garden on a working farm, this spacious, elegant cottage is enveloped in privacy.

Pender Island ❷

✕ Medicine Beach Market   Deli $

(☎250-647-5505; 5827 Schooner Way; mains CAN$7; ⏰10am-6pm Tue-Sat, noon-4pm Sun) A shop-cum-deli next to a beach for picnics. The ciabatta sandwiches will keep you full till dinner.

🛏 Poet's Cove   Resort $$$

(☎250-629-2100; www.poetscove.com; 9801 Spalding Rd; r/villa/cottage from CAN$300/460/480; 🚗) In a secluded harbor, these rooms and villas offer endless views – even from the tubs. Classy details, fireplaces and wooden beams make it a lovely escape.

Mayne Island ❸

✕ Wild Fennel   International $$

(☎250-539-5987; 574 Fernhill Road; lunch/ dinner CAN$11/22; ⏰11:30am-9pm Wed-Sun; 🖶) This relaxed, family-friendly place speaks diner fare but dishes up gourmet meals.

Salt Spring Island ❹

✕ House Piccolo Restaurant   European $$$

(☎250-537-1844; 108 Hereford Avenue, Ganges; mains CAN$25-30; ⏰from 5pm Wed-Sun)

Silverware clinks and candlelight flickers in the hush before the performance, starring scallops in creamy coconut-ginger sauce and Pacific crab cakes with citrus aioli.

🛏 Oceanside Cottages   Cottages $$

(☎250-653-0007; www.oceansidecottages. com; 521 Isabella Rd; cottages from CAN$135) These four unique cottages are nooks of bliss. Each is exceedingly private and filled with eclectic artwork and creative flourishes.

Botanical Beach ❻

✕ Tomi's Home Cookin'   Cafe $

(☎250-412-6099; 7152 Parkinson Rd, Port Renfrew; mains CAN$6-10; ⏰9am-5pm) Friendly and homey, with a big sunny deck, Tomi's serves up delicious muffins, soups, wraps and burgers that will fuel you up for the drive ahead.

Sooke ❽

🛏 Sooke Harbour House   Resort $$$

(☎250-642-3421; www.sookeharbourhouse. com; 1528 Whiffen Spit Rd; d from CAN$200) Whether you opt for the Emily Carr or Blue Heron room, each of the 28 guest rooms has a divine soaker tub, wood-burning fireplace, balcony and giant sea views.

Victoria ❾

✕ The Mint   Fusion $$

(☎250-386-6468, 1414 Douglas St, mains CAN$16; ⏰11:30am-4pm & 5pm-2am Mon-Sat, 5pm-2am Sun) Head downstairs to this hip, urban lounge for artfully blended South Asian and West Coast cuisine, plus divine cocktails.

🛏 Abigail's Hotel   Historic Hotel $$$

(☎]50-388-5363; www.abigailshotel.com; 906 McClure St; d from CAN$230) This 1930s heritage hotel offers unique, boutique rooms; the fireside rooms are particularly beautiful. Homemade cookies and a three-course breakfast add to the charm.

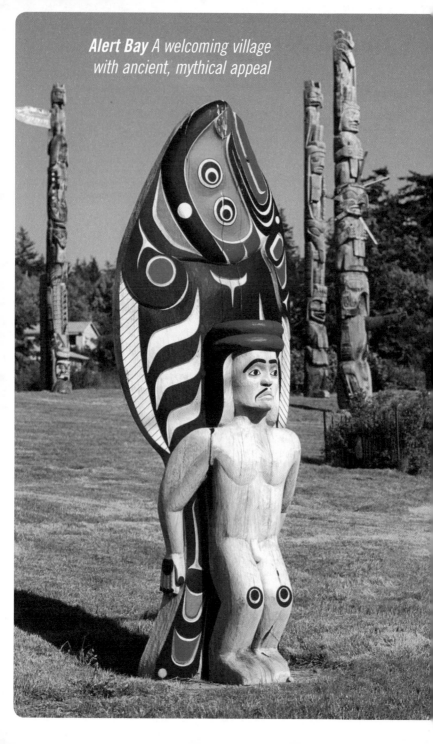

Alert Bay *A welcoming village with ancient, mythical appeal*

Vancouver Island's Remote North

29

Throw yourself head-first into Vancouver Island's natural side. Ancient forests, diving orca, wild sandy beaches, quaint villages and a peek into Native cultures make it a well-rounded trip.

TRIP HIGHLIGHTS

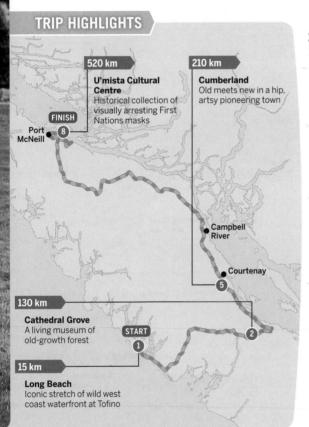

520 km

U'mista Cultural Centre
Historical collection of visually arresting First Nations masks

FINISH
8
Port McNeill

210 km

Cumberland
Old meets new in a hip, artsy pioneering town

Campbell River

Courtenay

5

130 km

Cathedral Grove
A living museum of old-growth forest

START
1

2

15 km

Long Beach
Iconic stretch of wild west coast waterfront at Tofino

2–3 DAYS
336 MILES/537KM

GREAT FOR...

BEST TIME TO GO
May to September for the most sunshine and least chance of snow.

 ESSENTIAL PHOTO

The forest of totem poles watching over the sea at Alert Bay.

 BEST FOR STORM WATCHERS

Watch massive waves crashing in from the wide-open Pacific at Long Beach in winter.

29

Vancouver Island's Remote North

Following this trip is like following Alice down the rabbit hole – you'll feel you've entered an enchanted land, beyond the reach of day-to-day life. You'll see moss-covered trees so huge and ancient that they leave you feeling tiny. Bald eagles swoop above and around you like pigeons. Bears munch on dandelions, watching you mischievously. And totem poles stand like forests, whispering secrets of the past. Go on. Jump in.

TRIP HIGHLIGHT

❶ Tofino

Once a simple, hardworking fishing village and later a hippie haven, Tofino has gently morphed into a sleepy soft-eco resort town. Packed with activities and blessed with stunning beaches, the small town sits on Clayoquot (clay-kwot) Sound, where forested ground rises from roiling waves that batter the coastline in a dramatic, ongoing spectacle. This is where

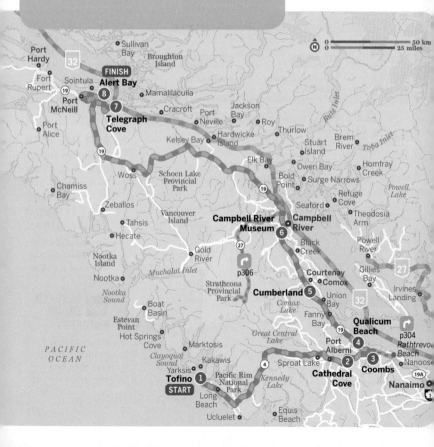

people come to surf, whale watch, kayak, hike, watch storms and hug trees. To get the scoop on these activities, go to the **visitor centre** (www.tourismtofino.com; 1426 Pacific Rim Hwy; ⏱10am-6pm May-Sep, reduced off-season). There's a satellite branch in town at 455 Campbell St.

The area's biggest draw is magnificent **Long Beach**, part of the Pacific Rim National Park and the epitome of west coast scenery. Easily accessible by car along the Pacific Rim Hwy, this wide sandy beach has untamed surf, lots of beachcombing nooks and a living museum of old-growth rainforest. There

LINK YOUR TRIP

27 A Strait Hop
From Qualicum Beach, travel south on Hwy 19 to Nanaimo where you can hook up with this tour, either heading across the Strait of Georgia to Gibsons or south on Hwy 1 to Victoria (p283).

32 Up the Inside Passage
From Port McNeill, continue north on Hwy 19 to Port Hardy where you can catch a ferry to Prince Rupert and head up the Inside Passage (p327).

TOP TIP: PACIFIC RIM PARK PASS

First-timers should drop by the **Pacific Rim Visitor Centre** (www.pacificrimvisitor.ca; 2791 Pacific Rim Hwy; ⏱10am-4pm, reduced off-season) for maps and advice on exploring this spectacular region. If you're stopping in the park, you'll need to pay and display a pass, available here or from the yellow dispensers dotted along the highway.

are plenty of walking trails; keep your eyes peeled for swooping bald eagles and shockingly large banana slugs, tread carefully over slippery surfaces and never turn your back on the mischievous surf.

The **Wickaninnish Interpretive Centre** (Wick Rd; admission included with park pass fee; ⏱9am-5pm mid Mar-mid Oct) houses exhibits on the region, including a First Nations canoe and a look at what's beneath the watery depths.

While you're in Tofino, don't miss Roy Henry Vickers' **Eagle Aerie Gallery** (royhenryvickers.com; 350 Campbell St; ⏱10am-5pm), housed in an atmospheric, traditional longhouse. Vickers is one of Canada's most successful and prolific Native artists. Check the website for storytelling events.

Also visit **Tofino Botanical Gardens** (www.tbgf.org; 1084 Pacific Rim Hwy; adult/child CAN$10/free; ⏱9am-dusk), 12 acres (4.8 hectares) of forest

and coast complete with unique pocket gardens, art installations, a historic homestead and a storytelling hut.

A short trip from town is the **Maquinna Marine Provincial Park** (www.bcparks.ca; admission CAN$3), where 1.2 miles (2km) of boardwalks lead to natural hot springs. Transportation is readily available from Tofino. Also accessible from Tofino is the mesmerizing **Meares Island**, home to the **Big Tree Trail**, a 1300ft (400m) boardwalk through old-growth forest that includes a stunning 1500-year-old red cedar.

🍴 🛏 p307

The Drive » Follow Pacific Rim Hwy 4 southeast, and then north as it turns into the Mackenzie Range. This road is well serviced but winding, with jaw-dropping scenery. Mountains rise up on the right as you pass the unfathomably deep Kennedy Lake (there are a number of vehicles resting unreachable at its bottom). The road carries on along the racing Kennedy River. Continue on to the next stop, just past Port Alberni.

TRIP HIGHLIGHT

② Cathedral Grove

To the east of Port Alberni, **Cathedral Grove** (www.bcparks.ca) is the spiritual home of tree huggers and the mystical highlight of MacMillan Provincial Park. Look up – way, waaaaay up – and the vertigo-inducing view of the swaying treetops will leave you swooning with an understanding of the grove's name. Extremely popular in summer, its accessible forest trails wind through a dense canopy of vegetation, offering glimpses of some of British Columbia's oldest trees, including centuries-old Douglas firs more than 10ft (3m) in diameter. Try hugging that.

The Drive >> Continue east of Hwy 4, past Cameron Lake, with swimming beaches and supposedly a resident monster. From Hwy 4, follow Hwy 4A for Coombs.

③ Coombs

The mother of all pit stops, **Coombs Old Country Market** (www.oldcountrymarket.com;

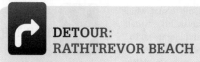

DETOUR:
RATHTREVOR BEACH

Start: ③ Coombs

Not far off the route, it won't take you long to get here – but it'll take you forever to leave. Visit Rathtrevor Beach when the tide is out and you'll be faced with a massive expanse of sand. Bring buckets, shovels and the kids, who will spend hours digging for gooey neck clams, catching crabs and hunting for shells. The beach is in a provincial park, just east of Parksville, and is backed by a forested picnic area.

2326 Alberni Hwy, Coombs; ☻9am-7pm Jul & Aug, reduced off-season) attracts huge numbers of visitors on balmy summer days. You'll get inquisitive looks from a herd of goats that spends the season on the grassy roof, as has been the tradition for decades. Nip inside for giant ice-cream cones, heaping pizzas and all the deli-makings of a great picnic lunch, then spend an hour or two wandering around the stores, which are filled with unique crafts, toys and antiques.

The Drive >> Continue east on Hwy 4A, crossing Hwy 19 to Parksville on the coast. Turn left, following the coastline west past pretty French Creek and on to Qualicum Beach.

④ Qualicum Beach

A small community of classic seafront motels and a giant beachcomber-friendly bay, Qualicum Beach is a favorite family spot. This coastline is thick with shellfish; many of the scallops, oysters and mussels that restaurants serve up come from here. Wander the beach for shells, and look for sand dollars – they're readily found here.

✗ ⌂ p307

The Drive >> While it's slower than Hwy 19, Hwy 19A is a scenic drive, following the coast north past the Fanny Bay Oyster Farm (stop in for a cookbook) and Denman Island (site of the famous chocolate factory). Just past of Union Bay, turn left, connecting with Hwy 19. Turn right, continuing north and taking the exit for Cumberland.

✓ TOP TIP:
VANCOUVER ISLAND NORTH

For blogs, maps, activities, tide charts and photos to inspire you, visit www.vancouverislandnorth.ca.

TRIP HIGHLIGHT

⑤ Cumberland

Founded as a coal-mining town in 1888, Cumberland was one

Coombs A goat grazes on the roof of the Coombs Old Country Market

of BC's original pioneer towns, home to workers from Japan, China and the American South. While Cumberland has retained that small-town feel, with a main street still lined with turn-of-the-century wood-built stores, it's also moved swiftly with the times. Instead of blacksmiths and dry goods shops, you'll find cool boutiques, espresso bars and even tattooists. One of Vancouver Island's most intriguing communities, Cumberland has a surprisingly youthful population. Stop by **Dark Side Chocolates** (www. darksidechocolates.com; 2722 Dunsmuir Ave; ⊙9:30am-4:30pm Tue-Sun) for truffles and bars, and the **Silk Soap Company** (2726b Dunsmuir Ave; ⊙ 9:30am-5pm Mon-Sat) for chai and lavender soap that smells good enough to eat.

Be sure to visit the evocative and very impressive **Cumberland Museum** (www.cumberland museum.ca; Dunsmuir Ave; ⊙10am-5pm Tue-Sat). Explore more than 40 exhibits including a replica coal mine and Company Store along with intriguing stories of Cumberland's early residents.

🍴 p307

The Drive » Carry on north on Hwy 19, with mountain and island views. Turn right onto Hamm Rd, heading east across farmland and passing a bison farm. Turn left onto Hwy 19a, which skirts Oyster Bay. The next stop is on your left, on the outskirts of Campbell River.

- - - - - - - -

⑥ Campbell River Museum

Stretch your legs and your curiosity with a wander through the award-winning **Campbell River Museum** (www. crmuseum.ca; 470 Island Highway; adult/child CAN$6/4; ⊙10am-5pm summer, noon-5pm Tue-Sun winter; ♿). Hop behind the wheel of an early logging truck, explore a settler's cabin, see First Nations masks and watch footage of the removal of the nearby legendary, ship-destroying Ripple Rock, which was blasted with the largest non-nuclear explosion in history.

The Drive » From Campbell River, head northwest on Hwy 19. As you head into the wilderness, it feels like the forest is swallowing you whole. Many islanders consider Campbell River as the last post of civilization. As you reach the north coast of Vancouver Island, turn right, following the signs and an increasingly narrow road for 10 miles (16km) to Telegraph Cove. En route, pass Beaver Cove with its flotilla of logs waiting to be hauled away

DETOUR: STRATHCONA PROVINCIAL PARK

Start: 6 Campbell River Museum

BC's oldest protected area and also Vancouver Island's largest park, **Strathcona** (www.bcparks. ca) is only a short jump from Campbell River. Centered on Mt Golden Hinde, the island's highest point (7218ft/2200m), it's a magnificent, pristine wilderness criss-crossed with trail systems that deliver you to waterfalls, alpine meadows, glacial lakes and looming mountain crags.

On arrival at the main entrance, get your bearings at **Strathcona Park Lodge & Outdoor Education Centre** (www.strathcona.bc.ca). It's a one-stop shop for park activities, including kayaking, guided treks, yoga camps, zip-lining and rock climbing for all ages.

for milling. It's a beautiful drive, but isolated. Be sure to fuel up before you head out.

- - - - - - - - - - - - - -

7 Telegraph Cove

Built on stilts over the water, Telegraph Cove began in 1912 as a one-room station for the northern terminus of the island's telegraph. A salmon saltery and small sawmill were later added. The boardwalk and houses have been restored and each has a plaque outside telling about the original resident living here around the turn of the century. From mid-June though October, the waters off the cove are home to orca whales. See (and hear!) them with **Stubbs Island Whale Watching** (☎250-928-3185; www.stubbs-island. com; 24 Boardwalk; adult/child CAN$84/79). You might

also encounter minke and humpback whales, dolphins and porpoises.

✕ ⌷ p307

The Drive » Return to Hwy 19 and carry on to Port McNeill, from where you can catch a BC Ferry (www.bcferries.com) to Alert Bay on Cormorant Island.

- - - - - - - - - - - - - -

TRIP HIGHLIGHT

8 Alert Bay

This welcoming village has an ancient and mythical appeal. Its First Nations community and traditions are still prevalent, with a palpable history. In some respects the village is like an open-air museum. On the southern side is an old pioneer fishing settlement and the traditional **Namgis Burial Grounds**, where 18 totem poles stand like a forest of formidable art.

The north of town is where the native Namgis population was segregated. Looming on the shoreline is the former St Michael's Residential School which operated from 1929 until the early '70s. Next to it is the impressive **U'mista Cultural Centre** (www.umista. ca; adult/child CAN$8/1; ⊗9am-5pm daily May-Sep, Tue-Sat Oct-Apr) with a collection of ceremonial Kwakwaka'wakw masks and other potlatch items repatriated from museums around the world.

Continue over the hill to reach the Big House, where **traditional dance performances** (adult/ child CAN$15/8; ⊗1:15pm Thu-Sat Jul-Aug) are held for visitors. One of the world's tallest totem poles is also here, carved in the Big House in the '60s. Alert Bay is home to a handful of professional Native carvers; see them at work in their galleries in and around town.

Head to the **visitor center** (www.alertbay.ca; 116 Fir St; ⊗9am-4:30pm Mon-Fri, reduced off-season) for heaps of information. They'll also give you tips on seeing orca; from mid-June until mid-October they're resident in the bay and sightings are common.

⌷ p307

Eating & Sleeping

Tofino

✕ Sobo — Seafood $$

(www.sobo.ca; 311 Neill St; lunch/dinner mains CAN$12/30) Sobo – meaning 'sophisticated bohemian' – is a popular bistro-style restaurant. Spicy fish tacos, smoked wild fish chowder and seared halibut with gnocchi and carrot-orange emulsion are a few of the treats on offer.

🛏 Wickaninnish Inn — Hotel $$$

(☎250-725-3100, 800-333-4604; www.wickinn. com; Chesterman Beach; r from CAN$399) Popular with winter storm-watchers, 'the Wick' is worth a stay any time of year. With the ambience of a place grown rather than constructed, the sumptuous guest rooms have fireplaces, two-person hot tubs and floor-to-ceiling windows.

🛏 Ecolodge — Lodge $$

(☎250-725-1220; www.tbgf.org; 1084 Pacific Rim Hwy; twin/suite CAN$149/199) Stay in the depths of the Botanical Gardens in warmly decorated, comfortable rooms. Suites sleep four and a welcoming lounge and kitchen are perfect for soaking up the serenity. Twin rooms have shared bathrooms.

Qualicum Beach ④

✕ Fish Tales Cafe — Seafood $$

(www.fishtalescafe.com; 336 W Island Hwy, Qualicum Beach; mains CAN$8-21) This Qualicum fixture has the look of an old-school English teashop but it has been reeling in visitors with its perfect fish 'n chips for years. If you arrive early enough, you can grab a table in the garden.

🛏 Free Spirit Spheres — Cabins $$

(☎250-757-9445; www.freespiritspheres. com; 420 Horne Lake Rd, Qualicum Bay; cabins from CAN$125) Suspended by cables in the trees, this clutch of three spherical treehouses enables guests to cocoon themselves in the forest canopy. Compact inside, Eve is smaller and basic, while Eryn and Melody are lined like little boats with built-in cabins, nooks and mp3 speakers. Book early for summer.

Cumberland ⑤

✕ The Wandering Moose — Cafe $

(☎250 336-8863; 2739 Dunsmuir Ave; mains CAN$8; ⊙10am-5pm Mon-Sat) The stately exterior of Cumberland's original post and customs house belies the interior of the town's coolest hangout. Warm and inviting with a kid's corner and seating on the patio, the Moose will satisfy coffee lovers with its locally roasted beans and refuel you with wraps, salads, gelato and baked treats.

Telegraph Cove ⑦

✕ Seahorse Cafe — Cafe $

(☎250-527-1001; www.seahorsecafe.org; mains CAN$9; ⊙8:30am-7pm May-Sep) This popular little dockside cafe has plenty of outdoor picnic tables for you to relax at while digging into barbecued Bavarian smokies, bison burgers, salmon burgers and home-cut fries. Breakfast brings pancakes, breakfast burritos and homemade granola.

🛏 Telegraph Cove Resort — Cabins $$

(☎250-928-3131; www.telegraphcoveresort. com; cabins from CAN$150) Stay in a restored hospital, manor or bunkhouse. The outside of the houses retain their original appearance while indoors a few extra comforts have been added. Each cabin or house is entirely unique. Check them out online and book ahead.

Alert Bay ⑧

🛏 Janet's Guest House — Hotel $

(☎250-974-5947; www.alertbayvacationrental. com; 667 Fir St; B&B CAN$65-90, house CAN$200) A heritage house from 1910 with simple but charming rooms, Janet's is a great deal. A wood stove, down duvets, use of the kitchen and even a piano will make you feel at home. Relax on the verandah or set out on the trails across the wooded property.

Okanagan Valley Picturesque
vineyards and pretty towns

Classic Trip

Okanagan Valley Wine Tour

30

Weave your way between green hills and the shimmering Okanagan Lake. This route will leave you with a trunkful of first-class wine and a belly filled with juicy cherries and peaches.

TRIP HIGHLIGHTS

0 km

Mission Hill Family Estate
This wine finds its way into many a restaurant across BC; try it at its source

3 km

Old Vines
Dishing up all kinds of gourmet-prepared local produce on a vineyard terrace

● Kelowna

① ②
START

⑤

FINISH
⑦

Carmelis Goat Cheese Artisan
Whether in blue or gelato form, it's handmade and delicious

35 km

Summerhill Pyramid Winery
The pyramid experience is intriguing, as is the wine

29 km

**2 DAYS
22 MILES/35KM**

GREAT FOR...

BEST TIME TO GO

July and September bring hot sunny days that are perfect for a slow-paced meander.

 ESSENTIAL PHOTO

Snap the view from the terrace at Mission Hill Family Estate winery.

 BEST FOR FOODIES

Stop for fresh peaches, nectarines, apricots, cherries, raspberries and watermelons.

Classic Trip

30 Okanagan Valley Wine Tour

Filling up on sun-ripened fruit at roadside stalls has long been a highlight of traveling through the Okanagan on a hot summer day. Since the 1980s, the region has widened its embrace of the culinary world by striping its hillsides with grapes. Over 100 vineyards take advantage of the Okanagan's cool winters and long summers. Icewine, made from grapes frozen on the vine, is a unique take-home tipple. And when you're done soaking up the wine, you can soak up the scenery at the countless beaches along the way.

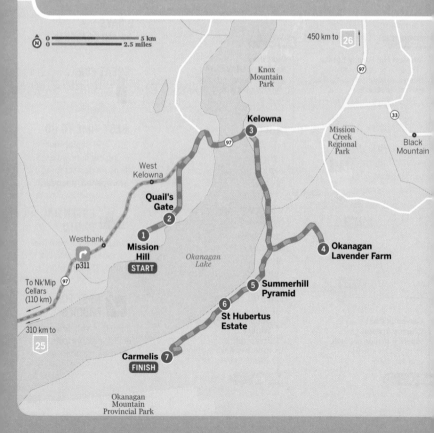

TRIP HIGHLIGHT

❶ Mission Hill

Begin your leisurely taste-tripping trawl on the western shore of the 62-mile (100km) long Okanagan Lake, the region's centerpiece. Following Boucherie Rd north, between the lake and Hwy 97, will bring you to Westbank's award-winning **Mission Hill Family Estate** (📞250-768-6448; www.missionhillwinery.com; 1730 Mission Hill Rd, Westbank; ⏰9:30am-7pm Jul & Aug, with seasonal variations). The estate is a modernist reinterpretation of mission buildings, reached through imposing gates. Several

LINK YOUR TRIP

25 **Vancouver & the Fraser Valley**

Follow Hwy 3A and then Hwy 3 from the southern end of the Okanagan Lake to Hope (p265).

26 **Sea to Sky Highway**

Head northwest from the north of Okanagan Lake on Hwy 97 through Kamloops to Hwy 99 which leads southwest to Whistler via Lillooet (p273).

DETOUR: NK'MIP CELLARS

Start: ❷ Quail's Gate

Add a day to your visit and sample one of the region's most distinctive wineries at **Nk'Mip Cellars** (www.nkmipcellars.com), North America's only First Nations–owned and operated winery when it opened in 2003. Rather than being a novelty producer, it has since created some celebrated tipples from its pueblo-style, desert-fringed site in the town of Osoyoos. Park yourself on the view-filled patio and enjoy the inspired lunch menu with wine pairings. Or knock back some Pinot Blanc for a little courage before checking out the rattlesnake enclosure at the adjoining **Nk'Mip Desert Cultural Centre** (www.nkmipdesert.com). The winery is about 70 miles (112km) south of Westbank along Hwy 97.

The Drive » Return to Boucherie Rd and continue north, following the coast.

TRIP HIGHLIGHT

❷ Quail's Gate

Continuing north will bring you to **Quail's Gate Estate Winery** (📞250-769-4451; www.quailsgate.com; 3303 Boucherie Rd, Westbank; ⏰9am-7pm Jun-Sep, with seasonal variations). Charming stone and beam architecture reigns at this warm and welcoming spot. Chill at vine-side picnic benches with a bottle. Tours run throughout spring and summer and begin in an on-site pioneer home built in 1873. There is also a free three-tipple tasting held throughout the day – the rhubarby Chenin Blanc and pleasantly peppery

tours and tastings are available, including some that include lunch. Highlights of the tours include a film on the creation of wine in the region, a peek at an amazing Chagall tapestry hanging in one of the rooms, and a visit to the barrel cellars where the only natural light comes from an oculus that sits above ground.

Outside is a terrace where you can sip wine and take in a great valley view, as well as a grassy amphitheater that hosts music concerts in the summer (accompanied by wine, of course). You can also visit the shop for souvenir bottles. Look out for Oculus, the winery's premium and unique Bordeaux-blend.

Classic Trip

LOCAL KNOWLEDGE
ERIC VON KROSIGK
WINEMAKER, SUMMERHILL PYRAMID WINERY

The Okanagan Valley is a semi-arid desert region with over 60 types of grapes growing and winemakers from every part of the world. The presence of sagebrush surrounding vineyards in the south of the valley often shows up as a note of sage in the wine. Most wineries (160 in the region) have tasting rooms and offer tours. Grape varieties of note include Pinot Noir, Syrah, Merlot, Riesling, Chardonnay, Gewurztraminer, Pinot Gris and Pinot Blanc.

Above: Merlot grapes, Kelowna
Right: Wine at Summerhill Pyramid Winery

reserve Pinot Noir are recommended. The on-site Old Vines restaurant is a foodie favorite, with a menu showcasing seasonal British Columbia ingredients and a commitment to sourcing sustainable seafood.

✖ p317

The Drive ≫ Cross the lake at the new William R Bennett Bridge and head for the 'east

coast' town of Kelowna, the Okanagan capital.

❸ Kelowna

The wine industry has turned Kelowna into a bit of a boomtown. Property prices are surprisingly high for this part of the world, as is the growing skyline. A wander around (and especially along Ellis Street) will unearth plenty of art galleries and lakeside parks, along with cafes and – predictably – wine bars.

Continue your wine education at the **BC Wine Museum** (☎250-868-0441; www.kelownamuseum.ca; 1304 Ellis St, Kelowna; admission by donation; ⏰10am-6pm Mon-Fri, 10am-5pm Sat, 11am-5pm Sun). Housed in the historic Laurel Packinghouse, the museum offers a look at celebrated bottles, labels and equipment along with an overview of winemaking in the region. This is also the place to pick up surprisingly well-priced wines from producers throughout the valley. Ask at the counter and they'll point you toward some rarities.

Classic Trip

TOP TIP:
WINE ONLINE

Get the full scope on the region's 63 wineries, events and new releases at www.okanaganwines.ca.

With vineyards cozied up to Knox Mountain, **Calona Vineyards** (☎250-762-9144; www.calonavineyards.ca; 1125 Richter St, Kelowna; ⊙9am-6pm daily Jun-Sep, with seasonal variations) was the Okanagan's first winery when it kicked off production in 1932. Its cellar-like tasting room is an atmospheric spot to try the ever-popular, melon-note Pinot Blanc, along with the port-style dessert wine that makes an ideal cheese buddy. You'll find it north of Hwy 97.

 p317

The Drive » Head south of Kelowna on Lakeshore Rd, keeping the Okanagan Lake on your right. Take a left onto Dehart Rd and follow it to Bedford Rd. Turn right and then right again so that you're heading south on Takla Rd.

- - - - - - - - - - - - - -

④ Okanagan Lavender Farm

Visiting **Okanagan Lavender Farm** (☎250-764-7795; www.okanaganlavender.com; 4380 Takla Rd, near Kelowna; ⊙9:30am-5pm Jul & Aug, with seasonal variations; 👫) is a heady experience. Rows and rows of over 60 types of lavender waft in the breeze against a backdrop of the Okanagan Lake. Take the self-guided tour and pop into the shop for everything from bath products to lavender lemonade. Your wine-soaked palate will be well and truly cleansed.

The Drive » Retrace your route back to Lakeshore Rd, heading south and then veering left onto Chute Lake Rd.

- - - - - - - - - - - - - -

`TRIP HIGHLIGHT`

⑤ Summerhill Pyramid

In the hills along the lake's eastern shore, you'll soon come to one of the Okanagan's most colorful wineries. **Summerhill Pyramid Winery** (☎250-764-8000; www.summerhill.bc.ca; 4870 Chute Lake Rd, near Kelowna; ⊙9am-9pm, with seasonal variations) combines a

THE OGOPOGO

For centuries, traditional Native legends have told of a 50-foot-long sea serpent living in the Okanagan Lake. Called the N'ha-a-itk, or Lake Demon, it was believed to live in a cave near Rattlesnake Island, just offshore from Peachland. Natives would only enter the waters around the island with an offering, otherwise they believed the monster would raise a storm and claim lives.

Beginning in the mid-1800s, Europeans also began reporting sightings of a creature with a horse-shaped head and serpent-like body. Nicknamed Ogopogo, the serpent has been seen along the length of the 80-mile (129km) lake, but most commonly around Peachland. In 1926, 30 car-loads of people all claimed to have seen the monster and film footage from 1968 has been analyzed, concluding a solid, three-dimensional object was moving through the water.

Cryptozoologist Karl Shuker suggests the Ogopogo may be a type of primitive whale like the balsiosaurus. Keep your eyes peeled but if you don't have any luck spotting it, you can visit a statue of the Ogopogo at Kelowna's City Park.

Okanagan Lavender Field

traditional tasting room with a huge pyramid where every Summerhill wine ages in barrels, owing to the belief that sacred geometry has a positive effect on liquids. The many medals awarded to the winery don't argue.

'The Pyramid has become a landmark and it's part of all our wines now,' says twinkle-eyed founder Stephen Cipes. 'The conditions are great here for making sparkling wine and we're also organic – the absence of toxins really make it a health drink.' It's hard to argue when you quaff some of his delightful Peace Chardonnay icewine.

✖ p317

The Drive » Return to Lakeside Rd and continue south. The next stop is across from Cedar Creek Park.

- - - - - - - - - -

6 St Hubertus Estate

Further south, lakeside **St Hubertus Estate Winery** (📞250-764-7888; www.st-hubertus.bc.ca; 5205 Lakeshore Rd, near Kelowna; ⏲10am-5:30pm May-Oct,

TOP TIP: WINE FESTIVALS

The Okanagan stages four seasonal wine festivals (www.thewinefestivals.com) throughout the year. Time your visit right and dip into one of these:

Winter Wine Festival Mid-January, five days

Spring Wine Festival Early May, 10 days

Summer Wine Festival August, nine days

Fall Wine Festival Early October, 10 days

(with seasonal variations) takes another twist on the winery approach. Visiting is like being at a traditional northern European vineyard, complete with Bavarian architectural flourishes.

'It's like Switzerland on steroids here,' says a jocular Andy Gebert, who owns the winery with his brother. 'We produce lots of Germanic varieties, including Riesling, which is not exactly the Pamela Anderson of wines. Actually, it's more like Mother Teresa.' But St Hubertus isn't conservative: try its floral, somewhat spicy Casselas and the rich Marechal Foch. While there are no formal tours, you can stroll around the vineyard or head to the complimentary tasting room to try four different wines. There's also a shop selling artisan foods and, of course, wine.

TOP TIP: WHAT'S RIPE WHEN

Say that 10 times fast. It's even trickier when you've got a mouthful of plump raspberries. Farms sell their ripened fruit in stalls along the road and fresh fruit and veggie markets are plentiful. Harvest times bring lower prices and top nosh. Here's what to watch for when:

Strawberries Mid-June to early July

Raspberries Early to mid-July

Cherries Mid-June to mid-August

Apricots Mid-July to mid-August

Peaches Mid-July to mid-September

Pears Mid-August to late September

Apples Early September to late October

Table Grapes Early September to late October

The Drive » Continue south on Lakeside and then take the left turning onto Rimrock Rd. Follow it to a T-junction and take a right onto Timberline Rd.

TRIP HIGHLIGHT

7 Carmelis

End your tour by treating your driver to something they can sample at **Carmelis Goat Cheese Artisan** (☎250-870-3117; www.carmelisgoatcheese.com; 170 Timberline Rd; ⏰10am-6pm May–mid-Oct, 11am-5pm April-May, closed Nov-Feb; 🚻). Call ahead to book a tour of the dairy, milking station and cellar. Even without the tour, you can sample soft-ripened cheeses with names like Moonlight and Heavenly, or the hard-ripened Smoked Carmel or Goatgonzola. For those with a milder palate, there are super-soft unripened versions like feta and yoghurt cheese. And then there's the goats-milk gelato!

Eating & Sleeping

Quail's Gate ❷

✕ Old Vines   Local $$

(☎250-769-4451; www.quailsgate.com; 3303
Boucherie Rd, Westbank; mains CAN$17-25;
⏰9am-7pm Jun-Sep, with seasonal variations)
Using only the freshest ingredients available,
this terrace-style restaurant draws crowds.
At brunch, try the Dungeness crab cakes with
coconut, cilantro and pineapple and daikon
radish salad. Or dig into smoked quail or prawn
risotto at lunch. And wash it all down with some
of the region's top wine.

Kelowna ❸

✕ RauDZ   Fusion $$

(☎250-868-8805; www.raudz.com; 1560 Water
St; mains CAN$12-25; ⏰5-10pm) This casual
bistro is a temple to Okanagan produce and
wine. The dining room is as airy and open as
the kitchen and the seasonal menu takes global
inspiration for Med-infused dishes good for
sharing, as well as steaks and seafood. Suppliers
include locally renowned Carmelis Goat Cheese
Artisan.

✕ Rotten Grape   Tapas $$

(☎250-717-8466; 231 Bernard Ave; mains
CAN$8-15; ⏰5pm-midnight Wed-Sun) Enjoy
flights of local wines without the frou-frou in the
heart of town. If you utter 'tannin, the hobgoblin
of pinot' at any point, be quiet and eat some of
the tasty tapas.

✕ La Bussola   Italian $$$

(☎250-763-3110; 1451 Ellis St; mains CAN$15-
30; ⏰5-10pm Mon-Sat) The Cultural District
location is fitting. Since 1974 Franco and
Lauretta Coccaro have worked to perfect their
Italian supper house. The menu spans the boot,
from pesto to red sauce, veal to seafood. Dine at
the sidewalk tables or in the stylish dining room.

🛏 Hotel Eldorado   Hotel $$$

(☎250-763-7550; www.eldoradokelowna.com;
500 Cook Rd, Kelowna; r CAN$290-445)
This dockside hotel offers a sumptuous place
to base yourself. South Beach–style rooms
feel comfortably posh, with both antique and
contemporary touches and views over the
sparkling lake. This makes a great base for
exploring the region.

🛏 A View of the Lake   B&B $$

(☎250-769-7854; www.aviewofthelake.com;
1877 Horizon Drive, Kelowna; r CAN$130-160) Set
on the edge of Kelowna, on the west side of the
lake, this B&B offers privacy and magnificent
views. Book the Grandview Suite for a lake vista
extending even to the air-jetted bathtub. Rooms
are peaceful, beds are comfy and the three-
course breakfast on the deck is gourmet.

Summerhill Pyramid ❺

✕ Sunset Organic
Bistro   Restaurant $$$

(☎250-764-8000; www.summerhill.bc.ca;
4870 Chute Lake Rd, near Kelowna; ⏰11am-
9pm, with seasonal variations; four-course
dinner/with wine CAN$48/73) With organic
delicacies like barley-stuffed quail, asparagus
risotto, a daily pick 'n' catch of fresh veggies
and seafood and desserts like rhubarb
parfait, this is no ordinary bistro. Wine
pairings are masterful and the Sunday
brunch (adult/child CAN$30/15) goes on
and on and on.

Haida Gwaii *Feel closer t
nature than ever befor*

Haida Gwaii Adventure

31

Far-flung and isolated, the lush Haida Gwaii ('Islands of Beauty') are steeped in superlatives – most stunning scenery, tastiest seafood and most accessible First Nations culture.

TRIP HIGHLIGHTS

2 DAYS
85 MILES/137KM

GREAT FOR...

BEST TIME TO GO

Visit in July and August when the sun is more likely to shine and the wind is less vicious.

ESSENTIAL PHOTO

Capture the islands' wilderness from the viewpoint on Tow Hill.

BEST FOR CULTURE

Gain some insight into local Native culture at the phenomenal Haida Heritage Centre.

103 km — 4

Masset
Towering totem poles and local Native art galleries

FINISH
5

151 km

North Beach
Dramatic sandy coast that feels like the edge of the earth

3 — **63 km**

Golden Spruce
A story about the mystery of nature and the strength of Haida culture

● Tlell

8 km

Haida Heritage Centre
Look into a culture that has survived for thousands of years

1

START

TODD LAWSON / ALAMY ©

31 Haida Gwaii Adventure

You'll be welcomed to what feels like the edge of the earth with a warm, hearty greeting. Once known as the Queen Charlotte Islands, this rugged northwestern archipelago maintains its pioneering spirit, evident in its quirky museums, rustic cafes, down-to-earth art and nature-loving locals. You'll also feel closer to the natural world than ever before.

Columbia's best First Nations attraction. Check out ancient carvings and artifacts recalling 10,000 years of Haida history and look for the exquisite artworks of the legendary Bill Reid – his glorious painted canoe bobs in the adjoining bay.

Hitting Hwy 16, head north to explore the distinctive settlements that make latter-day Haida Gwaii tick. You'll wind along stretches of rustic waterfront and through shadowy woodland areas while a permanent detachment of beady-eyed eagles follows your progress.

 p325

The Drive » Follow Hwy 16 north along the shoreline. At around 20km, watch for orange-and-white leading marks on the inland side of the highway, marking the end of the long bar which extends north all the way from Sandspit. At 22 miles (35km) you'll enter into the flat, arable land around Tlell River.

❷ Tlell

Just before Tlell, the charming **Bottle and Jug Works** (☎250-559-4756; 858 Hwy 16) exemplifies the region's pioneer spirit. Friendly potters John and Jennifer Davies will happily chat to you about life on the island as you peruse their selection of fat-bellied, Hobbit-friendly mugs and handsome rustic teapots. It's open

TRIP HIGHLIGHT

❶ Skidegate

Arrange a hire car far in advance of your BC Ferries arrival in Skidegate on Graham Island; try **Budget** (☎800-527-0700; www.budget.com), then spend some time perusing the clapboard houses or fueling up at the home-style pub or coffee shop near the dock. Save an hour or two for the area's highlight: the **Haida Heritage Centre** (www.haidaheritagecentre.com; Second Beach Rd; adult/youth/child CAN$15/10/5; ◷10am–6pm daily Jun–Aug, 10am–5pm Tue–Sat Sep–May; ♿), a striking crescent of totem-fronted cedar longhouses that's arguably British

TOP TIP: GETTING THERE

From mainland Prince Rupert in northern BC, take the **BC Ferries** (www.bcferries.com; adult/child/vehicle CAN$43/22/153) service to Skidegate on Graham Island. The crossing usually takes seven to eight hours.

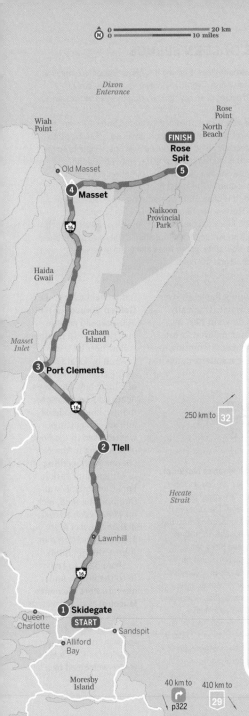

irregular hours and by appointment from Monday to Saturday.

🍴 p325

The Drive » Continue northwest along Hwy 16. This incredibly straight route was a walking trail until 1920 when a road was built by placing wooden planks end-to-end along the ground. Watch for shrub-like Shore Pines along the now-paved route.

TRIP HIGHLIGHT

3 Port Clements

Just before you reach Port Clements, head down Cedar Ave to Bayview Ave and onto the logging road for 3 miles

S LINK YOUR TRIP

32 Up the Inside Passage

From Skidegate, it's a six-hour ferry ride to Prince Rupert and a further 5½ hours to Ketchikan where you can pick up the northern half of this tour (p327).

29 Vancouver Island's Remote North

After a six-hour boat ride from Skidegate to Prince Rupert you travel along the inside passage on a 22-hour ferry to Port Hardy. From here drive 25 miles (40km) along Hwy 9 to Port McNeill to pick up this Trip (p301).

321

THE STORY OF THE GOLDEN SPRUCE

Long ago a harsh blizzard hit a small village, burying it in snow. Supplies diminished and villagers died of cold and starvation. Eventually only a young boy and his grandfather remained and, with hopes of surviving, they dug themselves out and began trekking.

As they walked in search of a new village, the blizzard ended and spring arrived. The grandfather warned his grandson: 'Don't look back. If you do, you will go into the next world. A world where people can admire you, but will not be able to speak with you. You will be standing in this sacred place until the end of the world.'

Missing his home, the boy stole one last glance in the direction of the village they'd left behind. The boy was rooted to the forest floor. Seeing what had happened, the grandfather said, 'It is okay. Future generations will come and see you and remember your story'. The boy had become the Golden Spruce.

And the grandfather was right. Many did come to marvel at the Golden Spruce, a tree that defied the laws of nature, with needles that should not have been able to absorb the sunlight but thrived among the green trees along the shoreline. It was a tree that stood between this world and the next.

(5km). This brings you to a signposted, easy 2-mile (3.2km) trail through the forest leading to the banks of the Yakoun River and a felled tree hanging haplessly over the water. Tragically cut down in 1997 by an unemployed forest engineer attempting to make a statement against industrial logging, the **Golden Spruce** – a 150ft, 300-year-old genetic aberration with luminous yellow needles – was revered by local Haida as the transformed spirit of a little boy. The tree's death was traumatic for many island residents and several cuttings where taken in the hope of replacing it. You can see one such seedling in Millennium Park in Port Clements. For an illuminating read, pick up *The Golden Spruce: A True Story of Myth, Madness and Greed* by John Vaillant (2006).

Head back to Hwy 16 to the village and nip into **Port Clements Museum** (www.portclements museum.org; 45 Bayview Rd; admission CAN$2; 11am-4pm Mon-Fri Jun-Sep, 2-4pm Sat & Sun Oct-May), where you're welcomed by a

DETOUR: GWAII HAANAS NATIONAL PARK RESERVE

Start: ❶ Skidegate

Famed for its mystical élan, **Gwaii Haanas National Park Reserve** (www.pc.gc.ca/gwaiihaanas) covers much of Haida Gwaii's southern section, a rugged region only accessible by boat or floatplane. The reserve is the ancient site of Haida homes, burial caves and the derelict village of Ninstints with its seafront totem poles (now a Unesco World Heritage Site). Visitors often remark on the area's magical and spiritual qualities, but you should only consider an extended visit if you are well prepared. Facilities are sparse; other than three water hoses, composting toilets and maintained cultural sites, you're on your own.

Contact **Parks Canada** (250-559-8818; www.pc.gc. ca/gwaiihaanas; Haida Heritage Centre at Qay'llnagaay, Skidegate; 8:30am-noon & 1-4:30pm Mon-Fri) with questions on planning a visit and a list of tour operators.

Gwaii Haanas National Park Reserve Sea lions

forest of rusty logging machinery. Learn about early logging practices and check out toys and tools from pioneering days. You'll also encounter a stuffed albino raven, another genetic aberration that was also revered until it electrocuted itself on local power lines.

🛏 p325

The Drive ›» Head north along Hwy 16, which hugs Masset Inlet to the northern coast.

- - - - - - - - - - -

TRIP HIGHLIGHT

❹ Masset

Continue north to the settlements of Masset and **Old Masset**. Masset primarily occupies the rather stark, institutional buildings of a disused military base and the adjoining Old Masset is a First Nations' village where wood-fired homes are fronted by broad, brooding totem poles. There are several stores here where visitors can peruse and buy Haida carvings in argillite, a glasslike slate that is found only in this corner of the world.

Also in Masset is the **Dixon Entrance Maritime**

RETURN OF THE HAIDA

The Haida are one of Canada's First Nations peoples, and had lived here for thousands of years before Europeans turned up in the 18th century. Centered on the islands, these fearsome warriors had no immunity to such diseases as smallpox, measles and tuberculosis that were brought by the newcomers, and their population of tens of thousands was quickly decimated. By the early 20th century, their numbers had fallen to around 600.

Since the 1970s, the Haida population – and its cultural pride – has grown anew, and the Haida now make up about half of the 5000 residents on the islands. In 2009, the Government of British Columbia officially changed the name of the islands from the Queen Charlottes to Haida Gwaii as part of the province's reconciliation process with the Haida. Today the Haida continue to live by their traditional laws which encompass the stunning nature of the islands and embrace both the past and the future.

The Council of the Haida Nation outlines the importance of Haida Gwaii: 'Our culture is born of respect and intimacy with the land and sea and the air around us. Like the forests, the roots of our people are intertwined such that the greatest troubles cannot overcome us. We owe our existence to Haida Gwaii. The living generation accepts the responsibility to ensure that our heritage is passed on to the following generations.'

To learn more about the Haida, visit www.haidanation.ca.

Museum (2182 Collinson Ave; admission CAN$2; ⏱1-5pm daily Jun-Sep, 2-4pm Sat & Sun Apr-Jun). Housed in what was once the local hospital, the museum features exhibits on the history of this seafaring community, with displays on shipbuilding, medical pioneers, military history and nearby clam and crab canneries. Local artists also exhibit their work here.

🛏 p325

The Drive » Head east off Hwy 16 along a well-marked logging road signposted for Naikoon Provincial Park.

TRIP HIGHLIGHT

⑤ Rose Spit

The region's wild northern tip is home to **Naikoon Provincial Park** (www.env.gov.bc.ca/bcparks). This dense, treed park has more than 60 miles of white-sand beach and is the area's most popular destination for summertime nature fans.

Continue along the tree-lined dirt road until you reach **Tow Hill**, a steep, dense and mercifully short forest walk (0.6 miles/1km each way). Look out for trees where strips of bark have been carefully removed for Haida basket-making over the decades, then catch your breath at the summit while you gaze over the impenetrable coastal forest stretching into the mist.

Finally, head for the park's extreme coastal tip and **North Beach**. Leave the car here and tramp along the wave-smacked sandy expanse, where locals walk in the surf plucking Dungeness crabs for dinner. With the wind watering your eyes, you'll feel closer to nature than you've ever felt before.

🍴 🛏 p325

Eating & Sleeping

Skidegate ❶

✕ Keenawi's Kitchen
Haida $$$

(📞250-559-8347; 237 Hwy 16; dinner feast CAN$60; 🕑by appointment) Delectable Haida seafood dishes (and songs) prepared and served by the family in Roberta Olson's waterfront home. Feast on crunchy dried seaweed, chunky shrimp chowder and dishes of butter-soft halibut and spring salmon. Reservations required.

Tlell ❷

✕ Rising Tide Bakery
Cafe $

(📞250-557-4677; 37580 Hwy 16; mains CAN$4-9; 🕑8am-5pm) This bright and sunny bakery is where the locals chat over home-baked goodies; look for the daily lunch specials.

Port Clements ❸

🛏 Golden Spruce Motel
Motel $

(📞250-557-4325; www.goldenspruce.ca; 2 Grouse St; r CAN$66-86) While a little Spartan, this clean and comfortable motel gives a warm welcome and has a good breakfast cafe. Some rooms have kitchenettes and there are fire pits outside for guest use.

Masset ❹

🛏 Copper Beach House
B&B $$

(📞250-626-5441; www.copperbeachhouse. com; 1590 Delkatla Rd; r CAN$100-140) This excellent B&B has five cozy, atmospheric rooms with names like The Retreat and Cloud Nine. The culinary treats are divine, with freshly baked goods and homemade gourmet delicacies like crab pate, sushi and inventive soups. The owners are a wealth of knowledge on the challenges and attractions of island life.

Rose Spit ❺

✕ Moon Over Naikoon
Cafe $

(📞250-626-5064; Tow Hill Rd, Naikoon Provincial Park; mains CAN$4-8; 🕑8am-5pm Jun-Aug) Seemingly constructed from driftwood and bleached whale bones, this rustic art- and artifact-lined coffee stop is nestled in the forest and features organic oven-fresh baked treats and ever-changing pizza and pasta specials.

🛏 All The Beach You Can Eat
Cabins $$

(📞604-313-6192; www.allthebeachyoucaneat. com; 15km marker Tow Hill Rd; cabins CAN$85-120) On beautiful North Beach, two cabins are perched in the dunes, back from the wide swath of sand that runs for miles east and west. One has views that seem to reach to Japan. There is no electricity; you cook and light your way with propane.

🛏 Agate Beach Campground
Campground $

(📞250-557-4390; www.env.gov.bc.ca/bcparks; Naikoon Provincial Park; campsites CAN$16) This rustic, wind-whipped campground gives you the opportunity to commune with nature for the night. The 43 waterfront sites have basic facilities (cold faucets and pit toilets) and are open mid-May to mid-September only.

Inside Passage Board a ferry and enjoy a constant visual feast

Classic Trip

Up the Inside Passage

32

Set sail on an Alaska Ferry from Bellingham, Washington, tracing the lush Canadian coastline before slipping into the foggy emerald maze of Alaska's wild, remote Inside Passage.

TRIP HIGHLIGHTS

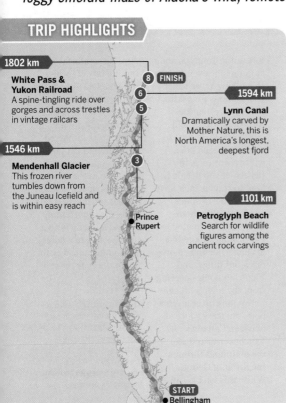

1802 km

White Pass & Yukon Railroad
A spine-tingling ride over gorges and across trestles in vintage railcars

1546 km

Mendenhall Glacier
This frozen river tumbles down from the Juneau Icefield and is within easy reach

8 **FINISH**

6

5

1594 km

Lynn Canal
Dramatically carved by Mother Nature, this is North America's longest, deepest fjord

3

1101 km

Petroglyph Beach
Search for wildlife figures among the ancient rock carvings

● Prince Rupert

START
● Bellingham

4 DAYS
1119 MILES/1800KM

GREAT FOR...

BEST TIME TO GO
June to September – the snow has melted and wildflowers bloom.

 ESSENTIAL PHOTO
Totem poles, tall pines and soaring eagles at Chief Shakes Island.

 BEST FOR WILDLIFE
Bears, bald eagles, whales and sea lions – they're all out there waiting to be spotted.

Classic Trip

32 Up the Inside Passage

Of the 27 All-American Roads, the Alaska Marine Hwy is the only one that takes to the water on a car ferry. Churning 3500 nautical miles from Bellingham and out to the far tendril of the Aleutian Chain, some of the highway's most dramatic scenes are pressed into the steep fjords, forests and waterlogged fishing towns of the Inside Passage. By land it takes 98 hours to reach Skagway from Bellingham, with lots of long, empty stretches where the forest seems to swallow you completely. By sea, it's a constant visual feast.

---

① Bellingham

In Bellingham, head to the brick-paved, historic **Fairhaven District**. Make sure to give yourself at least an afternoon to explore this city neighborhood, stamped onto several blocks and charmingly crammed with flower shops, cafes and bookstores. This is also where you board the **Alaska Ferry** (☎907-465-3941, 800-642-0066; www.alaska.gov/ferry; vehicle/adult/child/under 6 to Skagway US$820/363/199.50/free, to Ketchikan US$515/239/119.50/free; ⊞); you can walk, bike, or drive onto the vessel. A three-day trip ends in Skagway, traveling through the US's largest national forest, the Tongass, and stopping in several ports. If you have more time, your options for taking detours are countless. A through-ticket will give you a little time to explore in each port, while point-to-point tickets let you decide how long to stay in each town.

As the ferry slides out into **Bellingham Bay**, you'll be treated to views of meringue-like Mt Baker, sienna-colored brick buildings, and Victorian homes peering from the town's hillside.

Not long after leaving port, the ferry squeezes between Canada's Vancouver Island and the mainland through the Strait of Georgia. While this isn't a cruise ship, it's comfortable and the mix of locals and travelers gives it the feeling of an authentic voyage. You'll find the solarium filled with adventurers hunkered down under heat lamps, while brightly colored tents flap in the wind on deck. The snack-bar fare is what you'd expect of public transportation, but warming up with a cup of coffee in a booth is a comfortable way to watch the coast pass by.

✕ ⍩ p335

The Drive ≫ This is like autopilot in the extreme. Sit back and watch the amazing scenery pass by as you travel past lighthouse stations and between islands with wild coastlines, watching for eagles and even the occasional whale.

8 Skagway
FINISH
7 Haines
Teresa Island
Lynn Canal 6
Teslin Lake
Juneau 5
Glass Peninsula
USA
CANADA
37
Petersburg 4
LeConte Glacier
Wrangell 3
Marelle Islands
Prince of Wales Island
p331
Spatsizi Plateau Provincial Wilderness Park
ALASKA
p330
2 Ketchikan
Haida Gwaii
37
Masset
31
Heceta Strait
Prince Rupert
Terrace
Babine Lake
Skidegate
Kitimat
Juan Perez Sound
Houston
Harvey Islands
Don Peninsula
Tweedsmuir Provincial Park
Natalkuz Lake
Queen Charlotte Sound
Scott Islands
BRITISH COLUMBIA
Port Hardy
Brooks Peninsula
Vancouver Island
Chilko Lake
Coast Mountains
PACIFIC OCEAN
Campbell River
Strathcona Provincial Park
Powell River
99
Whistler
Garibaldi Provincial Park
CANADA
1
Vancouver
Hope
25
Victoria
USA
Bellingham
5 **START**
0   200 km
0   100 miles

2 Ketchikan

Thirty-eight hours after departing Bellingham, the ferry makes its first stop in Ketchikan. Here you'll skim along the town's thin band of colorful buildings (with equally colorful histories) before docking north of the town center. The ferry stays in port long enough for you to explore the historic, albeit touristy, **Creek Street**. Though this boardwalk is now safe for families, in Ketchikan's early boomtown years the street was a clatter of brothels and bars. Pop into **Dolly's House Museum** (www. dollyshouse.com; 24 Creek St; adult/child $5/free; ⏰8am-5pm), where you can get an insider's view of what was a working parlor.

LINK YOUR TRIP

31 Haida Gwaii Adventure

Hop on a ferry from Prince Rupert for a jaunt over to these remote, gorgeous islands (p319).

25 Vancouver & the Fraser Valley

From Bellingham, head north on I-5 across the Canadian border and follow Hwy 99 to Vancouver to take in the surrounding valley that's lush with vineyards, fruit and culture (p265).

Namesake Dolly Arthur operated the brothel until prostitution was outlawed in 1953, and lived here until her death in the '70s.

For an introduction to a different kind of wildlife, head to the **Southeast Alaska Discovery Center** (www.alaskacenters.gov/ketchikan.cfm; 50 Main St; adult/child $5/free; ⏲8:30am-5pm daily;). The center houses excellent exhibits on various aspects of the Southeast region (simply called 'Southeast' by locals), including ecosystems, artwork and Native Alaskan traditions, while downstairs a re-created rainforest looms. This is a great place to help you identify what you're seeing from the windows of the ferry.

 p335

The Drive » From Ketchikan, the ferry hums north through Clarence Strait to Wrangell.

- - - - - - - - - -

TRIP HIGHLIGHT

❸ Wrangell

Several hours after departing Ketchikan, you'll arrive at tiny, false-fronted Wrangell. You'll be greeted by the town's children, who set up folding tables (even in the rain) to sell their wares – deep-purple garnets that they've mined from the nearby Stikine River.

Wrangell practically spills over with historic, cultural and natural sights, including **Petroglyph Beach**. Less than a mile from the ferry terminal the beach is dotted with boulders depicting faces and figures that were carved thousands of years ago. Lifelike whales and owls peer up at you, while some spirals eerily resemble crop circles. If you're just popping off the ferry during its quick stop, you can jog there and back for a speedy examination of the stones.

More recent Tlingit culture is showcased on the other side of town at **Chief Shakes Island and Tribal House**, an oddly peaceful site in the middle of the humming boat harbor. Here, six totem poles tower among pines, and eagles often congregate in the trees' branches. The island is always open for walking, though the tribal house usually only opens for cruise ship groups.

Just after leaving Wrangell, the ferry enters the 22-mile long **Wrangell Narrows**. Too skinny and shallow for most large vessels, the Narrows (dubbed Pinball Alley) requires nearly 50 course corrections as boats thread between more than 70 channel markers. The ferry M/V *Columbia* is the largest boat to navigate the Narrows, as water depth can get as shallow as 24ft at low tide.

🛏 p335

DETOUR: PRINCE OF WALES ISLAND

Start: ❷ **Ketchikan**

The third-largest island in the US, mountainous Prince of Wales Island isn't a well-known mountain-biking destination, but that's due more to its remote location than its lack of spectacular terrain. Veined with over 1300 miles of mostly unpaved road and spotted with tiny villages, POW also has 21 public-use cabins scattered along its inlets and alpine lakes. There are dispiriting clear-cuts, but they're the reason for all those roads.

For an island guide, check out www.princeofwalescoc.org. The **Inter-Island Ferry** (www.interislandferry.com) has services from Ketchikan, Wrangell and Petersburg. Adult/child fares from Ketchikan are CAN$37/18, vehicles from CAN$5 per foot.

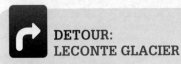

DETOUR: LECONTE GLACIER

Start: ❹ Petersburg

Complement a layover in Petersburg with a kayak tour to LeConte Glacier, at the head of serpentine LeConte Bay. Constantly calving, the glacier is somewhat infamous for icebergs that release under water and then shoot to the surface like icy torpedoes. If you're lucky you'll see one – from afar.

The Drive » After maneuvering through the Narrows, the ferry continues northwest to Petersburg.

❹ Petersburg

At the end of the Narrows sits Petersburg, a fishing village with blond roots. Petersburg's thick Norwegian history is evident not just in the phonebook full of Scandinavian names, but also in the flowery rosemaling, a decorative Norwegian art form found on buildings throughout town. To really get into the heart of Petersburg, walk the docks of its **North Boat Harbor**. Here fisherfolk unload the day's catch from small purse seiners, distinguishable by the large nets piled in the sterns.

 p335

The Drive » From Petersburg, the ferry heads north alongside the densely forested Admiralty Island to the port of Juneau.

TRIP HIGHLIGHT

❺ Juneau

After brushing through quiet fishing towns, arriving in Juneau can be somewhat surprising. This is the only US capital with no road access, yet it still bustles with the importance of a government center. It's also postcard perfect, with massive green cliffs rising above the city center. Be sure to stroll past the **Governor's Mansion**, its assertive columns and landscaped shrubs a contrast to the usual rainforest-rotted cabins of Southeast.

If the political climate gets to be too much, head to the laid-back **Alaskan Brewing Company** (www.alaskanbeer.com; 5429 Shuane Dr; ☻11am-6pm May-Sep, 11am-5:30pm Tue-Sat Oct-Apr) for a tour and a sample of their beers. The brewery is in the same neighborhood as the massive **Mendenhall Glacier**, which tumbles

BC'S STAFFED LIGHTHOUSES

The misty stretch of Canada between Washington and Alaska is home to 40 lighthouses, more than half of which require keepers. Watch for **Addenbroke Island Lightstation**, an outpost called home by a family with three children. The ferry then glides by picturesque **Dryad Point Lightstation**, which features an old-school style lighthouse perched on the northeastern tip of Campbell Island. Further north, **Boat Bluff Lightstation** is a simple aluminum skeleton, but the red-roofed outbuildings hug a small hillside and the keepers often emerge to wave to ferry passengers. After passing Prince Rupert, keep an eye out for **Triple Island Lightstation** where the lighthouse clings to the top of what appears to be more of a large rock than an island. This station has been kept since 1920 despite the lack of space or vegetation on the island. For an in-depth and often fascinating look at the history of the lighthouses, pick up a copy of *Lights of the Inside Passage* by Donald Graham (Harbour Publishing, 1987).

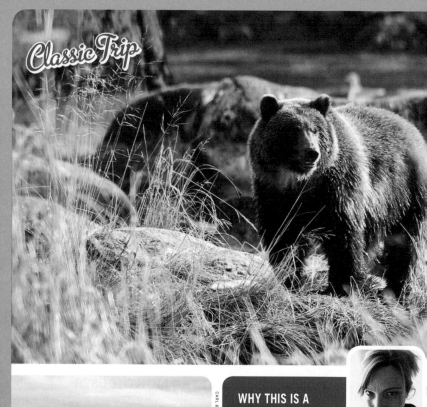

Classic Trip

CARL & ANN PURCELL / CORBIS ©

WHY THIS IS A CLASSIC TRIP
KORINA MILLER, AUTHOR

As the ferry enters the Inside Passage, you feel an undeniable spark of excitement. It's like following in the wake of the first European explorers. You appreciate the remoteness of it all. Catching a glimpse of a bear or a wolf on the shoreline, watching the bald eagles swoop overhead and stopping off at communities only accessible by water – quite quickly I realized this was no ordinary trip. The word 'remarkable' came to mind.

Top: Brown bear, Chilkoot River, Haines
Left: Mendenhall Glacier
Right: Petroglyph Beach, Wrangell

down from the Juneau Icefield and is one of the few glaciers in Southeast you can drive up to. The visitor's center offers a movie about the glacier, plus hiking trails and a salmon-viewing platform.

🛏 p335

The Drive ≫ The route continues north, hugging the coastline into the Lynn Canal.

TRIP HIGHLIGHT

❻ Lynn Canal

From Juneau, the ferry travels up the Lynn Canal, North America's longest (90 miles/145km) and deepest (2000ft) fjord. Glaciers and waterfalls make the canal a visual feast. It was first mapped in 1794 and was later a major route to the boomtown of Skagway during the gold rush. This was also the scene of one of the worst maritime disasters in the Pacific Northwest: in 1918 a passenger ship grounded on a reef and sunk along with all of its 343 crew and passengers.

Because of its high use, lighthouses were once scattered along the inlet; still standing are the octagonal **Eldred Rock Light** and the church-like **Sentinel Island Light**. The canal is now used less for freight and more by ferries, cruise lines and humpback whales.

The Drive ≫ The trip north from Juneau via the Lynn Canal to Haines takes about 4½ hours.

Classic Trip

❼ Haines

Seventy-five miles from Juneau lies Haines, where most passengers with cars disembark as the town is the main link to the Alaska Hwy. Haines has a laid-back vibe with almost extravagant scenery. You can't miss the huge hammer outside the **Hammer Museum** (www.hammermuseum.org; 108 Main St; adult/child $3/free; ⏰10am-5pm Mon-Fri May-Sep), which displays 1500 versions of humanity's first tool and chronicles history through them. Not surprisingly, this is the world's first (and only) museum dedicated solely to the humble hammer.

Between September and December, Haines' population grows by over 3500 when thousands of migrating bald eagles descend on the area. This is the largest gathering of bald eagles in the world and the town celebrates with the mid-November **Alaska Bald Eagle Festival** (www.baldeagles.org/festival). If you arrive at the same time as these white-headed guys, you'll undoubtedly be wowed.

The Drive » A short one-hour trip north along the coast brings you to Skagway.

IN SEARCH OF AURORA BOREALIS

Glowing green and red across the sky like fluorescent curtains, the Northern Lights were named after Aurora, the Roman goddess of dawn, and Boreas, the Greek name for north wind. The Native Cree call them Dance of the Spirits.

The Northern Lights can be seen to some extent anywhere above 60° north latitude, within what is known as the aurora oval. However, you can sometimes catch a glimpse as far south as Juneau.

Sightings are hindered by the perpetual twilight that dominates the night skies from late April until September. The best time to see the Northern Lights is around the 22nd of September or March, on a new moon, late at night or very early in the morning. Head to the ferry deck and await the performance.

TRIP HIGHLIGHT

❽ Skagway

At the turn of the 20th century, Skagway boomed with the gold rush, when the population went from two to 10,000 in just a few years. Sandwiched between forested slopes, it now booms with tourism; if you want to see can-can girls or pan for gold, this is the place to do it. The ferry deposits you about 100yd from **Broadway Street**, where you'll find women dressed in feathered hats and bright satiny dresses. The rest is history.

Since Skagway is likely your last ferry stop, it's worth boarding the **White Pass & Yukon Railroad** (www.wpyr.com; depot on 2nd Ave; Yukon Adventure adult/child $249/119.50 return, White Pass Summit Excursion $113/56.50), a narrated sightseeing tour aboard vintage parlor cars. This dramatic ride rumbles through Glacier Gorge and over White Pass (a 2885ft climb).

Whether you end your trip in Skagway or another port, you'll need to backtrack on the ferry, or fly south, to get home. There are few commercial flights from smaller towns, and to catch a major airline flight to Seattle you'll first need to fly to Juneau, Ketchikan or Sitka. Unless you brought your car on board, in which case you're in for a scenic road trip home. A one-way ticket from Skagway to Juneau with **Wings of Alaska** (www.wingsofalaska.com) is about US$120 and takes just under an hour.

🛏 p335

Eating & Sleeping

Bellingham ❶

🍴 Colophon Café & Deli — Cafe $
(☎360-647-0092; 1208 11th St; mains $7-10; ⏰9am-10pm Mon-Sat) Renowned for its rotating menu of 35 different soups (from African peanut soup to New England clam chowder) as well as for its peanut-butter pie, this cafe – with a welcoming garden – is the perfect place to make yourself at home.

🛏 Fairhaven Village Inn — Hotel $$$
(☎360-733-1311, 877-733-1100; www.fairhavenvillageinn.com; 1200 10th St; r $190-220) A vintage hotel that's perfectly located in the Fairhaven District and a class above the standard motel experience. Enjoy wonderfully comfortable beds and views over the sea or a park.

Ketchikan ❷

🍴 That One Place — Seafood $
(☎907-225-8646; 207 Stedman St; mains $6-12; ⏰8am-4pm) Practically everything on the lunch menu is seafood related. Let's face it – if you're in Alaska long enough you'll eventually order halibut tacos. You might as well do it here, where the locals rave about them.

Wrangell ❸

🛏 Alaskan Sourdough Lodge — Motel $$
(☎907-874-3613, 800-874-3613; www.akgateway.com; 1104 Peninsula St; s/d $104-114) For an overnight stay – and Wrangell is certainly worth it – this family-owned lodge has 16 basic but spotless rooms, a sauna and a steam room. It's a good place to thaw out if you've been exploring in the cold. They also offer a free shuttle from the ferry, and home-cooked evening meals served family-style.

Petersburg ❹

🍴 Rooney's Northern Lights Restaurant — Seafood $$
(☎907-772-2900; 203 Sing Lee Alley; breakfast $5-10, dinner $16-30; ⏰6am-9pm) Plant yourself at a window seat where you can watch fisherman in the harbor unload your potential dinner – here you can sample locally caught crab, halibut and shrimp.

Juneau ❺

🛏 Silverbow Inn — Hotel $$
(☎907-586-4146; www.silverbowinn.com; 120 2nd St; r $90-210) If your trip calls for a night in town, cozy up at the artsy, six-room Silverbow Inn where the smell of fresh bread from the bakery downstairs will wake you in the morning. Amenities at this historic hotel include a rooftop hot tub, full breakfast and a bottomless cookie jar.

Skagway ❻

🛏 At The White House — Hotel $$
(☎907-983-9000; www.atthewhitehouse.com; 478 8th Ave; r $125-155) A small, 10-room inn that retains its 1902 character with details like hand-crafted quilts. All rooms have a private bath, and in the morning you wake up to a breakfast of fresh baked goods and fruit.

Kootenay National Park
Prepare to be awestruck

Circling the Rockies

33

Taking you through Kootenay, Banff and Yoho National Parks and dipping into Alberta, this trip shows off Mother Nature at her best – lofty snowy peaks, deep forests and natural hot springs.

TRIP HIGHLIGHTS

179 km

Takakkaw Falls
Thundering, misty and utterly mesmerising

122 km

Lake Louise
Unbelievably stunning lake with a backdrop of snowy peaks and a looming glacier

8

5

FINISH
Golden

Castle Junction

3

93 km

Marble Canyon
Teeter above this gorgeous, somewhat dizzying, wonder of nature

3 km

Radium Hot Springs
Soak in the scenery and the curative, bubbling waters

1 START

3 DAYS
163 MILES/261KM

GREAT FOR...

BEST TIME TO GO
July and August when the snow has melted and all of the roads are open.

 ESSENTIAL PHOTO

Mt Temple Viewpoint in Banff National Park for postcard-perfect mountain shots.

 BEST FOR WILDLIFE

Watch for bears, elk, big horn sheep and plenty of moose.

33 Circling the Rockies

This route will give you a new perspective on nature. This is where mountains stretch up to the stars and where bears and moose own the woods (and sometimes the road). Waterfalls, canyons and gem-colored lakes lay deep in the forest, waiting to be discovered. It's impossible not to be awed, not to feel small, and not to wish you had longer to explore.

TRIP HIGHLIGHT

❶ Radium Hot Springs

Set in a valley just inside the southern border of Kootenay National Park, the outdoor **Radium Hot Springs** (☎250-347-9485; www.hotsprings.ca; adult/child CAN$6.30/5.40; open 9-11pm with seasonal variation; ♿) has a hot pool simmering at 102°F (39°C) and a second pool to cool you off at 84°F (29°C). Originally sacred to Natives for the water's curative

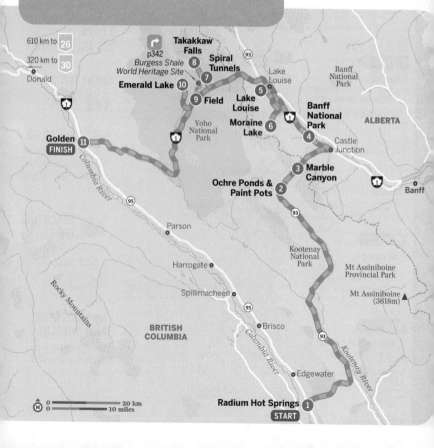

powers, these springs are uniquely odorless and colorless. The large tiled pool can get crowded in summer. You can rent lockers, towels and even swimsuits.

The Drive » From the junction of Hwy 95 and 93, follow Hwy 93 54 miles (86km) east to the hot springs.

2 Ochre Ponds & Paint Pots

As the road delves down into the woods along Hwy 93, a signpost leads to a short, flat interpretive trail. Follow this to the intriguing

LINK YOUR TRIP

30 Okanagan Valley Wine Tour

Head north on Hwy 97 from Kelowna to Sicamous and then east on Hwy 1, through Glacier National Park. From Golden, follow Hwy 95 south alongside the Columbia River to Radium Hot Springs (p309).

26 Sea to Sky Highway

Mountain-hop to the Coast Mountains by heading west from Golden on Hwy 1 and then on to Hwy 99 southwest to Whistler (p273).

TOP TIP: ROAD CONDITIONS

Weather is very changeable in the mountains. Be sure to carry chains outside of the summer months of June, July and August. For recorded, up-to-date road conditions, call ☎403-762-1450.

---

red-and-orange Ochre Ponds. Drawing Kootenay Natives for centuries – and later European settlers – this iron-rich earth was collected, mixed with oil and turned into paint. Further along the trail are three stunning crystal-blue springs that are known as the Paint Pots.

The Drive » Continue north along Hwy 93 for 1.9 miles (3km) to the next stop.

TRIP HIGHLIGHT

3 Marble Canyon

This jaw-dropping stop is not for the faint-of-heart. An easy 15-minute trail zigzags over Tokumm Creek, giving phenomenal views deeper and deeper into Marble Canyon below. The limestone and dolomite walls have been carved away by the awesome power of the creek, resulting in plunging falls and bizarrely shaped cliff faces. The trail can be slippery. Take sturdy shoes and your camera.

 p343

The Drive » Continue north along Hwy 93 and across the provincial border into Alberta to the junction with Hwy 1 (Castle Junction). Head west.

---

4 Banff National Park

More of a drive than a stop, the stretch of Hwy 1 running from Castle Junction to Lake Louise is one of the most scenic routes through Banff National Park. The highway runs through the Bow Valley, following the weaving, green Bow River and the route of the Pacific Railway. The craggy peaks of the giant Sawback and Massive mountain ranges sweep up on either side of the road. The resulting perspective is much wider than on smaller roads with big open vistas.

There are several viewpoint pull-offs where gob-smacked drivers can stop to absorb their surroundings. Watch for the unmissable **Castle Mountain** looming in its crimson glory to the northwest. The Panorama Ridge then rises in the south, after which the enormous **Mount Temple** comes into view, towering at 11,620ft (3542m). Stop at the **Mt Temple Viewpoint** for a good gander.

This stretch of the highway is only two lanes with no fencing to stop wandering animals from venturing into the road. Drive with caution.

The Drive ≫ The turnoff for Lake Louise Village is 14.9 miles (24km) from Castle Mountain Junction.

TRIP HIGHLIGHT

❺ Lake Louise

With stunning emerald-green water and tall, snowy peaks that hoist the hefty Victoria Glacier up for all to see, Lake Louise has captured the imaginations of mountaineers, artists and visitors for more than a century. You'll notice the lake's color appears slightly different from each viewpoint and with each visit.

Follow the **Lakeshore Trail**, a 2.4 mile (3.8km) round trip, or head up the gorgeous (though somewhat more difficult) route to **Lake Agnes** and its sun-dappled teahouse, perched 4.4 miles (7km) from Lake Louise's shore. For a more relaxed experience, rent a canoe from **Lake Louise Boathouse** (hour/half hour CAN$40/30; ◷8:30am-8pm with seasonal variation) and paddle yourself through the icy waters.

The **Lake Louise Gondola** (☎403-522-3555; www.skilouise.com; off Hwy 1A; adult/child CAN$27.75/13.75; ◷9:30am-5:30pm with seasonal variation; 🚡) lands you at a lofty 6850ft (2088m) for a view of the lake and the surrounding glaciers and peaks. En route you'll sail over wildflowers and possibly even a grizzly bear or two. At the top is the **Wildlife Interpretation Centre**, which hosts regular theater presentations and guided walks. Travel the 14-minute ascent in either an open ski lift or an enclosed gondola.

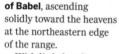 🍴 🛏 p343

The Drive ≫ From Lake Louise Drive, head south along Moraine Lake Rd for 8.75 miles (14km).

---

❻ Moraine Lake

You'll be dazzled by the scenery before you even reach Moraine Lake, set in the Valley of the Ten Peaks. En route, the narrow, winding road gives off fabulous views of the imposing **Wenkchemna Peaks**. Look familiar? For years this scene was carried on the back of the Canadian $20 bill. In 1894, explorer Samuel Allen named the peaks with numbers from one to 10 in the Stoney Indian Language (wenkchemna means 'ten'); all but two of the mountains have since been renamed. You'll quickly notice the **Tower**

of Babel**, ascending solidly toward the heavens at the northeastern edge of the range.

With little hustle or bustle and lots of beauty, many people prefer the more rugged and remote setting of Moraine Lake to Lake Louise. The turquoise waters are surprisingly clear for a glacial reservoir. Take a look at the surrounding mountains through telescopes secured to the southern shore (free!) or hire a boat and paddle to the middle for a 360-degree view. There are also some great day hikes from here and,

HANS-PETER MERTEN / GETTY IMAGES ©

Moraine Lake

to rest your weary legs, a cafe, dining room and lodge. The road to Moraine Lake and its facilities are open from June to early October.

The Drive » Return to Hwy 1 and continue west, across the provincial border and into Yoho National Park.

7 Spiral Tunnels

Upon completion of the railway in 1885, trains struggled up the challenging **Kicking Horse Pass**, which you'll cross soon after the Alberta–British Columbia provincial border. This is the steepest railway pass

in North America and wrecks and runaways were common. In 1909 the Spiral Tunnels were carved into Mt Cathedral and Mt Ogden and are still in use today. If you time it right, you can see a train exiting from the top of the tunnel while its final cars are still entering at the bottom. Watch from the main viewing platform on the northern side of the highway.

🛏 p343

The Drive » Continue west on Hwy 1 and then turn north onto Yoho Valley Rd (open late June–October). This road climbs a number of tight switchbacks.

TRIP HIGHLIGHT

8 Takakkaw Falls

Named 'magnificent' in Cree, **Takakkaw** (804ft/245m) is one of the highest waterfalls in Canada. An impressive torrent of water travels from the Daly Glacier, plunges over the edge of the rock face into a small pool and jets out into a tumbling cloud of mist.

En route to the falls you'll pass a second **Spiral Lookout** and the **Meeting of the Rivers**, where the clear Kicking Horse runs into the milky-colored Yoho.

DETOUR: BURGESS SHALE WORLD HERITAGE SITE

Start: **9** Field

In 1909, Burgess Shale was unearthed on Mt Field. The fossil beds are home to perfectly preserved fossils of marine creatures, dated at over 500 million years old and recognized as some of the earliest forms of life. The area is now a World Heritage Site and accessible only by guided hikes, led by naturalists from the **Yoho Shale Geoscience Foundation** (☎800-343-3006; www.burgess-shale.bc.ca; adult/child CAN$120/25). Reservations are essential, as is stamina: it's a 12-mile (20km) round trip, ascending 2500ft (760m).

The Drive >> Return to Hwy 1 and continue west to Field.

- - - - - - - - - -

9 Field

In the midst of Yoho National Park, on the southern side of the Kicking Horse River, lies the quaint village of Field. This historic but unfussy railroad town has a dramatic overlook of the river. While Field may be short on sights, it's a beautiful place to wander around.

This is also the place to come if you want to organize an activity in the park – from dog-sledding in winter to canoeing and white-water rafting in summer. Visit the **Field Visitor Centre** (☎250-343-6783; www.skilouise.com; Hwy 1; ☺9am-7pm with seasonal variation; ⓘ).

✕ 🛏 p343

The Drive >> Continue west on Hwy 1 and take the first right. Continue north for 6.2 miles (10km).

- - - - - - - - - -

10 Emerald Lake

Gorgeously green Emerald Lake gains its color from light reflecting off fine glacial rock particles that are deposited into the lake by grinding glaciers. It's a highlight of the park, so the lake attracts visitors year-round, either to simply admire its serenity or to fish, skate, hike or horseback ride. In summer, the water warms up just enough to have a very quick dip.

En route to the lake watch for the impressive **natural bridge** stretching across the Kicking Horse River.

✕ p343

The Drive >> Return to Hwy 1 and continue to Golden.

- - - - - - - - - -

11 Golden

With six national parks in its backyard, little Golden is a popular base. It's also the center for white-water rafting trips on the turbulent Kicking Horse River. Powerful grade III and IV rapids and breathtaking scenery along the sheer walls of Kicking Horse Valley make this rafting experience one of North America's best. Full-day trips on the river are about CAN$105; half-day trips CAN$65. Operators include **Alpine Rafting** (☎250-344-6778, 888-599-5299; www.alpinerafting.com).

Over 60% of the 106 ski runs at **Kicking Horse Mountain Resort** (☎250-439-5400, 866-754-5425; www.kickinghorseresort.com; 1-day lift pass adult/child from CAN$74/35) are rated advanced or expert. It's 8.7 miles (14km) from Golden on Kicking Horse Trail.

The **Northern Lights Wolf Centre** (☎250-344-6798; www.northernlightswildlife.com; 1745 Short Rd, Golden; adult/child CAN$12/6; ☺9am-7pm with seasonal variation) is a refuge for this misunderstood animal, which is being hunted to extinction. Meet a resident wolf or two and learn about their routines and survival.

Eating & Sleeping

Marble Canyon ③

🛏 Storm Mountain Lodge   Lodge $$$

(📞403-762-4155; www.stormmountainlodge.
com; Hwy 93; r CAN$140-290) Just inside the
border of Kootenay National Park and set amid
the forest, these luxury cabins were built in
1922 and have been gorgeously restored right
down to the copper piping in the bathroom.
They're cozy and romantic, with a big wooden
bed, fireplace and claw-foot bathtub. Meals in
the equally enchanting lodge are gourmet.

Lake Louise ⑤

🍴 Lake Louise
Station Restaurant   Canadian $$

(📞403-522-2600; end of Sentinel Rd; mains
CAN$12-30; ⏰11:30am-10pm) Dine in the
stationmaster's office surrounded by left
luggage and an old oak desk, opt for the
elegant dining cars, or lounge on the patio
overlooking the rails. This is one of Banff's most
atmospheric restaurants, a lovingly restored
railway station constructed in 1909. Reasonably
priced meals cover all the basics with flair.
Families are welcome.

🛏 Deer Lodge   Hotel $$$

(📞403-522-3991; www.crmr.com; 109 Lake
Louise Dr; r CAN$175-325) Lake Louise's most
atmospheric lodge was built in 1921 and is now
a maze of corridors connecting the many rooms
and towers of the shingled buildings. The hotel
has managed to keep its genuine alpine feel
intact. Restored lodge rooms are fairly tiny but
quaint, while spacious heritage rooms are in the
newer wing. To promote tranquility, you won't
find a TV anywhere.

Spiral Tunnels ⑦

🛏 Cathedral
Mountain Lodge   Cabins $$$

(📞250-343-6422; www.cathedralmountain
lodge.com; Yoho Valley Rd; r CAN$290-440)
Staying here is a treat. The beautiful, cozy log
cabins have giant tubs, vaulted ceilings, lots
of pillows, view-filled decks and a fireplace.
They've gone the extra mile with atmospheric
antiques, making you feel like you've stepped
into an alpine photo shoot.

Field ⑨

🍴 Truffle Pigs Bistro   Contemporary $$

(📞250-343-6303; 100 Centre Street; mains
CAN$12-30; ⏰7am-10pm with seasonal variation)
This award-winning upmarket bistro serves an
eclectic menu of gourmet-style meals, including
game and seafood. Tasty food is presented
artfully and the desserts are divine.

🛏 Kicking Horse Lodge   Hotel $$

(📞250-343-6303; 100 Centre Street; d
CAN$170-180; Jun-Sep) Rooms are simple
but fresh and clean and a steal for this part of
the world. There are also 'hikers' suites' with
kitchenettes and a family room.

Emerald Lake ⑩

🍴 Cilantro   Contemporary $$

(📞250-343-6321; www.crmr.com/emerald/
dining; Emerald Lake Lodge, Emerald Lake
Drive, Yoho National Park; lunch CAN$15-20)
Something of an institution among gourmets,
this lakeside restaurant has big picture windows
and a big fireplace. Sit out on the patio under
fairy lights and sip amazing cocktails, then
savor grilled salmon with yam or buffalo ragout.
Mmmm...

STRETCH YOUR LEGS
VANCOUVER

Start/Finish Gastown

Distance 6.2 miles

Duration Three to four hours

Wandering through Vancouver, with a constant backdrop of sparkling sea and snow-dusted mountaintops, you quickly realize there's more to this city than appearances. It's a kaleidoscope of distinctive neighborhoods, strongly artistic and just as bohemian as it is sophisticated. After this tour, make an unhurried beeline for Granville Island or Kitsilano for more cafes, unique shops and markets to explore.

Take this walk on Trip

Gastown

Crammed into a dozen cobbled street blocks, trendy Gastown is where the city began. Heritage buildings now house cool bars, hip boutiques and galleries, with the landmark **steam clock** (Water St) whistling to onlookers every 15 minutes. The notable building resembling New York's Flat Iron houses **Salmagundi West** (321 W Cordova St; ⊙10:30am-5:30pm), featuring the most eclectic array of antiques and objects that you will ever see. It's also home to **Brioche** (401 W Cordova St; ⊙7am-7pm Mon-Fri, 9am-6pm Sat & Sun), a colorful, comfy place to stop for superb coffee and drool-worthy baking.

The Walk ≫ Follow Water St east, turning right on Carrall St and heading south for three blocks to Pender St and Chinatown.

Chinatown

North America's third-largest **Chinatown** (www.vancouver-chinatown. com) is a highly wanderable explosion of sight, sound and aromas. Check out the towering **Chinatown Millennium Gate** (cnr W Pender & Taylor Sts) and visit the tranquil **Dr Sun Yat-Sen Classical Chinese Garden** (www. vancouverchinesegarden.com; 578 Carrall St; adult/child CAN$14/10; ⊙10am-6pm with seasonal variations). **The Chinese Tea Shop** (www.realchinatea.com; 101 E Pender St; ⊙12:30-6pm) has the makings for a perfect cuppa while **Pak Chong** (506 Main St; ⊙9:30-5pm) will give you a fascinating eyeful of traditional Chinese medicine.

Have lunch at the deservedly popular **Hon's** (☏604-688-8303; www.hons.ca; 268 Keefer St; mains CAN$8-13; ⊙11am-7pm), dishing up noodles and rice since 1972.

The Walk ≫ Follow Keefer St west, crossing over the roundabout at the road's end and continuing along the footpath that leads to Beatty St. Turn left and walk three blocks to Robson St. Turn right, heading northwest and crossing Granville St. From here, Robson is the city's main shopping drag. Continue two blocks to Hornby St.

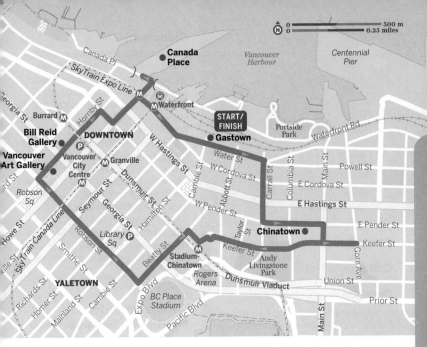

Vancouver Art Gallery

Standing on the corner of Robson St, the **Vancouver Art Gallery** (www.vanart gallery.bc.ca; 750 Hornby St; adult/child CAN$22.50/7.50; ⏲10am-5pm Wed-Mon, to 9pm Tue) houses contemporary exhibitions, work by time-honored masters, and blockbuster international traveling shows. Check out **Fuse** (admission CAN$19.50), a quarterly late-night party where you can hang out with the city's young arties over wine and live music.

The Walk ›› Walk two blocks northeast along Hornby St.

Bill Reid Gallery

The **Bill Reid Gallery of Northwest Coast Art** (www.billreidgallery.ca; 639 Hornby St; adult/child CAN$10/5; ⏲11am-5pm Wed-Sun) showcases carvings, paintings and jewelry from Canada's most revered Haida artist and his fellow First Nations creators. On the mezzanine floor you'll see an 8.5m-long bronze of intertwined magical creatures.

The Walk ›› Continue up Hornby St to Pender St. Turn right and then left on Howe St. Follow this to the water.

Canada Place

Shaped like a series of sails jutting into the sky over the harbor, Canada Place (www.canadaplace.ca; 999 Canada Place Way) is a cruise-ship terminal, convention center and pier where you can stroll the waterfront for some camera-triggering North Shore mountain views. If you have kids in tow, duck inside for the **Port Authority Interpretation Centre** (www.portvancouver.com; admission free; ⏲8am-5pm Mon-Fri;), a hands-on illumination of the city's maritime trade. Check out the grass-roofed expansion next door and the tripod-like **Olympic Cauldron**, a permanent reminder of the 2010 Games.

The Walk ›› Backtrack up Howe St for one block and turn left on Water St and back into Gastown.

STRETCH YOUR LEGS
VICTORIA

Start/Finish Chinatown

Distance 3.8 miles

Duration Four to five hours

It's not sugar-coating – the seaside provincial capital really is as charming and beautiful as it first appears. Filled with funky boutiques, excellent museums, unique neighborhoods and a jewel of a park, wandering Victoria is bliss.

Take this walk on Trips

Chinatown

Settled in 1858, Chinatown is announced with a bright, traditional gate, and stretches two packed blocks along Fisgard St. Grocers and shops display unfamiliar veggies, fans, fortune cookies and teapots. Pop into **Fantan Trading Ltd** (www.fantantrading.ca; 551 Fisgard St; ⏱10am-5:30pm) for a maze of made-in-China goods or **Fan Tan Gallery** (www.fantantrading.ca; 541 Fisgard St; ⏱10:30am-5:30pm Mon-Sat, noon-4pm Sun) for beautiful wooden and woven goods, lanterns and soap. Dine at **Fan Tan Cafe** (☎250-383-1611; 459 Fisgard St; ⏱11am-10pm), a local institution, and look for **Fan Tan Alley** running south next to the cafe. It's home to small boutiques and vintage shops.

The Walk ≫ At Chinatown's gates, turn right onto Government St.

Government Street

With everything from designer shops to ice-cream parlors, Government St is a great stretch of pavement to pound. Visit **Silk Road** (1624 Government St; ⏱10am-6pm) for heavenly teas, and lower Johnson St for quirky designers like **Smokin' Lily** (569 Johnson St; ⏱11am-5:30pm). Hungry? Sneak a block up Yates St and around the corner onto Broad St for the phenomenal **Pagliacci's** (☎250-386-1662; 459 Broad St; ⏱11:30am-10pm), a pasta place locals try to keep secret.

The Walk ≫ Continue eight blocks south on Government St.

The Inner Harbour

Watched over by the **Empress Hotel** (where the Queen stays when she visits!), the **Legislative Buildings** (Belleville St; ⏱8:30am-5pm) and the **Royal BC Museum** (p284), the Inner Harbour is Victoria's most photographic location. Walk down along the water to check out the yachts bobbing like eye-candy and watch street performers.

The Walk ≫ Continue south on Government St to Toronto St. Turn left and follow this east for two blocks to Beacon Hill park.

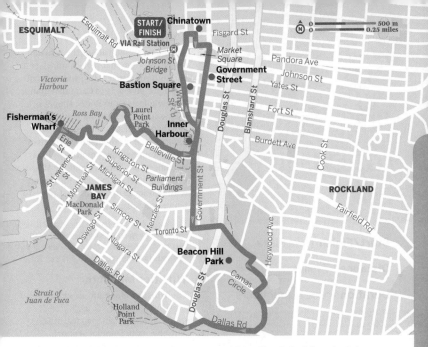

Beacon Hill Park

An ideal combination of planted garden areas and wild and woody sections, Beacon Hill Park is naturally popular. There's a fabulous water park, a petting zoo, a playground and a heron-nesting zone. Head south and you'll find one of North America's tallest totem poles and eventually Dallas Rd and its oceanside walkway, where whale sightings aren't uncommon.

The Walk » Follow Dallas Rd to its end.

Fisherman's Wharf

At **Fisherman's Wharf** (www.fishermans wharfvictoria.com), fishing boats share dock space with a floating community living in eccentric, colorful houseboats. Wander along the boardwalks and visit eclectic galleries. Award-winning **Barb's** (meals $10-20; ⊗11am-dusk Mar-Oct) is hard to resist for fish 'n chips and kids' eyes will pop at the counter of **Jackson's Ice-Cream**. The entrepreneurial fishmonger next door to Barb's sells whole fish to feed the wharf's resident seals. (They'll jump up in appreciation!)

The Walk » Follow the footpath east along the water from Fisherman's Wharf, all the way back to the Inner Harbour. Alternatively, jump on one of the cute Harbour Ferries ($5) to the Empress Dock. From the Inner Harbour, follow Wharf St north.

Bastion Square

The multi-level **Bastion Square** (www. bastionsquare.ca) hosts an **artisan market** (⊗11am-5:30pm Thu-Sat May-Oct) and Sunday farmers' market, along with countless cafes from where you can take in the many live performances. This is also the place to come for dinner. **Rebar** (☎250-361-9223; www.rebarmodernfood.com; 50 Bastion Sq; mains $10-15; ⊗4pm-1am) is a favorite among Victorians for good reason. Even meatatarians drool over the taste-infused veggie dishes and hearty, heavenly desserts. Be sure to pick up a cookbook on the way out.

The Walk » Carry on up Wharf St to Fisgard St to complete the loop.

STRETCH YOUR LEGS
WHISTLER

Start/Finish Town Plaza

Distance 1.7 miles

Duration Three to four hours

Whistler's not just for the über-active. This gable-roofed village sits amid stunning scenery, has a fantastic museum, ace shopping and superb restaurants where you can rub shoulders with ski bunnies and bike barons. And if you are feeling energetic, the outdoor pursuits are virtually endless.

Take this walk on Trip

Town Plaza

There's something about the Whistler shopping scene that makes money run through your fingers like water. From boutique hat shops to Canadian giants like Lululemon and Roots, shopping makes for an interesting (and often worthwhile) distraction. You'll find plenty of the prerequisite sports gear and souvenir shops, among less likely neighbors like Tiffany's and the Whistler Cigar Company. Town Plaza is ringed with boutiques and is the best place to begin browsing.

The Walk >> From Town Plaza, head west directly opposite the gazebo, between Deer Lodge and the Delta Whistler. Walk a block down Main St and swing a right to the museum.

Whistler Museum

The **Whistler Museum** (www.whistler museum.org; 4333 Main St; adult/youth/ child $7/4/free; ☺11am-5pm) features paraphernalia from local sports legends, plus displays on geology and wildlife and the history of the village. Look for the exhibit on Myrtle Philip, one of the first pioneers to settle in Whistler. 'She battled bears, birthed babies and bakes pies out on the trail.' A legend in her own time.

The Walk >> Return east up Main Street to the Village Stroll and carry on north to Olympic Plaza.

Olympic Plaza

Surrounded by cafes and home to a fantastic children's playground, Olympic Plaza is a great place for a coffee. For something stronger, the Plaza's **Whistler Brewhouse** (www.markjamesgroup.com; 4355 Blackcomb Way) offers smooth drinks such as Lifty Lager and Twin Peaks Pale Ale.

In summer, catch a performance at the Plaza's outdoor theatre. Also here is **Millennium Place** (www.artswhistler.com; 4335 Blackcomb Way), home to the free **Scotia Creek Gallery**, showcasing local artists. Check out what's playing in the acoustically amazing theatre and grab some tickets if you can.

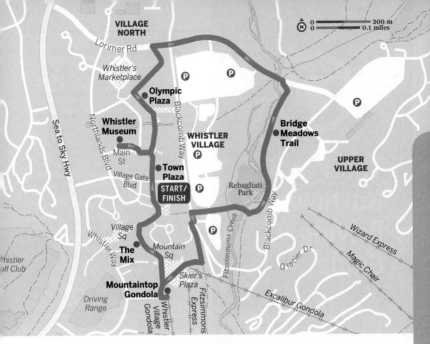

The Walk ›› Follow the footpath at the end of the Village Stroll. This leads to Lorimer Rd. Turn right and follow it over the bridge.

Bridge Meadows Trail

Beginning alongside the water beside the phenomenal **Squamish Lil'wat Cultural Centre** (p280), the Bridge Meadows Trail is a lovely escape into nature. Follow it south along Fitzsimmons Creek and through the woods. Hang a right at the covered wooden bridge and cross to the tiny Rebagliati Park, with a picnic area, more forest and a waterside meadow. Continue west across the next bridge and carry on through the woods until you reach Blackcomb Way.

The Walk ›› Cross over Blackcomb Way and follow the footpath south until you reach a set of stairs. Turn right and descend back to Village Stroll.

Mountaintop Gondola

Hop on Whistler Village Gondola, sans skis. At the top, the **Peak 2 Peak Gondola** (4545 Blackcomb Way; adult/child $42.95/18.95; ◷10am-4:45pm), links Whistler with Blackcomb. As you travel between mountaintops, ponder that this is the longest, highest unsupported lift span in the world – 1.9 miles (3km) at a height of 1427ft (436m). For further contemplation (and amazing, brave views) wait for one of the silver, glass-bottomed cabins.

The Walk ›› Return down to Whistler and the Village Stroll, heading north.

Cocktails at The Mix

If your knees are a little wobbly after the glass-bottomed gondola ride, steady them with a drink at **The Mix** (4154 Village Green; ◷4pm-1am). With a cool Latin vibe, low lights and candles, this is a great chill-out spot to sit with a martini in hand. They also serve tapas to complement the well-stocked bar. And if you're hungry for more, **21 Steps** (p281) is just around the corner.

The Walk ›› Continue on the Village Stroll to your starting point.

The Pacific Northwest's Driving Guide

Short on interstates, long on scenic byways, the Pacific Northwest yields some of the most beautiful drives on the continent.

Driving Fast Facts

→ **Right or left?** Drive on the right

→ **Legal driving age** 16

→ **Top speed limit** 75 mph US, 110 km/h Canada

→ **Best bumper sticker** Sasquatch for President

DRIVER'S LICENSE & DOCUMENTS

If you're stopped by the police, you'll be expected to provide a valid driver's license and proof of insurance. Foreign visitors can legally drive a car in the USA for up to 12 months using their home driver's license. However, an International Driving Permit (IDP) will have more credibility with police, especially if your home license doesn't have a photo or isn't in English. Your national automobile association can provide one for a small fee, and they're usually valid for one year. Always carry your home license together with the IDP.

Driving rules in Canada are similar to the United States, although they vary slightly from province to province. Just like in the US, you will need a driver's license and proof of insurance. A foreign license will suffice, though an IDP can save you headaches if your license is in a foreign language.

INSURANCE

Don't put the keys in the ignition if you don't have insurance, which is required by law. You risk financial ruin and legal consequences if there's an accident. Basic liability insurance covers damage you may cause to another vehicle. Rental companies are required by law to provide the minimum level set by each state, but it usually isn't enough in the event of a serious accident.

Many Americans already have enough insurance coverage under their personal car-insurance policies; check your own policy carefully. Foreign visitors should check their travel-insurance policies to see if they cover foreign rental cars. Rental companies charge about $15 per day for extra accident insurance.

Insurance against damage or loss to the car itself, called Collision Damage Waiver (CDW) or Loss Damage Waiver (LDW), can cost up to around $25 per day (and may have a deductible). The CDW may be voided if you cause an accident while breaking the law, however. Again, check your own coverage to see if you have comprehensive and collision insurance.

Some credit cards cover CDW for rentals up to 15 days, provided you charge the entire cost of the rental to the card. Check with your credit-card company to determine the extent of coverage.

RENTING A CAR

Major international rental agencies have offices throughout the Pacific Northwest. To rent a car, you must have a valid driver's license, be at least 21 years of age and present a major credit card or a large cash deposit. Drivers under 25 must pay a surcharge over the regular rental rate.

Agencies often have bargain rates for weekend or week-long rentals, especially outside the peak seasons or in conjunction with airline tickets. Prices vary greatly depending on the type or size of car, pickup and drop-off locations, number of drivers etc. In general, expect to pay from $30 to $60 per day for a midsize car, more in peak seasons. Rates usually include unlimited mileage, but not taxes or insurance.

For rates and reservations, check the internet or call toll-free:

Alamo (☎800-327-9633; www.alamo.com)

Avis (☎800-230-4898; www.avis.com)

Budget (☎800-527-0700; www.budget.com)

Dollar (☎800-800-3665; www.dollar.com)

Enterprise (☎800-261-7331; www.enterprise.com)

Hertz (☎800-654-3131; www.hertz.com)

National (☎877-222-9058; www.nationalcar.com)

Rent-A-Wreck (☎877-877-0700; www.rentawreck.com)

Thrifty (☎800-847-4389; www.thrifty.com)

BORDER CROSSING

The main (and busiest) overland point of entry from Washington to Vancouver, British Columbia (BC) is at the Blaine–Douglas crossing, on the northern end of I-5, which continues as Hwy 99 in Canada.

Commercial trucks (and regular vehicles) use the Pacific Hwy crossing, 3 miles (5km) east of Blaine–Douglas; from I-5, take exit 275. If you're entering Canada with duty-free goods, you'll need to cross here.

A good choice during busy times (although closed from midnight to 8am) is the little-known Lynden–Aldergrove crossing, about 30 miles (50km) east of Blaine–Douglas. Take exit 256 off I-5, just north of Bellingham, and follow Hwy 539.

Lastly there's Sumas–Huntingdon, 62 miles (100km) east of Blaine–Douglas. It's best for heading to BC's interior; take exit 255 off I-5, just north of Bellingham, and follow Hwy 542 and then Hwy 9.

Road Distances (miles)

	Seattle	Portland	Vancouver	Spokane	Eugene	Ashland	Seaside	Bend	ONP	Walla Walla	Whistler
Portland	172										
Vancouver	141	315									
Spokane	280	351	410								
Eugene	283	110	424	462							
Ashland	460	285	599	637	180						
Seaside	194	80	334	432	181	356					
Bend	330	159	470	396	120	186	247				
ONP	90	146	128	370	265	425	150	305			
Walla Walla	270	245	408	158	352	470	322	286	350		
Whistler	215	390	70	495	498	675	409	640	305	485	
Mt Rainer	85	136	179	212	204	325	279	195	175	173	300

Driving Problem-Buster

What should I do if my car breaks down? If it's a rental, call the service number of the rental company. If it's your own car, membership in an automobile association such as AAA will offer 24-hour roadside assistance.

What if I have an accident? If there are no serious injuries and your car is operational, move over to the side of the road. If there are serious injuries, call 911 for an ambulance. Exchange information with the other driver, including names, contact and insurance info, and license tag numbers. Then file an accident report with the police or Department of Motor Vehicles.

What should I do if I get stopped by the police? Stay in your car and keep your hands visible. (Policemen like that sort of thing.) They'll want to see your driver's license and proof of liability insurance. As long as you're not a serious threat, you probably won't end up in the pokey, although you'll probably get either a ticket or a warning if you've broken a road rule.

What if I don't have a room booked for the night? Not everyone reserves hotel rooms in advance. After all, spontaneity is a key ingredient of any road trip. Chain motels along the highway are a convenient solution if you're willing to give up amenities. You can try to book a last-minute bargain on websites like www.priceline.com or www.hotwire.com.

During the week, expect to wait five to 20 minutes; on weekends and holidays, an hour or more. For details check www.vancouver.hm/border.html (tips and directions) or www.borderlineups.com (wait times, web cams and hours).

Many travelers also cross the border by ferry, principally on journeys from Anacortes to Sidney, BC (near Victoria) and from Port Angeles to Victoria.

FERRIES

Washington and BC have two of the largest state-owned ferry systems in the world. Some boats are passenger-only, while others take vehicles and passengers. Summertime ferry routes can have long waits if you're in a car. Bring snacks, as ferry offerings are limited and expensive. You can almost always find a bathroom on board. For general information on the area's schedules and routes, check www.youra.com/ferry.

BC Ferries (☎888-223-3779; www.bcferries.com) Operates most of the ferries in BC. Primary links are between Tsawwassen (south of Vancouver) and Swartz Bay (on Vancouver Island), and to Nanaimo from Tsawwassen and Horseshoe Bay. BC Ferries services also link Gulf Islands to Tsawwassen.

Black Ball's Coho Ferry (☎Washington 360-457-4491, BC 250-386-2202; www.cohoferry.com) Privately operated; connects Victoria, BC with Washington's Port Angeles (on the Olympic Peninsula).

Clipper Navigation (☎206-448-5000; www.clippervacations.com/ferry_schedule) Privately operated; operates the *Victoria Clipper*, a passenger ferry that connects Seattle with Victoria, BC. Stops at the San Juan Islands in summer.

Washington State Ferries (WSF; ☎206-464-6400; www.wsdot.wa.gov/ferries) Operates most of the ferries that run in the Puget Sound area. Popular routes go to Bremerton, Bainbridge and Vashon Islands from Seattle. WSF also operates the ferry system through the San Juan Islands and on to Sidney (near Victoria, on Vancouver Island) from Anacortes. Check its website for fares, schedules and route maps, plus links to other ferry services.

MAPS

For a good road atlas or driving maps, try **Rand McNally** (www.randmcnally.com) and its Thomas Brothers city guides; both are stocked at many bookstores and some gas stations. If you are a member of an automobile association it will provide high-quality maps for free at regional offices. **Google Maps** (maps. google.com) is great for finding directions and figuring out driving times online.

ROAD-TRIP WEBSITES

Automobile Associations

American Automobile Association (www.aaa.com) Get 24-hour roadside assistance anywhere in the US plus free maps, trip planning and travel discounts.

Canadian Automobile Association (www.caa.ca) Same as AAA, but for Canada. The CAA honors AAA membership.

Better World Club (www.betterworldclub. com) Offers roadside assistance, plus donates 1% of revenue to assist environmental cleanup.

Road Rules

Oregon Department of Transportation (www.oregon.gov/ODOT/DMV/forms/ manuals.shtml)

Washington State Department of Transportation (www.wsdot.wa.gov/ LocalPrograms/Traffic/Laws)

British Columbia Regulations (www. vancouverisland.com/information/details. asp?id=6)

Conditions & Traffic

Oregon Trip Check (www.tripcheck.com)

Washington State Department of Transportation (www.wsdot.com/traffic)

Drive British Columbia (www.drivebc.ca)

Pacific Northwest Playlist

Kissing the Lipless The Shins

Roll on Columbia Woody Guthrie

You're No Rock 'N' Roll Fun Sleater-Kinney

Float On Modest Mouse

Come as You Are Nirvana

Mass Romantic New Pornographers

ROADS & CONDITIONS

During winter months – especially at higher elevations – roads are sometimes closed to cars without chains or 4WD, so keep a set of chains in the trunk. Make sure they fit your tires, and practice putting them on *before* you're out in the snow. Many car-rental companies prohibit the use of chains on their vehicles.

Deer and other wildlife can be a hazard on roads all around the region. Pay attention to the roadside, especially at night.

ROAD RULES

Cars drive on the right-hand side of the road. The use of seat belts and child safety seats is required. It's illegal to talk or text on a mobile phone while driving, unless you're on a hands-free device. The maximum blood-alcohol content for drivers is 0.08%; in Canada, it's 0.05%.

Speed limits vary depending on the type of road: in the United States, it's generally 55–65mph on highways, up to 75mph on the interstates, 25–35mph in cities and towns, and as low as 15mph in school zones. It's forbidden to pass a school bus when its lights are flashing.

In Canada, speed limits are expressed as kilometers per hour, so if you see a sign that says 'Maximum 60', they don't mean 60mph. If you're watching your US odometer, you shouldn't be traveling at more than 37.28mph.

Speed limits are generally 70–90km/h on highways (or 43–56mph), up to 110km/h (68mph) on expressways, 40–50 (25–31mph) on residential streets, and 30–50km/h (19–31mph) in school zones.

For tips and rules on driving in the USA, get an Oregon or Washington Driver Handbook at any Department of Motor Vehicles (DMV) office.

FUEL

Oregon law prohibits you from pumping your own gasoline – all stations are full service, so just sit back and enjoy it. Tips are optional and not expected.

Gas prices are fairly uniform, but tend to get more expensive in remote rural areas or near airports where rental-car returners don't mind paying extra. Within a given area, prices might differ by about 10 cents per gallon from one place to the next.

BEHIND THE SCENES

SEND US YOUR FEEDBACK

We love to hear from travelers – your comments help make our books better. We read every word, and we guarantee that your feedback goes straight to the authors. Visit **lonelyplanet. com/contact** to submit your updates and suggestions.

Note: We may edit, reproduce and incorporate your comments in Lonely Planet products such as guidebooks, websites and digital products, so let us know if you don't want your comments reproduced or your name acknowledged. For a copy of our privacy policy visit lonelyplanet.com/privacy.

OUR READERS

Many thanks to the travelers who used the last edition and wrote to us with helpful hints, useful advice and interesting anecdotes: Matt Albee, Thomas Guignard, Amy Larsen, John Neirinckx, Teresa Savin, Taylor St John, and Mick & Julie Tapley.

AUTHOR THANKS

MARIELLA KRAUSE

Thanks to Tim Bauer for being a great road-trip companion and for helping me sample all those microbrews (42 of them, I believe it was). And thanks to Heather Howard at Lonely Planet for sending me on this grand adventure!

CELESTE BRASH

Most thanks to my family for coming with me on many of these trips, and to Danny Palmerlee for his excellent base text and advice. Thanks also to Heather Griggs and Dana Robinson for Willamette Valley Pinot Noir. In Walla Walla thanks to Imbibe Tours for taking the wheel.

KORINA MILLER

Thanks to Heather, my coauthors, editors and cartographers for their wisdom and assistance. Thanks to friends and family for sharing their love of this region and to the helpful staff at visitor centers en route. Thank you to my mum for copiloting and to the bear for the peaceful encounter.

BRENDAN SAINSBURY

Thanks to all the untold gas-station cashiers, restaurateurs, national-park rangers, weather forecasters and innocent bystanders who helped me during my research, particularly to Arlene Wagner and Scott Davies for granting me interviews. Thanks also to my wife Liz and six-year-old son Kieran for their company on the road.

PUBLISHERS THANKS

Climate map data adapted from Peel MC, Finlayson BL & McMahon TA (2007) 'Updated World Map of the Köppen-Geiger Climate Classification', *Hydrology and Earth System Sciences*, 11, 163344.

Cover photographs: Front (clockwise from top): Mt Shuksan and Picture Lake, North Cascades National Park, Washington, Dennis Walton/ Lonely Planet Images; Kaka'solas Kwakwaka'wakw totem pole by Ellen Neal and Mungo Martin, Brockton Point, Stanley Park, Vancouver, BC, Chris Cheadle/ Corbis; 1950s Buick, Vancouver Island, BC, Kathy deWitt/Alamy. Back: Mt Humbug, Oregon, John Elk III/Lonely Planet Images.

THIS BOOK

This 2nd edition of Lonely Planet's *The Pacific Northwest's Best Trips* was researched and written by Mariella Krause, Celeste Brash, Korina Miller and Brendan Sainsbury. The 1st edition was written by Danny Palmerlee, Mariella Krause, John Lee and Bradley Mayhew. This guidebook was commissioned in Lonely Planet's Oakland office, and produced by the following:

Commissioning Editor Heather Howard **Coordinating Editors** Monique Perrin, Luna Soo **Coordinating Cartographer** Brendan Streager **Coordinating Layout Designer** Frank Deim **Managing Editors** Martine Power, Angela Tinson **Senior Editor** Andi Jones **Managing Cartographers** Mark Griffiths, Alison Lyall **Managing Layout Designer** Chris Girdler **Assisting Editors** Janet Austin, Paul Harding, Anne Mulvaney **Assisting Cartographers** Gabriel Lindquist, David Kemp, Cameron Romeril **Cover Research** Timothy O'Hanlon **Internal Image Research** Kylie McLaughlin **Thanks to** Jennifer Bilos, Lucy Birchley, Laura Crawford, Sally Darmody, Janine Eberle, Ryan Evans, Jennye Garibaldi, Joshua Geoghegan, Liz Heynes, Laura Jane, Jennifer Johnston, Wally Lien, Anna Lorincz, David McClymont, Wayne Murphy, Trent Paton, Raphael Richards, Jessica Rose, Mik Ruff, Julie Sheridan, Laura Stansfeld, Matt Swaine, John Taufa, Gerard Walker, Juan Winata

INDEX

Korina Miller Road trips have been an essential life ingredient since Korina was a small child growing up on Vancouver Island. While her friends were darting off to Hawaii and Florida, Korina's parents were packing the car and taking her on month-long journeys across Canada and up and down the Pacific Coast, from Alaska to Mexico. Korina has since traveled to more than three dozen countries, writing over two dozen Lonely Planet titles en route. She still includes road trips whenever she can, exploring India on the back of a motorbike, cruising through Sicilian villages and zipping down Japanese motorways.

My Favorite Trip 29 **Vancouver Island's Remote North** for its wild beaches, giant trees and roaming bears.

Brendan Sainsbury UK-born Brendan lives in White Rock, BC, 1 mile from the 49th parallel. The San Juan Islands and Olympic Mountains beckon from his kitchen window. He has been writing about the region for Lonely Planet since 2007 with books on the Pacific Northwest and the USA. He once ran 100 miles nonstop across the Cascade Mountains in an esoteric race. For finishing he received a rock with the words 'Plain 100' painted on it. It is one of his most prized possessions.

My Favorite Trip 6 **Cascade Drive** for the opportunities it offers to jump out of the car and sample some short but epic hikes.

OUR WRITERS

OUR STORY

A beat-up old car, a few dollars in the pocket and a sense of adventure. In 1972 that's all Tony and Maureen Wheeler needed for the trip of a lifetime – across Europe and Asia overland to Australia. It took several months, and at the end – broke but inspired – they sat at their kitchen table writing and stapling together their first travel guide, *Across Asia on the Cheap*. Within a week they'd sold 1500 copies. Lonely Planet was born.

Today, Lonely Planet has offices in Melbourne, London and Oakland, with more than 600 staff and writers. We share Tony's belief that 'a great guidebook should do three things: inform, educate and amuse'.

Mariella Krause Mariella loves a good road trip, and feels lucky to live just six hours south of the Oregon border (especially now that she knows all the best places to go). Researching this book was her second major tour through the Pacific Northwest, having traveled through Washington state for the first edition. This is her eighth title for Lonely Planet.

My Favorite Trip 13 Highway 101 Oregon Coast for the laid-back pace and the amazing hikes that reward you with ocean views.

Celeste Brash Locals have a hard time believing it, but the beauty of the Pacific Northwest is what coaxed Celeste back to the US after 15 years in Tahiti. She was thrilled to explore and imbibe the treasures of her new backyard for this book and to get in touch with her cowboy and Indian roots. Up until now her award-winning travel articles and stories, which have appeared in publications such as *Travelers' Tales*, *LA Times* and *Islands* magazine, have focused on Southeast Asia and the South Pacific.

My Favorite Trip 16 Columbia River Gorge & Mt Hood because of its ever-changing spectacular scenery.

 ## MORE WRITERS

Published by Lonely Planet Publications Pty Ltd
ABN 36 005 607 983
2nd edition – Feb 2013
ISBN 978 1 74179 815 9
© Lonely Planet 2013
Photographs © as indicated 2013
10 9 8 7 6 5 4 3
Printed in China

MIX
Paper from
responsible sources
FSC™ C021741

Paper in this book is certified against the Forest Stewardship Council™ standards. FSC™ promotes environmentally responsible, socially beneficial and economically viable management of the world's forests.